Ernest Cruikshank

The documentary history of the campaign upon the Niagara frontier in the year 1813

Part II (1813)

Ernest Cruikshank

The documentary history of the campaign upon the Niagara frontier in the year 1813
Part II (1813)

ISBN/EAN: 9783337147723

Printed in Europe, USA, Canada, Australia, Japan

Cover: Foto ©ninafisch / pixelio.de

More available books at **www.hansebooks.com**

THE DOCUMENTARY
History of the Campaign

UPON THE

Niagara Frontier

IN THE YEAR 1813.

PART II. (1813)
JUNE TO AUGUST, 1813.

COLLECTED AND EDITED FOR

THE LUNDY'S LANE HISTORICAL SOCIETY

By LIEUT.-COL. E. CRUIKSHANK,

Author of the "Story of Butler's Rangers," &c., &c.

PRINTED AT THE TRIBUNE, WELLAND

The Documentary History of the Campaign on the Niagara Frontier in 1813.

PART II.

June to August, 1813.

Jasper Parish, Indian Agent for the United States, to Major-General Lewis.

CANANDAIGUA, May 2, 1813.

SIR,—I received your letter of the 27th ult. At the time of delivering your letter to the Secretary of War I had some conversation with him on the subject of the war, and of employing such of the Indians as have firearms and were offering their services to the United States last fall. He observed that they may be of service and would refer the matter to the President.

The President has given no permission to employ the Indians or even accept of their services. He has sent a speech to the Six Nations by me giving his advice to them to retire from the lines during the war, to Alleghany, where they may sleep in safety.

(From Ketchum's History of Buffalo and the Senecas, Vol. II., pp. 427-8.)

Major-General John Armstrong, Secretary of War, to Major-General Dearborn.

WASHINGTON, 15th May, 1813.

DEAR GENERAL,—Your affair of the 27th ult. is matter of public and private congratulation, much qualified, however, by the loss of Pike and the escape of the frigate, the capture or destruction of which was, according to the Commodore's calculations, to give him a decided and permanent ascendency on the lake. Another drawback upon it, less apt to be noticed by ordinary critics but in itself very vexatious, is the escape also of Sheaffe with the main body of his regular force. Under the present circumstances of Great Britain, bound as she is neck and heels to the prosecution of the war in Europe, she can ill afford to send to this country either men or money to support the *petite guerre* in which she has so inconsiderately involved herself with us. From information, the most direct and respectable, I am assured that her regular force in both the Canadas has at no time since the declaration of war exceeded three thousand men, and that at the present time, by casualties, (death, desertion, &c.,) always at work thinning the ranks of an army, this force is reduced at least one-fifth. Taking then this fact for granted, we cannot doubt but that in all cases in which a British commander is constrained to act defensively his policy will be that adopted by Sheaffe—to prefer the preservation of his troops to that of his post, and thus, carrying off the kernel leave us only the shell. To counteract this policy becomes therefore a special duty on our part—requiring the strictest attention as well in projecting as in executing our attacks. On this head my distance from you and my very insufficient knowledge of the topography of the country in which you act, make it improbable that any suggestion I could make has not already presented itself to your mind. As a general maxim, however, I may be permitted to say that in concentrating our whole force on any given point of an enemy's position, we necessarily leave all others open to him for escape, whence it follows that to deprive him of this advantage two attacks, (if our force permit it,) should be made, and one of these so directed as to shut him out from all means of retreat, or at least to force him into roads where, finding little or no accommodation, he may sustain the greatest possible loss. In your late affair I have thought, (perhaps erroneously,) that had the descent been made between the town and the barracks things would have turned out better. On that plan the two batteries you had to encounter would have been left out of the combat, and Sheaffe, instead of retreating to Kingston, must have sought refuge at Fort George. In the affair before you nothing will, I hope, be omitted, nor anything be misunderstood, and that with regard to the garrison in particular it will not be permitted to escape to-day that it may fight us tomorrow. For obvious reasons I have made this letter private. On the records of the War Department it would appear to carry with it an official censure, whereas it is in truth nothing more than the suggestions of one who, both for your sake and his own, wishes you the fullest and most unqualified prosperity.

(From Notices of the War of 1812. By John Armstrong, late a Major-General in the army of the United States and Secretary of War. Vol. I., pp. 226-8. Appendix No. 18. New York, Wiley and Putman, 1840.)

General Order.

G. O.   HEADQUARTERS, KINGSTON, June 6, 1813.

The following detachments of troops to be held in readiness to proceed at the shortest notice to join the forces under Brigadier-

General Vincent: The flank companies of the 104th Regiment, one company Glengarry Light Infantry, each 60 rank and file, a select detachment from the recruits of the King's and 49th Regiment. All men sufficiently recovered, belonging to the Regiments above Kingston, are to join their corps; the detachment under command of Major De Haren, Canadian Fencibles, is to be provided with camp equipage and ten days' provisions.

Lieut.-Colonel Hamilton, 100th Regiment, to proceed to Prescott with four companies of the 100th Regiment, where the grenadier company will join Major Taylor with four companies to garrison Isle Aux Nois, together with such further force as may be deemed expedient. Captain Hall, Canadian Fencibles, is to proceed to the station of Brigadier General Vincent with a detachment of 1 subaltern, 1 sergeant, 1 trumpeter and 24 troopers, to march to-morrow morning.

Major-General De Rottenburg will deliver over the command of the troops and the civil administration of the Province of Lower Canada to Major-General Glasgow, and is to arrive at Kingston on the 20th inst.

Major-General Sir R. Sheaffe will meet Major-General De Rottenburg at Cornwall on the 15th and from thence proceed to Montreal to assume the command of the troops in that district.

Major Smelt, 103rd Regiment, is appointed to command the 2nd Light Battalion, forming at Chambly.

EDWARD BAYNES, A. G.

General Order.

KINGSTON, 6th June, 1813.

The following detachment of troops to be kept in perfect readiness to proceed from Kingston to the head of the lake at the shortest notice, the whole under the command of Major De Haren, Canadian Fencibles: The flank companies of the 104th completed to 60 rank and file, one company of Glengarry Light Infantry 60 rank and file, a select detachment of the recruits of the 8th or King's Regiment and such men as are fit to resume duty; the recruits of the 49th Regiment.

Eleven batteaux to be furnished for the troops, who are to take ten days provisions, camp equipage sufficient for the detachment, all the militia clothing remaining in store, shoes, stockings and 100 felt caps are to be sent for the supply of the forces with Brigadier-General Vincent.

Lieut.-Colonel Hamilton with four companies of the 100th Regt. is to march from the Isle Aux Noix to Prescott where he will be joined by the grenadier company.

Major Taylor, with four companies, 100th Regt., is to remain at Isle Aux Noix with such further reinforcements as may be deemed expedient.

Captain Hall will select a detachment of one subaltern, one sergeant, one corporal and 20 dragoons and proceed to-morrow morning by easy marches to join Brigadier-General Vincent at the head of the lake.

General Dearborn to the Secretary of War.

HEADQUARTERS, FORT GEORGE, June 6, 1813.

SIR,—I have received an express from the head of the lake this evening with the intelligence that our troops were attacked at two o'clock this morning by the whole British force and Indians and by some strange fatality, though our loss in numbers was small and the enemy was completely routed and driven from the field, both Brigadier-Generals Chandler and Winder were taken prisoners. They had advanced to ascertain the situation of a company of artillery when the attack commenced. General Chandler had his horse shot under him and was bruised by the fall. General Vincent, their commander, is supposed to have been killed. Colonel Clark was mortally wounded and fell into our hands with sixty prisoners of the 49th. The command devolved on Colonel Burn, who has retired to the Forty Mile Creek. If either of the general officers had remained in command, the enemy would have been pursued and cut up, or if Colonel Burn had been an officer of infantry. The loss of the enemy in killed, wounded or prisoners must exceed two hundred and fifty. The enemy sent in a flag next morning with a request to bury their dead. Generals Lewis and Boyd set off immediately to join the advanced army. I never so severely felt the want of health as at present, at a time when my services might perhaps be most useful. I hope General Hampton will repair here as soon as possible.

June 8, 1813.

There was a mistake in the arrival of the express mail—since writing the above the enemy's fleet has passed, consisting of two large ships and four heavy schooners. I have consequently deemed it prudent to *concentrate the forces at this point.*

(American State Papers, Military Affairs.)

Lieut.-Colonel Harvey to Colonel Baynes.

BURLINGTON HEIGHTS, Sunday, 6th June, 1813.

MY DEAR COLONEL,—The enemy having dared to pursue, as he arrogantly termed it, this division by moving a corps of 3,500 men with four field pieces and 150 cavalry to Stoney Creek, (within ten miles of this position,) I strongly urged General Vincent to make a forward movement for the purpose of beating up his encampment. In the course of yesterday afternoon, our advanced post at Davis's, (eight miles from hence towards Forty Mile Creek,) consisting of the 49th Regt., was driven in. I instantly went out for the purpose of reconnoitering, and found the enemy had again withdrawn to his camp at Stoney Creek. I therefore recommended to the General to move the five companies of the King's, (say 280,) and the 49th Regiment, (say 424,) total 700 men, which was accordingly done at half-past 11 o'clock. General Vincent accompanied these troops, the conduct and direction of which he was so good as to give to me. The troops moved in perfect order and profound silence, the light companies of 49th and King's in front, the 49th Regiment in the centre and the King's as a reserve. In conformity with the directions I had given, the sentries at the outskirts of the enemy's camp were bayonetted in the quietest manner and the camp immediately stormed. The surprise was tolerably complete, but our troops incautiously advancing and charging across the line of camp fires, and a few muskets being fired, notwithstanding my exertions to check it, our line was distinctly seen by the enemy, whose troops in some degree recovered from their panic and formed upon the surrounding heights, poured a destructive fire of musketry upon us, which we answered on our part by repeated charges whenever a body of the enemy could be discerned or reached. The King's Regiment and part of the 49th charged and carried the four field pieces in very gallant style, and the whole sustained with undaunted firmness the heavy fire which was occasionally poured upon them.

In less than three-quarters of an hour the enemy had completely abandoned his guns and everything else to us. Our loss has been severe, but that of the enemy much more so. Our trophies, besides the three guns and howitzer, (two of the guns, by the bye, were spiked by us and left on the ground for want of means of removing,) are two brigadier-generals, one field officer, three captains, one lieutenant and about 100 men prisoners.

General Vincent being too much hurried and fatigued to write to-day has desired me to forward to you with this letter the returns of killed and wounded, as well as those of the prisoners and ordnance, etc., taken. The Brigadier-General's despatch will be forwarded to-morrow. In the meantime, he desires me to congratulate His Excellency on the complete and brilliant success of this enterprise, and on the beneficial results with which it has been already attended. Information has just been received that the enemy has entirely abandoned his camp, burnt his tents, destroyed his provisions, ammunition, etc., and retired precipitately towards the Forty Mile Creek. Our advanced posts occupy the ground on which his camp stood.

P. S.—This is sent by Capt. Milnes, who proceeds with Brigadier-Generals Chandler and Winder, and who, from having been present both in the action of this and that of the 27th ultimo and all the intermediate operations, is perfectly qualified to give His Excellency every satisfactory information on these subjects.

J. H.

The circumstances in which I write will, I hope, excuse this hasty and inaccurate scrawl, of which, moreover, I have no copy.

(Canadian Archives, C. 679, p. 38.)

Brigadier-General Vincent to Sir George Prevost.

BURLINGTON HEIGHTS, HEAD OF LAKE ONTARIO,
6th June, 1813.

SIR,—Having yesterday received information of the enemy having advanced from the Forty Mile Creek with a force consisting of 3,500 men, eight or nine field pieces and 250 cavalry, for the avowed purpose of attacking the division under my command in this position, and having soon afterwards received a report that he had passed the swamp and driven in my advanced posts from Stoney Creek and Brady's, Lieut.-Col. Harvey, D. A. G., immediately went forward with the light companies of the King's and 49th Regiment, and having advanced close to and accurately ascertained the enemy's position, sent back to propose to me a night attack on his camp. The motives which induced Lieut.-Col. Harvey to make and me to agree to this proposal were these: This position, though strong for a large body, is far too extensive for me to hope to make any successful stand against the superior force understood to be advancing against me in three separate points, viz.: By the lake, by the centre road and by the mountain on my right. The attack I knew would not be delayed; I had neither time or inclination precipitately to retreat from my position. I therefore embraced the proposition of Lieut.-Col. Harvey as an alternative, not only more worthy of the gallant troops under my command but as offering the best chance of crippling the enemy and disconcerting all his plans, as well as gaining time for retreat should that measure still be found necessary.

The enemy's camp was distant about seven miles; about half-past 11 I moved forward with the five companies of the 8th, (King's,) and 49th Regts., amounting together to only 704 firelocks. Lieut. Col. Harvey, who conducted it with great regularity and judgment, gallantly led on the attack. The enemy was completely surprised and driven from his camp, after having repeatedly formed in different bodies and been as often charged by our brave troops, whose conduct throughout this brilliant enterprise was above all praise. The action terminated before daylight, when three guns with one brass howitzer, with their tumbrils, two Brigadier-Generals, Chandler and Winder, first and second in command, and upwards of 100 officers, non-commissioned officers and privates remained in our hands.

Not conceiving it prudent to expose our small force to the view of the enemy, who, though routed and dispersed, was still formidable as to numbers and position, he having fled to the surrounding heights and having still four or five guns, the troops were put in motion at daybreak and marched back to the cantonments. After we had retired and it had become broad day, the enemy ventured to return and occupy his camp, only, however, for the purpose of destroying his encumbrances, such as blankets, carriages, provisions, spare arms, etc., after which he commenced a precipitate retreat towards the 40 Mile Creek, where he effected a junction with a body of 2,000 men on their march from Niagara to reinforce him. I cannot conclude this despatch without calling Your Excellency's attention to the following officers:

To Lt.-Col. Harvey, the Dept.-Adjt. General, my obligations are particularly due; from the first moment the enemy's approach was known he watched his movements and afforded me the earliest information; to him indeed I am indebted for the suggestion and plan of operations. Nothing could be more clear than his arrangements, nor more completely successful in the result. The conduct of Major Plenderleath, who commanded the 49th Regt., was very conspicuous; by his decision and prompt efforts the surprise of the enemy's camp was complete, and all his efforts to make a stand were rendered ineffectual by the bayonet, which overthrew all opposition. A party of the 49th Regt., with Major Plenderleath at their head, gallantly charged some of the enemy's field pieces and brought off two six-pounders. Major Ogilvie led on in the most gallant manner the five companies of the King's Regt., and whilst one-half of that highly disciplined and distinguished corps supported the 49th Regt., the other part moved to the right and attacked the enemy's left flank, which decided our midnight contest. I have also received the greatest assistance from Major Glegg, Brig[ade] Maj[or] to the forces, and beg leave to mention the names of Capts. McDouall and Milnes, Your

Excellency's aides-de-camp, who accompanied me in the attack and upon all occasions have volunteered their services. I have likewise to acknowledge the assistance of Capt. Chambers of the 41st Regt., who had arrived four days before from Amherstburg, and Mr. Brock, P[ay]m[aster], 49th, who assisted me as acting aide-de-camp.

To Mr. Hackett, Acting Staff Surgeon to this army, I feel myself particularly indebted for his judicious arrangement by which the wounded have received every attention, and are, most of them, likely to be restored to the service.

It would be an act of injustice were I to omit assuring Your Excellency that gallantry and discipline were never more conspicuous than during our late short service, and I feel the greatest satisfaction in assuring you that every officer and individual seemed anxious to rival each other in his efforts to support the honor of His Majesty's arms and to maintain the high character of the British troops.

On leaving this position to march against the enemy it was immediately occupied by Lt.-Col. Bisshopp, with detachments of the 41st Regt., Glengarry, and Newfoundland and militia and the artillery under Major Holcroft, who were in a situation to move towards my support or to either flank, as circumstances might require.

I directed Capt. Fowler, the Dept. A. Q. M. G., to remain in the rear with a view of reconnoitring the country, collecting the resources and keeping open the communication.

I am happy to assure Your Excellency that had any extreme case happened I felt the fullest confidence in the zeal and exertions of those officers for making the most judicious arrangements.

I beg leave to refer Your Excellency to the enclosed reports for particulars respecting our loss, which I regret to say has been very severe.

(Canadian Archives, C. 679, p. 27.)

General Return of Killed, Wounded and Missing in Action with the Enemy Near the Head of Lake Ontario, 6th June, 1813.

Staff—One fort major wounded.
8th (or King's) Regt.—One lieutenant, 2 sergeants, 7 rank and file killed ; one major, 2 captains, 2 lieutenants, 4 sergeants, 51 rank and file wounded ; 13 rank and file missing.
49th Regt.—One sergeant, 12 rank and file killed; 1 major, 3 captains, 1 ensign, 1 adjutant, 5 sergeants, 2 drummers, 62 rank and file wounded ; 3 sergeants and 39 rank and file missing.
Staff—Fort Major Taylor, severely.

8th—Lieut. Hooker, killed; Major Ogilvie, severely, not dangerously; Captain Munday, severely, not dangerously; Capt. Goldrick, slightly; Lieut. Weyland, do.; Lieut. Boyd, do.

49th—Major Plenderleath, severely, not dangerously; Bt. Major Clerk, dangerously; Bt. Major Dennis, slightly; Captain Manners, do.; Ensign Drury, dangerously; Adjutant Stearn, slightly.

J. HARVEY,
Deputy Adj. General.

(Canadian Archives, C. 679, p. 28.)

Return of American Prisoners of War Captured near Stoney Creek in the Action of the 6th inst.

BURLINGTON HEIGHTS, 7th June, 1813.

2 Brigadier Generals.
1 major.
5 captains.
1 lieutenant.
116 non-commissioned officers and privates.

(Sgd.)   J. HARVEY,
Dep'y. Adj. General.

(Canadian Archives, C. 679, p. 30.)

Return of Ordnance, &c., &c., Captured from the Americans by a Division of the Troops under the Command of Brig.-Genl. Vincent in Action on the 6th June, 1813, at the Head of Lake Ontario.

Ordnance, 6 pounders, iron................................. 3
　　5½ inch howitzers................................. 1
Carriages, lumber, 6 pounder............................... 1
　　Tumbril with 6 pounder, ammunition complete......... 1
Harness, thill setts....................................... 4
　　Trail setts................................... 4
Horses, artillery.. 9

(Sgd.)   WM. HOLCROFT, Major,
Comd'g Royal Artillery.

N. B.—Two of the above 6-pounders were spiked and left on the ground in consequence of the impossibility of removing them.

(Canadian Archives, C. 679.)

Memo. by Lieut.-Col. Glegg.

HEADQUARTERS, BURLINGTON HEIGHTS,
6th June, 1813.

Return of American prisoners of war captured in the action with the enemy on the morning of the 6th June, 1813:
2 Brigadier Generals, (Chandler and Winder.)
1 Major—Vandeventer.
3 Captains—Steel, 16th Infy., Van Vechten, 23rd, McEwan.
1 Lieut.—Swearingen.
94 non-commissioned officers and rank and file.

Return of American prisoners of war captured near Stoney Creek in the action of the 6th inst:

Burlington Heights, 7th June, 1813.

2 Brigadier Generals.
1 major.
4 captains.
1 lieutenant.
105 non-commissioned officers and privates.
N. B.—1 captain and 11 privates brought in after the return of yesterday.

(From memorandum book in possession of Lieut.-Col. Turner, Reading, England.)

Memo. by Lieut.-Col. Glegg.

Thomas Hunt, an American prisoner of war taken on the 6th June at the battle of Davies' Mills, and Sergt. McDonald, 41st Regt., is ready to swear that he is a deserter from the 2d Battn., 60th.

(From memorandum book in possession of Lieut.-Col. Turner, Reading, England.)

From Lieut. James FitzGibbon to the Reverend James Somerville of Montreal.

BURLINGTON BAY, 7th June, 1813.

REVEREND AND DEAR SIR,—

Three days ago we discovered that the Americans were following us with about 3,000 men. On the evening of the 5th their advanced guard was engaged with the Lt. company, 49th, then our rear guard, which killed and wounded 8 of their cavalry. We lost one, killed. Our little army was paraded, according to custom, at 6 p. m. About 11 at night the King's and 49th, (about 700,) were ordered towards the enemy. After 3 miles we were informed that it was intended to

surprise the Yankeys and that the work was to be done entirely by
the bayonet—not a shot to be fired. The night was almost pitch
dark—calm and, except for a shower in the beginning of the march,
dry. They had no post in advance—only 3 sentries about 200 yards
on the road through the wood leading towards our position. The 2
first were surprised and secured in succession by the Lt. company of
the 49th, which led—the third resisted and was bayonetted. Their
picquet at the entrance to the open space heard the noise and a shot
was fired by them. In an instant our Lt. company was upon them.
Up to this moment everything succeeded most favorably. But just
as the Lt. company dashed upon the enemy's picquet some of the
staff officers in front began huzzaing. The company which I commanded was the 5th from the head of the column. I therefore distinctly heard every noise in front. The moment I heard the shout
spread amongst the men I considered our situation as very critical.
For I was aware that it would be almost impossible to make the men
silent again, and that consequently orders could not be heard or
obeyed. I instantly turned to my men and charged them not to take
up the shout then coming from the front, and by the assistance of my
3 sergeants I succeeded in keeping them silent and in good order until
a late stage of the affair, when firing on our side became general.
Then, shouting, we rushed into the open ground occupied by the enemy
and wheeled to the left from whence you see "road" on the annexed
slip along the lane to where is written "49th." The King's formed to
the right of the road where you see "King's." Their numbers apparently about 200*. Ours about 500. We had arrived upon this
line in column of sections. About this time the enemy commenced firing, which he might have done sooner had he been prepared,
but he was taken completely by surprise, many of his men being
bayonetted by our Lt. company before they could get away from the
fires. The crosses which I have marked thus upon the accompanying
slip you may suppose the fires which guided the enemy much in their
firing upon us, as we had to form amongst them, the fires. Just as
we had reached the left and before we formed line the enemy commenced firing. Our men never ceased shouting. No order could be
heard. Everything was noise and confusion—which confusion was
chiefly occasioned by the noise. Our men returned fire contrary to
orders and it soon became apparent that it was impossible to prevent
shouting and firing. The scene at this instant was awfully grand.
The darkness of the morning, 2 o'clock, made still more dark by the
flashing of the musketry and cannon. The officers could no longer
control their men and they soon began to fall back. The company I
commanded, up to this moment, was kept in good order, neither
shouting nor firing, but when I saw the men falling back and no field

officer near, I ran along the line to the left to prevent the men retreating, although I was almost convinced that their remaining under the enemy's fire could be of no use. Yet I had some hopes that good order might be restored. Major Plenderleath came immediately after to that portion of the line which I had quitted, and with the men I had left in charge of a sergeant and a few others he rushed forward against the guns and took 4 of them—2 and a tumbril were brought away. The others c[oul]d not, our men having bayonetted the horses. Major P[lenderleath] pushed on with about 20 men, following the main road, the men stabbing every man and horse they met with. Generals Chandler and Winder were close to this road where you see "guns" written on the slip. They were taken and secured—one of them was in the act of presenting his pistol at a young man, Sergt. Fraser of the 49th, when the Sergt. raised his fusee and said: "If you stir, Sir, you die." The General took his word for it and threw down his pistol and sword saying: "I am your prisoner." The Sergeant stabbed 7 Americans, and his brother, a young lad of the co[mpan]y I belong to, stabbed 4. This handful of men with Major Plenderleath took at this dash besides the 2 Generals, 5 field officers and captains and above 100 prisoners and brought them off. The people on the left and I believe every other portion of the line were in total confusion, shouting and firing, and ultimately breaking and flying into the woods in their rear. I am of opinion that had not Major Plenderleath made the dash he did the Americans would have kept their ground and our ruin would have been inevitable, but finding our people so far advanced in their centre they broke and fled in every direction and their fire consequently ceased at a time when our line was, as it were, entirely routed. For the fire of the enemy while it lasted was most heavy, and tho' not destructive, owing to the darkness, the men thought it terrible and fled.

Here then we find both parties leaving the scene of action, each believing the others the conquerors. I am convinced that it was Major P[lenderleath]'s party which drove the enemy off the field—that saved us and gave us time to bring off our prisoners and guns. Our people thus made the best of their way from the field as the day began to dawn. 2,000 Americans landed on the lake shore the evening before, about 2 miles to his, the enemy's, right, and after daylight pushed on to the scene of action, which was deserted. They occupied it, burnt some waggons with flour, arms, accoutrements, blankets, in short everything which they found on the field, and then retreated to the 40 Mile Creek with their main body.

Their loss we cannot ascertain. I found this morning on the field 19 dead Americans and 22 dead British, and from observations I made on the spot I am convinced they must have carried off many of

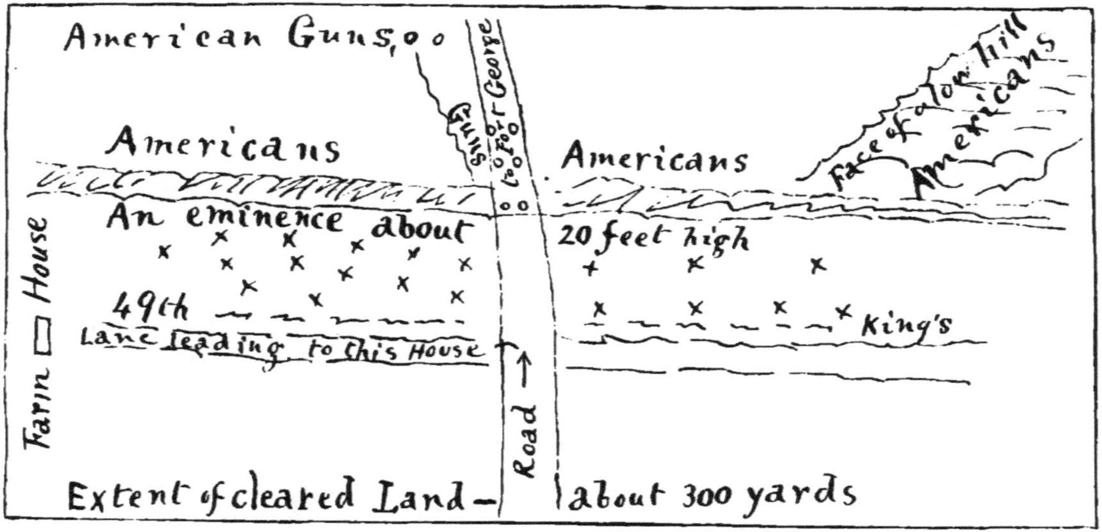

American Guns
Guns
to Fort George
Americans
Americans
Face of a low Hill
Americans
An eminence about
20 feet high
49th
King's
Farm House
Lane leading to this House
Road
Extent of cleared Land—
about 300 yards

their dead. For in situations of the road, where there was little done by us, I found many of them dead, and in the road where they must have suffered most I found but one dead man. But from the road it was easy to carry them off, and I am now told that 12 bodies are discovered in a spot about ¼ mile in rear of the field in the line of their retreat. A man of the 49th came in this morning from the bush where he lost himself, and he tells me he counted above 30 of their wounded lying in the woods and one only by a ball, the others were by the bayonet. Of the 49th, 13 are killed, 74 wounded and 32 missing. Many of the latter were left wounded on the field and were carried off by the enemy. I don't know the loss of the King's; it is said to be greater than ours in proportion. I counted 22 of the British on the field, of whom 9 must be of the King's.

This business was, I think, very ill executed by us, and the great error was shouting before the line was formed for the attack. Had we maintained silence and not fired I believe we sh[oul]d have taken and destroyed four-fifths of the Americans, and with all their guns, 7 in number. The instant I heard their shout I considered our affair ruined, and after circumstances confirmed this opinion, for the conduct of Major Plenderleath and the pusillanimity of the enemy alone saved us from destruction. General Vincent with the whole left of the line retreated, or I may say fled into the woods, and not until noon next day did we know what was become of him. A flag of truce was sent to enquire if he was taken but the Americans knew nothing of him. Indians were sent in search of him but without success. He at length found a road and joined us. Numbers of officers and men were lost for a time in the woods, so difficult is it to *navigate* these forests. This affair is much praised and the Americans think it a brilliant one on our part, but for myself it is an evidence most convincing of the deficiency of our officers in general. This is a severe observation, but if we meet again I will find little difficulty in convincing you of its justness. Never was surprise more complete—never was anything more brilliant than it would have been had we kept silence and not fired, but our officers began that which they should have watched with all their care to prevent; for they ought to have known that in darkness and noise confusion must be inevitable. I think I could have killed some of them had I been near them at the moment.

Major Ogilvie, King's, wounded slightly; Lt. Hooker, do., killed; Major Plenderleath, 2 severe wounds in the left thigh; Major Clerk I fear dangerously wounded. He is in the next room suffering incessant and great pain. Ens[ign] Drury, mortally wounded by a musket ball in the back of the head; Captains Manners and Dennis, slightly; also the Adjutant Ens[ign] Stearn.

8th June—Our fleet is now working up to the Head of the Lake with troops on board.

We hear little from below since we left Fort George. I wish some of your merchants would be enterprising enough to send us up supplies of shoes, shirts, stockings, &c., &c. Not one in 20 has an article more than what is on his person. Adieu. Yours entirely,

JAMES FITZGIBBON.

The Rev'd Jas. Somerville, Montreal.

(From MS. in possession of Rev'd W. C. Plenderleath, Mamhead Rectory, Exeter, England.

From a Memorandum of the Services of Lt..Colonel Charles Plenderleath, C. B., Sent to his Widow after his Death, on Jan. 1, 1854, by Colonel James FitzGibbon.

On the 27th of May, 1813, the American army crossed the Niagara River and drove the British from Fort George and from the whole frontier up to Fort Erie. The several frontier detachments were united at the Beaver Dam, some 10 miles back from the frontier, and thence retreated towards Burlington Heights at the head of Lake Ontario. The American army soon followed, and on the evening of the 5th of June bivouacked for the night at Stoney Creek, within 3 or 4 miles of the British. Late in the evening the British commander determined on attacking the Americans before day on the following morning; and for which purpose his small force, about 700 bayonets, was countermarched, and whilst it was yet dark commenced the attack. The enemy, about 3,000 strong, fled from around their fires in the open farm grounds where they were sleeping and formed out of view in the rear and commenced a heavy fire of cannon and musketry, while the British, endeavoring to form in extreme darkness upon unknown and rough ground covered with rail fences, fallen trees and stumps, soon fell into inextricable confusion and broke and fell back into the surrounding woods. Major P[lenderleath], who was with that part of the force which formed on the high road, soon discovered what was passing on the partially cleared ground on his right and left and decided on charging the guns in his front, in the road, then beginning to fire upon him. He called aloud for volunteers to follow him, upon which a young Scotch sergeant named Fraser, only 19 years of age, sprang forward, followed by about 30 men and led by the Major they charged the gunners, killing or dispersing every one of them. At this moment the 2 American Generals, Chandler and Winder, rushed forward, followed by some of their officers and men, but they were received on the points of the bayonets of our soldiers, who killed many of them and took the 2 Generals with 5 other officers and 75 men prisoners. These they brought off together with 2 of the field pieces, of which there were 4, but 2 had to be left behind for want of men to drag them away. The Major's horse was killed under him and he was severely wounded. On rising from the ground he laid hold of a soldier, who at this moment was near him, to help him on his feet and soon found he had hold of an American, but the man immediately surrendered on being ordered to lay down his arms.

In justice to Sergeant Fraser it ought to be stated that he stabbed 7 Americans, and his younger brother, a lad of 17, stabbed 4. The Sergeant also captured General Winder, who was in the act of raising a pistol to fire at him, but Fraser promptly put his bayonet to the General's breast and commanded him to throw the pistol down, which the General did and surrendered. Fraser is now a half-pay lieutenant and a Colonel of Militia in Upper Canada.

The Major then brought off his prisoners and guns and in the retreat was joined by scattered troops, who were now, by returning daylight, enabled to find their way back from the surrounding woods to the road.

* * * * * * * *

The advance thus made by Major P[lenderleath] saved that small army, and consequently most probably the whole of Upper Canada. For had it not been so made the Americans would have maintained their ground till daylight, when they would have discovered that our force was dispersed in the woods and liable to be easily made prisoners in detail as they issued from them to the high road individually or in small parties.

(From MSS. in possession of Rev'd W. C. Plenderleath, Mamhead Rectory, Exeter England.)

John McGillivray to Simon McTavish.

Extract of a letter from Montreal, dated 7th June, 1813:

The first ships from Quebec are to sail on the 10th inst., at least a month later than I expected, for I thought our Governor would have been solicitous to send off a vessel early with an account of our political situation, which must excite a little interest even in England.

Since the navigation opened in April the enemy has carried on his operations unmolested for the subjugation of the Upper Province. The recent surrender of Niagara has gone far towards the completion of his wishes, as we are thereby cut off from all communication with the country beyond it, and I am very apprehensive that in return for the bravery and gallant conduct of General Procter, who has so successfully fought and so repeatedly beat the enemy and with very little assistance has hitherto kept possession of not only our own territory but that of Michigan, is doomed to become the prey of an overwhelming force, or be forced to surrender for want of supplies of provisions and ammunition. He may save himself if the Indians soon join him in force, by pushing off to the River La Tranche and uniting with General Vincent at the head of Lake Ontario, but it is dubious if the latter will be able to maintain his position, and it is certain he will not if we do not beat the enemy on the lake. A failure in the latter instance would enable the Americans to land troops and cut him off from Kingston, which would be a fatal blow to him and General Procter. Our ships have sailed to supply our little army with provisions and ammunition.

An attempt may perhaps be made by General Vincent to go to the assistance of Procter, but it would be a bold measure and its success in keeping Detroit, &c., must depend on their being strongly supported by the Indians.

Dickson is expected to arrive at Detroit with a considerable number about this time, but I am afraid they will be indifferent when they find us without supplies and hear of our disasters lower down.

As the events that have been passing in this Province since the commencement of the war seem to have excited little or no alarm for our safety, it may be that Government will be a little surprised when they learn what has happened. But that will be singular, for the enemy has proclaimed his intentions, his preparations have been seen and known since October last, if not sooner, and nothing else could be expected. Believe me, that after General Brock defeated Hull and rendered abortive the designs of the American Gov't on the breaking out of the American war, every misfortune which has befallen us has arisen from the infatuation of our own Government in not sending troops and a few sailors to the province, and rendering not only unavailing but injurious to us, (by exhausting our small force), the very victories that we have so hardly and with so much difficulty obtained.

At the commencement of the war we had on Lake Ontario five fine ships carrying ten to twenty guns, when the enemy had only one 18-gun brig and four or five paltry schooners.

Strange, however, to relate, we had not a sailor nor captain to command them that had ever seen a shot fired, and when sent to capture, with our whole force, the enemy's brig they ran away because a 32-pounder was fired at them from the shore and they were afraid it would hit their vessels. It is also a fact that two of our vessels of 12 and 15 guns each would not approach a schooner with one gun, and the latter got off in triumph, loaded, too, with military stores.

When the enemy found us thus despicable they set seriously about recruiting their navy, and had so far succeeded by the end of October that they took all our merchant ships but one and blockaded our ships of war in Kingston. Had Government been pleased during the summer to have sent us about 250 sailors to fight our ships the force of the enemy would have been annihilated, their harbor rendered useless, and they never could have had it in their power to enter into competition with us on the lakes, where they have only one fort. Thus the very foundation of our misfortunes would have been destroyed, for without ships they could not have collected such large bodies of troops at any given place, nor have made any descent on our side of the lake, nor yet have prevented us from reinforcing, as was required, such points as they threatened with attack. But not a sailor was sent us till this spring and, tho' they arrived after a most fortunate passage and were sent off with uncommon expedition and exertion, yet they were only 450 in number and the blow struck beforehand. This deficiency of sailors was soon perceived, but other causes within our own control succeeded to distress us. The first was the armistice between General Prevost and General Dearborn, whereby General Brock was stopped in the career of victory and the enemy got time to strengthen their works, collect their forces and prepare for us the battle of Niagara in October. This sanguinary contest, in which that excellent and ever-to-be-lamented officer General Brock lost his life, was so favorable for us that the whole of the enemy were killed or taken, and what did his successor Major-General Sheaffe do? He liberated all his prisoners but the regulars and made an immediate armistice to give them time to collect forces for another attack. This they did in the face of our garrison, which could have destroyed their whole fortifications and taken their cannon with 100 men, so reduced were they after the action.

But as soon as General Smyth had collected 6 or 7000 men and brought his boats to a convenient spot for crossing he informed us that the armistice was at an end and again attacked us. He was defeated and their line was subsequently left to the care of about 500 men, but, as on former occasions, we were not allowed to attack them. "We would *irritate* them," said some of our wise men, "and that would unite them and then they would be sure to conquer us." The same policy has been adopted by our Government throughout. They have allowed the enemy to inflict misery on us when and where he chose and have prevented us from retaliating when in our power. In one solitary instance, at Ogdensburg, we retaliated and the Governor's General Order apologized for it. Till the end of February the whole of the enemy's navy lay in Sackett's Harbor guarded by only about 500 men, and tho' only about 40 miles distant from Kingston, and at least 2,000 men could easily have been sent over, yet the golden opportunity was neglected, the enemy perceived his danger and sent several thousand troops to guard against it.

From that time they began their preparations, which have ended in the capture of our whole line with all our valuable stores, guns and provisions at Niagara, with the sacrifice of 3 to 400 valuable lives and the pillage and ruin of all the inhabitants in that part of the country. The grand outset at York cost them, (the enemy,) 700 men, that of Fort George near 3 to 400, so that they have not obtained a bloodless conquest.

Another and very serious piece of misconduct on our part was the building a new ship, (a frigate,) *at York*, where there was neither fortifications nor troops to defend it and where it could be destroyed without the enemy's landing. There was not a man in the country besides them who laid it down that did not predict that it would be burnt on the opening of navigation, and such was the unhappy fate of this ship that had it not been burnt it was next to certain there was not water to launch it or soil to support the ways, for tides do not rise in the lakes and a deep marsh is not well calculated for supporting a heavy weight. It would also have been necessary that we should have been masters of the lakes to be enabled to transport to York the guns, anchors, cables and other materials, and if previously masters of the lake there was no occasion to build that ship.

The expense of building there was also double what it would have been at Kingston, where it would have been in company with the rest of our ships and in perfect security.

This ship, which if we had guns and sailors would now have been ready to go out, would undoubtedly have made us complete masters on the water, and the want of it may not only occasion our defeat but endanger or even cause the loss of Upper Canada.

With such ships as we possess Sir Jas. Yeo sailed from Kingston to assist General Vincent on the 3rd inst., and if Commr. Chauncey, with his 19 sail against our six, feels bold, a battle must very soon take place. I have all the confidence in Sir James that his high character deserves and hope success, tho' the odds in ships, metal and guns are much against him. I am not yet of opinion because the American frigates have beat ours that we are not superior to them, and tho' Chauncey is deemed a good officer I think Sir James is at least his match. A drawn battle will not suit us, for the enemy can soon recruit both ships and men, but we cannot. We have only a schooner on the stocks, they have a frigate.

If Chauncey does not come out till the new frigate is ready, which will be in a month, we shall be badly off for he will then have a superiority we cannot oppose. We ought in such a case to send 3 or 4,000 men down to Sackett's Harbor and I am confident with the assistance of our fleet we will destroy them. If we can do that we may recover Niagara, but I am afraid we cannot do it otherwise.

Indeed it would be folly to attempt it with less than 4,000 regulars, aided by our fleet, the militia and Indians.

The Americans have at least 10,000 men on our side and can destroy batteries, carry off guns and render the post untenable, but by superior numbers. If the enemy beats our fleet we must try to keep Kingston, which it will be difficult to do as they can cut off the communication between that place and Montreal and prevent supplies from being forwarded. Thus our situation is not the most agreeable and we have little prospect of its being better. A great part of the intended reinforcements for this country is to come from Halifax, yet strange to say tho' the troops were there since March, if not sooner, none of them have yet appeared, altho' the sailors arrived from Europe a month ago.

Those from Cadiz have not arrived nor any others but 1,500 men from Ireland, partly raw recruits. One would really imagine that Government expects this extensive country to be maintained against the population of the United States by a handful of men, for if only 6,000 troops come out this year they may indeed, with the sacrifice of every comfort of the inhabitants and of their ordinary pursuits, enable us to defend the Lower Province, but as to acting offensively it is a mere farce.

The enemy will be much elated with his late success and will readily get as many volunteers as he chooses, to molest us in the Upper Province and threaten us here. This will divide our small force and render it inadequate to any enterprise.

I shall not be surprised if in the course of three or four weeks we have 8 or 10,000 of them on our lines.

An alarm was given us the other day when two of their armed schooners of 11 guns each, attacked four gunboats we have a little beyond Isle Aux Noix. We luckily took them and they will be of great service to us on Lake Champlain, where we had not a vessel.

In general we are badly off for intelligence of the enemy's operations because economy will not admit the expense of obtaining it, while on the other hand we have a considerable number of Americans residing in the Province who give their countrymen all the information they can wish. The business of York has given such a disgust to General Sheaffe that he can never have the least influence in that Province. The enemy not only got the public stores there, but we did not remove the military chest in which there was £2,500; the Royal Standard was left, but fortunately must not have been found by the enemy, and we think was consumed in the Government House, and what may be more injurious to us still, no part of the correspondence of the Government or any of the public confidential papers were removed. The enemy got them all and a portion of them will very probably hereafter decorate the columns of the American Gazette. I shall say nothing of the manner in which the defence of the place was conducted, as opinions are divided, but it is very harshly censured.

To come to our actual situation, I shall confine myself to observing that nothing but a naval victory can save any part of the Upper Province above Kingston, and if we are beat the latter place as well as the whole of that country must, I fear, fall.

The system hitherto pursued of not attacking the enemy, however fair the opportunity, has been our ruin, and if continued must involve us all in distress and cause our subjugation. Should we fortunately obtain a decided naval victory we shall probably be able to drive the enemy out of the Upper Province, as we need not keep a strong garrison at Kingston, and our whole force may be directed to one point. I am not without hopes of success and am convinced that Sir James Yeo will beat them if anybody can. They have at least 1,000 good sailors, which is more than double our number. But we are not disheartened, as the disposition of the people is good, and both by water and land we shall give many hard blows before we surrender. The 8th Regt. has suffered severely in the action at York and Fort George and the officers in general have borne their share of the misfortunes of the day. None of our friends at Niagara are killed, &c., &c.

Endorsed:

"Mr. McGillivray, 10th Aug't, 1813."

(Apparently communicated to Lord Bathurst on that day.)

(Canadian Archives, Q. 125, p. 87.)

Colonel John Vincent to Sir George Prevost.

BURLINGTON BAY, 8th June, 1813.

SIR,—After having closed my despatch of the 6th instant to Your Excellency I regret to find that I have omitted the name of Mr. Hackett, Acting Staff Surgeon to the army. It is but justice to him to say that by his judicious arrangement the wounded have received every attention and are most of them likely to be restored to the service.

(Canadian Archives, C. 679.)

Major Charles A. Plenderleath, 49th Regiment, to General Vincent.

ST. DAVIDS, 23d July, 1813.

SIR,—I have much satisfaction in relating to you such of the particulars of the distinguished conduct of Sergeant Alexander Fraser of the 49th Regiment, Assistant Sergeant-Major, in the action at Stoney Creek, as fell under my own observation.

After our first advance and dispersion of the enemy on the right I was proceeding across the meadow, guided by a fire of musketry, to find the enemy more to the left, when the discharge of a field piece pointed out the position of his guns upon the top of the hill at a very inconsiderable distance. Another having been fired, without doing any injury, altho' so close upon them, I told the men about me the moment must be seized to charge the guns before they were reloaded, when Sergeant Fraser very gallantly advanced, setting a noble example to about fifteen or twenty men, who rushed forward with him and carried a howitzer and three six-pounders, killing at the same time a great many of the enemy. The party afterwards charged and put to flight a body of infantry formed immediately in rear of the guns, which gave us possession of the caissons and some of the horses. General Winder surrendered to and gave up his sword to Sergeant Fraser, who immediately presented it to me, and I afterwards delivered it to Lieut.-Colonel Harvey.

I have been informed that Brigadier-General Chandler was also made a prisoner at the guns. There were some officers taken but their names were not reported to me.

Sergeant Fraser is the son of a soldier of the Royal Veterans and a young man whose general character is not unknown to you. I consider it only necessary to mention that at the age of twenty-three he has been for the last six months Assistant Sergeant-Major of the regiment.

(Canadian Archives, C. 679.)

Col. James Burn, 2d Light Dragoons, to Major-General Dearborn.

(Extract.)

(No. 2.)

In the afternoon of the 5th our advance guard, consisting of the light infantry under the command of Captains Hindman, Biddle and Nicholas, a part of the rifle corps under Captain Lytle and a detachment of the 2d Dragoons under Captain Selden, commenced a sharp skirmish with the advance of the enemy, said to be a detachment of the 49th Regiment, which soon retreated, covered by a thick woods, having, however, several wounded on both sides and one dragoon horse killed. In the evening our advance returned behind Stoney Creek, where the army took a position for the night. The light infantry and part of the rifle corps on the right of the 25th Regiment formed the right wing. The artillery under Captains Towson and L. Leonard the centre. The 5th, 16th, 23d and some riflemen the left wing and the cavalry in the rear. A strong picket guard was posted some distance in front, also strong flank and rear guards, in such a manner as to surround the whole encampment with sentinels. The troops lay under arms without any covering. Our troops in the field did not exceed one thousand—three hundred effectives of the 13th and 14th Regiments having encamped on the borders of the lake, about three miles distant, for the protection of the boats. The enemy forced our picket and attacked us about two o'clock in the morning, (which was very dark,) with their army and Indians, expecting no doubt to throw us into confusion. Their views were in this instance, however, completely frustrated, and when the day dawned none were to be seen except their killed and wounded, who covered the field of battle. The attack began on our right and was gallantly repelled by the fire of the light troops and 25th Regiment, commanded by Major Smith. In a few minutes it became general along the whole line and was nobly returned by the artillery of the centre, commanded by Captains Towson and L. Leonard, and again by the troops of the left wing, viz.: The 5th under Lieutenant-Colonel Milton; the 23d, commanded by Major Armstrong, and the 16th. The fire continued with little intermission for one hour, during which time the enemy attempted by frequent charges to break our line, but without effect, being obliged to give away by the well directed fire of our brave troops.

The 13th and 14th Regiments, (which had been detached the preceding evening,) were active in making prisoners and advanced with much ardor to the field in hopes of sharing with the gallant 5th and 25th, 23d and light troops the glory of another combat. But the unfortunate capture of Brigadier-Generals Chandler and Winder, who were taken in the action unknown to any part of the army, and hurried into the enemy's lines, prevented the future operations from being carried into effect with the promptitude which would assuredly have taken place had either of those officers been present to command.

You will be surprised to find our loss so small; that of the enemy exceeds ours much. They lost in killed about sixty, many wounded and upwards of seventy prisoners, all regulars and principally of the 49th Regiment. Several of their officers were killed, wounded and missing. A flag was sent by Colonel Harvey asking permission to make inquiries for them, also to be allowed to send a surgeon to attend their own wounded, which I readily granted. On the return of daylight I found the command of the army had devolved on me, and being at a loss what steps to pursue in the unpleasant dilemma occasioned by the capture of our Generals, finding the ammunition of many of the troops nearly expended, I had recourse to a council of the field officers present, of whom a majority coincided in opinion with me that we ought to retire to our former position at the Forty

Mile Creek, where we could be supplied with ammunition and provisions and either advance or remain until further orders.

Every aid was afforded by the staff. The Assistant Adjutant General, Major Johnson, and Brigade Majors Jones and Whartenby exerted themselves in rendering all the assistance in their power.

The army on this occasion has proved its firmness and bravery by keeping its position in a night attack, in which the yells of the Indians, mingled with the roaring of cannon and musketry, were calculated to intimidate. The enemy charged repeatedly, and so dark was the night that our army could not distinguish friend from foe; in one of these they succeeded in carrying off a six-pounder, a howitzer and a caisson, to the great mortification of our brave artillery. I presume it was on that occasion also that we lost our Generals, who were distinctly heard encouraging our men to fight. The squadron of dragoons remained formed and steady at their post, but could not act on account of the darkness of the night and the thickness of the adjacent woods. Much credit is due to the troops generally, but too much praise cannot be said of the conduct of the 5th and 25th Regiments.

(American State Papers, Military Affairs.)

Report of the Killed, Wounded and Missing, in the Action of the 6th of June at Stoney Creek.

Killed—1 sergeant, 1 corporal, 15 privates.

Wounded—1 captain, 1 sergeant, 2 corporals and 34 privates.

Missing—2 brigadier-generals, 1 major, 3 captains, 1 subaltern, 9 sergeants, 4 corporals and 80 privates.

Total killed, wounded and missing, 154.

Correct return from the reports of the different corps in the action of the 6th instant at Stoney Creek.

J. JOHNSON, Asst. Adj. Gen.

(From the Historical Register of the United States, 1814, Vol. II., pp. 240-1.)

General John Chandler to General Dearborn.

MONTREAL, June 18, 1813.

SIR,—I deem it my duty to improve the earliest opportunity possible to give you a more detailed account of the affair of the 6th instant, near Stoney Creek, than I have before had it in my power to do.

On the morning of the 5th I arrived at Forty Mile Creek. The detachment under General Winder was then under marching orders for Stoney Creek. After a short halt the whole marched for that place and arrived there between five and six o'clock p. m., at which place a small picket of the enemy was posted, but retired on our approach. The advanced guard pursued, and soon fell in with a picket of about one hundred strong under Colonel Williams. A skirmish ensued. I hastened the main body. Williams retreated and our advance pursued. The pursuit was continued rather longer than I could have wished, but returned to their proper place in the line of march not far from sunset. I had ordered the 13th and 14th, who were in the rear, to take a position for the night near the mouth of the creek to cover the boats, (should they arrive,) which would be on the route which I intended to pursue the next morning, and a favorable position presenting itself I encamped with the rest of the troops, (except Captain Archer's company of artillery which accompanied the 13th and 14th,) on the spot where we had halted, with an advanced picket from half to three-quarters of a mile in front, with express orders for them to keep out constantly a patrol. A right and left guard and a rear guard were also posted. I gave positive orders for the troops to lay on their arms. Contrary to my orders fires were kindled, but there are doubts whether this operated for or against us, the fires of the 25th, which were in front, and by my orders had been abandoned, enabled us to see a small part of the enemy, while the fires on our left enabled the enemy to see our line. On the whole I think it operated against us. I did expect the enemy would attack us that night if he intended to fight, but perhaps this was not expected by all. I had my horse confined near me and directed that the harness should not be taken from the artillery horses. I directed where and how the line should be formed in case of attack. About an hour before daylight on the morning of the 6th an alarm was given. I was instantly up, and the 25th, which lay near me, was almost as instantly formed, as well as the 5th and 23d, which were on the left under the immediate eye of General Winder. Owing to the neglect of the front picket or some other cause, the British officers say that they were not hailed nor an alarm given until they were within three hundred yards of our line. The extreme darkness prevented us from seeing or knowing at what point they intended to attack us until an attack was made on our right. A well directed fire was opened on them from the 25th and from nearly all the whole line. After a few minutes I heard several muskets in our rear in the direction of the rear guard, and then expected that the enemy had gained our rear by some path unknown to me and were about to attack us in rear. I instantly ordered Colonel Milton with the 5th to form in our rear near the woods to meet such circumstances as might take place, knowing that I could call him to any other point if necessary at any moment. I had observed that the artillery was not covered, and directed General Winder to cause the 23d to be formed so far to the right that their right should cover the artillery. At this moment I heard a new burst of fire from the enemy's left or our right, and not being able to see anything which took place, I set out full speed towards our right to take measures to prevent my right flank from being turned, which I expected was the object of the enemy. I had proceeded but a few yards before my horse fell under me, by which fall I received a serious injury. Here was a time when I have no recollection of what passed, but I presume it was not long. As soon as I recovered I recollected what my object was, and made my way to the right and gave Major Smith such directions as I thought proper to prevent his right being turned by surprise. I was then returning toward the centre, and when near the artillery heard men who, by the noise, appeared to be in confusion, it being the point at which I expected the 23d to be formed. I expected it was that regiment. I approached there and as soon as I was near enough I saw a body of men, whom I thought to be the 23d, in rear of the artillery, broken. I hobbled in amongst them and began to rally them and directed them to form, but I soon found my mistake. It was the British 49th, who had pushed forward to the head of their column and gained the rear of the artillery. I was immediately disarmed and conveyed down the column to its rear. It was not yet day and the extreme darkness of the night, to which was added the smoke of the fire, put it totally out of our power to see the situation of the enemy. This was all that saved their columns from sure and total destruction, of which some of their officers are aware. After seeing the situation of the column I did hope and expect that General Winder, on the first dawn of light, would see their situation and bring Colonel Milton with the 5th, (who I had still kept in reserve until I could have daylight to discern their situation,) to attack this column, which I am sure he would have done to advantage; but to my mortification I soon learned that he had fallen into the same mistake as myself, and by endeavoring to learn what was taking place in the centre he was also taken, as well as Major Van De Venter. To the extreme darkness of the night, the enemy's knowledge of his intended point of attack and our not knowing where to expect him, must be attributed his partial success, and not to a want of strength or bravery in our troops, who generally behaved remarkably well under all the circumstances, and, however unfortunate the event as it relates to myself, I only ask that all the circumstances may be taken into consideration in making up your opinion upon the conduct of General Winder and myself in this affair, which I am sure you will do, and I flatter myself you will see no cause of censure. I regret that my decrepit situation and the rapidity with which we have been brought to this place has put it out of my power to give you a detailed account of the affair earlier. I am now able to walk some with the aid of a cane, and hope I shall continue to recover.

(American State Papers, Military Affairs.)

(From the Buffalo Gazette, 8th June, 1813.)

BATTLE AT NEWARK.

The following comes from a respectable and indisputable source and may be relied on as perfectly correct :

To the Editor of the Buffalo Gazette :

SIR,—That the public may have a correct idea of the descent on Canada at Newark, I enclose you an extract from the General Order:

A corps of light infantry, consisting of 400 men, Forsyth's riflemen, the flank companies of the 15th infantry, accompanied by one 3-pounder, are to form the advance under Colonel Scott. It is intended that corps should first effect a landing, scour and possess the shore and cover the landing of the troops who are to follow. The riflemen to advance in front and on the flanks or obliquely to the flanks, according to circumstances. It is not intended that Colonel Scott should advance beyond 300 paces before he is supported by the first brigade.

Boyd's brigade, (the first,) will follow quickly in support to advance or display, [i. e., deploy,] according to the disposition and movements of the enemy. Lieut.-Colonel Porter's corps of light artillery to accompany this brigade, and the volunteers will be on its flanks. In like manner Winder's brigade will follow in quick succession to advance in column and display on Boyd's left or remain in column, as may be deemed expedient by General Lewis. Chandler's brigade and Colonel Macomb's corps to constitute the reserve. As soon as the main line is formed Colonel Scott will advance, not more than 300 paces, in front of the infantry, and if the enemy appear in force the light troops will fall back and form on the flanks. The direction of the boats and the embarkation of the troops will be arranged by Commodore Chauncey.

By order of the Major-General, Commanding in Chief,

W. SCOTT, Adj. Gen.

The charge of the light troops and Boyd's brigade upon the enemy on the bank was so impetuous that Winder's brigade and the reserve were not gratified in coming into action. The enemy fled, leaving 260 of his regulars killed and wounded on the field, among whom were Colonel Myers of the 49th and several officers of distinction. The cannonade commenced at dawn of day; the day was fine and the American bank covered with spectators. On a signal given by General Dearborn* from the *Madison* the advance pushed for the shore; the different brigades of boats under cover of the shipping followed in rapid succession. The enemy was drawn up in battle array on the hostile shore, and as the boats advanced the water appeared in foam from the impression of his fire; after fifteen or twenty minutes struggle the American arms again triumphed in Canada. The tremendous cannonade kept up by the shipping—the atmosphere filled with fire and shells from Fort George and Niagara —Fort George, in flames from our hot shot, still keeping up a spirited fire of grape and shrapnel shells on our troops, now formed in rear of the town—these combined with the contest on the bank contributed to render it one of the most grand and interesting spectacles that has ever been witnessed.

Further Particulars—From an intelligent officer we learn that the American loss in the action was 39 killed and 110 wounded; 105 of the enemy's regulars were found on the field of battle and buried by our troops; 163 wounded were taken into hospital and 115 prisoners, (not wounded,) were taken from the enemy, exclusive of officers.

The inhabitants of Canada opposite to us appear to be well suited in the recent change of affairs. We learn that nearly all the militia from Chippawa to Point Abino have come in and received their parole from Colonel Preston at Fort Erie.

At Fort George multitudes of the Canadians have come in and claimed the protection of the Commander in Chief.

The fleet under Commodore Chauncey left Niagara on Sunday week for Sackett's Harbor. So we may soon expect to hear of *compliments* passing between the gallant Chauncey and Sir James L. Yeo.

The British army, it appears by recent advices from Niagara, is now at 40 Mile Creek near the head of Lake Ontario, at a stronghold about 6 miles from the lake, at a pass in the mountain which extends from Queenston Heights to the head of the lake. It is said they have several pieces of artillery with them, that their force is about 2,000 regulars and a few Indians. We also understand that Generals Boyd, Winder, and Chandler have marched against the enemy. It is expected that General Procter is on his march from Malden to the head of the lake.

---

*General Dearborn had been confined several days to his room by a fever and, contrary to the advice of his physician, insisted on being conveyed on board the *Madison* where he might superintend every movement*.

Our flotilla on Lake Erie will soon be ready for sailing. The vessels at Erie are rapidly fitting out. Those at Black Rock are now armed and rigged complete, only waiting a wind to make up the rapids.

(File in Buffalo Public Library.)

(From the Baltimore Whig.)

FORT GEORGE, June 8th, 1813.

Yesterday the British squadron of two large ships and four smaller vessels hove in sight. At one time they appeared to be standing towards the head of the lake, at another standing for this place. We were, of course, on the alert. Towards night the fleet bore away N. W., but as we were suspicious of their intentions and knew the facility with which they might return and land a force, all remained at their posts. About 2 o'clock in the morning several guns were fired from one of our picket guards. An alarm was fired from our forts, and all paraded and marched to the assigned spot with the utmost imaginable promptitude. It proved a false alarm, occasioned by some boats rowing down along shore from Forty Mile Creek with our wounded and 52 British prisoners on board. They were fired on by our pickets . . . .

. . . .

Very heavy cannonading was heard all this morning. It must either proceed from our army or the enemy's squadron.

(File in Philadelphia Library.)

Battle of Stoney Creek.

DEAR SIR,—With regard to your enquiries I can assure you that I am happy in being able to give a considerable detailed account of our Northern army on the Canada frontier, during the early part of the year 1813, so far as they affect the military reputation of General Chandler. I shall do this with the greater satisfaction as I have noticed with some solicitude for the credit of the late army and our country those incorrect statements, (and some of them under the imposing character of "official reports,") to which you allude as having been so injurious to the reputation of that valuable officer. On this account, in regard to the veracity of its narration, you may implicitly rely. For you, Sir, I am persuaded this assertion will be sufficient. If it were not I could produce the testimony of others of the most respectable kind in support of every material part.

Among the first operations connected with our subject was the capture of Fort George, situated on the British side of Lake Ontario and near its upper end, which took place on the 27th of May. Pursuant to the arrangements made by the Commander-in-Chief for effecting this object, the light troops under Colonel Scott were to form the advance and consequently occupy the first line of boats for the purpose of landing. The second line was to contain the brigade of General Boyd and the third that of General Winder. These were to be followed by the reserve in the fourth line under the command of General Chandler, embracing his own brigade and Colonel Macomb's corps of artillery. The orders provided that the several lines should observe a proper distance from each other, in order to avoid the confusion which might arise from any succeeding line arriving before the troops of the preceding had disembarked. Owing to the extreme and protracted indisposition of Major-General Dearborn he was under the necessity of remaining on board the flotilla, ordering Major-General Lewis to assume the immediate command as soon as the troops should arrive at the shore.

Agreeably to these dispositions Scott's command first landed under cover of the fire from the fleet of Com. Chauncey, and commenced the attack with promptness and gallantry. The remaining lines arrived, disembarked, and formed to sustain them in as rapid succession as was practicable. The conflict was severe but of short duration. When the enemy discovered that the troops of the first and second lines had effected a landing, that those of the third were disembarking, and that the reserve was in readiness to land whenever space should be made for that purpose, he commenced a retreat.

About this time in consequence of the repeated intimations from the commanding general of the importance of a more prompt attention to orders and expressing, it is said, extreme solicitude on account of the procrastinating disposition discoverable in the part of the officer to whom he had committed the charge of the expedition, Gen. Lewis found himself on shore.

Brig. Gen. Chandler having landed almost at the same moment at the head of his command, with the alacrity characteristic of the good soldier immediately despatched Capt. Tobey, his orderly officer, to inform Gen. Lewis that by the time he should receive the communication his line would be formed and waiting his orders, expecting, doubtless, that they would be for an immediate and rapid pursuit of the enemy, which must have resulted in the capture or complete destruction of the whole British force. Such, however, was not the case. The remainder of the day was occupied in fruitless preparations which tended to protract rather than forward any practicable object, and indicated a disposition rather to assume the *appearance* of activity than to hazard the consequences of its reality. Consequently the reserve was not brought into action during the day, but in furnishing boats for the landing of the artillery it, however, suffered some inconsiderable loss. It is perhaps difficult for one who has never been exposed to the same mortification to judge how much the feelings of officers, particularly of a commander, must suffer for being thus improperly deprived of an opportunity of rendering essential service to his country, and of gratifying that laudable desire of fame which always inhabits the bosoms of the brave.

The Commander-in-Chief, to his mortification and disappointment, having learned that General Lewis had neglected to pursue the advantage that had been gained, ordered him the next morning to commence an immediate pursuit of the retreating enemy with the brigades of Generals Chandler and Winder, a part of Colonel Burn's dragoons and a corps of riflemen. After having wasted as much of the forenoon as could with any decency be consumed in *preparation*, he commenced his march and proceeded, during the day, as far as Queenstown, a distance of *seven miles!* Finding very convenient lodgings, he took up his quarters for the night at this place, retaining General Winder's brigade, and ordering that of General Chandler's, with part of the dragoons and riflemen, to advance as far as St. David's, where they arrived just before dark and encamped.

It was now, however, too late to pursue the enemy by this route, and as Major General Dearborn had received intelligence that he was endeavouring to gain Burlington Heights he ordered General Lewis to fall back upon Fort George with a view, it appeared, of ordering a detachment to pursue the route by the lake road, as that was most practicable and afforded a prospect of cutting off the retreat of the British to York. General Chandler received orders to return to Fort George on the following morning and arrived at that post a little before night on the same day. General Winder was then ordered to march by the lake road for Forty Mile Creek with the 5th, 13th, 14th and 16th regiments of infantry, two companies of artillery, part of Col. Burn's regiment of dragoons, and part of a company of riflemen, in the whole amounting to about 1400 men. On the 3rd of June General Chandler received orders to join General Winder with the 9th, 23rd and 25th regiments of infantry, one company of artillery and part of a company of riflemen, and assume command of the whole. He effected a junction with General Winder's detachment at Forty Mile Creek on the morning of the 5th, and at 11 o'clock took up the line of march for Stoney Creek, eleven miles beyond, with the intention, it is believed, of crossing the neck of land between Lake Ontario and Burlington Bay, intercepting the communication between York and Burlington Heights, where the enemy had now established his headquarters, and thus cutting off his retreat.

When we had nearly arrived at Stoney Creek, where the road is little more than a mile from the lake, his advance fell in with a strong British picket under the command of Col. Williams and a skirmish ensued. Gen. Chandler, being then marching by his left, ordered the 25th to the support of his advance. On the approach of this regiment the enemy broke, scattered and fled, and it was not till after sunset that the pursuit was abandoned. Finding his position tenable the General concluded to halt here for the night. The 13th and 14th Regiments, with a company of artillery, were ordered to take a strong station on the lake shore near the mouth of Stoney Creek and something over a mile from the encampment, in order to protect the ammunition, baggage and provisions, which were expected to arrive in boats from Fort George. The position selected for the encampment was near a small meadow by which it was in some measure defended in front as well as by the almost perpendicular ascent on the rear or southerly side of the same to the upland and on the brow of which was a fence, partly of logs and partly of rails, and in addition to which, near the borders of the meadow, the timbers having been felled but not cleared away was so overgrown with briars and small bushes as to be rendered nearly impassable except in the wood. On the left the mountains and woods shut down so close upon the meadow as to render that flank quite secure, and the right was equally protected by a swamp which approached it on that quarter. Little danger was apprehended in the rear as there was no passage known by which it could be gained by the enemy. The guards were posted by Col. Burn, who was officer of the day. The 9th Regiment, being very small and in rear, formed the rear guard. The advance picket was posted from half to three-quarters of a mile in advance of the meadow. The right flank guard was posted on the right of the meadow near the swamp, and the left on the opposite flank near the mountain.

That General Chandler expected an attack during the night, and that at the very point it was afterwards made, is evident from the disposition of his guards and his subsequent precautionary measures. Indeed, so far from "having been taken by surprise" he is known to have declared to General Winder that if the enemy intended to fight them he would commence the attack before morning, and with this expectation the arrangements were made.

The troops had no opportunity to cook their provisions for the day; the General deemed it prudent for them to occupy ground and build fires for that purpose at stations considerably distant from those selected for the encampment, from which they should be removed into the line whenever they should be refreshed, so that the enemy should not be able to calculate from reconnoitering in the evening what their position would be in the latter part of the night. He therefore ordered the 25th infantry and the light troops in advance to form a line and kindle their fires at about 150 yards in advance of the high ground in rear of the meadow, where he intended to await the attack, if it should be made in front as was expected. The other regiments were ordered to form on a ridge of ground in the rear of the meadow and on the left of the road, and extended to line of their fires from north to south. The artillery was likewise posted on the upland in rear of the meadow, in a position to rake the road, which was nearly straight for a distance of half a mile.

As soon as the troops had finished their cooking and were refreshed, when it was near midnight, the General ordered that part of his forces which were in advance of the meadow to leave their fires burning, fall back to the upland and form on the right of the road near the fence with the left of the 25th resting on the right of the artillery. The regiments on the left were at the same time ordered to advance in an oblique direction toward the road and fence by wheeling them practically to the left so as to form three lines, by each succeeding regiment being a little in the rear and to the left of the preceding, somewhat in the *eschellon* form, having the 23rd in front on the left of the artillery and near the road and fence. Colonel Burn's dragoons were ordered to post themselves in rear of the whole and also near the road. In the event of an attack in the front the 23rd was to form so as to cover the artillery with its right on the left of the 25th. The 16th was to form to the left of this regiment, the 5th to the left of the 16th, and the light troops to the left of the whole. The dragoons of Colonel Burn were to act as circumstances should require. The whole forces were likewise ordered to ground and lie upon their arms, so that on being ordered to rise they would be formed into platoons and sections as when they halted.

By these arrangements the General would not only prevent the enemy from gaining a knowledge of his position and have his own forces in constant readiness for action, but by leaving the fires in front would also gain the double advantage of deceiving him and of availing himself of the light to regulate his own movements and discover those of his opponents if they should advance within the first line of fires. Had the rear line on the left been permitted to remain its light would have given them the same advantage in that quarter. Several times, however, contrary to orders, some of these fires were rekindled, but they were again extinguished the moment they were discovered by the General, who was constantly on his guard and did not suffer himself to sleep during the night, which was as dark and gloomy as can well be imagined. It was cloudy, misty and perfectly calm, and the fog which arose from the low land completed the obscurity.

About an hour before daylight the discharge of a musket was heard by the General, who was then in his tent on the left of the 25th. Immediately he with his Assistant Adjutant General, Johnson, who was then in his tent, was mounted and gave orders to form for action, which was done with the greatest facility by the troops under his more immediate command, as they had only to stand upon the ground they then occupied. Major Johnson was forthwith despatched to General Winder, who commanded the left wing, with orders to cause the infantry on the left to advance to the fence in rear of the meadow, where the ground was too wet to admit their laying down upon it, there to await the attack. This was scarcely done when the head of the British column was seen by the light of the fires in front, advancing to their line, expecting doubtless to find the Americans sleeping by them and intending to deploy to the left and dash in upon them.

The 25th, the light troops upon the right and nearly at the same time the artillery now opened their fire upon him, which considerably checked his progress. Soon after, the 5th and light troops on the left also commenced their fire, and as the enemy was between the advance line of fires and our troops they enjoyed an advantage which was well improved by those who were brought into action. The excessive darkness of the night, however, rendered it impossible for the General to ascertain whether his own troops had all been formed or what was the number and exact position of the enemy. Shortly after the commencement of the action therefore, hearing the discharge of muskets in the rear in the direction of his rear guard, and apprehending that quarter might have been gained by some route unknown to him and he might there be attacked, he ordered the 5th to form in that direction, at some distance from the line, in order to protect it. He now observed that the fire near the artillery was not as brisk as he expected, and riding up to ascertain the cause discovered that the 23d had not taken the position to which they had been directed. He therefore again ordered them to be formed so as to cover the artillery according to his previous arrangement. By this time the enemy appeared to be completely broken, and the General had every reason to suppose he could keep him employed and at bay until daylight, when there could be no doubt of obtaining a decisive victory. He was thus anxiously expecting the first glimmer of dawn, when a new burst of fire was heard upon his right. Having just before despatched Major Johnson, as also his Brigade Major and his aid, to other parts of the line, he unfortunately had now no officer about him by whom to transmit orders or gain intelligence. Apprehending, however, that the enemy might have received a reinforcement and endeavor to turn his right, and being aware of the importance of ascertaining this point as soon as possible, he attempted to repair thither himself with all the rapidity of which the ground would permit. He had not proceeded far when his horse was killed under him while in full speed, and himself severely wounded by the fall. Stunned, as he must have been, by the shock, he perhaps was not himself sensible how long he remained on the field before he was able to recover himself. He arose as soon as possible, and passing the 25th, whom he encouraged in the performance of their duty with perfect coolness, arrived on the right and ordered Major Smith to wheel the platoon on his right to the left backward, (the fence in front not permitting it to be wheeled forward,) and by this means prevent the enemy from gaining the rear of his right by surprize. The fire of the British had now considerably subsided, and the General was about returning to the centre, there appearing to be some convulsion about the artillery and on the ground where he had repeatedly ordered the 23d to be formed. Knowing this regiment to be new and undisciplined, he naturally concluded it might have broken and thereby occasioned the confusion he had discovered. Instead of the 23d, this confusion was occasioned by a body of the enemy who, owing to the 23d not having been formed according to orders, had penetrated his centre, but were broken and now retreating. But from the unusual darkness, which prevented his distinguishing one corps from another, he did not learn his mistake till he was surrounded by this body of British, and by calling on the name of an officer who was not in their service discovered to them that he was an American. He was then immediately seized, disarmed and taken into their rear. Almost at the same moment General Winder from similar causes likewise fell into the hands of the enemy.

Unquestionably there was not, at this time, an entire platoon in the whole British forces. Captain Miles (Milnes), an aid to Governor Prevost, who had a command on that night, repeatedly acknowledged that their troops broke at the commencement of the action, and that it was not possible to form them again until they had retreated from the scene of action next morning, and that in the excessive darkness he had himself lost his command and did not find it again during the night. He likewise stated that General Vincent was also driven from his command and did not recover it until the afternoon of the succeeding day, and then at the distance of seven miles from the field of battle, and that he passed the forenoon in concealment among the woods, concluding that his own forces were totally destroyed and that his only chance for safety lay in secreting himself until the American forces should be withdrawn. Certain it is, he only joined his army at the time and place above stated. It is also certain that Colonel Harvey, the next in command, must have supposed him either killed or wounded or taken, as he sent in several flags during the next day with a view of ascertaining his situation, although in doing this he might have had the further object of learning whether the American forces were advancing.

The British must have considered their fall as inevitable for some time after the action, since their loss was more than four times greater than that of the Americans, being little less than five hundred in killed, wounded and missing; and since, from the circumstance of their having made every preparation for retreat by slinging their knapsacks and putting every horse which they could muster to the waggons, it is evident they had abandoned all ideas of further resistance and would have fled on the first appearance of pursuit. From every consideration it is obvious that the remnant of the enemy owed its safety to the misfortune of the Americans in losing their commanders.

Indeed, the Americans, although very possibly dispirited by the unfortunate loss of their Generals, were unbroken, as the greater part of them had not suffered in the slightest degree. The 13th and 14th Regiments, which were the strongest, being at a distance from the scene of action, had nothing to do with it except in collecting a considerable number of prisoners whom on their return next day they found scattered through the woods in every direction. The 9th infantry and Colonel Burn's dragoons being in the rear were not at all engaged, nor was the 23rd, notwithstanding the exertions of the commanding Generals. The 16th, likewise, was only partially engaged, for when the enemy on the first fire set up an hideous Indian yell this regiment broke and only a small part of them could again be formed and brought into action—who, however, displayed great bravery. The whole loss of those who were engaged on the American side did not exceed thirty in killed and wounded, and was something less than one hundred prisoners. It is not, however, intended by these observations to censure Colonel Burn, on whom the command devolved, for not pursuing the enemy, nor in any measure to impeach the bravery of this officer, or to question the correctness of his conduct on the present occasion.

The occasion of the British having approached so near our lines before they were discovered was afterwards learned from themselves. Major Mundy [Munday], who led their advance and was severely wounded, stated to several American officers that he did not fall in with our advance guard at all, and that they must have been asleep in the church near which they were posted, and that the first centinel with whom he fell in near the church was totally ignorant of his duty, and was taken without noise. From him the Major unquestionably obtained the countersign, as he stated that no difficulty was experienced in capturing the other centinels except the one who was posted next the line, who did his duty faithfully and by discharging his piece gave the first notice of their approach.

Such, Sir, were the events of that part of the campaign of 1813 for his conduct in which General Chandler has been censured. How little he has deserved this you will judge. For myself and on the authority of a respectable number of officers under his command, and of several engineers and other officers who have since visited the position chosen for his encampment on the night of his rencounter with the enemy, I can safely avow my belief that but for the misfortune to which any officer, however able or intelligent, must have been equally liable, he would have obtained a most brilliant and decisive victory, and in the words of an order of Major Johnson issued immediately subsequent to the action, "have been covered with glory." Indeed, had it not been for the lamented death of that valuable officer the calumnies to which you refer would have been as ephemeral as the characters of those who originally propagated them.

(From Niles' Register, volume 11, pp. 116-119. Oct. 19th. 1816. Probably inspired by General Chandler himself.)

General Chandler and the Affair of Stoney Creek.

General Chandler has made an appeal to the public on his military conduct at Stoney Creek, for the two-fold purpose, it would seem, of repelling what he terms calumnies and of fixing a stigma on the reputation of his then superior officer, Major-General Lewis. Had his statement been confined to the single object of self-justification, his ignorance and errors might have quietly accompanied him into obscurity unnoticed and undisturbed, but having indulged in malice unprovoked, in assertion unwarranted and in vanity unparalleled, to exhibit him as he is becomes a duty.

The appeal, which may be seen in a late number of the Boston *Patriot*, the *Aurora* of the 12th ult., and the eighth number of the 11th vol. of *Niles' Weekly Register* I do not hesitate to ascribe to General Chandler himself. Not that I mean to charge him with having written anything so voluminous, but I do assert on its intrinsic evidence that he furnished the material for the fabrication, the miserable attempt at deception imprinted on its front to the contrary notwithstanding.

Enveloped in Cimmerian darkness, with "no officers about him by whom to transmit orders or gain intelligence," what wizard discovered that "his horse was killed under him while in full speed; that, stunned with the shock and perhaps not sensible how long he laid on the field, he arose as soon as possible," &c., that afterwards, unable from the darkness to distinguish friend from foe, "he was captured in the rear of the artillery, seized, disarmed and taken to the rear of the British forces." These facts, if facts they are, could be known to the General only or to some one endued with that spirit which inspired the Grecian bard to sing the visions of the Thracian king, wrapped in his sleep of death: "So dreamed the monarch and awaked no more."

The attention of the reader is here called to a slight shade of difference between the present account of the direful fate of the General and his steed and that contained in his official report under date of the 18th of June, 1813, and published by order of the House of Representatives of the United States. The misfortune of Bucephalus was then represented as less severe than now. He was not stated to have fallen *to rise no more*. In that the General simply says: "My horse fell under me." But that the General's horse was *killed* under him will sound better in story.

That the first account was most correct is held the better opinion. The transaction was then recent, of course fresh, in the General's memory. Besides, the circumstances of neither horse, saddle nor bridle being found next morning after the most diligent search justifies the conclusion that a courser in full speed, over ground covered with fallen trees and briers, with no other light to mark his devious way than that which, like the flashes from Phlegeton, rendered darkness more visible, may stumble and dismount his rider without the aid of a British bullet.

Another evidence that the report and appeal is of one common origin may be derived from the similarity not only of style but form of expression. The report—"I heard a new burst of fire from the enemy's left on our right." The appeal—"When a new burst of fire was heard on his right." If these proofs are not sufficient, on closer comparison many more may be discovered.

The appeal charges General Lewis with having made, in his official letters, incorrect statements injurious to the credit of the army and the country. Let us look at it. As far as relates to the affair at Stoney Creek, the only statements given as his own are in the words following: "The gallantry of the 5th, 25th, part of the 23rd, and light troops saved the army. Lieut. M'Chesney's gallantry recovered a piece of artillery and prevented the capture of others. The highest officers in grade with the 16th were two captains, Steel and McCuen; both were captured and the command of the regiment devolved on Lieut. McChesney." General Lewis therefore compliments all the infantry in the action, a new mode of injuring the credit of the army and the country.

But the letter was accompanied with sundry documents on which the writer ventured an opinion. A military officer transmits to his government an account of a singular disaster (or as General Chandler terms it, "a partial success of the enemy," or, in the language of General Dearborn, "a strange fatality,") sustained by a portion of the army under his command. Was it not his duty to endeavor to account for it and to ascribe it to what he supposed its cause? He wrote not for a gazette but for the information of his government, and if the representatives of the people thought proper to give publicity to his communication it was their affair not his. It had been prudent in General Chandler, previous to an indulgence in remarks neither liberal nor courteous, to have enquired into the nature and authority of these documents. It would have hid them from the public eye and perhaps have saved him some uneasiness—the contrary conduct has rendered the development unavoidable.

On the capture of the Generals the command of the troops devolved on Colonel Burn of the 2nd Dragoons. This officer, with the characteristic candor and delicacy of a gentleman, applied for the particulars of this disastrous affair to those only who were most nearly connected with or acting most immediately under the orders of General Chandler. His informants were Major Smith, who commanded the 25th Regiment, and the officers of the General's staff and family. The information consisted of: 1st—A report from Major Smith with a sketch of the encampment and field of battle. 2nd—A report from Lieut. Frazer, acting Aid-de-Camp to General Chandler, with a diagram of the encampment, battle ground, march of the British troops, disposition of the American forces, accompanied with various references. 3rd—A report from Major Johnson, acting Adjutant-General—the officer whose death the General justly regrets, for he was honest, generous and brave. 4th—A report of Capt. Jones, his Brigade-Major.

These documents, except the last, which was subsequently received, accompanied the letter of Col. Burn to Gen. Dearborn, extracts from which may be seen, page 32 of the pamphlet publication of the President's message, of the 2nd February, 1814. On the 9th of June, General Lewis, in obedience to the orders of General Dearborn, brought back to Fort George the remains of General Chandler's discomfited army. On the 10th General Dearborn resigned the command-in-chief to General Lewis, and on the 12th sent to him by his aid, Colonel Pinkney, the letter of Colonel Burn and its accompaniments, which were forwarded on the 14th to the war office, with a remark predicated on Frazer's diagram and the facts reported. "The very head and front of General Lewis's offending hath this extent, no more."

Had General Chandler been treated with more severity no injustice would have been done him. If ignorance merited censure, a large portion of it was his due. Before he set out on his command he knew that the British army, consisting of nearly 1700 regulars, a body of incorporated and ordinary militia, with the Grand River and Missassaga Indians had gained Burlington Heights on the evening of the 30th May, and that it had been subsequently reinforced by a battalion of the 8th or King's Regiment 300 strong. On the morning of the 5th of June, according to Major Johnson's report now before me, his own force at the Forty Mile Creek amounted to 2,643 men, who, in the course of the day, were disposed of as follows:

Left sick at Forty Mile Creek	90
Left at that place as guards	90
Rearguard halted three miles in rear of Stoney Creek	95
4 picquets at a distance from the field of battle, which could not have come into action	240
Colonel Christie's command on lake, 2½ miles distant from the field of action	800
	1315
In the action	1328
Total	2643

(Signed) J. JOHNSON, Ass't Adj't-Gen.

It will be recollected that the appeal states Christie's command to have been at a distance from the scene of action *something over a mile*. Johnson's official report says 2½ miles; others have computed it at *three*. The appeal gives General Chandler credit for the ground he selected; by his own shewing accident placed him on it.

"The 25th, (says this singular production,) did not return from the pursuit of the enemy's picquet till after sunset, and the General, finding his position tenable, concluded to halt there for the night." That the position was a strong one will be admitted, and that in the hands of an experienced soldier or a man of even decent talents it was tenable against the efforts of a superior force cannot be denied. But the march from the anvil and the dram shop in the wane of life to " the dearest actions of the tented field " is not to be achieved in a single campaign. Had it been possible for the unfortunate gentleman to have learnt scientifically the art of blundering he could not have exhibited a more complete series of errors.

Advancing to the attack of an enemy equal if not superior to him in numerical force, he idly fritters away his own, places one-half of it *hors de combat*, his two strongest regiments on a duty to which a subaltern's guard was competent, and with the remainder encamps in the face of the enemy where, from the gross want of foresight, he is compelled to light fires and cook provisions by night. Under these circumstances and expecting, (as he declares,) an attack on the very point at which it was made, would not a commander of the most ordinary capacity have brigaded his artillery and made his order of encampment his order of battle? Instead of which, his artillery is placed in park on the margin of the high road, unsupported by a single battalion. The 25th infantry is advanced 150 yards in front on the opposite side of the road with the *elite*, composed of three companies, on its right. His three remaining regiments are encamped in line from three to four hundred yards on the left of the road, fronting to and parallel with it, its left flank towards the enemy and on a line with the artillery. This was the first position which was taken, (he informs us,) with intent to be changed afterwards as a deception on the enemy. The second position was taken after midnight, when surrounded by impervious darkness. A circumstance extremely favorable to the echellon movement he so scientifically describes. It appears, however, that the regiments on the left were not so far advanced in front of their first position as to prevent the frequent rekindling of their fires to his great annoyance.

The second position, as regards the 25th, was certainly judicious. But was it a part of the General's original plan? Is he entitled to the credit of it? Let us hear Major Smith and Lieut. Frazer on the subject. The first reports as follows: "The 25th encamped in a lane on the right of the road, 100 yards in advance of the artillery and of all the other regiments of infantry. It was in low land, in an unsafe position and exposed by our fires. With *consent* of General Chandler, precisely at one o'clock, I left that ground and posted the regiment immediately on the right of General Chandler's tent and on the brow of a hill which overlooked and commanded its first position, &c." Frazer says: "Previous to the commencement of the action probably two hours, I suggested to General Chandler the propriety of our men removing from our fires, that in case we were attacked the Indians would be upon us unawares. He *then* gave *me* directions to order out *some* fires and the 25th to remove on the bank, which was immediately done." Thus was this regiment removed, and, it is believed, without even notice to the *elite*, who were left in this exposed situation to shift for themselves. Fortunately they were led by men of talent and information.

Under the orders of General Winder the third position was taken up by the troops on the left when the alarm was given. The 5th and 16th were wheeled to the left and advanced to the fence. The 23rd wheeled in like manner and was directed to wait further orders. No further orders were received. Its commander, surprised at the circumstance, sent Ensign Tappan in quest of the Generals to inquire the cause; neither of them was to be found. As General Chandler casts imputations without reserve to entitle himself to credit, he should give some evidence *by whom* and *to whom* his orders were sent and delivered. This omission, connected with a few facts, leaves room to doubt the correctness of the General's statement as to the repeated breaches of orders by the 23d.

The facts referred to are:

1st—That the General in his official of the 18th June does not state, (as in the appeal,) the designation of the 23d to cover the artillery as a part of his original plan, but as a thing which happened to him after the action had commenced from observing that the artillery was not covered, neither does he there state that any orders were given to the 23d but to General Winder, who, I am told, has since induced him to retract that assertion. Look at his own words. After describing the fire in the rear he proceeds: "I had observed that the artillery was not covered, and directed General Winder to cause the 23d to be formed so far to the right that *their* right should cover the artillery."

2d—That Lieutenant Fraser in his report, after mentioning an attempt to rally in rear of the artillery some troops which were in confusion, (doubtless British,) says: "And at the same moment ordered me to go to General Winder and order him to send a regiment to support the artillery. I ran and could not find General Winder; the general opinion was that he was taken. I went to report the same to General Chandler where I left him, and found myself when I arrived there in company with guests I did not like, one of which claimed me as a prisoner. I, however, declined the honor."

With one single observation I dismiss this calumny on the 23d. When day appeared it was found on the ground Gen. Winder placed it on, and the 5th, finding its right flank no longer covered, fell back with Towson's artillery and formed on its right.

Notwithstanding General Chandler's pompous display of his foresight and precautionary measures, when the attack actually commenced all his dispositions, (except as to the 25th,) were to be made. After General Winder had placed the 5th and 16th Regiments at the fence on the bank of the creek to oppose the main attack, a firing is heard in his rear and General Chandler immediately orders the 5th Regiment to that point, where his reserve ought to have been instead of where they were, at three miles distance. Fortunately this injudicious order did not reach Col. Milton. Had it been otherwise the artillery, which was then actually in possession of the enemy, had been irretrievably lost. For, if the statement of General Chandler be true that "the 16th broke on the first yell of the savages," the whole left wing would have been *hors de combat* on the removal of the 16th.

For the truth of the fact that his artillery was then in possession of the enemy I refer to his own authority. In a letter written by him at Kingston, seven days after the affair, viz., on the 13th, speaking of his capture, he thus expresses himself: "To my surprise I found it to be the British 49th, who had advanced with charged bayonets *and taken the pieces.*" And here let me ask how this accords with his subsequent statement that "the confusion was occasioned by a body of the enemy who had penetrated his centre and *were broken and retreating ?*"

As an additional proof of the General's inaccuracy, I shall mention a fact or two more, in other respects of little moment: "Our loss, (says he,) did not exceed thirty killed and wounded." Major Smith on the contrary reports 42 of the 25th alone to have fallen in their ranks: "42 brave fellows of our regiment fell, either killed or wounded, in their ranks," are his words. Nor is the General more accurate with respect to the operations and loss of the enemy, a circumstance not a little singular as he was so long among them. In his report of the 18th he speaks of their column and the 49th's having pushed forward the head of their column, (a movement of no very military cast,) and gained the rear of the artillery, and in the appeal he states the British loss to have been little less than 500. It is at this day well known that the British force engaged in the sortie consisted of 200 men of the 8th (King's) Regiment, under the command of Major Ogilvie, and a column of 430 of the 49th, under Major Plenderleath, the whole under Lieut.-Col. Harvey. The 49th marched direct for the artillery, the 8th to the attack of the 25th but failing to force it concentrated with the 49th in the road. A loss of nearly 500 out of 710 is incredible. The returns on either side make the loss nearly equal on each. In killed there appears not to have been the difference of a man.

On the preceding exposition candor is called on to decide whether General Chandler, who charges the 23d with repeated disobedience to orders, and the 16th with having deserted their colors on the first Indian yell, or General Lewis who applauds the troops though not their commander, detracted most from the credit of the army and the country. And further, whether from the General's own shewing his centre was not his weakest point, whether his line was not cut at that point, and whether the arrangement of his camp was not among the principal causes of his misfortunes. Should the decision be, (as surely it must,) in the affirmative, wherein, I ask, has General Lewis misrepresented or even misconceived ?

As soon as leisure will permit I shall examine General Chandler's statements as to the attack on Fort George, when, if his feelings can be affected by anything short of a blow from his own sledgehammer, I think I shall make an impression on them.

ONE OF THE STAFF.

(From Niles' Weekly Register, 4th January, 1817, Vol. 11, pp. 308-11.)

Notes by Capt. Wm. H. Merritt.

They, [the Americans,] kept pressing on. The 5th and 6th June [they] drove in our pickets as far as Aickman's, nearly. On the 6th [I] dined with Gordon, who remained at Dundas. After returning to my quarters [I] was ordered to fall in with the main body at Barnard's, where the troops were formed in order of battle expecting the enemy on every moment. Col. Harvey and Mr. McKenney went on in advance as far as Davis's, made one or two prisoners and found that the enemy had encamped at Stoney Creek and a party on the lake shore of 1500. Mr. George, an ensign [in the] militia, who was with them, suggested the practicability of attacking them in their camp, (insert McKenney's version, who claims the suggestion.) Col. Harvey approved of it and on his return proposed it to Gen. Vincent. After a little deliberation he carried it into effect. Most of the officers were laying on the grass, some, of which I was one, fast asleep. The order came to move forward. We had to march 6 miles before we came upon their pickets. Our force consisted of 590 men, a field piece in the rear, which was no manner of use. All my hopes depended on the success of this bold enterprise. Had we not attacked them, the next morning they would have advanced. In all probability we would have retired without risqueing an action, as our force was not one-fifth of theirs. Consequently Procter and the whole upper country would have fell. On our arrival at Davis's we heard the report of a gun from their picket. The detachment was halted, formed into sections, the loading drawn from each gun, the l[igh]t comp[anie]s of the 49th and King's in advance, Gen. Vincent and staff at the head of the column in their rear. I was attached to him for the night. The enemy were encamped in Gage's fields in a very advantageous position, 2000 on the hill on the right of the road, 500 in a lane on the left in advance of their artillery, which was situated on a hill directly in front of the road our troops must come, their pickets nearly half a mile in advance, in the wood. Those we made prisoners without giving the alarm. On our opening the clearing we were fired on by the second picket, which was more alert. The fires of the 500 on our left was the first that was discovered. The Gen[eral] ordered a change immediately. The men set up a tremendous shout, continued along the whole line, and was the cause of throwing the men in the greatest confusion imaginable. The two light comp[anies] routed the 500 before the [main] body had time to come up. George was by my side; told me the fight was over. I happened to cast my eye round [and] discovered the fires of the main body which I showed him, likewise Col. Harvey and the Gen[eral]. The officers were using every exertion to get the men formed, when the enemy opened a most tremendous fire on us from the hill, likewise opened their guns. Our men dispersed in every direction, and had not Col. Plenderleath charged and captured their guns with 30 men we would have been completely defeated. I never heard so rapid a discharge of musquetry. The hill was a continual sheet of fire. However, after capturing their artillery and both their Generals, they thought proper to retire off the field. At the appearance of daylight we followed their example, fearing when they discovered their force they would renew the attack. After we left the field Col. Harvey desired me to return and, if possible, find the General who was missing, he supposed dead or wounded on the field. On my return [I] was looking at the dead and wounded, not thinking of the enemy till I was challenged by a sentry under old Gage's, near the house. [I] was on the point of surrendering as my pistols were both in my holsters. Trusting to my blue coat [I] hoped to evade him by stratagem. Without answering him [I] asked him who placed him there and rode up to him. He answered me his captain, who had just went in the house with a party of men. I enquired if he had found the British General, pulled out my pistol [and] made him drop his gun. At that moment a man without his gun ran down the hill. I called him, he came to me and I had the good fortune to bring them both off, owing entirely to the dress, as they took me for one of their own officers. That stratagem had once taken before by accident or I should not have thought of it. The enemy retreated early on the morning of the 7th. When the Indians discovered it they came on in droves. The fleet likewise made their appearance, which was a very fortunate circumstance for us. The militia raised *en masse*, made a number of prisoners. The Americans had already given them a sample of their policy by countenancing traitors and making prisoners of the most respectable inhabitants.

(From a Letter to the Editors of the Baltimore Whig.)

FORT GEORGE, 8th June, 1813.

From the Forty Mile Creek we learn that the affair at Stoney Creek was very serious. The confusion was great. Some spy or deserter procured the countersign at our encampment, went to the British camp and in 5 minutes after he entered General Vincent's tent the English army was in motion. Our camp was entered without opposition by means of the above mentioned treachery; the light artillery near the front was seized and turned upon our men, when Winder, &c., riding up to prevent what they thought a mistake in firing against themselves, found themselves seized and carried off by the enemy. Captain Towson, (an ornament to Maryland,) soon opened a fire from his light artillery, (which was more to the rear,) and threw the enemy into disorder. The advanced corps, the 5th and the 25th, and a squadron of Colonel Burn's light horse bore the brunt of the action. The enemy retreated but renewed the assault, it is said, three times, when about daylight our horse, &c., pursued and cut down immense numbers. For two miles the roads and woods are strewed with dead or British, (desperately wounded.) Our loss in killed is comparatively very trifling. General Vincent was missing on the part of the British but is not taken by us. So his fate remains unascertained at present. They lost Colonel Clark, a zealous and loyal partizan, killed. Generals Winder and Chandler and Captain Steele, (a brave officer,) have been captured. Next day it was deemed proper to fall back to a strong and convenient place. Yesterday about 2 o'clock, it is supposed, General Boyd arrived and our army shouted with exultation at the news of his approach.

Very heavy cannonading was heard all this morning—it must either proceed from the army or the enemy's squadron. May the result retrieve what we lost on the 27th ult., when we ought to have slain or taken the very troops that have since given us so much trouble.

Of Procter we have heard no recent intelligence worthy of belief. It is supposed he shall find it a hard task to retreat—his Indians may turn upon him if he offers to fly. Harrison will capture him if he remains in the upper country. Such is the opinion of some shrewd men whom I saw today from the mouth of Grand River.

June 9, 1813. I walked down to the beach yesterday morning to see some English prisoners bro't in boats the night before from a place called Forty Mile Creek. They are very clean, smart looking fellows.

General Chandler had taken the command before our army was surprised by Gen. Vincent. Our camp, they say, was badly and loosely laid out. The British advanced silently with fixed bayonets, not a musket was allowed to be loaded for fear of blowing their design. Some officers and men advanced at some distance ahead of them, who hailed, amused, and stabbed some of our centinels, pretending to give the countersign. The advanced guard were first alarmed by hearing the dying groan of a sentry who had been run through. Five pieces of light artillery were seized and fired against our troops, and they say that General Winder was made prisoner in making a desperate attack on the British to retake them.

The regiments in the centre and rear never got to the assistance of the front. The 16th Regiment, when formed, was broken through by our cavalry that had cut their way through the 49th (British) Regiment and could not stop. Owing to that and the darkness some of its companies unfortunately engaged their own men. Col. Pearce, a very good man, was left sick at this place, and Colonel Dennis had cleared out for Philadelphia after being only two or three days on the lines. Capt. Steele had the command. He was wounded and taken prisoner, but in the end our army killed three or four to one and made the red coats scamper. Colonel Burn and Colonel Milton are said to have saved the army.

(From Niles' Weekly Register, of Baltimore, Md., 12th June, 1813. Vol. IV., pp. 262-3.

New York Statesman, June 24th, 1813.

Extract of a letter from an officer in the army to his friend in Philadelphia:

We took possession of Queenston with some artillery, remained there one night and returned to Fort George next evening, where we remained two days, when General Winder's brigade was ordered to pursue the enemy. Capts. Hindman, Biddle and Nicholas, with their companies and the riflemen, joined the brigade again as an advance party.

We left Fort George on the 2d inst. and followed the enemy's retreat, but on our near approach they possessed themselves of a stronghold about 46 miles from Fort George and fortified it, in consequence of which our army was checked one day within 15 miles of them. The next we continued our march and our advanced party drove in the enemy's picquets with a slight loss on both sides, after which we, with General Chandler's brigade, took our ground about three miles from the enemy, and notwithstanding the opinion of all the officers that an attack would certainly be made that night, yet Generals Chandler and Winder permitted us to encamp without any order or regularity. One brigade of 800 men was three miles from the other. No order of battle, no watchword, not a rallying post assigned. In this situation about 2 o'clock in the morning the enemy, with Indians, surprised with loud yelling and attacked our advance guard, which we composed. We were able to make but a feeble resistance, as the enemy was not more than 15 yards from us when Capt. Henderson formed the advance. Notwithstanding our danger we gave them three or four rounds of musketry, which they warmly returned and obliged us to retire in great confusion, as it was quite dark. You can imagine my astonishment and regret when at the approach of day we could not muster more than 60 of our brave companions, the rest were killed, wounded or made prisoners. Out of our fine battalion of artillery, which you saw leave Philadelphia, not more than 75 were left. Capt. Biddle's fine company musters only about 20 men.

(File in New York Society Library.)

Captain John Johnson, 5th U. S. Infantry, Assistant Adjutant-General, to ———

CAMP, FORTY MILE CREEK,
June 7, 1813.

It is with extreme regret that I announced to you the loss of our brave and worthy friend, General Chandler, who was made prisoner yesterday morning in the action with the enemy near Stoney Creek. Unfortunately General Winder was also taken, both about the time victory was ours. The morning was extremely dark, so much so that we could not distinguish a red coat from a blue one at the distance of three paces. This induces me to believe that they were lost by entering the enemy's line supposing it to be their own. They both behaved throughout the action with the utmost coolness and bravery, and it is with great satisfaction that I can assure you that they were not taken by surprise or alarm. They anticipated an attack and had made their arrangements accordingly. Our troops slept on their arms in line of battle, formed to the best advantage the ground would admit of.

The Generals spent the previous evening together until 12 o'clock in General Chandler's tent making arrangements for the victory they expected the next day.

After the departure of General Winder and our guides, General Chandler and myself lay down but did not sleep. About 20 minutes past 2 o'clock in the morning our outposts and guards were fired on by the head or advance of the enemy's column. They immediately after advised us of their approach by a tremendous savage yell. General Chandler and myself were mounted instantly, and the line formed and waiting for the enemy by the time they were within musket shot. Gen. Chandler immediately took post in the rear of the left flank of the right wing where he issued his orders with the utmost coolness, and occupied his leisure moments by encouraging his troops to perform acts of valor. I carried his orders frequently to General Winder, who commanded the left wing, where I found him busily employed and with great energy encouraging his men and giving orders.

In carrying these orders I lost sight of General Chandler and did not know he was taken until daylight. His horse was shot under him in the heighth of the action.

The officers and men behaved like veterans, and if we had not lost our Generals we should have been covered with glory.

(From Niles' Weekly Register, 10th July, 1813, Vol. IV., pp. 307-8. Reprinted from the Boston Patriot.)

(From the United States Gazette of Philadelphia, 8th July, 1813.)

Letter from an officer in the United States army to the Editor of the *United States Gazette*:

FORT GEORGE, UPPER CANADA, June 22, 1813.

SIR,—Our army with the exception of two regiments marched from this place in pursuit of the British and advanced as far as Stoney Creek and halted, on the evening of the 5th inst., within a few miles of the enemy and about 47 from this post towards the head of Lake Ontario. About half-past two o'clock the very next morning after we halted, our camp was surprised by a few hundred British under the command of General Vincent, who, after taking two pieces of cannon, two Brigadier-Generals, three captains and one Assistant Quartermaster General, with about three hundred and fifty rank and file retreated to their former position with the loss of only a hundred in killed, wounded and taken prisoners. About forty of the latter we took in the woods after the action, who had lost their way owing to the darkness of the night. Two of our regiments happened to have good positions; they kept up a fire until daylight, at which time the 6th Regiment, under command of a subaltern, (Lieut. Machesney,) discovered the enemy taking off our cannon and made a successful charge and retook two pieces with their caissons. This was done without any orders. In fact there was not a solitary instance of any officer excepting the above attempting to retake either our officers, men or cannon, but they stood as the British retreated, waiting, as they said, for orders when both our Generals were taken prisoners.

Picture to yourself an army of between two and three thousand infantry, with artillery and cavalry halted on their arms, each commanding officer choosing such ground and place as he thought proper, some on a hill, others in a hollow, some one way, some another. No order of battle, no watchword. View this army attacked by at most seven hundred British regulars. What was our confusion! The horses of the cavalry and infantry bursting in amongst us at every direction. General Chandler running about crying: "Where is the line? Where is the line?" General Winder in the same manner exclaiming: "Come on!" &c., and both in among the British soldiers.

No orders passing from or to any corps or any officer. May my eyes never witness such a scene again. Everything appeared to add to the confusion and disorder.

I did not think my anticipations of our Generals would have come to pass so soon, nor that the consequences would have been quite so fatal. But when I informed you some time since that Chandler was coming on with his *undisciplined regulars* I hinted and dreaded the consequences, knowing him when at Plattsburg to have been a particular favorite of General Dearborn, who entrusted to his charge and command the whole of the above expedition. As to General Winder, if he had one or two years experience in the field as a platoon or field officer he might then have made a tolerable good General. But Chandler has neither sense nor discretion, and is without any military knowledge at all. This I assure you is a fact known to every officer who has had as good an opportunity of witnessing his folly as myself. Thank God, he is now where he can do us no more harm and General Dearborn is sick. General Lewis left here on the 19th for Sackett's Harbor. General Boyd is commanding officer of the army. Colonel Miller takes Boyd's brigade. A Colonel Milton commands the second brigade. I have been with Colonel Miller and find him a most excellent officer. He and General Boyd went up from this place and brought the army back from Stoney Creek.

. . . .

The British fleet is now out and has the command of Lake Ontario. It consists of two ships, a brig and two schooners, all of which were cruising off here on the 13th and 14th instant. It has committed many depredations on our side of the lake, particularly in the Genesee river, where a great quantity of public stores were taken. Our fleet is expected here about the first of July and is now only waiting for a large new ship, which will be ready for sea by that time in Sackett's Harbor.

The names of the officers who were taken prisoners to my knowledge are: Brigadier-Generals Chandler and Winder, Captain Van Vechten, *(who had command of the picket guard,)* of the 23d Regiment, and Captains Steel and McEwen of the 16th Regiment, and Major Van De Venter, Assistant Quartermaster General. Many of the inhabitants of this country, when we were up towards the head of the lake, showed us every favor and every attention. But on our retreating the scene was truly distressing. To see them of every age and sex weeping and bewailing their fate, nothing more than an anticipation of their distress; they believed the tales we told them too soon. Many of them have been thrown on board the British fleet, whilst others have had their property given up to pillage and destruction. I feel it the more sensibly as the inhabitants on this side have been infinitely more kind than those on the other.

Many of the officers have resigned, who will be now enabled to give those particulars in detail which I cannot express.

(File in Philadelphia Library.)

Sir George Prevost to Earl Bathurst.

HEADQUARTERS, KINGSTON, UPPER CANADA,
6th June, 1813.

No. 66.

MY LORD,—Since I had the honour of addressing Your Lordship on the 3d instant, I have received from Colonel Vincent the intelligence herewith transmitted, together with a letter which accompanied it from the commander of the American forces, relating to the British subjects who were taken in arms at Queenston in October last and sent to England in His Majesty's ship *Jason*.

I have taken measures for the immediate reinforcement of our army at the head of the lake with the flank companies of the 104th Regiment and a detachment from the Glengarry levy. This is all that the force I possess at the present moment will allow me to do until the promised succour arrives. Your Lordship cannot fail to observe the eagerness with which the enemy are pressing forward in very superior numbers for the conquest of Upper Canada before I can possibly receive a sufficient support to enable me to withstand them, and I am very apprehensive that when the expected reinforcements arrive they will come so much in detail and at such uncertain periods as not to produce to me the means of making one grand effort to arrest the progress of the American army and drive it out of His Majesty's territory.

To enable Your Lordship to appreciate the importance to our cause of the Indian chief Norton, I enclose the original letter addressed to me by him after the late unequal contest at Niagara, in which I have the heartfelt satisfaction of assuring Your Lordship the character of the British soldier was well supported. Our flotilla is on Lake Ontario with a reinforcement of troops and supplies of ordnance stores and provisions for Colonel Vincent. I cannot learn that the American fleet has ventured out to contest with us for the ascendency on that lake.

The period has arrived when, from the uncertain state of affairs, paper money loses its effect and specie alone can command the hidden resources of the country.

Your Lordship has long been aware of the total deficiency of specie in the Canadas, and I must now beg leave to inform you that among the many difficulties I have to encounter this is becoming one of excessive magnitude, in consequence of the small quantity of provisions which can be obtained in these provinces for the maintenance of the troops.

(Canadian Archives, Q. 121, p. 262.)

General Orders.

KINGSTON, 8th June, 1813.

No. 3.

Captain McIntosh of the Embodied and Captain Davy of the Incorporated Militia are appointed each to command a gunboat. Colonel Cartwright is directed to furnish crews from the militia to man these gunboats, one sergeant, one corporal and 24 privates for the *Thunder* gunboat; *Black Snake* gunboat, one sergeant, one corporal and twenty privates. Two gunners from the Royal Artillery to be attached to each gunboat. Captain Wallace, R. A., will select these men. Captains McIntosh and Davy will receive written instructions for their guidance from Lt.-Col. Drummond, Acting Deputy Qr. Mr. General.

Major De Haren will be furnished a pilot by Colonel Cartwright

---

General Orders.

HEADQUARTERS, KINGSTON,
8th June, 1813, 5 o'clock P. M.

His Excellency the Commander of the Forces has just received an express announcing that a strong division of the enemy had advanced to the Forty Mile Creek with the intention of attacking the position occupied by Brigadier-General Vincent at the head of Burlington Bay. The enemy's plan was, however, anticipated by the gallant General and completely defeated by a spirited attack at daybreak on the 6th instant on the American army, which was completely defeated and dispersed. Twelve officers, two of whom were Generals, and five pieces of cannon were taken, and the fugitives were pursued in every direction by a numerous body of Indians under the Chief Norton. The enemy's force is stated at 200 cavalry and 4000 infantry, besides a strong force in boats.

The intelligence was communicated off York at 2 p. m. to Commodore Sir James Yeo, who had sailed with the fleet on the 3d instant to co-operate with General Vincent, and immediately proceeded with reinforcements on board to support the General's further attack upon the enemy. Further reinforcements under Major De Haren proceeded this day from Kingston to join General Vincent. The British loss has been very slight. The official despatch is hourly expected.

EDWARD BAYNES, Colonel,
Adjutant General.

Colonel John Vincent to Sir George Prevost.

BURLINGTON BAY, 8th June, 1813.

SIR,—In consequence of our attack on the enemy's camp on the 6th inst. they have made a movement to their rear and retired back to the 40 Mile Creek, which has given me an opportunity of pushing out my patrols to their late camp.

I have had the honor to receive your letter of the 2d instant with a memorandum enclosed. The fleet are this moment reported. I am therefore perfectly secure in this post as long as we have the lake open to us. I have this morning made a change of position to a place named Coot's Paradise, in which I am throwing up a strong fortification in my front. All other parts are so strong as to secure themselves from an attack of the enemy. In my situation I am determined to hold out, if their whole force of twelve thousand is brought against me. Colonel Harvey and Captain McDouall will write very fully on the subject of this new situation to Colonel Baynes.

I have to report the arrival of Sir James Lucas Yeo. He informs me that this morning he cannonaded a camp at 40 Mile Creek, which he dispersed with some batteaux. I had already given orders for the detachment of the 8th to be disembarked, when I received a private express from the 40 Mile Creek, that in consequence of our fleet being upon the lake the enemy struck their tents and are retiring towards Fort George. I have therefore sent this detachment back to the 40 Mile Creek with the Commodore, and I have pushed forward my outposts with some Indians to co-operate with our fleet to take up their quarters this night at the 40 as my advanced post.

I can assure Your Excellency that a troop of dragoons will be of the greatest service in this country. I have to make an excuse for the hasty manner of writing this letter.

(Canadian Archives, C. 679.)

General Dearborn to the Secretary of War.

HEADQUARTERS, FORT GEORGE,
June 8, 1813.

SIR,—I have been honored with your letters of the 26th and 27th ult., and a duplicate of one of the 19th April. My ill state of health renders it extremely painful to attend to the current duties, and unless my health improves soon I fear I shall be compelled to retire to some place where my mind will be more at ease, for a short time. Colonel Macomb proceeded with two hundred men with the Commodore to Sackett's Harbor. Lieutenant-Colonel Ripley has also gone by the way of Oswego to the harbor with his regiment, where he will be joined by several hundred recruits. He took charge of the provisions to Oswego. The Commodore will probably not venture out until his new ship is fit for sea. The enemy has now the command of the lake, and as long as that is the case any offensive operations below this must be suspended. I had intended placing a small garrison at Fort Erie and a stronger one at Fort George, but as you have directed otherwise I shall select Fort George as guarding the only harbor on the southern shore of the lake. Detroit will be the safest harbor on Lake Erie. I have by request of Commodore Chauncey detached 200 men to aid Captain Perry in moving his armed vessels from Black Rock to Presque Isle. Commodore Chauncey is unwilling to approach Malden unless he can have a reinforcement to General Harrison of our regulars. As my command does not extend to Malden I ask your directions on this subject. The Commodore is anxious that his fleet on Lake Erie should proceed with troops to Michilimackinac and St. Joseph as soon as the business shall be decided at Detroit. On taking possession of this place the inhabitants came in in numbers and gave their paroles. I have promised them protection. A large majority are friendly to the United States and fixed in their hatred against the Government of Great Britain. If they should generally be made prisoners of war and taken from their families it would have a most unfavorable effect on our military operations in the Provinces. The whole country would be driven to a state of desperation and satisfy them beyond a doubt that we had no intention of holding the Provinces. The same effect would be produced on the Indians, who are now principally quiet for fear of losing their valuable tract of land on Grand River. I had authorized the civil magistrates to combine in the *due* exercise of their functions and cannot with propriety revoke this authority unless specially directed.

The whole of our troops, officers and men in the action of the 27th discovered a degree of ardor and readiness for action which evinced a determination to do honor to themselves and country. The animating example set by Colonel Scott and General Boyd in landing and repulsing the enemy deserves particular mention. I am greatly indebted to Colonel Porter, Major Armistead and Captain Totten for their judicious arrangements and skilful execution in demolishing the enemy's forts and batteries, and to the officers of the artillery generally who had the direction of the guns.

(American State Papers, Military Affairs.)

Major Thomas Evans to Colonel John Vincent.

FORTY MILE CREEK, half-past seven o'clock p. m., 8th June, 1813.

SIR,—I have the honor to report to you that part of the force of which you honored me with the command has taken possession of the post hastily abandoned this morning by the American army under Major-General Lewis. So precipitate has been their flight that their tents were in part left standing, and various articles of stores, arms, ammunition and provisions have been secured. The naval part of our force has captured fourteen or sixteen boats laden with supplies. Many prisoners have been made. The American force is stated to have consisted of from 4 to 5,000 men and represented as in a *sickly* condition. I have stationed my force as best calculated for its immediate security and pushed on the Indian force in hopes of intercepting the enemy's course and troubling his rear. I enclose for your information a return of ammunition, &c., arrived for the use of the army in the *Lady Gore*.

P. S.—The detachment of the 41st and 49th, under Lieut.-Colonel Dennis, arrived in time and took possession of the post abandoned by the enemy at Milton's.

(Canadian Archives, C. 679.)

Anne Powell to Justice William D. Powell.

YORK, 8th June, 1813.

. . . . Mrs. Claus and her family arrived this morning. I have seen her. She confirms the cause of the firing. She was at Mrs. Brandt's when two soldiers from the picket at the outlet alarmed her by saying they had escaped from the Americans, who had cut off the guard at that place: 27 boats had arrived with troops and artillery. Coffin waits to carry the event of the contest. I dread it; this shall be ready for him. A message from Cameron announced the arrival of Col. Evans at Major Allan's; the fleet is just below, but I fear their aid at the 40 will be ineffectual. Mrs.

Claus says there were various opinions amongst the officers, some for, others absolutely rejecting a retreat. The fleet does away our immediate apprehensions, but leaves Kingston exposed to an implacable enemy, who wants but the conquest of that important post to perfect his laurel wreaths. A drizzling summer rain with fog and calm impede the progress of our ships, and every moment increases the importance of their speedy movements. Mrs. Claus saw John P[owell] at home the night of the battle. He had been struck by a spent ball but not materially hurt. She says they were at tea and the Americans went and took such things as they liked. He was supposed to have been premature in spiking his gun. General Vincent vindicates him by saying that it was useless before he did spike it. This, Mrs. Claus says, you know as well as I what credit may be given to it. From another quarter I hear Major Holcroft was the person with whom the censure originated. . . . .

The report this morning is that the enemy are beaten and driven to Stoney Creek; that we have taken two Generals and some artillery and are in hopes that the fleet, (which left Colonel Evans behind last night,) will complete the destruction of the whole force.

(From the Powell Papers, Toronto Public Library.)

Anne Powell to Justice W. D. Powell.

YORK, June 8th, 1813.

(Extract.)

Sir J. Yeo sailed to intercept the return of the beaten enemy to his strong post at Niagara. A heavy cannonading at night, and with little cessation till this time (1 o'clock) gives us reason to believe something of moment has taken place. It is said that from St. George's house the ships were seen to attack the gunboats and must take them. God grant it, but such ill fortune has as yet marked our measures that I cease to be sanguine. Well may Sackett's Harbor throw into the background the York mishap, for it sure merits no harsher term—in one instance the attempt was voluntary and ought not to have been made without means fully adequate to its important consequences; in the other the means were insufficient, and there existed no possibility of obtaining an increase of what was necessary to defend us against an overwhelming enemy, who, however, repulsed by land, had the command of the water and from it would have let loose his vengeance. Then those who have now untouched property and a roof to shelter them would have execrated the madness of a general whose obstinacy, in an unequal contest, sacrificed the King's troops and deprived of all they possessed and exposed to an enemy the inhabitants of a town the safety of which should have been an object of consideration. Could he by the destruction of the town have destroyed the enemy, there ought to have been no hesitation, but it was not the case, and a general of popular manners would be applauded for the conduct which has in him caused the most unjustifiable censure.

(From the Powell papers, Toronto Public Library.)

Earl Bathurst to Sir Roger H. Sheaffe.

DOWNING STREET, 8th June, 1813.

No. 1, 31 Dec'r 1812.
" 2, " " "
" 3, " " "
Unnumbered,
    15 Jan'y, 1813.
    14 Feb'y, 1813.
No. 3, 15 Mc'h, 1813.
" 4, " " "
" 5, 16 " "
" 6, 17 " "

SIR,—I have received and laid before the Prince Regent your despatches of the dates and numbers specified in the margin. His Royal Highness views with entire approbation, the conduct of the Legislature of the Province and the zeal which they have manifested for the defence of their country against the enemy, and the liberal provision which they have made for carrying on the war with vigor and effect. His Royal Highness is deeply sensible of the inconveniences which have resulted to the inhabitants of Upper Canada from the length of time which it was [during] the last year necessary to detain the Militia from their families and their ordinary occupations. The Bill passed by the Legislature for the formation of Incorporated Regiments, and the large reinforcements which have been lately ordered to Canada, will, I trust, have the effect of relieving them from so extended a service in future years. You will of course partake of the anxiety which His Royal Highness feels, not to interfere with the ordinary occupations of the inhabitants beyond what may be necessary for the defence of the Province, and by demanding no sacrifices beyond what are absolutely required to ensure their being easily and cheerfully borne.

I have already on many occasions expressed to Sir George Prevost the entire approbation of His Royal Highness of the conduct of the troops employed in Upper Canada whenever they have encountered the enemy, and it is therefore unnecessary for me to repeat what His Excellency will not have failed to communicate to you at an earlier period.

A part of the supply of Indian presents required in your letter of the 31st December, had been despatched from this country previous to its receipt. I have only ordered by the next fleet such additional quantity as may make up the difference between those already transmitted and those specified in the enclosure in your despatch.

I have not failed to lay before the Prince Regent the addresses of the House of Assembly of Upper Canada on the subject of a grant of land to the representatives of General Brock, and am commanded to signify His Royal Highness' pleasure that you should make them such a grant and under such conditions as may best fulfil the intentions of the House of Assembly.

(Canadian Archives. Q, 293A, pp. 224-5)

Lieut.-Colonel James B. Dennis to ——

8th June, Evening.

MY DEAR SIR,—

In three hours after quitting you I possessed myself of the enemy's camp and fortunately secured from 2 to 300 tents with various articles of stores, &c. I fear the Indians are too insubordinate to be used otherwise than to effect intimidation, of which I shall avail myself to its fullest extent.

(Canadian Archives, C. 679.)

Brigadier General John Vincent to Sir George Prevost.

BURLINGTON BAY, 9th June, 1813.

SIR,—I had the honor of writing to Your Excellency yesterday that the enemy, in consequence of our fleet appearing off the 40 Mile Creek, had been reported to me as returning towards Fort George. I immediately pushed out our outposts, consisting of the Grenadier company of the 49th Regiment and a strong company of the 41st Regiment, under the command of Lieut.-Colonel Dennis, with two three-pounders, to take post at Milton's on the mountain at the 40, and Major Evans with the detachment of the 8th Regiment not yet being disembarked from our fleet, Commodore Sir James L. Yeo immediately got under way in hopes of cutting off their boats.

I have now the pleasure of reporting from letters I received, dated seven o'clock last night, from the Commodore and Major Evans, that they were in possession of the 40 Mile Creek and the *Wolfe* at anchor within musket shot of the shore.

We have got into our possession a number of their boats, a quantity of baggage and more than 200 tents.

I herewith forward for Your Excellency's information Major Evans's letter.

I have directed the boats and camp equipage to be forwarded to this post without delay.

It is my intention to keep possession of the 40 as long as I possibly can. If the troops there are kept on the alert they will at all times have an opportunity of retiring on me here.

I have taken the liberty of opening Brigadier-General Procter's letter to Your Excellency and I find his want of the remaining companies of the 41st Regiment is so great that I think it advisable to send him the whole of the detachment of this corps at present with me, and they can be parted with at this present moment better than at any other period, as I can now defend myself where I am in my present situation, and more especially as I do not intend to act on the offensive until I receive reinforcements.

(Canadian Archives, C. 679.)

From the Canadian Courant of Montreal, July 10th, 1813.

To Brigadier-General John Vincent, Commanding His Majesty's forces on the Niagara frontier in Upper Canada:

We, the magistrates and principal inhabitants of York, His Majesty's loyal and faithful subjects, feel it a duty we owe to our country to notice in the most public manner the signal victory obtained over the enemy by the brave troops under your command on the 6th inst., an achievement history must select as one worthy of her page.

However we may grieve at the battle of Fort George, a disaster inflicted upon us by an army in numbers immensely superior to ours and aided by a fleet and powerful artillery, we nevertheless are fully sensible how much applause is due to you when we consider that in the defence of that place the glory of the British arms was nobly sustained, that your retreat in front of the numerous foe was effected with safety to all the troops with adequate artillery, ammunition and stores, and that without sustaining any loss on your march you had taken a judicious position where you have effectually checked the further advance of the enemy. But, Sir, peculiar pride in our country and gratitude to you and your brave officers and soldiers engross all our feelings when we perceive you taking the great resolution of surprising the pursuing enemy in his camp, a resolution not of rashness but of judgment, as vigorous in its execution as bold in idea, as prompt as it was important, not only anticipating by a few hours the enemy in his meditated attack upon you, but completely foiling him in all his hopes.

We beg you, Sir, to accept this tender of our confidence, and be assured that it flows from honest pride in the glory of our mother country, and that however long this war may be, whatever privations, griefs or losses it may bring upon us, we only wish for its termination in the expulsion of our unprovoked and malicious invaders in adding splendor to the British arms, and in peace comporting with the dignity of the empire.

(Sgd.) WM. CAMPBELL,
Chairman,
and all the principal inhabitants of York.

June 16, 1813.

ANSWER.

GENTLEMEN,—

The very gratifying expression of the approbation of the principal inhabitants of York of the services of the gallant troops under my command during the late operations, and particularly in the attack on the enemy's camp at Gage's on the 6th inst., shall be immediately communicated to and will be duly appreciated by them. The merit you so flatteringly impute to myself I feel a pride in referring to the troops; with them and for them I offer you my most grateful thanks. The approbation of our distinguished fellow-subjects will not relax the efforts the army is about to make to expel the enemy from our territory and carry the war into their own.

JOHN VINCENT,
Brigadier-General.

District General Orders by Major-General Sir Roger H. Sheaffe.

KINGSTON, June 9th, 1813.

Commanders of districts are as early as practicable to transmit the following reports and returns to the headquarters of the Major-General commanding and President.

1st—Returns of the several corps and detachments within the limits of their commands, whether of the line or militia.

2d—Of arms, ammunition and other ordnance stores.

3d—Of provisions, either in their possession or contracted for.

4th—Of the supplies of provision that the district can probably furnish.

5th—Of military stores of all kinds and what the district may be capable of supplying.

6th—Of the persons employed in the several departments, their salaries and allowances.

7th—Of barracks and block houses, what number calculated for, and other public buildings for what purpose used and their state, to which is to be added a report of the defences and their present condition, and of all other such matters as the commanding officers of districts may deem beneficial to His Majesty's service, to be communicated to the Major-General.

Major Thomas Evans to Lieut.-Col. Harvey.

40 MILE CREEK, 10th June, 1813.

SIR,—Conformable to the wish of Brigadier-General Vincent, commanding, I herewith transmit a concise and connected narrative of the late operations of the detachment of which he honored me with the command. In consequence of your orders, given immediately after my arrival, (8th June,) I embarked in company with Sir James L. Yeo and proceeded for the squadron then lying off the mouth of Burlington, which on our reaching it was ordered by signal to weigh and stand for the 40 Mile Creek. A steady breeze soon enabled us to gain and come to anchor close in with the enemy's position with which we had a brush on passing in the morning. By the excellent arrangements of the Commodore the whole of my detachment, composed of about 220 of the King's, was on shore and in possession of the enemy's encampment by half-past seven p. m., little more than three hours after receiving my instructions. Lieut.-Colonel Dennis, with the detachment ordered on by land, joined me soon after and the Indians quickly followed. The enemy's flight and terror is best evidenced by the precipitate manner in which he abandoned everything which was valuable or could be called to constitute his equipment for field operations. Aware from the nature of the country that a further co-operation of the naval force could not be expected, I lost no time in taking measures for a close pursuit by the Indians, detaching Lieut.-Colonel Dennis with the grenadier company of the 49th and part of a company of the 41st to the Twenty, with directions to that officer to push his dragoons and Indians just to the skirts of Fort George. That movement, tho' not coming up to my expectations by the capture of the enemy's cannon, was otherwise productive of the most beneficial results. Many prisoners were taken, the spirit of the loyal part of the country aroused, the little remaining baggage of the enemy destroyed, his panic increased and confirmed, and what is of the utmost consequence, intelligence of all his movements obtained. On the evening of the 9th the enemy set fire to and abandoned Fort Erie, withdrew his force from Chippawa and Queenston, concentrating them at Fort George and hastily began throwing up field-works either there to defend himself or cross the river by means of boats, (which he holds in a constant state of readiness,) according to circumstances. Yesterday I had information of the militia having taken a depot of arms, &c., in the neighborhood of Queenston, and in the evening had actually possessed themselves of the town. I have everything to say in praise of the good conduct of my officers and men, but have most particularly to remark the zeal, spirit and ability with which Lieut.-Colonel Dennis conducted his share of the operations.

(Canadian Archives, C. 679.)

FORTY MILE CREEK, June 10, 1813.

Return of camp equipage, provisions, arms, ammunition and ordnance stores belonging to the enemy captured and destroyed by the squadron under the command of Commodore Sir James Lucas Yeo, and a detachment of the army commanded by Brigadier-General Vincent under the immediate orders of Lieut.-Colonel Evans:

CAPTURED.

Tents	200	
Ditto, taken by the Indians	180	
Ditto, carried off by inhabitants	120	
		500
Camp kettles		200
Boats		3
Waggons		1
Horses		6
Flour, barrels of		140
Pork, do		10
Medicine chests		1
Arms and appointments, stands		100

DESTROYED.

Boats	17
Arms and appointments	50

TOTAL TAKEN AND DESTROYED.

Tents, 500; camp kettles, 200; boats, 20; waggons, 1; horses, 6; barrels flour, 140; barrels pork, 10; medicine chests, 1; arms and appointments, 150; exclusive of a great quantity of public and private baggage destroyed by the enemy.

ROBT. NICHOL,
Q. M. Gen., Militia.

(Canadian Archives, C. 679.)

Return of prisoners of all degrees captured on the enemy's retreat from Forty Mile Creek, on the 8th, 9th and 10th June, 1813:

Forwarded to York 43
In the Provost guard at Forty Mile Creek 37
                                                              ——
                                                              80

ROBT. NICHOL, Lt.-Col.,
Q. M. Gen., Militia.

(Canadian Archives, C. 679.)

From the Quebec Mercury, 15th June, 1813.

Sir James Yeo received intelligence off the harbor at York at 2 o'clock p. m., on the 16th inst., of General Vincent's victory, and bore away immediately with the fleet to cut off the retreat of the American boats employed in the expedition. Sir James laid to and remained off Sackett's Harbor on the 2d June some hours awaiting Commodore Chauncey, who, however, thought proper to continue in port, thus acknowledging our superiority on the lake.

(File in the Library of Parliament, Ottawa.)

Brigadier General Procter to Captain McDouall.

SANDWICH, June 10th, 1813.

MY DEAR SIR:—

By my last letter to you I trust you will perceive the expediency of sending me the remainder of the 41st Regiment. I did flatter myself that they were on the route hither from your letter to me. I do think that the remainder of the 41st Regt. should be sent here without delay, to, in any degree, insure the safety of this District. There has always been the greatest reluctance in the Niagara District to the sending here any regulars. I stand very little chance at this end of the line if I am to receive only reinforcements that can be spared. I informed the Indians in council that four hundred troops were on the march here, and I can assure you that it might have the worst effect were they to conceive I was deceiving or amusing them. I am really very anxious to hear of Dickson, as I fear the Americans may have found employment for him. You will have plenty of Indians without my sending more. I should run some risk in parting with any more. You have some very fine fellows among them, whom perhaps I may miss. I am very anxious to have our new vessel in the water, where she will be much safer. Every effort should be made to send us seamen before the vessels at Presque Isle are ready.

If reinforced I shall have some confidence, but I know that the cry has been always against sending men here. The consideration for me will be apparent in sending Lieut.-Colonel Short, who brought his baggage to us and left provisions, and the baggage of the 41st Regt., to be destroyed, or fall into the possession of the enemy. I shall endeavor to do my duty. The bearer of this despatch, who is a very good subject on the Thames, only stops to take this hasty scrawl, which he promises to forward. I understand that from the bad roads most of the horses are completely done up.

(Canadian Archives, C. 679, p. 110.)

General Orders.

KINGSTON, June 10th, 1813.

His Excellency the General in Chief and Commander of the Forces is pleased to appoint Lieutenant and Interpreter St. Germain to be captain in the Indian Department from the 25th May. Lieut. Anderson is appointed lieutenant and interpreter in the Indian Department of Upper Canada from the 25th April.

All women and children belonging to corps in Upper Canada are to be sent to Montreal by the returning batteaux, where appropriate accommodation is to be hired for them and the usual allowance of rations and fuel issued. After the 24th instant no rations are to be issued to soldiers' wives except to such as are employed as nurses in the hospitals or who from some sufficient cause have received the commanding officer's special permission to remain with the corps.

The officers commanding at Quebec and Montreal are to make such arrangements as may be found expedient for the distribution of soldiers' wives and children in quarters. Orders to be issued for the regular delivery of their rations and allowances.

EDWARD BAYNES,
A. G.

General Order.

HEADQUARTERS, KINGSTON,
ADJUTANT GENERAL'S OFFICE, 11th June, 1813.

His Excellency the Commander of the Forces has the highest gratification in publishing to the forces a district general order issued by Brigadier-General Vincent. His Excellency avails himself of the words of the Brigadier. He is at a loss for language to do justice to the distinguished bravery and good conduct of the troops engaged.

A Royal Salute is to be fired in celebration of the splendid achievement.

By His Excellency's command.

EDWARD BAYNES,
Adjutant General.

District General Orders.

HEADQUARTERS, BURLINGTON, 7th June, 1813.

D. G. O.

Brigadier-General Vincent congratulates the troops on the success which crowned the attack made by the King's and 49th Regiments on the enemy's position and camp at Gage's yesterday morning, when his force, consisting of not less than 3,500 men advantageously posted and protected by a considerable number of guns, was completely routed and driven off the field, 4 pieces of cannon with their tumbrils, horses, &c., 2 brigadier-generals, 5 field officers and captains and upwards of 100 prisoners were the trophies of this brilliant enterprise. Immediately after our troops had retired towards their cantonments the enemy abandoned the position to which he had fled, and after burning and destroying a quantity of baggage and provisions, carriages, blankets, arms, &c., commenced a precipitate retreat and did not halt until he reached Forty Mile Creek 12 miles (through the worst possible roads) from the scene of action; here he effected a junction with a reinforcement which was on its march to join him.

Brigadier-General Vincent is at a loss for language to do justice to the distinguished bravery and good conduct of the troops engaged.

To Lieutenant-Colonel Harvey, Deputy Adjutant General, who planned the enterprize and conducted the column to the attack, every degree of praise is due, and his distinguished services are duly appreciated. The 8th (King's,) and 49th Regiments he was rejoiced to observe vied with each other in acts of intrepidity and gallantry, though at the unavoidable expense of many of their valuable officers and men.

To Major Ogilvie and the officers and men of the 8th and to Major Plenderleath and the officers and men of the 49th Regiment the Brigadier-General offers his grateful thanks.

To the officers of the staff as well as to Captain Chambers and to His Excellency's aides-de-camp, Captains MacDouall and Milnes, Brigadier-General Vincent feels great obligations.

To the Royal and Provincial Artillery under Major Holcroft and the 41st Regiment and detachments of the Glengarry, Newfoundland and militia under Lieutenant-Colonel Bisshopp was confided, during the absence of the other troops, the important trust of the defence of this extensive position, menaced on the right by the enemy's riflemen and on the left by a numerous brigade of boats filled with troops.

Had the threatened attack been made the Brigadier-General feels the utmost confidence that those troops would have gallantly discharged their duty.

JOHN VINCENT,
Brigadier-General, commanding.
J. B. GLEGG, Lieut.-Col. B. M.

Lieut.-Colonel Harvey to Colonel Baynes.

FORTY MILE CREEK, 11th June, 1813.

MY DEAR COLONEL :—

General Vincent has desired me to forward to you the enclosed report from Lieut.-Colonel Evans accompanying returns from Lieut.-Colonel Nichol, Q. M. Gen'l. of Militia, who have been actively and successfully employed here for this day or two. The panic of the American army, you will perceive, has been most complete, and had the whole of this division been at hand to take advantage of it doubtless many prisoners might have been taken and probably some more guns, but I am not aware that any further results could rationally have been hoped for. It was quite impossible, however, for us to know to what degree the panic prevailed, and even if we had, to move sufficiently rapidly with all the troops to take advantage of it. What we could do was, however, done, and I think you will be of that opinion when you know that the enemy only retired from this post at 12 o'clock on the morning of the 8th, and our advanced troops, (amounting to 400 men,) were in possession of it and *advancing from it* after the enemy by *seven o'clock* the same evening. The distance is 20 miles from our position at the head of the lake.

The principal objects General Vincent has had in view in making a forward movement with the greatest part of the troops to this place are to communicate and give every support and assistance in his power to Sir James Yeo and the fleet and be at hand to take advantage of the success which we sanguinely anticipate from his approaching encounter with Commodore Chauncey, to give encouragement to the militia and yeomanry of the country, who are everywhere rising upon the fugitive Americans and making them prisoners, and withholding all supplies from them, and lastly, (and perhaps *chiefly,*) for the purpose of sparing the resources of the country in our rear and drawing the supplies of this army, as long as possible, from the country in the enemy's vicinity. Our position here secures all these important objects, and so long as our fleet is triumphant it is a secure one. Should any disaster (which God forbid) befall that we have no longer any business *here* or in this part of *Canada.* We have just been (Gen'l. Vincent and myself) on board the *Wolfe.* She is a *war* vessel indeed, and, Sir James Yeo says, admirably manned, as are, I understand, the rest. We have given them, however, 60 volunteers from the King's to assist, and a few gunners and bombardiers for the heavy carronades. Sir James, I am happy to observe, is fully impressed with the necessity of having a *commanding* breeze before he makes his attack. In a light one or calm the enemy's flotilla of small vessels would have an incalculable advantage. There is scarce a breath of air at this moment. The moment there is wind he proposes sailing to attack. The anxiety with which we shall witness and await the result you may readily conceive.

N. B.—Be careful of exchanging *Genl. Winder,* (my prisoner.) He possesses more talent than all the rest of the Yankee Generals put together.

P. S.—The return of captured articles is transmitted rather for the purpose of shewing to what a degree the enemy has suffered in his equipment, &c., as the greatest part of the articles are in the hands of the *Indians,* or scattered through the country. They are, however, collecting as fast as possible.

(Canadian Archives, C. 679.)

General Orders.

KINGSTON, June 10th, 1813.

A detachment of the Eighth Regiment, consisting of one captain, four subalterns, two sergeants and 56 rank and file and two companies of the Second Battalion, 41st Regiment, is to be held in readiness to embark in batteaux at gun-firing on Saturday morning to proceed by water to the head of the Bay of Quinte, and from thence to march to York by a route to be furnished by the Acting Deputy Qr. Mr. Genl., when further orders will be received from Major-General Vincent. A supply of rations is to be issued to the troops. If any remains on their arrival at the head of the Bay of Quinte they are to be carried on but are not to be made use of except a regular supply of fresh provisions are not furnished on the road.

A detachment of one officer, one sergeant and 20 militia is to embark for the purpose of conducting the boats, guarding them when the troops land, and assist in bringing them back to Kingston. Of the militia, half is to precede this movement and to make the arrangements for provisions and quartering the troops in conformity to the route they will be furnished with.

General Order.

KINGSTON, 11th June, 1813.

G. O.

A draft of one hundred rank and file of the 2d Battalion, 41st Regiment, will proceed to join the 1st Battalion under Major-General Vincent.

Lieut.-Colonel Evans and all officers belonging to the 1st Battalion will join by this opportunity. The men's accounts to be settled to the 24th June inclusive, from which date they will be transferred to the 1st Battalion. Brevet-Major Frend is to command the 2nd Battalion.

Major Moodie, with the battalion company of the 104th Regiment, is to proceed by water to join the forces under Brigadier-General Vincent.

Lieut.-Colonel Bruyeres, Royal Engineers, is to proceed to Montreal to take charge of the engineer department in that district until further orders.

EDWARD BAYNES,
A. G.

General Order.

KINGSTON, June 11th, 1813.

Lieutenant Ketcheson and ten men to be on the parade at gun-firing to-morrow morning with four days provisions, for the purpose proceeding with a detachment of troops to the head of the Bay of Quinte. A sergeant from Captain Clark's company to be attached to the gunboat commanded by Captain McIntosh.

Major Samuel S. Conner, A. D. C., to the Secretary of War.

HEADQUARTERS, FORT GEORGE,
June 12, 1813.

SIR,—As the General is unable to write I am directed by him to inform you that in addition to the debility and fever he has been afflicted with, he has within the last twenty-four hours experienced a violent spasmodic attack in his breast, which has obliged him to relinquish business altogether, and the command is given over to Major-General Lewis, who will in future make the necessary communications to the Department of War. The British fleet still rides triumphant in this section of the lake.

(American State Papers, Military Affairs.)

General Order.

KINGSTON, 12th June, 1813.

G. O.

Lieut.-Colonel Battersby is appointed to command the 1st Demi-Brigade to consist of the 1st Light Battalion, the Glengarry Light Infantry and Voltigeurs.

The detachment of the 8th, (or King's,) Regiment left at Kingston is to be attached to the 1st or Royal Scots till further orders.

EDWARD BAYNES,
A. G.

General Orders.

KINGSTON, June 12th, 1813.

Sergeant ——— and ten militia men are to be on the parade to-morrow morning at 4 o'clock, with four days provisions, for the purpose of proceeding to the head of the Bay of Quinte with a detachment of troops.

(No. 1.)
Orders.
ADJUTANT GENERAL'S OFFICE,
HEAD QUARTERS, FORT GEORGE, June 10, 1813.

By reason of the temporary indisposition of Major General Dearborn, the command of the troops on this frontier, and of the Ninth Military Department of the United States, devolves on Major General Lewis. All persons concerned are notified accordingly.

By command,
W. SCOTT, Adjutant General.

Lieut.-Colonel DeBoucherville to Sir George Prevost.

13 June, 1813.

SIR :—

. . . .
. . . .

About noon on the 5th instant [I] set off on my way down and got to the head of the lake Wednesday morning. Saw General Vincent and a number of his officers. Stayed at said place but the necessary time to receive the letters of the Gen'l. to Your Excellency. They contain all the news. All I have to observe is that I found the troops in high spirits, but am sorry at the same time to observe that the disaffection of the settlers is shocking and deserves an exemplary chastisement. At York I saw Lt.-Cols. Ogilvy and Plenderleath. These gentlemen are doing very well, as well as the rest of the wounded.

Few miles above Kingston,
　　13 June, 1813.
(Canadian Archives, C. 679, p. 88.)

From the Independent Chronicle, June 28th, 1813.

Extract from a letter from a gentleman at Newark, U. C., to the editor of the Albany *Argus*, dated June 13th.

The dragoons and riflemen are out every day in scouting parties, and seldom return without prisoners. The day before yesterday they brought in 14 of the militia who had been paroled and were caught with arms. One of the fellows confessed that he had assisted in taking 23 of our men when the army moved down from the 40 Mile Creek. With this fellow it will go hard, and I hope a more rigorous course will be pursued with the inhabitants who are opposed to our course. This class are principally Scots and Orangemen, and many of them obtain all the information they can and forward it to the enemy.

(Lenox Library, New York.)

Lieut.-Colonel Harvey to the Officer Commanding the United States Troops at Fort George.

NIAGARA, 13th June, 1813.

SIR,—With reference to a paper bearing the signature of W. Scott, Adjutant General, purporting to be instructions to an Ensign Ingersoll to proceed on an armed mission to search for an American officer, Captain Mills, who is wounded and a prisoner:

I have the direction of Brigadier-General Vincent to apprise you that if the person who signed the paper above referred to be the Lieut.-Colonel Scott who was taken at Queenston on the 13th of October last, it is impossible that he can be recognized in any other capacity than a British prisoner of war, he having given his parole of honor, (of what value is now proved,) not to serve again until regularly exchanged.

Lieut.-Colonel Scott cannot but be aware, however, of what the custom and usage of nations have prescribed should the chance of war again place him and others similarly situated in our hands.

(Canadian Archives, C. 689, p. 94.)

Sir George Prevost to Major-General Dearborn.

HEADQUARTERS, KINGSTON, 14th June, 1813.

SIR,—I have been given to understand that Lieutenant-Colonels Scott, Christie and Miller and Captain King are now serving in the forces of the United States invading this Province under the command of yourself and of Major-General Harrison, in direct violation of their parole of honor not to serve against Great Britain or her allies during the war until regularly exchanged.

I am the more surprised at this information as Your Excellency must have been aware from my last communication to you by Major Murray that I had publicly disavowed the pretended exchange of those officers, declared to have taken place under the authority of the American Government alone, and had solemnly protested against its validity.

Under these circumstances I deem it necessary to caution Your Excellency against the consequences which may result to these officers being again taken in arms by the forces under my command.

As your Government has not yet thought proper to make any reply to my last communication upon this subject, Your Excellency will, I have no doubt, see the propriety of those officers withdrawing from the army, at least during the time the question respecting their exchange remains in discussion, a measure which I trust after this letter is made known to them they will not hesitate to adopt, as the only means of preventing that severity of treatment which I shall, however reluctantly, be compelled to observe towards them should the fortune of war place them again at my disposal.

(Canadian Archives, Q. 122, p. 39.)

Return of the Troops, 13th June, 1813.

Corps.	Majors.	Captains.	Lieuts.	Ensigns.	Adjts.	Q. Mrs.	Pay Mrs.	Surgeons.	Serg'ts.	Drs.	R. & F. fit for duty	Sick.	Total.	Remarks.
Royal A[rtiller]y		2	2						1		73		73	
Artillery Drivers		1	2						1		28		28	
8th King's	1	1	9	1	1		1	3	24	13	406		406	
41st Regt		5	7	5	1	1	1	1	29	15	384	9	393	
49th Regt	1	6	9	2	1	1	1	1	27	14	439	52	491	
Royal Newfoundland		2	3	1					3	2	61		61	
Glengarry Regt		1	1						6		61		61	
Colored Corps									2		27		29	
Dragoons		1							1		23		23	
	2	19	33	9	3	2	3	5	94	44	1502	61	1563	

(From Memorandum of Lt.-Col. Glegg in possession of Lt.-Col. Turner, Reading, England.)

Brigadier-General Vincent to Colonel Baynes.

FORTY MILE CREEK, 14th June, 1813.

SIR,—I have just been informed by a confidential friend at Fort George that the greatest part of the enemy's force have returned to Fort Niagara and that line, and at present the force on this side is not more than six thousand, numbers of whom are in a sickly state. If this is a correct statement, and on my next communication with the fleet and our reinforcements have arrived, I am determined, if Sir James Yeo thinks he can co-operate with us, to push on and retake Fort George. I can see none of our fleet on the lake. I have therefore to suppose they have made a run on Kingston for provisions, but if this circumstance has taken place it will not in the least change my intentions or situation, as I am confident from Sir James's experience he would not be many days absent from this army.

The enemy have passed a brig up the rapids at Fort Erie on the 10th inst. They have two brigs and six large gunboats at Presqu' Isle not yet ready, but expected in three weeks. I have sent this information to Amherstburg.

Notwithstanding I cannot well spare troops, but supposing that Brigadier-General Procter may be in more want than myself, I have ordered one hundred rank and file, with the headquarters of the 41st Regiment, to proceed by land, which I hope will meet with His Excellency's approbation.

By a letter I received from the Brigadier-General the 10th inst., I have every reason to expect some hundreds of Indians are on the march to join, and I make bold to say one thousand men more added to this army will drive every part of the enemy out of this country.

I have to request shoes may be sent. We are more in want of them than any other article.

(Canadian Archives, C. 679, p. 92.)

Major-General Morgan Lewis to the Secretary of War.

NIAGARA, June 14, 1813.

SIR,—You will perceive by the enclosed copy of orders marked 1, that General Dearborn, from indisposition, has resigned the command not only of the Niagara army but of the district. I have doubts whether he will ever again be fit for service. He has repeatedly been in a state of convalescence but relapses on the least agitation of mind.

In my last I mentioned the unfortunate circumstances of the capture of our two Brigadiers, Chandler and Winder; the particulars are detailed in the report of Col. Burn, which he gives from the best information he could collect. His corps lay a considerable distance from the scene of active operations, as you will perceive by the enclosed diagram, which is on a scale of 100 yards to the inch. The light corps spoken of were Captains Hindman's, Biddle's and Nicholas's companies of the 2d Artillery, serving as infantry. These three gentlemen and Captains Archer and Towson of the same regiment and Leonard of the light artillery are soldiers who would do honor to any service; their gallantry and that of their companions was equally conspicuous on this occasion as in the affair of the 27th ult. A view of Gen. Chandler's encampment will be sufficient to show that his disaster was owing to its arrangement, its centre being its weakest point, and that, being discovered by the enemy in the evening, received the combined attack of his whole force and his line was completely cut. The gallantry of the 5th, 25th and part of the 23d and light troops saved the army. Of the 5th it is said that when the day broke not a man was missing, and that a part of the 23d under Major Armstrong was found sustaining its left flank; their fire was irresistible and the enemy was compelled to give way. Could he have been pressed the next morning his destruction was inevitable; he was dispersed in every direction and even his commanding General was missing without his hat or horse. I understand he was found the next morning at a distance of four miles from the scene of action.

Lieut. Machesney's gallantry recovered a piece of artillery and prevented the capture of others; he deserves promotion for it.

On the evening of the 6th of June I received the order No. 4, and joined the army at 5 in the afternoon of the 7th. I found it at the Forty Mile Creek, 10 miles in rear of the ground on which it had been attacked, encamped on a plain of about a mile in width with its right flank on the lake, and its left on a creek which skirts a perpendicular mountain of a considerable height. On my route I received Nos. 5 and 6 enclosed.

At 6 in the evening the hostile fleet hove in sight, though its character could not be distinguished with precision. We lay on our arms all night—at dawn of day struck our tents and descried the hostile squadron abreast of us about a mile from the shore. Our boats, which transported the principal part of our baggage and camp equipage, lay on the beach. It was a dead calm, and about 6 the enemy towed in a large schooner which opened her fire on our boats. As soon as she stood for the shore, her object being evident, I ordered down Archer's and Towson's companies with four pieces of artillery to resist her attempts. I at the same time sent Capt. Totten of the Engineers, (a most valuable officer,) to construct a temporary furnace, which was prepared and in operation in less than 30 minutes. Her fire was returned with vivacity and effect, (excelled by no artillery in the universe,) which soon compelled her to retire.

A party of savages now made their appearance on the brow of the mountain, (which being perfectly bald exhibited them to our view,) and commenced a fire on our camp. I ordered Col. Christie to dislodge them, who entered on the service with alacrity, but found himself anticipated by Lieut. Eldridge, the adjutant of his regiment, who, with a promptness and gallantry highly honorable to that young officer, had already gained the summit of the mountain with a party of volunteers and routed the barbarian allies of the defender of the Christian faith. This young man merits the notice of government.

These little affairs cost us not a man. Sir James L. Yeo being disappointed of a tragedy next determined in true dramatic style to amuse us with a farce. An officer with a flag was sent to me from his ship, advising me that as I was invested with savages in my rear, a fleet in my front and a powerful army in my flank he and the officers commanding His Britannic Majesty's land forces thought it their duty to demand a surrender of my army. I answered that the message was too ridiculous to merit a reply.

No 7 was delivered to me about 6 this morning. Between 7 and 8 the four wagons we had being loaded, first with the sick and next with ammunition, &c., the residue of the camp equipage and baggage was put in the boats and a detachment of 200 men of the 6th Regiment detailed to proceed in them. Orders were prepared to be given them to defend the boats, and if assailed by any of the enemy's small vessels to carry them by boarding. By some irregularity, which I have not been able to discover, the boats put off without the detachments, induced probably by the stillness of the morning. When they had progressed about three miles a breeze sprung up and an armed schooner overhauled them. Those who were enterprising kept on and escaped; others ran to the shore and deserted the boats. We lost 12 of the number, principally containing the baggage of the officers and men.

At 10, I put our army in motion on our return to this place. The savages and incorporated militia hung on our flanks throughout the march and picked up a few stragglers. On our retiring the British army advanced and now occupies the ground we left.

The enemy's fleet is constantly hovering on our coast and intercepting our supplies. The night before last, being advised that they had chased into Eighteen Mile Creek two vessels laden with hospital stores, &c., I detached at midnight 75 men for their protection. The report of the day is, though not official, that they arrived too late for their purpose and that the stores are lost.

(American State Papers, Military Affairs.)

Papers Referred to in General Lewis's Letter to the Secretary of War of 14th June, 1813.

GENERAL DEARBORN TO GENERAL LEWIS.

(No. 4.)

HEADQUARTERS, NIAGARA, June 6, 1813.

DEAR GENERAL:—
You will please to proceed with as little delay as may be and take command of the advanced army. Brigadier Generals Boyd and Swartwout and Colonel Scott will accompany you. I have ordered an additional escort of light artillery, to be equipped as cavalry, to attend you. You will attack the enemy as soon as practicable. Your force will ensure success. Every possible effort should be made for preventing the enemy's escape.

May success and glory attend you.

(American State Papers, Military Affairs.)

(No. 5).

GENERAL DEARBORN TO GENERAL LEWIS.

NIAGARA, June 6, 1813.

DEAR GENERAL:—
A ship having appeared this morning, steering towards the head of the lake, which is undoubtedly one of the enemy's ships, (others are appearing) you will please to return with the troops to this place as soon as possible.

P. S.—The object of the enemy's fleet must be to cover the retreat of their troops or to bring over a reinforcement.

(No. 6.)

GENERAL DEARBORN TO GENERAL LEWIS.

June 6, 1813.

It is possible the fleet in sight may be our own; a few hours will probably enable you to determine and act accordingly.

(American State Papers, Military Affairs.)

(No. 7.)

GENERAL DEARBORN TO GENERAL LEWIS.

DEAR GENERAL:—
I am induced to suspect that the enemy's fleet have an intention on this place. Two small schooners have been examining the shore very minutely for three or four hours this afternoon. They have

gone on towards the head of the lake and their ships appear to have taken the same course. They may take on board additional troops near the head of the lake and be here before you reach this place. You will please to send Milton's detachment and 500 of Chandler's brigade, and Colonel Burn's light dragoons, with all possible despatch; they ought, if possible, to be here sometime to-morrow forenoon. You will follow with the remainder of the troops as soon as practicable. It will be necessary to take care that your boats are not taken or lost. General Swartwout and Colonel Scott should return as soon as they can.

(American State Papers, Military Affairs.)

Report of the Killed, Wounded and Missing in the Action of the 6th June at Stoney Creek.

Killed—1 sergeant, 1 corporal, 15 privates.
Wounded—1 captain, 1 sergeant, 2 corporals and 34 privates.
Missing—2 Brigadier-Generals, 1 major, 3 captains, 1 subaltern, 9 sergeants, 4 corporals, 80 privates.
Total killed, wounded and missing—154.
Correct return from the reports of the different corps in the action of the 6th inst. at Stoney Creek.

J. JOHNSON, Asst. Adj. Gen.

(From Niles's Weekly Register, Baltimore, Md., 26th June, 1813. Vol. IV., p. 272.)

Sir George Prevost to Brigadier-General Procter.

KINGSTON, 14th June, 1813.

SIR,—I have had the honor of your different letters of the 14th of May by Lieut.-Colonel Boucherville, containing the report of your successful resistance to the attack of the enemy on the 5th of that month, and must heartily congratulate you on the skill and bravery so invariably displayed by yourself and the troops under your command and which have led to so fortunate a result. I have also to acknowledge the receipt of your letter of the 10th inst. and beg leave to assure you that I have not been unmindful of your situation and wants. Brigadier-General Vincent has already received directions, and I have reason to think he has already adopted measures for supplying them as far as lies in his power, and whenever the Indian goods, which are now on their way from Quebec, shall have reached this post they shall be forwarded to you without delay. As you have not acknowledged the receipt of my instructions transmitted to you, by desire of Major-General Sheaffe, to avail yourself of any favorable opportunity of retaliating upon the enemy for the attack upon York by endeavoring to annoy their settlements upon Lake Erie, I fear his letter has not reached you. The arrival of Captain Barclay, who, I trust, with a small reinforcement of seamen, is with you long before this, will, I hope, enable you to place your marine on such a footing as to check any attempts of the enemy to gain a superiority on Lake Erie. I am very solicitous to receive from you a correct statement of the whole of your marine establishment and what is wanted to render it complete.

(From Some Account of the Public Life of Lieutenant-General Sir George Prevost, Bart., London, 1823. Appendix No. XXIII., pp. 66-7.)

Sir George Prevost to Lord Bathurst.

KINGSTON, UPPER CANADA, 14th June, 1813.

(No. 70.)

MY LORD,—I have again the high gratification of having to transmit to your Lordship the particulars of a feat of distinguished valor and enterprise achieved near Burlington Bay on the 6th instant by a division of the army commanded by Colonel Vincent of the 49th Regiment, who is acting as Brigadier-General in Upper Canada until His Royal Highness the Prince Regent's pleasure is known.

To the just measure of praise given by Colonel Vincent to Lieutenant-Colonel Harvey for the zeal, intelligence and gallantry displayed by him on this occasion, I have to add that so great was the desire of that meritorious officer to arrive at his post and share in the arduous duties of the army to which he had been appointed, that he walked on snow shoes in the depth of last winter through the wilds laying between the Canadas and New Brunswick. In addition to Colonel Vincent's report of the affair at Stoney Creek, I have the honor to inform Your Lordship that the enemy made a movement to their rear in consequence of the attack of their camp, and had retired to the 40 Mile Creek when Sir James Yeo's flotilla had appeared in the offing.

The Commodore, after communicating with Colonel Vincent, proceeded with the reinforcement of troops I had put on board his vessels at Kingston towards the enemy's second camp, and when the last intelligence left him his squadron had so successfully cannonaded it that the mass of the Americans were retreating with precipitation, and our troops pressing upon them; several of their boats had fallen into our possession. The attack made upon Sackett's Harbor on the 29th ult., which terminated in the destruction of the naval stores accumulated at that post, induced the enemy's fleet to cease operating with the army and to return suddenly into port, since which time Commodore Chauncey has not ventured upon the lake.

Captain McDouall, my aide-de-camp, will have the honor of delivering to Your Lordship this despatch. He is an officer of great merit and intelligence, and having been sent forward with instructions to Colonel Vincent, had the good fortune to be present in the last action, in which that division of the army so highly distinguished itself. He was also at the attack made on Sackett's Harbor, and was employed on an arduous mission to Colonel Procter when the movement of the American army under General Harrison towards the Detroit frontier took place in February last. He is therefore well qualified to give Your Lordship any information you may require respecting the state of affairs in the Canadas, and deserving of any mark of favor it may graciously please His Highness the Prince Regent to confer upon him.

Captain McDouall will also have the honor of delivering to Your Lordship the colors taken from the enemy at Ogdensburg, that they may be laid at the feet of His Royal Highness the Prince Regent.

(Canadian Archives, Q. 122, p. 22.)

Indictment of Andrew Patterson.

Home District.

The jurors for our Lord the King upon their oath present that on the first day of June in the fifty-third year of the reign of our Sovereign Lord George the Third, by the Grace of God of the United Kingdom of Great Britain and Ireland King, Defender of the Faith, and for a long time before open and public war existed and was carried on between our said Lord the King and the United States of America, and does still exist and is carried on, and that Andrew Patterson of the Township of Whitchurch, yeoman, being an ill-designing and seditious person and greatly disaffected to the Government of our said Lord the King and of this Province of Upper Canada, on the first day of June in the said fifty-third year of the reign of our Lord the King at the Township of Whitchurch in said district in the presence of divers good liege subjects of our Lord the King, did pull off his hat and hurra for the United States, enemies of our Lord the King, and wish them success, and did then and there cry out, " Huzza to the United States," (public and declared enemies of our Lord the King,) " for their, (meaning the United States,) great success in taking Fort George," (meaning Fort George in the District of Niagara in the Province of Upper Canada, taken in open war and by arms by the forces of the United States, public and declared enemies of our Lord the King, from our Lord the King, on the twenty-seventh day of May in the year aforesaid, or words to that effect and meaning, and did then and there openly and loudly in presence and hearing of the said liege subjects of our Lord the King, express great joy at the success of the enemies of our Lord the King over the arms of our Lord the King in the taking of Fort George aforesaid on the day aforesaid, to the great scandal and disgrace of the Government of this Province of Upper Canada, to the evil example of all others in the like case offending and against the peace of our said Lord the King, his Crown and Dignity.

 Endorsed—The King against Andrew Patterson, sedition.
    Witnesses—Edward Sanders, John Wideman, Jacob Wideman.
    TRUE BILL—Alexander Wood, foreman.

Prisoner arraigned and traversed to the next assize, 20th Oct., 1814. The jury by their foreman, Abram Legg, brought a verdict *Guilty.* Thos. Scott, C. J.

Abstract of Indictment of Elijah Bentley.

Home District.

The jurors present Elijah Bentley of the Township of Markham, an Anabaptist preacher, in that while the forces of the United States were in possession of the town of York, on the 2d day of May, 1813, at Markham, in a certain large congregation of good and faithful liege subjects of our Lord the King, assembled to hear the said Elijah Bentley preach and hold forth on religious matters, he, the said Elijah Bentley, did say, "I thank God there never has been such freedom for poor people in York as there has been since General Dearborn set his foot in it," to the great scandal and disgrace of the Government of this Province of Upper Canada, to the evil example of all others in the like case offending and against the peace of our said Lord the King, his Crown and Dignity.

The jury brought in a verdict *Guilty.*

Sentenced to be imprisoned in gaol for the term of six calendar months, and to give bonds to keep the peace for five years.

(Original in Osgoode Hall, Toronto.)

Captain Robert McDouall to Brigadier-General Procter.

         Headquarters, FORTY MILE CREEK,
           June 14th, 1813.

MY DEAR GENERAL,—We every day look for a reinforcement of about 400 men from Kingston. On their arrival, and should the fleet continue with us, it is intended to advance the army to 20 Mile Creek and throw forward the whole body of Indians and the light troops, (considerably augmented,) to feel the pulse of the enemy. We have various accounts as to his force, and none to be depended upon, but his fears are said to be as strong as ever and a *ruse* of the nature above mentioned might operate so powerfully upon him as might induce him to think that his own side of the river is the only place of safety.

Our Indians prove themselves right worthy and right useful auxiliaries. Macbeth says: "'Tis the eye of childhood that fears a painted devil." But it is so far lucky that our opponents are mere infants in the sublime science of war. Now, as you are perhaps encumbered with too many mouths, considering your scanty means of filling them, you might perhaps be able to prevail on two or three hundred more of your swarthy warriors to join us here. They would be invaluable under the present circumstances, and you might fairly tell them that a great effort is to be made to drive their enemy and ours across the St. Lawrence, and once effected I do most positively believe they will never renew the attempt. Remember me to Col. Warburton, Dixon and Mockler.

(From Niles' Weekly Register, Baltimore, Md., 15th January, 1814. Vol. V., p. 328. Said to have been taken in General Procter's baggage on 5th October, 1813.)

Proclamation.

By His Excellency Lieutenant General Sir George Prevost, Baronet, Governor General and Commander-in-Chief in and over His Majesty's North American Provinces and Commander in the Forces in the said Provinces, &c., &c., &c.

A PROCLAMATION.

His Excellency the Commander of the Forces in the said Provinces having seen a public declaration made by Lieut.-Colonel James P. Preston of the 12th Regiment of United States Infantry, dated at Fort Erie the 30th of May last, in which he professes to hold out the protection of the United States to all those who shall come forward and voluntarily enroll their names with him, and threatening with rigorous and disastrous consequences those who shall have the spirit and loyalty to pursue a different course of conduct, His Excellency deems it necessary to caution His Majesty's subjects in this Province against listening to this insidious offer of the enemy, or trusting to their assurances of protection, which subsequent events have clearly proved they are so little able to afford to themselves. With the bare possession of a narrow strip of our frontier territory, not obtained by them without a severe contest and corresponding loss, with an unconquered and unbroken army in their front at an inconsiderable distance from them, and ready to dispute every inch of ground over which they should attempt to advance into the country, it was hardly to be expected that the enemy's presumption would have led them to consider themselves as in possession of this Province, or have induced them, contrary to the established usages of civilized warfare, to treat its peaceable inhabitants as a conquered people.

The brilliant result of the action of the 6th inst., the rout and complete dispersion of a large division of the enemy's forces on that day, attended with the capture of their artillery and of their ablest Generals, their subsequent retreat and flight, with the loss of the whole of their baggage, provisions and tent equipage, before the victorious army of Brigadier-General Vincent, daily increasing in strength from the powerful reinforcements reaching it and assisted by the squadron under Sir James Yeo, now in undisturbed possession of the lake, all these events, which followed in rapid succession within a very few days after Lt.-Col. Preston's declaration, shew more strongly than any language can possibly describe the futility of the offers held out by it, and produce the strongest incentive to His Majesty's subjects to hold fast that allegiance from which the enemy would so insidiously withdraw them.

His Excellency therefore confidently calls upon all the loyal and well disposed in this Province, who are not under the immediate control or within the power of the enemy, to use every possible effort in repelling the foe and driving him from our soil, assuring them that they will be powerfully aided by the reinforcements daily arriving at this post and pressing on to their support. To those of His Majesty's subjects who are unfortunately situated within that inconsiderable portion of the territory occupied by the enemy, His Excellency recommends a quiet and peaceful conduct, such as shall neither afford a just cause to the enemy for treating them with the severity and rigor they have threatened, or incompatible with their allegiance to the best of sovereigns. His Excellency at the same time declares that he shall be compelled, however reluctantly, to retaliate upon the American prisoners in his possession every violation of the persons or property of any of His Majesty's subjects so peaceably demeaning themselves, and hereby publicly protests against such treatment as equally unsanctioned by the usages of war or by the example afforded by His Majesty's forces with regard to any of the American prisoners in his possession.

Given under my hand and seal at arms at Kingston this fourteenth day of June, one thousand eight hundred and thirteen.

By His Excellency's Command,
E. B. BRENTON.

GEORGE PREVOST,
Commander of the forces.

(Canadian Archives, Q., 122, p. 44.)

General Orders.

KINGSTON, 14th June, 1813.

G. O.

Major Macdonnell, of the Glengarry Light Infantry, is appointed to the command of the 1st Battalion of light infantry.

The senior captains of the flank battalions are to act as majors of the corps and to receive the forage allowance for one horse. A subaltern officer is permitted to act as adjutant to the battalion, and another as adjutant of the demi-brigade, who will each be allowed forage for one horse.

A depot of provisions is to be formed at York, for three months, for 1700 men and 200 horse. The Commissariat Department will make the necessary arrangements for this order being carried into effect.

All men of the 104th Regiment, fit for field service, are to be sent forward to join the 1st and 2d divisions of their regiment; all sick and convalescent men are to remain at Quebec.

EDWARD BAYNES, A. G.

Midland District Orders.

KINGSTON, 14th June, 1813.

No. 1—The officer commanding the Second Battalion, 41st Regiment, will immediately establish a regular system of drill, and practice the whole of his corps with ball-firing.

No. 2—The light companies are also to fire ball cartridge, each man to be practiced to fire at a given object, either on a level, up hill or down hill, on his knees or on his belly.

Brigadier General Procter to General Vincent.

SANDWICH, 15th June, 1813.

MY DEAR SIR:—

Your letter of the 10th inst. was the most agreeable one I have received for some time past, and I heartily congratulate you on the brilliant result of the judicious and gallant attack of the 6th inst. The enemy are indebted entirely to their flotilla for their late successes. We are anxiously looking for a reinforcement of seamen who, I hope, can be spared from the lower lake, tho' I am fully aware that the enemy are not idle at Sackett's Harbor, neither are they, I apprehend, at Presque Isle. Capt. Barclay is endeavoring to ascertain their real state. I am surprised they have not appeared on this lake. We are well aware of the necessity of giving the first blow, indeed, we owe everything to our having done so. Captain Barclay has, I believe, written urgently to Sir James Yeo on the necessity of our having seamen without delay. If I had a regular force on which alone I could place any reliance I could give an impulse to my Indian force that would enable them to feed at the enemy's expense. At present they are not half fed and would leave us if they were not warm in the cause. The want of meat does operate much against us, as does the want of Indian arms and goods. In short, our wants are so serious that the enemy must derive great advantage from them alone. Surely Mr. Couche need not have kept us so entirely without money as well as meat. I am, however, full of hope that we shall stand our ground, trusting that every aid and supply will be afforded us as soon as possible from the head of the lake. I should suppose that the land carriage is practicable, and thence by water to Long Point is certainly so. Provisions, Indian arms and goods can undoubtedly be sent, and some exertions may be expected, as these articles cannot be dispensed with. Col. Nichol is fully qualified to direct the transport in question. I have sent one of the commissariat to meet the 41st on the Thames, and also some boats for their conveyance.

The last letter I received from Dickson was dated the 22d of March, nor have they at Mackinac heard from him. He promised to be here in June, early. I am very anxious to hear from him, tho' every person speaks confidently of his soon coming. The enemy's emissaries are availing themselves with no little effrontery of circumstances unfavorable to us, and have effected the defection of a few Indians. They were sending wampum to Mr. Harrison. I hope we shall be able to remedy the evil and punish individuals. You will perceive the necessity for troops to inspire confidence and restrain the evil-disposed. I fear this circumstance may delay the Indians a couple of days longer. However annoying, it cannot be helped. I shall council with the Indians and endeavor to persuade them to take a few of Mr. Harrison's cattle. They are, however, very wild from being fired at often. I feel no small confidence of supplies, from your being where you are. Mrs. and Miss Procter desire to be kindly remembered to you, as does Harry.

The want of some officer here of the Adjutant-General's Department has caused me much dissatisfaction.

(Canadian Archives, C. 679, p. 197.)

(From the Buffalo Gazette, 15th June, 1813.)

CAPTURE OF GENERALS WINDER AND CHANDLER.

On Thursday evening last we issued an extra *Gazette* announcing this unpleasant intelligence and now add some further particulars. On Saturday evening, the 6th inst., (says our informant,) while our advanced guard, consisting of Winder's brigade and detachments of light artillery, dragoons and riflemen were lying encamped at Stoney Creek, a few miles from the 40 Mile Creek, where the enemy lay in force a sergeant, deserted from his post with the countersign, upon which General Vincent repaired to our encampment and passed the whole line of our centinels, made what discoveries he could and returned with all his disposable force, made a vigorous and desperate charge upon the picquet and other guards and penetrated into the heart of our camp with but little regular opposition, and succeeded in capturing Generals Winder and Chandler, Quartermaster C. Van de Venter and several other officers and about 150 soldiers. This affair happened about 2 o'clock in the morning and produced great confusion, but the command devolving upon Colonel Burn of the light dragoons, he and Lieut.-Colonel Milton had the address to retreat a short distance in as good order as the darkness of the night would allow of. The troops were formed and maintained their ground and at dawn of day they attacked the British, routed and pursued them a few miles and made nearly 100 prisoners and then returned unmolested.

Our loss in killed and dangerously wounded was between 30 and 40. The enemy lost not less than 200 in killed and badly wounded. *Our riflemen may well be termed sharpshooters.* General Vincent is said to have been badly wounded. Colonel Clark of the 49th and Major Glegg, late aid to General Brock, are said to have died of their wounds. The enemy are reported to have been about 1,500 strong before they made the attack.

On Monday 5 British vessels passed up the lake with a small reinforcement on board, and in their course destroyed 18 of our boats passing from Fort George up the lake with baggage and provisions for our troops. After the appearing of the enemy's fleet our army fell back on Fort George, as the enemy might with great facility take a force from the 40 Mile Creek to Newark in their vessels and do much mischief before our troops could march to the relief of that place.

Colonel Preston has marched from Fort Erie to Fort George, after which the public buildings at the former place were burnt.

Great exertions, we understand, are making in Canada to embody the militia, and that no respect whatever is paid to those who have been paroled by our officers.

(File in Buffalo Public Library.)

Major J. B. Glegg to William Jarvis.

40 MILE CREEK, 15th June, 1813.

DEAR SIR,—A wonderful change has taken place in our prospects since the nocturnal visit to the enemy's encampment at Stoney Creek on the 6th. We begin to carry on our arrangements as usual. We are all well and in the highest spirits.

(From the Jarvis Papers, Toronto Public Library.)

Midland District Orders.

KINGSTON, 13th June, 1813.

(No. 2.)

The commanding officers will immediately make themselves acquainted with the country round about their several posts, and take care that the communications to their front, flanks and rear are open and that their officers and non-commissioned officers are acquainted with them.

General Order.

KINGSTON, 15th June, 1813.

G. O.

The forces serving in Upper Canada are to be distinguished in the following manner:

The division serving under Brigadier-General Procter at Detroit to be styled the Right Division of the Army of Upper Canada. The forces at Niagara and York the Centre Division, and the troops at Kingston and below to form the Left Division of the Army of Upper Canada.

EDWARD BAYNES,
A. G.

General Orders.

ADJUTANT GENERAL'S OFFICE,
Headquarters, KINGSTON, June 15th, 1813.

The light company of the 100th Regiment is to proceed to Kingston to join the light battalion and the light company of the 89th Regiment is to form part of the Second Light Battalion. All of the 104th Regiment fit for field service are to be sent forward by detachments as they arrive at Quebec, to join their regiment.

The company of the Royal Sappers and Miners is directed to proceed to Kingston, leaving thirty men at Prescott of such description as the commanding engineer may direct.

Lieut.-Colonel Macdonnell of the Glengarry Light Infantry will take the command of the First Light Battalion vice Lieut.-Colonel Smelt, appointed to the Second Light Battalion.

The senior captains of the light battalions are to act as Majors to the corps and receive forage as such.

Augustus Porter to Peter B. Porter.

MANCHESTER, June 16th, 1813.

SIR,—I send Augustus up to Buffalo after the remainder of the abstracts, which I expect Mr. Lecroy has completed by this time. If they are not done I have directed Augustus to wait at your house until they are finished, as they are almost all the papers which I now wait for.

I have been to Niagara and obtained vouchers for all my provisions on hand that has arrived. Such as remain back at Genesee and Oswego Genl. Dearborn would not agree to receive. I expect a considerable quantity of them are taken by the British. So it goes, one day one thing and another the next. I shall not hereafter take the verbal promise of any man. If you are well enough I should be very glad to have you come down immediately and must wish to see you before I start for Washington, which will be in about five days. I have just received notice that two drafts which I lately made on the S. of W., one of 3,000 the other of 4,000 dollars, are protested. I find I have got more vouchers than I had expected. My issues and deposits here will not be much short of 1,400,000 rations.

(MSS. of Hon. Peter A. Porter.)

Captain F. Chambers, U. S. A., to Lieutenant-Colonel Harvey.

FORT GEORGE, 17th June, 1813.

SIR,—I am directed by Major-General Lewis to state to you for the information of Brigadier-General Vincent that the Colonel Scott who gave the instructions of Ensign Ingersoll is the identical Lieut.-Colonel Scott who was captured at Queenston. That while perfectly aware of the obligations of a parole, and of too nice honor ever to violate one, as a good citizen he places implicit faith in the assurance of his government and as a good soldier obeys its mandates. The American Government has officially announced to Colonel Scott his exchange for officers, &c., taken on board His Brittannic Majesty's ship, *Samuel and Sara*, (which troops are now understood to be in actual service,) and has been ordered. Should any misunderstanding exist as to the correctness of the exchange it may afford question for the two governments, but certainly not for the individual implicated, who is bound to obey his orders regardless of consequences.

(Canadian Archives. C. 689, p. 104.)

Captain R. H. Barclay to Brigadier-General Vincent.

H. M. S. *Queen Charlotte*,
LONG POINT, June 17th, 1813.

MY DEAR SIR,—

I had the pleasure of receiving your letter by Captain Finnis and most sincerely congratulate you on your late signal successes, so well timed to take ample satisfaction for the transient success of the enemy at Fort George.

I reconnoitered Presque Isle yesterday and found two corvettes in a very forward state indeed, they being both launched and their lower masts in. Such a force, with the very backward state which I am sorry to state the *Detroit* is in, must give the enemy a very great superiority on this lake, taking also into consideration the men I have, the tardy organization even of those, together with the great want of stores at Amherstburg renders the prospect rather gloomy. Nor can anything clear the cloud except an immediate reinforcement of troops to enable General Procter to join with me in an attack at Presque Isle and destroy the enemy's squadron before they get quite ready.

From the appearance of Presque Isle a considerable force will be necessary. There is a camp there sufficiently large to contain from 6 or 700 men. The entrance is defended by two blockhouses and a small redoubt, but I saw nothing to render the consequences of a vigorous attack even doubtful. I proposed the measure to General Procter, but he cannot spare the men. He will grant a large body of Indians, which will be a noble auxiliary to any force that may be sent for the desirable purpose of utterly destroying the only naval force the enemy have on this lake.

I have written to Sir James Yeo, and I hope that through him His Excellency the Governor General will afford you the means of assisting me in this enterprise, that the event may be honorable to His Excellency's arms and beneficial to the country.

I have thought fit to send Lieut. Garden of the Newfoundland Regiment with this despatch, fearing it might fall into improper hands, with which this country so much abounds.

I have the pleasure also to state the safety of 300 barrels of pork, which I have taken measures to get to Amherstburg immediately.

I beg that you will cause the letter addressed to the Commodore to be immediately forwarded, as I deem it of the utmost consequence that he should know the enemy's preparations on this lake that he may give me a proportionate force against them.

I hope soon to address you at Fort George.

P. S.—Captain Finnis gave me great hopes that there were four companies of the 41st Regiment coming here. I sent a militia officer to apprize them of my leaving here with part of the squadron, that I might save them a march of 200 miles by giving them a passage to Amherstburg. How much disappointed I was when I found there was only one company I leave you to imagine, as I thought of receiving the long wished for force to enable General Procter to assist me to destroy the nest at Presque Isle.

I shall send part on in battoes with the pork and take the rest with me in the *Queen Charlotte* in a few days. The officer met them at the Grand River. They will be here to-night.

(Canadian Archives, C. 730, pp. 10-14.)

General Order.

Headquarters, KINGSTON, 17th June, 1813.

G. O.

All officers arriving from Europe and all recruits and soldiers fit for active field service belonging to regiments in Upper Canada are to proceed to join their corps with the least possible delay.

Major Gordon and two effective companies of the Royal Scots are to embark on the fleet this afternoon at five o'clock.

All detachments and soldiers belonging to regiments above Kingston are to be attached to the Royal Newfoundland Regiment unless an officer of their corps is present in the garrison.

EDWARD BAYNES,
A. G.

Garrison Orders.

KINGSTON, 17th June, 1813.

(No. 6.)

One subaltern, one sergeant, one corporal and twenty rank and file of the Second Battalion of the 41st Regiment are to relieve the detachment of the 104th Regiment at Gananoqui. A gunboat is to take this party at six o'clock this evening and bring back the men of the 104th Regiment in the morning. On their arrival they will report to Major Heathcote.

The troops in the garrison are permitted to expend ten rounds of ball cartridge for practice for every rank and file. The commanding officers are particularly directed to attend personally to the instruction of their men in the act of firing and they are to report for the information of His Excellency the progress made by their respective corps at the time they report the expenditure of the ammunition.

EDWARD BAYNES,
Adjutant General.

Muster roll and pay list of a detachment of the 2d Norfolk Regiment of Militia, under the command of Lieutenant Titus Williams, captured by the enemy at Sugar Loaf Hill the 17th June, 1813:—

Lieut. Titus Williams.
Private John Widner.
" Jeremiah Green.
" Sobrigen Dominique.
" Angus McIntire.
" Charles Knight.
" Elijah Montonier.
" Alex. Logan.
" John Furry.
" Samuel Troup.

(From the Talbot Papers.)

Brigadier General Vincent to Sir George Prevost.

40 MILE CREEK, 18th June, 1813.

SIR,—I have just received the enclosed letter from Captain Barclay and I think it so very necessary that the remainder of the 41st Regiment should be sent forward immediately for the purpose of destroying the fleet at Presqu' Isle that I shall not hesitate in giving every assistance to Captain Barclay. Captain McDouall will explain to Your Excellency my intention.

(Canadian Archives, C. 679.)

Captain James P. Fulton to Sir George Prevost.

Headquarters, FORTY MILE CREEK, 18th June, 1813.

SIR,—I have so fully explained to Captain MacDouall for Your Excellency's information our resources for the accommodation of troops between Kingston and York, that it is unnecessary for me to enter into a detailed account of them.

On my arrival here I found the troops in great distress for necessaries, shirts, shoes and stockings. Most of the 49th are *literally naked.* General Vincent has informed me that he has made the necessary application for the *stores* required for the different departments.

At York the medical department want a supply of stores particularly. I am happy to have it in my power to add that the wounded officers and men are doing extremely well. Majors Plenderleath and Ogilvie hope to join their regiments on the 24th of this month.

(Canadian Archives, C. 679.)

General Dearborn to General P. B. Porter.

Headquarters, NIAGARA, June 18, 1813.

SIR,—You will please to assemble fifty or sixty men, duly officered, with as little delay as possible for the purpose of preventing any small depredating party from annoying the village of Buffalo or the public property at Black Rock and its vicinity, until other troops shall arrive.

P. S.—You will please to have as many cannon fitted and mounted as you can.

(From MSS. of Hon. P. A. Porter.)

General Order.

Headquarters, KINGSTON, June 19th, 1813.

A party of a subaltern, a sergeant and 20 rank and file of the 104th Regiment are to embark immediately on board the *Pultney* schooner to proceed in her in charge of provisions and stores towards the Head of the Lake; to take ten days provisions.

E. BAYNES,
Adjutant General.

Lieut. MacEwen, Royal Scots, to his Wife at Montreal.

KINGSTON, 18th June, 1813.

Colonel Stuart arrived here yesterday and seemed happy to see me. He informed me that he had seen you at Montreal and that you were all well when he came away. I have been obliged to sell him my horse, as we are again under orders to march to York, with two hundred men. Major Gordon, Captain Wilson, Clyne, Fox, Hendrick, Johnston and Rutledge embarked last night for same place. I have sold the horse for my own money, thirty guineas, which is thirty-five pounds currency.

(From A. Brymner's Excerpts, p. 5.)

Lieut. MacEwen to his Wife, at Montreal.

CARRYING PLACE, 23d June, 1813.

I again take the opportunity of a gentleman going down to Kingston to inform you that I arrived here this morning in good health after a march of nearly one hundred miles from Kingston. Our destination I cannot at present give you the smallest information of, as the whole of our army is on the march against the enemy, who are at Fort George, a place about three hundred miles from here. Our regiment has lost several men in the actions with the Americans, but we have always been the victorious party. We have destroyed one of their finest towns and plundered them of every article.

(From A. Brymner's Excerpts, pp. 5-6.)

From Poulson's American Daily Advertiser of Philadelphia, 20th June, 1813.

CANANDAIGUA, June 17, 1813.

The enemy visited the mouth of the Genesee River yesterday morning and took about 500 barrels of provisions and 1700 bushels of corn, as is said by a person who is from there this day. Apprehensions are entertained of a similar visit at Sodus and Oswego, and Colonel Swift's volunteer regiment has marched to the former place to-day. On their passage from the Head of the Lake several boats have been taken. Five laden with provisions are named among the number taken on Sunday.

(File in the Philadelphia Library.)

From Poulson's American Daily Advertiser of Philadelphia, 30th June, 1813.

CANANDAIGUA, June 22, 1813.

The naval force of the enemy on Lake Ontario are cruising from Niagara down the American side of that lake for the purpose, it would seem, of sweeping the coast, in which they were but too successful. On Saturday, the 12th inst., near the Eighteen Mile Creek, they captured two schooners and several boats, with valuable cargoes, bound from Oswego to Niagara. On Tuesday, the 15th inst., at 4 p. m., the force appeared off the mouth of the Genesee River, to which place they sent several boats, with about 300 men, 150 of whom landed, went into the village of Charlotte, placed sentries around the place to prevent the inhabitants from going out to give the alarm, and proceeded to execute their object. They entered the storehouse and took off between 400 and 500 barrels of flour, pork, etc., together with a large boat laden with 1200 bushels of corn, destined for our troops at Niagara. About 80 of the militia of Penfield turned out, but did not arrive in season for service. The enemy went off about 4 next morning, having met with no opposition except from the owners of the boat, Messrs. Spalding and Hildreth.

From this they proceeded to Sodus, before which they appeared on Saturday last, about 5 p. m., and sent a demand for the property there to be delivered up, accompanied with a threat to burn the place if refused. The property had been removed to a safe distance, and the enemy, being disappointed, executed their threat on Sunday by setting fire to several buildings. We have heard of but one man killed, Ab. Warren.

On the first alarm, Colonel Swift's regiment of militia was ordered out, but reaching the point of attack before the enemy appeared were dismissed. They have, however, been called out again, and we understand the artillery under Captain Rees and infantry of Captain A. Dox of Geneva have turned out with alacrity highly commendable.

P. S.—We have just heard that the enemy evacuated Sodus on Sunday afternoon, having burnt several valuable buildings belonging to Messrs. Merril, Wycan and others, and destroyed or carried off about 800 barrels of flour, &c.

(File in Philadelphia Library.)

From Poulson's American Daily Advertiser of Philadelphia, 22d July, 1813.

MONTREAL, June 26, 1813.

We understand by a report from the Upper Province that Sir James Yeo when he was last out landed a small part of his force at Sodus, a village belonging to the enemy, where with trifling loss he captured about 300 barrels of pork and a considerable quantity of clothing. The provisions he sent immediately to General Vincent, who with his gallant little army has entirely prevented the further advance of the American army into the Province.

In addition to the number of boats with provisions and stores taken and destroyed by the squadron and advance of Brigadier-General Vincent's army on the 6th and 10th inst., we have much pleasure in stating that by letters from Kingston of the 16th inst., received in town on Saturday evening, Sir James Yeo had returned to that place after having completely scoured the lake, and entering all the creeks and bays on the enemy's side, and capturing four American schooners having on board 400 barrels of pork and a quantity of merchandise intended for the enemy's army at Fort George.

Four companies of the Royals were embarked on board of the fleet to serve as marines, and were to sail from Kingston on Thursday last. The enemy's fleet was then still in Sackett's Harbor.

(File in Philadelphia Library.)

Lieutenant Wolcott Chauncey to Commodore Chauncey.

SACKETT'S HARBOR, 18th June, 1813.

SIR,—According to your orders of the 14th instant, I proceeded off Presque Isle in the schooner *Lady of the Lake*. On the morning of the 16th I fell in with and captured the English schooner *Lady Murray*, from Kingston, bound to York, loaded with provisions and ammunition.

Enclosed is a list of 1 ensign and 15 non-commissioned officers found on board, with 6 men attached to the vessel.

(From the Historical Register of the United States, 1814, Vol. II., p. 280.)

The Secretary of War to General Dearborn.

WAR DEPARTMENT, June 19, 1813.

(Extract.)

Your letters of the 6th and 8th instant have been received. There is indeed some strange fatality attending our efforts. I cannot disguise from you the *surprise* occasioned by the *two escapes of a beaten enemy ;* first on the 27th ultimo, and again on the 6th instant. Battles are not gained when an inferior and broken enemy is not destroyed. Nothing is done while anything that might have been done is omitted. This axiom is as old as the profession of arms, and in no walk of life applies with as much force as in that of a soldier.

Should Procter have retired from Malden and been able to effect a junction with Vincent's corps at the head of the lake it has been done for one of two purposes: either to dispute with you the possession of the peninsula, or more securely to effect their general retreat to Kingston. The latter is the more probable conjecture of the two, and is strengthened by the appearance of Yeo on the upper part of the lake and by the position which Vincent has taken there.

(American State Papers, Military Affairs.)

General Dearborn to the Secretary of War.

Headquarters, FORT GEORGE, June 20, 1813.

(Extract.)

SIR,—I have been so reduced in strength as to be incapable of any command. Brigadier-General Boyd is the only general officer present, and from resignations, sickness and other contingencies the number of regimental officers present fit for duty are far below what the service requires. A considerable proportion of our army being composed of new recruits, and the weather having been extremely unfavorable to health, the sick have become so numerous in addition to the wounded as to reduce the effective force far below what could have been contemplated, but if the weather should become favorable, which ought to be expected, a great part of the sick will probably be fit for duty in a short time. The enemy have been reinforced at the Head of the Lake with about 500 men of the 104th Regiment. A vessel carrying ammunition and other munitions of war was captured four days since by one of Commodore Chauncey's schooners, from which I conclude that the enemy will endeavor to keep up such a force at or near the Head of the Lake as to prevent any part of our force in this quarter from joining or proceeding to Sackett's Harbor for the purpose of attacking Kingston, and such is the state of the roads in this flat country, in consequence of continual rains, as to render any operations against the enemy extremely difficult, without the aid of a fleet for the transportation of provisions, ammunition and other necessary supplies. The enemy would probably retreat on our approach and keep out of our reach, being covered by one or more armed vessels which remain on this part of the lake. The whole of these embarrassments have resulted from a temporary loss of the command of the lake. The enemy has availed himself of the advantage and forwarded reinforcements and supplies.

(American State Papers, Military Affairs.)

From Poulson's American Daily Advertiser of Philadelphia, 2d July, 1813.

ERIE, June 20, 1813.

On Tuesday last the *Queen Charlotte* and a large armed schooner made their appearance off this harbor. They had coasted down this side of the lake from Cleveland, and at the mouth of Ashtabula [river] sent a boat ashore and took off an ox. They left 8 dollars for the owner of it, with written directions if it was not enough they would pay him the balance on their return.

It appears they were looking out for Captain Perry, who was coming up from Buffalo with five vessels which had been fitted up at the navy yard below Black Rock, and it was an object for them to prevent the junction of those vessels with the ones preparing here.

Captain Perry arrived here unmolested on Tuesday evening. The enemy had not kept a sharp lookout, for that morning both squadrons were seen off the mouth of Chautauqua at the same time, not more than 14 miles apart, by a boat that was about an equal distance from each. The enemy stood down the lake afterwards and chased a boat into the mouth of Cattaraugus the same afternoon. The boat has since arrived here; it came on after the enemy had passed.

It may be thought a very fortunate escape of Captain Perry, as the vessels he had with him were not able to contend with so superior a force, and had they been taken it might have frustrated all our operations on Lake Erie for this season. Three of them were brought over the bar yesterday, and the other two will be in to-day.

We have now a force here of 11 vessels, two of which will carry 20 guns each.

(File in the Philadelphia Library.)

General Orders.

Headquarters, KINGSTON, 19th June, 1813.

Major-General De Rottenburg being arrived will take upon himself the command of the troops in Upper Canada and the civil administration of the Province.

Major-General Sir Roger Sheaffe will proceed to Montreal and assume command of the troops in that district.

His Excellency the Governor in Chief and Commander of the Forces is pleased to approve of the following appointments in the Indian Department of Upper Canada:

Matthew Elliott, Junior, to be captain, vice his brother killed in action of the 22d Novr., 1812.

To be lieutenants in addition to their being interpreters:

Alexander McKee,
Barnet Lyons,
Jacob Gruserat,
Edward Sayers,
} Amherstburg.

Interpreter Charles Anderson to be lieutenant at Kingston, Lieut.-Colonel Claus, Deputy Superintendent General of the Indian Department at Niagara, and Lieut.-Colonel Elliott, superintendent of the same at Amherstburg, are to be allowed the allowance in lieu of forage for two horses, provided they have them, agreeable to the regulations on that head, from the 24th instant and until the Indians are disembodied.

The Commissariat Department is directed to provide provisions for six months for 2,000 men for the Right Division of the Army of Upper Canada, and the Deputy Barrack Master General is to provide barrack stores of 1000 men at the same place.

EDWARD BAYNES,
Adjutant General.

Extract from MSS. of Captain Wm. Hamilton Merritt.

On the 16th [June] FitzGibbon came down with his party and our advance pushed on to the 10 Mile Creek, which gave my men a great relief, as there was no field to act, only the mountain, where Fitz remained with his party. Cornet McKenney was attached to him with a few dragoons. The service had been so severe prior to this that our horses were completely knocked up. Capt. Hall arrived with a party of Can[adian] dragoons, which was likewise a very great relief. Col. Bisshopp, commanding the advance, whose headquarters were at the 20 Mile Creek, Major or Lt.-Col. Dehearn [DeHaren] at the 10 with 200 of the 104th and 300 Indians, principally Cognawagas, who had arrived from Lower Canada, his left at the lake, a strong picket on the Lake Road, his right at Turney's Cross Roads, near the German meeting house. FitzGibbons' headquarters [were] at DeCoo's, altho' he was always on the move, never slept twice in the same place. [The] dragoons [were] patrolling from the G[erman] meeting house to the lake. A circumstance that was ever fresh in my memory had been the means of giving me a perfect knowledge of every bye-road in this part of the country, which proved of the greatest service to me on many occasions.

On the 19th Fitz heard of Chapin's party being on their way to Chippawa from Fort George. [He] marched up Lundy's Lane with a design of ambushing them at or near Forsyth's wood. [He] left his men in rear of the mountain in the lane [and] proceeded on himself to get information of their movements. Mrs. Kerby, who lived at the corner, waved her h[and]k[erchie]f for him to return, ran out to meet him [and] informed him that Chapin with 2 or 300 men had that moment passed up. He discovered a dragoon horse near the inn, rode up near the door, dismounted [and] entered the house, in which were two Americans, a rifleman and [a] soldier. The former presented his piece on his entering the door. Fitz, without answering, gave him his hand, claiming an old acquaintance, which threw the man off his guard, (he had likewise a green coat on, as had all his men at times, [they] called themselves the Irish Greens or Bloody Boys,) with the other seized his gun. The soldier was in the act of firing when he fortunately caught his gun, brought both of them under his arm, by which means the muzzles of each were pointing at his comrade, both cocked, the friction of the two enabled him to keep them so firm that they could not with every exertion break his grasp. In this position he pulled and pushed them both out of the house, the steps of which were two or three feet high, he swearing and demanding them to surrender, they retorting the demand on him. Two or three inhabitants were standing by at the time and refused to assist him. Mrs. K[erby] begged and threatened them to no effect. A small boy of Doct[or] Flemming's threw brickbats at them, done everything in his power. After a short struggle the rifleman drew Fitz's sword from its sheath with his left hand and was in the act of thrusting it in his breast when the woman of the house, Mrs. Defield, who was standing in the door with her child in her arms, kicked it out of his hand. He stooped [and] recovered it, [but] she threw the child on the floor, ran out and wrenched it completely from him and hid it in the house. A few moments after her husband came up, knocked the flint out of one of the guns and disarmed the man. The other Fitz threw against the steps and disarmed him. [He] mounted his horse, led the other and drove the two gentlemen before him to his party. He had not left the place two minutes before the [American] party returned. Upon the whole it was a most gallant, daring and miraculous proceeding.

On the 20th I had two men surrounded and taken by a party of dragoons near Eastman's. They both made their escape, one by an excellent stratagem of Mrs. Gesso's (Gesseau?) She was a perfect heroine and deserves every credit for her patriotism. The young man's father was paroled, altho' near seventy years of age, which was the custom with the Americans. They paroled all males from 14 to 100 years of age. The son, who was named after the father, John Stiver, when brought in was taken over the river and put in close confinement, as they thought he had broken his parole. His father on hearing it came in to Gen. Dearborn with his parole and rectified the mistake. The General ordered his A. D. C. to destroy the old and give him a new one, likewise gave him a pass to cross over the river. He was boasting of his new parole and likewise of his pass to see his son. Mrs. G[esso] examined them, found they could answer the purpose of getting off the son, and explained it to him. He was fearful of undertaking it. She sent him out of the town, took his papers with a kettle of fresh butter, crossed the river, sold it to the com[mandin]g officer, inquired for Stiver, told him she had his parole and pass over the river. He liberated him. She gave him the parole which passed him through the guards. That night he joined the troop at the 10. It was very easy and simple as the papers were, but few would have had the invention of carrying it into effect.

General Orders.

ADJUTANT GENERAL'S OFFICE, KINGSTON,
19th June, 1813.

Two companies of the Royal Scots are to embark to-morrow morning at 6 o'clock in batteaux to proceed to the head of the Bay of Quinte, from thence they are to march to York, where they will receive further orders. The Acting Quartermaster-General will furnish a route and the depots of provisions. A detachment of the 104th, consisting of all the men belonging to that corps fit for field service, will embark at the same time, the whole under the command of Colonel Stuart, Royal Scots, six days' rations to be taken.

The Commander of the Forces finds it necessary to caution officers in the command of corps or detachments on the march, or commanding posts or stations by which troops pass, that no deviation is to be permitted to take place from the prescribed order of the route, as although in some cases possible inconvenience may arise to the detachment so deviating, yet as it will immediately entail delay and interruption to the general plan adopted for the troops and stores (it is, however to be understood to except in cases of emergency, and when the security of the post or detachment may justify), and all officers are called upon to prevent unnecessary delay, and to expedite by every possible means the quick passage of the batteaux, both in coming up loaded and on the return to Montreal for further supplies.

EDWARD BAYNES,
Adjutant General.

From the Quebec Mercury, 22d June, 1813.

MONTREAL, June 19, 1813.

By letters received from the 40 Mile Creek, dated 10th June, it is said that the advance of our army under Major Evans took possession of General Lewis's camp, baggage, stores, &c., and took up his position in the quarters from which the General had just flown; the General's horse was taken and the enemy pursued close to the Niagara line, which he has or will cross to-morrow. We have taken about 70 prisoners and 20 batteaux laden with supplies. Scott, Christie and King and a hundred others are acting with their army, although prisoners on parole. Information is just received that there are 6,000 of the enemy at Fort George, where sickness, discontent and famine prevail. In their flight they have burnt Fort Erie and abandoned everything.

By an express which arrived here yesterday from Kingston, it is said that General Vincent was within 12 miles of Fort George; that Sir James Yeo has taken in camp equipage, arms and ammunition nearly, or quite double to the quantity lost at Fort George; that the Americans have been driven from Fort Erie, Chippawa and Queenston; that an Indian had informed General Vincent that Fort George and the town was in flames. The express left York the 12th instant, and Kingston the 14th, early in the morning.

(File in the Library of Parliament, Ottawa.)

Sir George Prevost to Brigadier-General Procter.

Headquarters, KINGSTON, 20th June, 1813.

SIR,—In addition to my letter of the 14th inst. (whereof a duplicate is herewith transmitted), I have to inform you that Major-General DeRottenburg (whom I have appointed to the command of the forces serving in Upper Canada) has received my directions to push on the remainder of the 41st Regt. from the head of Lake Ontario to Amherstburg, and also the other reinforcements and supplies intended for the Right Division of the Army of Upper Canada which you command.

The supplies are to consist of £1,000 in specie, £2,000 in Army Bills, salt pork—as much as can be forwarded,—some clothing, and all the shoes which could be collected by Capt. Chambers, together with a proportion of entrenching tools and some articles for the naval dept.

Encourage as much as possible the exertions of the navy; bring forward the united power of both services to crush the enemy's endeavors to obtain the ascendency on Lake Erie, when a favorable opportunity presents itself; in short, persevere in those judicious exertions which [have] distinguished your command, are so honorable to yourself and acceptable to His Majesty and Gov't.

(Canadian Archives, C. 679, p. 113.)

Joseph Ellicott to General Peter B. Porter.

BATAVIA, June 21, 1813.

DEAR SIR,—Your favor covering an order for embodying two hundred and fifty militia was handed to me this morning by your express. I availed myself of the opportunity by the same conveyance to transmit the order to Colonel Churchill, commanding the Batavia regiment. The Colonel has since called on me and gave it as his opinion that it was most proper also to direct it to Brigadier-General Rea, which I complied with under the impression that possibly the whole brigade might furnish that number of volunteers without resorting to a draft.

If in future it should be necessary to call the militia into service from this country, let the order come directly from the Commanding General to the Brigadier-General. The present order, they think, has reached them in such an informal manner, when taken in connection with your letter, that they seem to hesitate whether or not they are, strictly speaking, authorized to furnish their quota. I am persuaded, however, they will take immediate measures to furnish the men.

From the tenor of your letter it would seem that mounted riflemen was the description of force wanted, but this they say was merely the request of a citizen, which they could not comply with, even if such a force could be obtained without taking the responsibility on themselves, and I feel very little inclination to take the responsibility on myself while the Government has persons under employ clothed with power to order all the militia out *en masse* if they deem the public exigencies require it; and really, Sir, there is no other way to carry on war systematically than by those who are commissioned to perform those duties, and unless it is conducted systematically many lives may be sacrificed to no good purpose.

In future I hope all requisitions of this nature will be forwarded to gentlemen holding military offices, which will be very much to the satisfaction of very respectfully,

Your most obedient servant,
JOSEPH ELLICOTT.

(From original in the Buffalo Historical Society's Library.)

Sir George Prevost to Hon. William Dummer Powell.

Headquarters, KINGSTON, 21st June, 1813.

DEAR SIR,—In your leisure moments would you have the goodness to ascertain the resources which the neighbourhood of York affords for the maintaining of an army, the accommodation remaining in the town for troops, and the probable effect the appearance of a military force would produce? It would also be very satisfactory to me to obtain your sentiments on the degree of confidence to be reposed in the functionaries of government residing at York. I mean in their energy; also, upon the state of the public mind on important points.

(From MSS. of George Murray Jarvis. Esq., Ottawa.)

Brigadier-General John Vincent to Sir George Prevost.

40 MILE CREEK, 22d June, 1813.

SIR,—I have the honor of enclosing a letter from General Dearborn to Your Excellency, which I have, according to the instructions before received, taken the liberty to open.

I have forwarded for Your Excellency's information a correspondence which has passed from this by flags of truce to the commanding officer of the United States troops at Niagara.

(Canadian Archives, C. 679.)

Erastus Granger to the Chiefs of the Six Nation Indians.

BUFFALO, June 22d, 1813.

BROTHERS,—I have just received a speech from General Dearborn, the commander at Niagara, requesting one hundred and fifty of the young men of the Six Nations to meet him at Fort George. It is therefore my request that forty or fifty of the young men of your village should turn out and come to this place as soon as possible. Let a sufficient number of chiefs come with them. Bring your guns along with you and come prepared to stay one or two months. When you get to this council fire the business will be more fully explained to you. Call on the Cattaraugus Indians and get as many of their young men to turn out as possible. I wish you to be here as soon as possible.

Your friend and brother,
ERASTUS GRANGER.

To the Chiefs at the Allegheny Village.

(MSS. of Colonel James N. Granger.)

New York Evening Post, June 28th, 1813.

CANANDAIGUA, June 22, 1813.

During and since the capture of Fort George there have been the most shameful acts of rapacity committed on the innocent inhabitants of the Province. We hear every day of quantities of plate and other valuable articles being brought from there and sold by the marauders at a small price. We are ashamed to record the commission of acts which stain our national character with such foul disgrace.

(File in Astor Library, New York.)

New York Evening Post, 9th July, 1813.

Extract of a letter to the Editor of *Baltimore Whig*, dated Newark, June 22d, 1813:

We are still encamped here and things remain almost in *statu quo*. General Dearborn has taken some precautionary measures respecting violent British partisans in this town and vicinity. The most conspicuous are taken up and sent over the river to be kept in the United States as hostages.

At the solicitation of the inhabitants who are friendly to our cause the General has agreed to introduce a few of our Indians to combat those of the enemy.

Flags have lately come in from the British commander. I am

told they commonly bring insolent demands or trifling pretences in order to protract our inactivity and cover some of their own movements.

Small parties of horse and riflemen ride out now and then and sometimes have a skirmish with a scouting party of English and Indians. In this sort of warfare our men seldom gain much, as the enemy is best acquainted with the paths, bye-roads, swamps and the country in general. There are various rumors about the reinforcements and situation of the enemy's army, but I can learn no authentic account of either.

The season is uncommonly wet. Old inhabitants say they have not seen so rainy a summer for twenty-five years. I dread the consequences to the health of our army.

It is probable our commander is waiting the arrival of Chauncey before he moves.

(File in Astor Library, New York.)

Regimental Orders.

KINGSTON, 22d June, 1813.

The officers commanding companies of militia will make out a list of such persons belonging to their respective companies as have died in consequence of diseases contracted while on duty, together with the situation of their families and the names and ages of the children they have left.

General Order.

ADJUTANT GENERAL'S OFFICE, KINGSTON,
22d June, 1813.

G. O.

The remainder of the Regiment De Watteville is to march from Montreal to Kingston immediately, two companies with a field officer to halt at Prescott and form the garrison at that post.

The detachment of the 100th Regiment at Prescott is to march to Kingston when relieved. The 2d Battalion, 41st Regiment, is to proceed to Montreal.

EDWARD BAYNES,
A. G.

Garrison Order.

KINGSTON, June 22d, 1813.

The convalescents of the 104th Regiment and such others as Doctor Macaulay may think proper to send are to proceed to Gananoqui at 12 o'clock this day, there to remain until further orders, under charge of Lieut. Rangeworth [Rainsford?] The *Retaliation* gunboat will be ready to receive them. She will remain at that station under the direction of the officer commanding that post. Lieut.-Colonel Heathcote will see that these men are complete in arms, accoutrements, ammunition and necessaries.

R. LEONARD,
B. M.

(From the Buffalo Gazette, 22d June, 1813.)

BATTLE AT STONEY CREEK.

To the Editor of the Buffalo Gazette:

SIR,—As no person has given an account of the action fought at Stoney Creek, near the head of the lake, I deem it proper to state a few particulars as far as my observation extended.

The troops on that day, under the command of General Chandler, advanced from their encampment at the Forty Mile Creek for the purpose of taking a position nearer the enemy. At nine the line of march commenced. About 3 o'clock the advance, under Captain Hindman, commanding the light troops, encountered the picquets of the enemy, consisting of Indians and regulars. They retired, but were pursued so rapidly that they took shelter in the woods, from whence the riflemen routed them after some time. They were obliged to make partial stands to give and receive fires. The captain was rapid in his movements, and had a smart firing at a sawmill on the road, where the enemy attempted to make a stand. Captain Hindman and Captain Little of the volunteers riflemen, being directly in advance of the enemy, were much exposed to their close fire. One of Captain Hindman's men was shot dead between him and Captain Little, and two or three wounded. The enemy were obliged to fly, losing some prisoners and leaving three redcoats dead. We advanced further, but were halted by General Winder. We then retired about a mile and halted for the night. We lay within seven miles of the enemy, and were encamped in detached parties, so that when the firing commenced we knew not where to look for the line of battle.

The enemy entered our camp about one o'clock in the morning, down the road leading to the position of our artillery. It seemed, from their manoeuvering, to be their principal object to take the cannon. The first we heard of the enemy was a partial fire, and instantly afterward the yell of the Indians and shouting of their troops. They were upon us in an instant. They made their attack upon the artillery, which was about the centre of our troops, and Captain Hindman, who was on the right of the whole. When the enemy first advanced to the right they were met by Captain Hindman, and all his officers supposed the enemy to be American troops, so that he did not fire. It was soon discovered that they were red coats from the light of our fires, over which they run, and that they were endeavoring to cut off Captain Hindman by turning his left flank. He instantly gave them a destructive fire, killed many men and one or two officers, checked their progress, saved his little band, and prevented the enemy from advancing further and doing much injury to our line. He suffered little loss in killed and wounded; one officer, Captain Mills, was mortally wounded. The enemy penetrated the centre, and after a severe struggle took one six pounder and a howitz[er.] General Chandler was made prisoner near the cannon. In like manner General Winder was made prisoner, after the fight was over. He walked down to the cannon and saw several persons standing near them, and thought they were Americans. Unfortunately he was hurried away without our knowledge. It was so dark that we dare not move from our position for fear of accident. The 5th Infantry, under Colonel Milton, behaved handsomely. He repulsed the enemy twice,—indeed, to Colonel Milton and Captain Hindman we are indebted for the glory of the fight. Our loss in prisoners at furthest does not exceed two hundred, our killed about 10; that of the enemy in killed one hundred, wounded sixty, prisoners fifty. Colonel Clark, of the 49th Regiment, was badly wounded and taken prisoner; Captain Manners wounded and prisoner, besides several dead on the field. Our troops behaved well, particularly the 5th Infantry, under Colonel Milton, and light troops under Captain Hindman. The gallant captain deserves much credit; in the battle at Fort George he was the first to land and commence the action, and afterwards the first ordered by Colonel Scott to occupy Fort George.

To the Editor of the Buffalo Gazette:

SIR,—A correspondent of yours having furnished for publication what he terms *extracts* from the General Orders of the 25th ulto., I presume it will be equally gratifying to you and the public to see those orders in an entire shape and therefore send them to you in the precise form in which they emanated from Headquarters, accompanied with a short detail of the events of the 27th, not doubting a place will be afforded them in your paper. The motive which induced your correspondent to give publicity to a mutilated copy cannot be mistaken. The preposterous idea of directing the movements of an army engaged in action by a General on a sick bed on board a ship three miles from the shore certainly never entered the head of General Dearborn. I am warranted in saying he had full confidence in the military abilities of General Lewis, (which the event shows was not misplaced,) and too much good sense to restrict him to a precise manoeuvre, a departure from which the events of a field of battle might render imperiously necessary. In truth, there was no one period of the action of the 27th to which the orders of the 25th could apply, and it is believed that it will not be asserted that any order arrived from the ship which bore the Commander-in-Chief after the troops landed. Each was given by the Commanding General *with* the troops. When the enemy brought his reserve into line had Colonel Scott, in strict observance of the orders of the 25th, fallen back on the flanks the day had probably been lost. This gallant soldier saw the consequence of such a retrograde movement. He therefore amused the enemy while he sent for orders, which were promptly given him, to charge. At the same instant Boyd's brigade was ordered to be thrown into double columns and advanced to his support. With equal promptitude was this duty performed, while the second brigade advanced in like order to support the left of the first, and Chandler's, with two twelve pounders, was directed to occupy the village of Newark, silence the remaining fire of Fort George, and turn the enemy's right. The rapidity of his retreat disappointed the effect of the latter movement. The two first corps were then ordered to continue the pursuit to the Five Mile Meadows and to carry a battery erected on the bank of the river, which prevented the crossing of the light dragoons. When they arrived they found the battery deserted. Their march was too rapid for the artillery, which was without horses and of course had to be drawn by hand throughout the day. The pursuit here terminated and the troops returned to Fort George. With no part of all this had the position of the Commander-in-Chief on board the *Madison* any connection.

An Acting Aid,
To the Commander-in-Chief.

Plan of Descent.

ORDERS.

ADJUTANT GENERAL'S OFFICE,
May 25, 1813.

A corps of light troops, consisting of 400 infantry. Forsyth's riflemen, the two flank companies of the 15th infantry, also one 3-pounder, to form the advance under Colonel Scott. It is understood that this corps should first effect a landing, scour and possess the shore and cover the landing of the troops which are to follow. The riflemen to advance in front on the flanks or obliquely to the flanks, according to circumstances. It is not understood that Colonel Scott should advance beyond 300 paces before he is supported by the first brigade.

2d.—Boyd's brigade will follow quickly in support to advance in column or display as may best suit the general purpose of the descent. Major Eustis's corps of light artillery to accompany this brigade, and Lieut-Colonel McClure's volunteers will be on its flanks.

3d.—In like manner Winder's brigade will follow in quick succession to advance in column and display on Boyd's left or remain in column, as may be deemed expedient by Major-General Lewis. Captain Towson's company of artillery will accompany this brigade. Major-General Lewis will land with any part of his division.

4th.—Chandler's brigade to constitute the reserve. It is to be embarked as soon as possible. Colonel Macomb with his artillery will land with the reserve and act as circumstances may require. Brigadier-General Chandler is to detach 100 men to remain at the point of landing as soon as the main line is formed. Colonel Scott, (who will be under the orders of Major-General Lewis,) will advance, but not more than 300 paces in front of the infantry. If the enemy appear in force the light troops are to fall back and form on the flanks and act as circumstances may require. The direction of the boats and debarkation of troops will be arranged by Commodore Chauncey. Each brigade will designate and mark its boats.

By command,
W. SCOTT,
Adjutant General.

Orders.

ADJUTANT GENERAL'S OFFICE
May 26, 1813.

The army will embark at three o'clock to-morrow morning The troops will be up at one, eat their breakfast at two, and be all on board their respective boats, ready to move, at half-past three o'clock. Each man will take his blanket and one day's provisions ready cooked.

By command,
W. SCOTT,
Adj. Gen.

On Tuesday last (15th June) Captain Perry left our waters for Erie, with five sail of armed vessels, which were lately fitted up at Black Rock. We understand that they have arrived safely. The British brig *Queen Charlotte* and schr. *Lady Prevost* lay at Long Point when our vessels passed up, and on Friday (18th June) they appeared off Point Abino, and during the night they made Sturgeon

Point. In the morning they discovered a boat passing up the lake, which had left Buffalo Creek the evening preceding, with considerable property on board. The vessels immediately put out boats in chase and fired several guns, but the boat succeeded in getting into Cattaraugus Creek and escaped. The enemy's boats landed and plundered Ingersol's tavern, at 18 Mile Creek, of all his liquors, some bedding and other articles, and 2 barrels of salt. The pillagers then paid a visit to several houses on Sturgeon Point, among which were (as we understand) Captain Gates' and Mr. Lay's (both of whom suffered pillaging last fall.) Captain Gates was taken on board the vessels, but after some detention was suffered to depart, with most of his effects. The pillaging party, in the course of their excursion, captured several swine, hens, &c.

On Wednesday last (16th June) Major C. Chapin of this village organized a small company of mounted riflemen, and crossed into Canada for the purpose of clearing the frontier of persons inimical to the States, and protecting the inhabitants from the outrages of the enemy and their property from the merciless plunderers. On Friday (18th June) a detachment from Chapin's corps, under command of Capt. E. Smith, captured a British boat near Point Abino, having a lieutenant and 14 men on board, with a quantity of provisions. Smith's force was only 11 men. Considerable public property has been secured.

We learn from Newark that General Lewis has left that place for Sackett's Harbor, and that Commodore Chauncey is not expected out until the new 32-gun frigate is ready for a cruise. There are no British vessels stationed off Newark.

On Sunday (20th June) a vessel arrived at Newark bearing a flag of truce, supposed to have come from the head of the lake.

A report is prevalent here that the British have taken a large quantity of flour and pork at the mouth of Genesee River, and burnt 100 tons of pressed hay.

(File in Buffalo Public Library.)

General Dearborn to General P. B. Porter.

NIAGARA, June 23rd, 1813.

SIR,—Your letter of the 23d has been received. Your proposition for taking command of the militia that are about assembling meets my full approbation, especially when your liberal conditions are considered, on which you offer to serve. You will therefore please to take the command accordingly. You will take post at Fort Erie or elsewhere at your discretion, but you will find it necessary to be extremely cautious and vigilant to prevent any surprise. The enemy will have an eye upon you, and will not fail of endeavoring to cut you up. It may be expedient for you to act in the character of a Lieut.-Col. You will have the corps regularly and correctly mustered. If an additional number to the amount of one or two hundred should be disposed to join you, so as to make your total force from 350 to 450, you are authorized to engage and employ them. I can say nothing at present in relation to our Indians, but should my proposition to them meet a favorable reception, you shall have a share of them. I am happy to learn that Captain Perry arrived safe at Erie. Permit me to repeat my caution against a surprise or an attack from a superior force.

P. S.—Your letter by Mr. Smith arrived before I had finished my letter.

(From MSS. of Hon. P. A. Porter.)

Garrison Order.

KINGSTON, June 23d, 1813.

A party of one sergeant and 12 men of the 104th Regiment to comprise an escort for batteaux, to be placed immediately under the command of Deputy Asst. Qr. Mr. General Captain Chambers. Strong, healthy men who understand the management of boats, are to be selected.

EDWARD BAYNES,
Adjutant General.

Colonel Wm. Claus to Lieut.-Colonel Bisshopp.

LOUTH, June 24th, 1813.

SIR,—I put under cover a letter received from Captain Kerr giving an account of an action this morning between a party of the Six Nations, the Seven Nations of Canada and some of the Lake Indians, consisting of about 450 chiefs and warriors, and a detachment of the American army under Colonel Bustler, with two field pieces. It is with pride I mention that, notwithstanding the severe loss the Indians have met met with in the death of five of the principal chiefs and warriors and upwards of twenty wounded, several prisoners were taken in the woods and brought in without the least injury to one of them. The number of the killed and wounded is not ascertained; we know of the above only at present.

(Claus MSS.)

Lieut.-Colonel J. B. Glegg to Colonel William Claus.

Headquarters, FORTY MILE CREEK,
June 24th, 1813.

SIR,—I return your requisition for 17,280 lbs. of flour approved. Your expenditure of powder is quite alarming and cannot be supported from our funds. Pigeon shooting and such idle sport must be given up. The schooner bringing up a supply of ammunition and a choice collection of every kind of stores has unfortunately been captured by the *Lady of the Lake* and carried into Sackett's Harbor. 'Tis an irreparable loss at this moment. The General begs you will make choice of a small party and send them quietly away to meet the Western Indians, who are reported to be very near Grand River. I have just received your letter of the 24th. From Merritt's report I expected to hear that the enemy was advancing, but your silence proves the absurdity of his intelligence. I hope we shall soon shake hands with our Western friends. Much depends, I am confident, on the men and warriors who first receive them. The General hopes this immense quantity of flour will be properly made use of.

(From the MS. Letterbook of Colonel Claus.)

Lieut. James FitzGibbon, 49th Regiment, to Major DeHaren.

TOWNSHIP OF LOUTH, 24th June, 1813.

SIR,—At DeCou's this morning, about 7 o'clock, I received information that about 1,000 of the enemy, with two field guns, were advancing towards me from St. Davids. I soon after heard a firing of cannon and musketry, and in consequence rode in advance about two miles on the St. Davids' road. I observed by the firing that the enemy was moving for the road on the mountain. I sent Cornet McKenney to order out my detachment of the 49th, consisting of a subaltern and 46 rank and file, and close upon the enemy to reconnoitre. I discovered him upon the mountain road, and took a position on an eminence to the right of it. My men arrived and pushed on in his front to cut off his retreat, under a fire from his guns which, however, did no execution. After examining his position, I found it difficult to approach him, there being no wood in the front or in the flank to cover the Indians, and his force, apparently 600, I could not approach. I was here informed that he expected reinforcements. I therefore decided upon summoning him to surrender. After the exchange of several propositions between Lieut.-Colonel Boerstler and myself, in the name of Lieut.-Colonel DeHaren, Lieut.-Colonel Boerstler agreed to surrender on the conditions stated in the articles of capitulation. On my return to my men to send an officer to superintend the details of the capitulation, you arrived.

(Canadian Archives, Q. 122, p. 59.)

Lieut.-Colonel Bisshopp to Brigadier-General Vincent.

BEAVER DAMS, 24th June, 1813.

SIR,—I have the honor to inform you that the troops you have done me the honor to place under my command have succeeded in taking prisoners a detachment of the United States Army under Lieut.-Colonel Boerstler.

In this affair the Indians under Capt. Kerr were the only force actively engaged; to them great merit is due, and I feel particularly obliged for their gallant conduct on this occasion. On the appearance of the detachment of the 49th, under Lieutenant FitzGibbon, and the light company of the 8th or King's Regiment and the two flank companies of the 104th under Major De Haren, and the Provincial Cavalry under Captain Hall, the whole surrendered to His Majesty's troops. To the conduct of Lieut. FitzGibbon, through whose address the capitulation was entered into, may be attributed the surrender of the American troops.

To Major DeHaren, for his speedy movements to the point of attack and execution of the arrangements I had previously made with him, I am much obliged.

I have the honor to enclose the capitulation entered into between Col. Boerstler and myself, and a return of the prisoners, exclusive of the wounded not yet ascertained. I lost no time in forwarding my Staff Adjutant, Lieut. Barnard, to you with this intelligence. He has been particularly active and useful to me upon all occasions. I take this opportunity of mentioning him to you, and I beg the favor of you to recommend him to Sir George Prevost as an active and meritorious young man.

(Canadian Archives, Q. 122, p. 57.)

Particulars of Capitulation.

24th June, 1813.

Particulars of the capitulation made between Captain McDowell, on the part of Lieut.-Colonel Boerstler of the United States Army, and Major DeHaren of His Britannic Majesty's Canadian Regiment, on the part of Lieut.-Colonel Bisshopp, commanding the advance of the British, respecting the force under the command of Lieut.-Col. Boerstler:

First—That Lieut.-Col. Boerstler and the force under his command shall surrender prisoners of war.

Second—That the officers shall retain their arms, horses and baggage.

Third—That the non-commissioned officers and soldiers shall lay down their arms at the head of the British column and become prisoners of war.

Fourth—That the militia and volunteers with Lieut.-Col. Boerstler shall be permitted to return to the United States on parole.

ANDW. MCDOWELL,
Capt. U. S. Light Artillery.

Handed to C. S. Boerstler, Lt.-Col. Comdg. Detacht. U. S. Army.

P. V. DEHAREN,
Major, Canadian Regt.

(Canadian Archives, Q. 122, p. 61.)

RETURN OF PRISONERS.

Return of American prisoners taken near Fort George on 24th June, 1813:—

Corps.	Lt.-Cols.	Majors.	Captains.	Lieutenants.	Cornets.	Surgeons.	Sergeants.	Drummers.	Rank and File.	Remarks.
Light Dragoons					1		1		19	Two field pieces taken.
Light Artillery			1	1			2		31	1 12-pounder.
6th Regt. Infantry			1	1			3		54	1 6-pounder.
14th do	1		3	11		1	15		301	2 cars.
20th do		1								Stand of colors of [14th U. S. Regt.
23rd do			1				4	2	57	
Total	1	1	6	13	1	1	25	2	462	30 militia, released on parole, not included in this return.

OFFICERS' NAMES AND RANK.

Lieut.-Colonel Boerstler, 14th Regt.
Major Taylor, 20th.
Captain McDowell, Light Artillery.
" Machesney, 6th.
" McKenzie, 14th.
" Cummins, 14th.
" Fleming, 14th.
" Roach, 23d.
Lieutenant Morris, Light Artillery.
" Shell, 6th.
" Saunders, 14th.
" Kearney, 14th.
" Waring, 14th.
" Mudd, ⎫
" Murdock, ⎪
" Goodwin, ⎬ Do.
" Clarke, ⎪
" Robinson, ⎪
" Rundall, ⎭
Cornet Bird, Light Dragoons.
Surgeon Young, 14th.

EDWARD BAYNES,
Adjt. Gen'l.

The loss of the enemy supposed to be about 100 in killed and wounded.

(Canadian Archives, Q. 122, p. 62.)

General Order.

Headquarters, KINGSTON, 28th June, 1813.

The Commander of the Forces has great satisfaction in announcing to the army that a report has just been received from Brigadier-General Vincent of a most judicious and spirited exploit achieved by a small detachment of the 49th Regiment, amounting to 46 rank and file, under Lieutenant FitzGibbon, and a band of Indian warriors, which terminated in the defeat and entire capture of a considerable detachment of the American regular army under the command of Lieutenant-Colonel Boerstler of the 14th United States Regiment, after sustaining considerable loss.

Lieutenant FitzGibbon on reconnoitering the enemy's position and finding him too numerous to oppose with his small force, with great presence of mind kept him in check. while he sent and summoned him to surrender in the name of Major DeHaren, and which he was fortunately enabled to enforce by the timely advance of the light division under that officer, by whose vigorous co-operation the capture of the enemy's force, consisting of one lieutenant-colonel, one major, six captains, fifteen inferior officers, twenty-five sergeants, two drummers and 462 rank and file, one 12-pounder, one 6-pounder, field pieces and a stand of colors, was effected on the field.

Not a single British soldier is reported to have fallen on this occasion. The Indian warriors behaved with great steadiness and courage, and His Excellency has great satisfaction in learning that they conducted themselves with the greatest humanity and forbearance towards the prisoners after the action.

By His Excellency's command.

EDWARD BAYNES,
Adjutant General.

From the Montreal Gazette of 6th July, 1813.

The intelligence last week from the theatre of war in Western Canada is not of a very sanguinary nature, but it is not the less interesting, and we have much satisfaction in communicating to the public the particulars of a campaign not of a *General* with his *thousands* but of a *lieutenant* with his *tens* only. The manner in which a bloodless victory was obtained by a force so comparatively and almost incredibly small with that of the enemy, the cool determination and the hardy presence of mind evinced by this highly meritorious officer in conducting the operations incident to the critical situation in which he was placed with his little band of heroes, and the brilliant result which crowned those exertions will, while they make known to the world the name of Lieutenant FitzGibbon, reflect new lustre if possible, on the well earned reputation of the gallant 49th Regt., and class the event with the most extraordinary occurrences of the present accursed war. We shall at present make no further comment, but refer our readers to the following detail of Mr. FitzGibbon's operations as communicated to us by a friend who had the particulars from the best authority.

Immediately after the gallant affair of our advance on the 6th ultimo., Lieut. FitzGibbon made application to General Vincent to be employed separately with a small party of the 49th Regiment and in such a manner as he might think most expedient. The offer was accepted and this little band has been constantly ranging between the two armies. Many events would naturally occur on such a service, which would be very interesting, but are necessarily proscribed in our limits of detail, and we will confine ourselves to two very extraordinary occurrences. About the 20th ult., Lieut. FitzGibbon went in pursuit of 46 vagabonds, volunteer cavalry, brought over by Doctor Chapin from Buffalo, and who had been plundering for some time the inhabitants round Fort Erie and Chippawa. He came near to them at Lundy's Lane, below the Falls, but he discovered that they had been joined by 150 infantry. His force was but 44 muskets—he did not think it advisable to attack, and therefore his party was kept concealed. He, however, rode into the village at the end of the Lane to reconnoitre. He could not perceive the enemy.

Mrs. Kerby, who knew him, ran out and begged him to ride off, for that some of the enemy's troops were in a house at a short distance. He saw a horse at a door and supposing there were none but the rider in the house he dismounted and approached it, when an infantry soldier advanced and presented his piece at him; he made a spring at him, seized his musket and desired him to surrender. The American resisted and held fast. At this instant a rifleman jumped from the door with his rifle presented to Lieut. FitzGibbon's shoulder, who was so near to him that he seized the rifle below the muzzle and pulled it under his arm, keeping its muzzle before and that of the musket behind him. In this situation Lieut. F[itzGibbon] called upon two men who were looking on to assist him in disarming the two Americans, but they would not interfere. Poor Mrs. Kerby, apparently distracted, used all her influence, but in vain. The rifleman finding that he could not disengage his piece, drew Lieut. F[itz-Gibbon]'s sword out of his scabbard with his left hand with the intention of striking at Lieut. F., when another woman, Mrs. Danfield (Defield?) seized the uplifted arm and wrested the sword from his grasp. At this moment an elderly man, named Johnson, came up and forced the American from his hold on the rifle, and Lieut F. immediately laid the other soldier prostrate. A young boy 13 years old, son of Dr. Fleming, was very useful in the struggle, which continued some minutes. Lieut. F., thus relieved, lost not a moment in carrying off his two prisoners and the horse, as the enemy's force was within 200 yards of him, searching a house round a turn of the road.

At 7 o'clock in the morning of the 24th ult. Lieut. F. received a report that the enemy was advancing from St. Davids with about 1000 men and 4 pieces of cannon to attack the stone house in which he was quartered at the Beaver Dam. About an hour afterwards he heard the report of cannon and musketry; he rode on to reconnoitre and found the enemy engaged with a party of Indians who hung upon his flanks and rear and galled him severely. Lieut. F. despatched an officer for his men; by the time of their arrival the enemy had taken a position on an eminence at some distance from the woods in front. He estimated the enemy's strength at 600 men and two field pieces, a 12 and a 6-pounder. To make the appearance of cutting off his retreat, Lieut. F. passed at the charge step across his front to gain his other flank, under a quick fire from his guns, which, however, did not the smallest injury. He took post behind some woods and saw that the Indians were making very little of the enemy, and it would have been madness in him with 44 musketeers to dash at them across open fields where every man he had could be so easily perceived. Many of the Indians were at this time taking themselves off and he began to think of his own retreat. He had a hope, however, that Col. DeHaren would soon join him, but fearing that the enemy would drive him off or make good their retreat, he determined to play *the old soldier* and summon the enemy to surrender. He tied up his handkerchief and advanced with his bugles sounding the "cease from firing." A flag was sent to him by a Capt. McDowell of the artillery. Lieut. F. said that he was sent by Col. DeHaren to demand their surrender and offer them protection from the Indians, adding that a number had just joined from the west, who could not be controlled, and he wished to prevent the effusion of blood. The captain sent back to his commanding officer, Lieut.-Col. Boerstler, and soon after returned saying that Col. B. did not consider himself defeated and would not surrender. Lieut. F. proposed that Col. B. should send an officer to see Col. DeHaren's force, when he would be better able to judge of the necessity. He soon returned with a proposal that Col. B. should himself be shown the British, and if he found the force such as to justify his surrender he would do so. To this Lieut. F. said he would return to Col. DeHaren and state Col. B.'s proposal. The real intention of showing to the enemy's officer our small force never existed, but appearances must be kept up in order to carry out the propositions of Col. B. Lieut. F. found on his return Capt. Hall, who happened to arrive with 12 dragoons. To him was communicated what had passed, and immediately Capt. H. assumed the rank of Colonel for the purpose. On this Lieut. F. returned and stated that Colonel Hall, being now the senior officer on the spot, did not think it regular to let the enemy see his force, but that it was perfectly ample to compel a surrender, and from motives of humanity five minutes would be allowed for acquiescence, and if he refused hostilities would be commenced at the expiration of this period. Col. B. agreed to surrender on condition that the officers should retain their horses, arms and baggage, and that some militia and volunteers, (among whom were Dr. Chapin and his marauders,) should be permitted to return to the States *en parole*. When the extent of our forces is considered it is no wonder that these conditions were immediately acceded to. Lieut. F. at this moment, most fortunately, met with Col. Clark of Chippawa, who came galloping up and who proceeded to assist him in disarming the enemy, as Col. Hall could not appear, and his only officer, (an ensign,) must remain with the men. Col. DeHaren immediately afterwards appeared with the flank companies of the 104th Regiment, and the whole affair was soon settled, thus putting into our possession 26 officers, one 12 and one 6-pounder, two caissons and two waggons and above 500 prisoners, including about 20 dragoons. Had not Col. DeHaren arrived at this moment this large number of the enemy would have yielded to 48 soldiers of the 49th Regiment, for all the arrangements were made previous to the arrival of that officer. The Indians behaved well; they killed and wounded during their skirmishing about 50 of the enemy. We are informed that at the time of the summons being sent many of the enemy had gone off. The number of Indians engaged did not exceed 80. Thus terminated a bloodless victory on our part. If promotion and reward await the officer selected to be the bearer of despatches announcing an enemy's defeat, we cannot doubt that the hero of this achievement will receive that favor from his sovereign to which his services have established so just a claim, and who, we believe, has no other patronage but his own distinguished merit.

On Saturday last arrived in this city four officers and 110 non-commissioned officers and privates, forming part of the American prisoners captured on the 24th ultimo by the gallant Lieutenant Fitz-Gibbon and his small party of the 49th Regt., in the advance of our army under General Vincent. The remainder arrived this morning *en route* to Quebec in charge of Captain Renvoisey, 3d Batt. Inc. Militia.

(File in Parliamentary Library, Ottawa.)

Memorial to Captain Wm. J. Kerr.

To His Royal Highness Frederick, Duke of York, Field Marshal and Commander-in-Chief of all His Majesty's land forces.

The memorial of William Johnson Kerr, Esquire, member of the Provincial Parliament of Upper Canada, and late a captain in the Indian Department, most respectfully sheweth:

That Your Royal Highness' memorialist was appointed a captain in the Indian Department at the commencement of the late war between Great Britain and the United States of America by the late Major-General Sir Isaac Brock, and served under the following officers, viz.: Major-General Sir Isaac Brock, Major-General Sir R. H. Sheaffe, Major-General Vincent, Lieut.-General Sir Gordon Drummond, Major-General Riall, Lieut.-Colonel Bisshopp, and Colonel Clark, of the militia of Upper Canada, and was in most of the actions fought on the Niagara Frontier.

That Your Royal Highness' memorialist had the honor to command about five hundred Indian warriors on the 24th day of June, 1813, and attacked a much larger force of the enemy under the command of Colonel Boerstler, and obliged them to surrender after a severe action of two hours, in which action were captured about six hundred prisoners of the regular army, two field pieces, one six and one twelve-pounder, two baggage waggons, two tumbrils, five hundred stand of small arms, forty horses and a stand of colors, and on which occasion there was not a single cartridge expended by His Majesty's regular forces, neither was there a soldier or militiaman killed or wounded.

That Major-General Vincent, in the official despatch of that officer, gave the whole credit to Lieut. FitzGibbon of the 49th Regiment, when in right it was due to Your Royal Highness' memorialist and the Indian warriors under my command, as will appear evident to Your Royal Highness from the letter of Colonel Harvey, Deputy Adjutant General at the time, as well as that of Lieut. FitzGibbon himself, who commanded a small detachment of the 49th Regiment, consisting of about fifty men, who were not in the action, although they arrived at its close. The report of the battle transmitted by Your Royal Highness' memorialist to Colonel Claus, Deputy Adjutant General of Indian Affairs, was not noticed by Major-General Vincent in his official despatch.

Your Royal Highness will perceive from the letter of Lieut.-Colonel Evans, then Major of Brigade, that the favorable result of that action effectually checked the enemy's marauding parties along the Niagara Frontier, to the great relief of the inhabitants His Majesty's subjects.

Your Royal Highness' memorialist was at the capture of Fort Niagara, Lewiston, Fort Schlosser, Black Rock and Buffalo on the enemy's shore, and was also in the battle of Chippawa, under Major-General Riall, in which action Your Royal Highness' memorialist was made prisoner and detained until the peace took place, when the department was reduced.

(Canadian Archives, Q. 330, p. 22.)

Captain James FitzGibbon to Captain William J. Kerr.

YORK, 30th March, 1818.

(Extract.)

With respect to the affair with Captain Boerstler, not a shot was fired on our side by any but the Indians. They beat the American

---

The colors alluded to were presented by Captain Kerr as a mark of respect to the principal woman of the Six Nations, Mrs. Brant, widow of the celebrated chief, Captain Joseph Brant.

detachment into a state of terror, and the only share I claim is taking advantage of a favorable moment to offer them protection from the tomahawk and scalping knife. The Indian Department did all the rest.

(Canadian Archives, Q. 330, p. 29.)

Lieut.-Colonel Thomas Evans to Captain William Johnson Kerr.

AMHERSTBURG, 4th June, 1818.

DEAR SIR,—I was only last week favored with your letter of the 31st of March, in reply to which it affords me much pleasure in bearing my testimony to your merits as an active and zealous officer of the Indian Department during the period you were known to me on the Niagara Frontier.

In the action at Chippawa, on the 4th of July, 1814, you had to contend with far superior numbers when, after a gallant but ineffectual struggle, you fell into the power of a too formidable opponent. On the 24th of June, 1813, your activity with the Indian warriors was by the army justly extolled, and whatever merit Mr. FitzGibbon might have in stepping forward, on the ground of Colonel Boerstler's dread of surrendering to the Indians, there can be no doubt remaining in the mind of any impartial person but the subjugation of that officer, with about five hundred prisoners, must be mainly ascribed to the destruction created in the enemy by the warriors directed by your activity and intelligence.

The best effects in checking the enemy's marauding parties resulted from the capture.

On the suppression of your despatch to the superintendent, or of yourself being unnoticed in the public despatch announcing that event, it is not for me to remark.

(Canadian Archives, Q. 338-2, pp. 596-7.)

Captain William Johnson Kerr to Colonel Claus.

FORT GEORGE, December 8, 1815.

SIR,—I have the honor of enclosing to you a return of Indians and such others as were present at the battle of the Beaver Dams on the 24th June, 1813, under my command.

(Canadian Archives, Q. 330, p. 35.)

Return of the Six Nations of Indians and such others as were engaged at the Battle of the Beaver Dams, on the 24th June, 1813, viz.:

Mohawks	72	men
Oneidas	9	"
Aughquagas	11	"
Tuscaroras	15	"
Cayugas	40	"
Onondagos	20	"
Delawares	25	"
Senecas	5	"
Tututies	4	"
Nanticokes	2	"
	203	
From the River Thames	12	
From the Rice Lakes	70	
From Lower Canada	180	
Grand total	465	men.

Officers—William J. Kerr, Captain Commanding; John Brant, Lieutenant; George Martin, Charles Aymard, Interpreters.

(Canadian Archives, Q. 330, 34.)

Notes by Capt. W. H. Merritt.

On the 21st in the afternoon, young Barnard, staff adjutant to Col. Bisshopp, FitzGibbon, McKenney, Cummings and myself, with a dragoon, were sent to Sugar Loaf, or rather Point Abino, for Mr. Tice Horn (Haun ?), as information had been lodged against him for giving information to the enemy. The enemy were in possession of Fort Erie and all the country above Chippawa. We arrived at the mouth of Lundy's Lane at 9 p. m., was near being fired on by a party of the inhabitants who were skulking from the Americans. Chapin had passed down an hour before. We were apprehensive of meeting that party on our return. It commenced raining and continued all night. We arrived at 2 o'clock at Horn's, surrounded the house and made him and one of Chapin's party prisoners. We could with difficulty mount or dismount our horses, the night was cold with the rain; we were completely chilled through. We returned to the 12 by 9 a. m. next morning. I went on to the Forty to make out muster-rolls, &c., against the 24th. I always remained at Mrs. Lewis's when at the Forty, as the Nelles's were crowded by every officer [who] could get in. Capt. Hall was sent on, with part of his own and my men, to Decoo's. I had a good rest for those two days, which was a very desirable thing, as I had not two nights regular sleep since the 6th inst. On the 24th Col. Boerstler came out to take FitzGibbon, with about 600 men, including Chapin's party. I gave an acc[oun]t of this in the other sheets; suffice it to say he got caught in the trap he intended for the other. But 6 men escaped; Totman was one. At 11 o'clock we heard of the enemy advancing. [I] was ordered on with my party to reinforce the advance. On our arrival at the 20 [we] had the satisfaction of hearing [that] the detachment was all made prisoners. [We] got down in time to form an escort to take them on to the 20. Early next morning we were all sent on to Decoo's, and dispersed from there to the lake. Nothing material occurred for a few days but slight skirmishing on the Swamp Road. Capt. Norton humorously observed on the battle of the Beaver Dams, "The *Cognawaga Indians* fought the *battle*, the *Mohawks* or Six Nations got the *plunder*, and *FitzGibbon* got the *credit*." The greater part of the Cognawagas were so much displeased [that] they returned home a few days later, which at this time was a very great loss.

(From the Merritt MSS.)

From "La Bibliothèque Canadienne."

By Michael Bibaud.

VOLUME 4, NUMBER 1.

December, 1826.

Montreal, 1826.

Lettre du Capitaine D. Ducharme sur la prise du Colonel Boerstler, &c.:

La capitulation du Colonel Boerstler ou l'affaire de Beaver Dam qui eut lieu le 24 Juin, 1813, est un des évènments interessants de la dernière guerre Americaine. On sait que les sauvages à qui la victoire fut principalement dû se montrérent très mécontents de l'ordre général qui fut publié à cette occasion. Le Capitaine Ducharme, leur principal commandant dans cette rencontre, instruit de ce mécontentement, fit ce qui dependait de lui pour le faire cesser, ou du moins pour faire connaitre la verité, en communiquant à l'editeur du *Spectateur Canadien* des details qui furent publies dans le numero du 22 Juillet. Il fut aussi public dans le *Spectateur* du 4 Avril, 1818, une lettre du meme Capitaine Ducharme contenant de nouveaux renseignements sur cette affaire. Enfin l'ètè dernier, un monsieur de cette ville, qui a à cœur de connaitre dans le detail tout ce qui doit entrer dans l'histoire de notre pays, ayant lu dans un journal ètranger* un exposé de cette meme affaire qui lui parut fautif, fit prier le Capitaine Ducharme de lui communiquer par ecrit tout ce qu'il en savait comme temoine oculaire. Il reçut du brave et obligeant Capitaine une nouvelle lettre qu'il a en la bonté de nous communiquer, et dont voici la substance.

---

*The "Soldier's Companion," article "Spirited Exploit."

Lac des Deux Montagnes.

5 Juin, 1826.

Monsieur,—Ayant su du Capitaine L ***** que vous desiriez avoir de moi un detail de la prise du Colonel Boerstler et de son armée, je vais tacher de satisfaire votre curiosité.

Le 26 Mai, 1813, j'eus ordre de Sir John Johnson de partir de Lachine a la tête d'un parti de 340 sauvages, savoir, 160 du Sault St. Louis, 120 du Lac des Deux Montagnes et 60 de St. Regis. J'étais accompagne des lieutenants J. B. DeLorimier, Gedeon G. Gaucher, Louis Langlade, Evangeliste St. Germain et Isaac Leclair.

Nous contumâmes le route jusqu'a la tête du lac (Ontario) ou nous fûmes mis sous le commandement du Colonel Clauss. Arrivés près de 40 Mile Creek, ce commandant nous fit accompagner du Capitaine Carr et du Lieutenant Brandt et de 100 Mohawks (ou Agniers.) Le 20 Juin nous fûmes camper a 20 Mile Creek ou Beaver Dam avec tous nos sauvages.

Le 23 je fus à la découverté sur la riviere de Niagara avec 25 de mes sauvages. Nous apperçûmes une berge remplie de soldats Americains, les sauvages firent feu dessus et tuèrent quatre hommes et en firent sept prisoniers. Comme nous étions à la vue de Fort George, j'ordonnai à mes sauvages de faire hater pas a leurs prisoniers. La cavalerie Americans ne manqué pas de nous poursuivre, et deux jeunes Iroquois étant restes derrière pour prendre, ils disaient, des chevaux l'un d'eux fût fait prisonier.

Le 24 vers les 8 heures du matin les decouveurs revinrent en faisant le cri de mort qui signifiait que nous étions frappes par l'ennemi. Aussitôt nous nous preparâmes, et je fus faire mon rapport au Colonel de Haren qui avait sous son commandement 100 hommes de troupes regulières. Il nous fit mettre en file. Je lui representai que la place qui nous occupions n'était pas avantageuse pour attendre l'ennemi, et que je desirais l'attaquer dans le bois. Il trouva l'avis bon, et dit qu'il nous suporterait. Nous courûmes au-devant de l'ennemi environ un demi-mille, et priniez notre position des deux cotes du grand chemin, le Lieutenant De Lorimier, à la droite avec le Lieutenant Leclair et 25 hommes, le Capitaine Carr avec ses Mohawks, à la gauche, et moi au centre. Nous apperçûmes aussitôt 20 dragons ennemis descendre une petite côté, en venant sur nous; j'ordonnai aussitôt a tirer et ces 20 hommes fut tous tués roides, a l'exception d'un seul que les sauvages achévèrent; après quoi ils se jetèrent sur les morts pour les depouiller, malgré je leur enjoinisse de n'en rien faire mais de rester a leur place. Le gros de l'ennemi arrive sur le côte, fit sur nous une décharge de trois pieces de canon chargées de mitraille; heureusement, le feu fit si mal dirigé, que nous, n'en recûmes presque aucun mal. J'ordonnai cependant aux sauvages de gagner le bois, et pendant le mouvement le feu de la mousqueterie ennemie nous tua et blessa plusieurs hommes. Alors les Mohawks se retirent; le Capitaine Carr et le Lieutenant Brandt nous laisserent aussi pour tacher de rallier leurs sauvages et pour demander le secours de troupes; mais ils ne reparurent pas dans l'engagement.

Le combat devint des plus vifs; les sauvages irritées de la perte de leurs frères se battrent en furieux; à la fin leurs cris affreux epouvantèrent les ennemis qui se retirérent precipitamment, infanterie et cavalrie dans une coulée. Notre feu devenant inutile, j'ordonnai aux Lieutenants Gamelin, Gaucher et Langlade de cerner la coulée ; se que fut executé avec ponctualité et diligence. On recommença alors a tirer avec effét ; les chevaux d'un canon furent tués ; le Colonel Boerstler reçut deux blessures grievés et eût son cheval tué sous lui. Enfin l'ennemi retraita encore. Mais arrète d'un côte par un marais et de l'autre par nos sauvages, il se vit hors d'etat de continuer ou le combat on la retraite et hissa le pavillon de tréve. J'ordonnai aux sauvages de cesser de tirer ; mais je fus mal ecouté ; le feu continua encore de leur part.

Sur ces entrefaites le Capitaine Hall de notre cavalerie étant venu nous trouver et voyant l'ennemi rendu, alla faire son rapport. Il rencontra le Lieutenant FitzGibbon du 49e Regiment, qui venait a notre aide avec 40 hommes. Celui-ci s'offrit à faire la capitulation et comme je ne parlais pas bien l'anglais nous l'acceptâmes, aux conditions qui les sauvages auraient toutes les depouillés. Le Lieutenant FitzGibbon, non plus que le Colonel de Haren ne prirent, aucune part au combat. La victoire fut entiérement dû aux sauvages, qui pourtant se virent frustrés alors non seulement des depouillés qui leur avaient été promisés mais de l'honneur et de la gloire qui devaient leur revenir.

Notre perte fut d'une quinzaine d'hommes tué et d'environ 25 blessés. Celle de l'ennemi en tués et blessés fut tres considerable, et presque tous ceux que ne furent pas tués dans le combat au nombre de plus de 500, y compris le commandant et une vingtaine d'officiers furent faits prisonniers.

Votre, &c.,

D. DUCHARME.

[Translation.]

A letter from Captain Ducharme on the capture of Colonel Boerstler, &c. :

The capitulation of Colonel Boerstler or the affair of Beaver Dam, which took place on the 24th June, 1813, is one of the interesting events of the last American war. It is known that the Indians, to whom the victory was principally due, were greatly discontented at the General Order which was published on that occasion. Captain Ducharme, their senior officer in that action, being informed of their dissatisfaction did everything in his power to remove it or at least to make known the truth by communicating to the editor of the *Spectateur Canadian* the details, which were published in the number for July 22d. There was also published in the *Spectateur* of 4th April, 1818, a letter from the same Captain Ducharme containing further information about this affair. Finally, last summer a gentleman of this city, who is deeply interested in the history of our country, having read in a foreign publication* an account of this event, which seemed incorrect, requested Captain Ducharme to relate in writing

---

*The "Soldiers Companion," article "Spirited Exploit."

what he knew about it as an eyewitness. He received from the gallant and obliging captain a letter which he has had the goodness to communicate to us, of which the substance is as follows:

"LAKE OF TWO MOUNTAINS, 5th June, 1826.

DEAR SIR :—

Having learned from Captain L * * * that you wish to obtain from me a narrative of the capture of Colonel Boerstler and his force, I shall endeavor to satisfy your curiosity.

On the 26th day of May, 1813, I was ordered by Sir John Johnson to set out from Lachine at the head of a body of 340 Indians, namely: 160 from Sault St. Louis, 120 from the Lake of Two Mountains and 60 from St. Regis. I was accompanied by Lieutenants J. B. DeLorimier, Gedeon G. Gaucher, Louis Langlade, Evangeliste St. Germain and Isaac Leclair.

We proceeded to the head of the lake (Ontario) where we were placed under the command of Colonel Claus. When we arrived near the 40 Mile Creek this officer sent with us Captain Carr, (Kerr), Lieutenant Brandt and 100 Mohawks (or Agniers.) On the 20th of June we encamped at 20 Mile Creek, or Beaver Dam, with all our Indians.

On the 23rd I went scouting to the Niagara River with 25 of my Indians. We discovered a barge filled with soldiers; the Indians fired upon it, killed four men and made seven prisoners. As we were within sight of Fort George I ordered my Indians to hurry away their prisoners. The American cavalry pursued us, and two young Iroquois, having remained behind, as they stated to capture horses, one of them was made a prisoner.

On the 24th, about 8 o'clock in the morning, our scouts returned, giving the death-cry, which signified that we were attacked by the enemy. We immediately prepared for action, and I made a report to Colonel De Haren, who commanded 100 regulars. He directed us to form up. I represented to him that the position we occupied was not an advantageous place to meet the enemy and that I desired to attack them in the woods. He approved of this and promised to support us. We ran forward towards the enemy about half a mile and took up our position on both sides of the main road, Lieutenant De Lorimier on the right with Lieutenant Leclair and 25 men; Captain Carr, with his Mohawks, on the left, and myself in the centre. We soon perceived 20 of the enemy's dragoons approaching us, coming down a slight declivity. I at once ordered them to fire, and the whole of these 20 men were killed stone dead except one, whom the Indians finished; after which they threw themselves upon the dead to strip them, although I warned them to remain quiet at their posts.

The main body of the enemy arrived upon the ridge and fired three cannon upon us loaded with grapeshot; fortunately their fire was so badly directed that it did us little harm. However, I ordered the Indians to take to the woods, and during this movement the enemy's musketry killed and wounded several men. Then the Mohawks retired; Captain Carr and Lieutenant Brandt also left us to try to rally their Indians and to demand assistance from the troops, but they did not reappear during the engagement.

The battle became warmer; the Indians, enraged at the loss of their brethren, fought savagely, and finally their horrible yells terrified the enemy so much that they retired precipitately, infantry and cavalry, into a hollow. Our fire becoming ineffective I ordered Lieutenants Gamelin, Gaucher and Langlade to surround the hollow, which was accomplished with much promptitude and diligence. They then recommenced their fire with effect; the horses of one of their guns were killed, Colonel Boerstler received two severe wounds and had his horse killed under him. Finally the enemy again retreated. But, hemmed in on one side by a swamp and on the other by our Indians, he found himself unable either to continue the action or his retreat, and showed a flag of truce. I ordered the Indians to cease firing but was not obeyed; they still continued to fire.

At this time Captain Hall of our cavalry having come up and seeing the enemy subdued, rode off to make his report. He met Lieutenant FitzGibbon of the 49th Regiment, who was coming to our assistance with 40 men. The latter offered to conclude the capitulation, and as I could not speak English very well we agreed, on the condition that the Indians should have all the booty. Neither Lieutenant FitzGibbon nor Colonel DeHaren took any part in the action. The victory was entirely due to the Indians, who were not only deprived of the booty which had been promised them but of the honour and glory which they had won.

Our loss amounted to fifteen men killed and about 25 wounded. That of the enemy in killed and wounded was very large and nearly all those who were not killed in the action, to the number of more than 500, including their commander and a score of officers, were made prisoners.

Yours, &c.,
D. DUCHARME,

(File in Toronto Public Library.)

Mrs. Laura Secord's Narrative.

I shall commence at the battle of Queenston, where I was at the time the cannon balls were flying around me in every direction. I left the place during the engagement. After the battle I returned to

Queenston and there found that my husband had been wounded, my house plundered and property destroyed. It was while the Americans had possession of the frontier that I learned the plans of the American commander and determined to put the British troops under FitzGibbon in possession of them, and if possible to save the British troops from capture or perhaps total destruction. In doing so I found I should have great difficulty in getting through the American guards, which were out ten miles in the country. Determined to persevere, I left early in the morning, walked nineteen miles in the month of June over a rough and difficult part of the country, when I came to a field belonging to a Mr. Decamp in the neighborhood of the Beaver Dam. By this time daylight had left me. Here I found all the Indians encamped; by moonlight the scene was terrifying and to those accustomed to such scenes might be considered grand. Upon advancing to the Indians they all rose and with some yells said, "Woman," which made me tremble. I cannot express the awful feeling it gave me, but I did not lose my presence of mind. I was determined to persevere. I went up to one of the chiefs, made him understand that I had great news for Capt. FitzGibbon and that he must let me pass to his camp or that he and his party would all be taken. The chief at first objected to let me pass, but finally consented, after some hesitation, to go with me and accompany me to FitzGibbon's station, which was at the Beaver Dam, where I had an interview with him. I then told him what I had come for and what I had heard—that the Americans intended to make an attack upon the troops under his command and would, from their superior numbers, capture them all. Benefitting by this information, Capt. FitzGibbon formed his plans accordingly and captured about five hundred American infantry, about fifty mounted dragoons, and a field piece or two was taken from the enemy. I returned home next day exhausted and fatigued. I am now advanced in years and when I look back I wonder how I could have gone through so much fatigue with the fortitude to accomplish it.

(From the Anglo-American Magazine, Vol. III., Toronto, November, 1853, No. 5, p. 467.)

(From the "Church," Published at Cobourg, Ont., April, 1845.)

To the Editor of the "Church":

QUEENSTON, 11th April, 1845.

SIR,—In the course of the late debate in the House of Assembly, relative to the propriety of granting Col. FitzGibbon £1000 for his services, in lieu of a grant of land, Mr. Aylwin said "he strongly opposed the grant, and gave as one reason that Col. FitzGibbon had monopolized honor which did not rightfully belong to him. He had received credit for the affair at the Beaver Dam, whilst in point of fact the party to whom that credit was due was Major Delorimier, a relative of his own, and a native of Lower Canada, but instead of being rewarded for his services Major Delorimier could not obtain the life of his son when he afterwards solicited it."*

Now I think it proper that Mr. Aylwin should be informed and that the country in general should know in what way Col. FitzGibbon achieved so much honour for the affair at the Beaver Dam. My mother, living on the frontier the whole of the late American war, a warm supporter of the British cause, frequently met with the American officers and upon the occasion of the capture of the American troops at the Beaver Dam, after our troops, consisting of a small detachment under Col. FitzGibbon, then Lieut. FitzGibbon of the 49th Regiment, and some Indians, had taken up their position at that place, overheard an American officer say to other of the officers that they intended to surprise and capture the British troops at the Beaver Dam. Without waiting for further information my mother, a lone woman, at once left her house to apprize the British troops of what she had heard, and travelled on foot the whole of the way, passing all the American guards and many of the Indian scouts who were placed along the road, until she arrived at the Beaver Dam, and enquiring for the officer in command was introduced to Col. FitzGibbon, (then Lieut. FitzGibbon, as I said before,) as the officer in command : she then told him what she had come for, and all she had heard,—that the Americans intended to make an attack upon them and would no doubt, from their superior numbers, capture them all. Col. FitzGibbon in consequence of this information prepared himself to meet the enemy, and soon after the attack being made the American troops were captured and one or two field-pieces taken—as the Colonel's certificate of my mother's services on that occasion, accompanying this communication, will shew. It might perhaps be as well for me while upon this subject further to state that I never heard my mother speak of Major Delorimier or any other officer being at the Beaver Dam at that time. Col. FitzGibbon was the only officer who appeared to be in command, to whom my mother gave the information, and who acted the part he so nobly did on that occasion.

I am, Sir, your most obedient servant,

CHAS. B. SECORD.

---

*Major DeLorimier was the Lieut. J. B. Lorimier mentioned in Capt. Ducharme's narrative and elsewhere in this volume. One of his sons was executed for participation in the insurrection of 1837-8 in Lower Canada.—Ed.

(Certificate.)

TORONTO, 23d February, 1837.

I do hereby certify that Mrs. Secord, wife of James Secord of Chippawa, Esquire, did in the month of June, 1813, walk from her house in the village of St. Davids to DeCoo's house in Thorold, by a circuitous route of about twenty miles, partly through the woods, to acquaint me that the enemy intended to attempt by surprise to capture a detachment of the 49th Regiment, then under my command, she having obtained such knowledge from good authority, as the event proved. Mrs. Secord was a person of slight and delicate frame and made this effort in weather excessively warm, and I dreaded at the time that she must suffer in health in consequence of fatigue and anxiety, she having been exposed to danger from the enemy, through whose line of communication she had to pass. The attempt was made on my detachment by the enemy, and his detachment, consisting of upwards of 500 men, with a field piece and 50 dragoons were captured in consequence. I write this certificate in a moment of much hurry and from memory, and it is therefore thus brief.

JAMES FITZGIBBON,

Formerly Lieut. in the 49th Regt.

(From a clipping in possession of C. C. James, Esq., Deputy Minister of Agriculture, Toronto, Ont.)

Narrative of the Expedition from Fort George to the Beaver Dams, U. C.

By Lieut.-Colonel Boerstler.

On June 23d, 1813, the *soi disant* Major Chapin called at the tent of Lieutenant-Colonel Boerstler on the plains of Newark, talked largely about having scoured all the country with his forty followers, that he had been to the Beaver Dams, that the enemy had fortified Decoo's stone house, that there were one company of regulars and from sixty to one hundred Indians at that post, that if this stronghold was destroyed the enemy could no longer show himself in this quarter: that five hundred men with a couple of field pieces could effect this, &c., &c.

Lieutenant-Colonel Boerstler, knowing this man to be a vain boasting liar, and suspecting his fidelity from various circumstances, amongst which was that of having joined a committee to remonstrate against the war, and that of coming forward as spokesman in favor of a man charged by many of his neighbors with giving intelligence to the enemy—he was heard by Lieutenant-Colonel Boerstler with indifference and dismissed with coolness. A messenger now arrived to inform Lieutenant-Colonel Boerstler that General Boyd desired to see him at his quarters. When arrived he was asked: "Have you seen Major Chapin?"

"Yes Sir."

"Has he mentioned anything of an expedition?"

"He talked (as above related.")

"It is intended to send five hundred men and two field pieces to capture or dislodge the enemy and batter down Decoo's house, and you are to have the command."

"Very well, Sir, when do I march?"

"This evening. You will call at the Adjutant-General's office for your orders."

He called and the Adjutant General having commenced to explain the object of the expedition he was interrupted with: "You are a soldier and will excuse me when I demand my orders in writing."

"Certainly, Sir."

They were written and Lieutenant-Colonel Boerstler marched about dark with five hundred men, consisting of Captain McDowell's company of light artillery, with a twelve and six-pounder, twenty dragoons under Cornet Burd, Major Chapin's thirty-eight or forty mounted militia and the rest composed of infantry of the Fourteenth, Sixth and Twenty-third Regiments. The riflemen ordered to join this expedition, (and which were all-important,) were by Lieutenant-Colonel Milton, the commander of the second brigade, contrary to all rule, placed on guard and could not be relieved.

The detachment arrived at Queenston about eleven o'clock p. m., in great silence. Patrols and pickets were immediately sent out to prevent citizens from escaping to give intelligence. No candles were suffered to be lighted and officers and men laid down on their arms. After daybreak the detachment proceeded, and near St. Davids an Indian scout was killed by a flanker, while another made his escape. At St. Davids the commander discovered that Major Chapin's knowledge of the roads was not to be relied on. He accordingly interrogated various inhabitants and proceeded several miles, when, arriving at a cross-road, he demanded of some of Major Chapin's men where that road led to? They replied they did not know. "How not know? Were you not here two days ago?" "No Sir, not within several miles as far."

The commander now perceived that the General had been inveigled to risk this detachment on doubtful intelligence.

Two British officers were discovered at some distance reconnoitering, and presently bugles and musketry conveyed the alarm in the direction of St. Catharines. The commander viewed the ground and observed: "Gentlemen, here we must fight on our return. The detachment proceeded until within a mile and a half of Decoo's house in the original order of march, that is, the mounted militia in front, the commanding officer at the head of the detachment from the Fourteenth Regiment—the artillery and waggons—Major Taylor at the head of the companies of the Sixth and Twenty-third Regiments, the dragoons in the rear and flankers out on the right and left from each company. Having passed the road from St. Catharines, where it crosses the mountain road by which the detachment marched, a piece of woods on either side of the road, some fields ahead, the Indians fired a volley on the rear-guard and killed and wounded three or four men. The detachment was forced to the right and in a moment the action became general. The waggons, artillery, horses and dragoons were ordered to the rear, out of the reach of the enemy's fire.

Some of the *soi-disant* Major Chapin's men now demanded: "Where is our commander? What are we to do?" The commanding officer looked for him in vain and replied: "You have no commander but myself, turn into the ranks and fight with my men." Some did so; others found it as convenient to join their commander in the hollow alongside the waggons.

The second-in-command, Major Taylor, was unhorsed the first fire and afterwards fought on foot. The surgeon remained until his horse was twice wounded, when he was ordered to the waggons. Thus the commanding officer alone was mounted and consequently compelled to carry his own orders to every point where they became necessary. He received a shot through the thigh in the early part of the action, which he concealed, fearing a bad impression might be made on his troops.

After the contest had continued some time the commanding officer endeavored to make it decisive, for which purpose he left orders with Major Taylor to protect the artillery, &c., and forming the Fourteenth into single file, a company on each flank thrown back *en potence*, a charge at quick step was commenced through the woods and part of the enemy driven across the field, where many fell. The charge having been made obliquely to the right in order to drive the enemy into the cleared ground—this was no sooner effected than a furious attack commenced on our left. The charge was now continued obliquely to the left and the enemy driven to a considerable distance, not, however, without keeping up a constant fire on us, which from the thickness of the woods and mode of fighting, where every combatant is his own commander, was perfectly in his power. Finding, in short, that musketeers unaccustomed to fighting in any other than a regular order, could not maintain so unequal a combat without great loss, a party of skirmishers were ordered and the troops retreated by filing to the rear from the right of companies. After reaching again the small field the line was again formed behind the fence, (the enemy having advanced as we retreated and the contest kept up until twenty-six rounds were expended.)

The commanding officer now dashed into the rear and found Major Chapin and a parcel of his men around the waggons. "For God's sake, Major, do something; if you do not fight your men then take them and furnish mine with ammunition and carry off the wounded to the waggons, that I may not be compelled to take men for this purpose out of my ranks."

Major Chapin appeared shortly after this in the rear of the line with a keg of cartridges on his horse: he called a soldier, handed it over and resumed his station in the *hollow*. This was the whole of his exertion, and the only time he appeared on the battle ground during three hours; this is the man who in an official document was called "the brave Major Chapin." The commanding officer now directed men to be detached from each company to carry off the wounded and get a supply of cartridges, which being effected, (the contest still continuing,) Captain McDowell was directed to limber his pieces and proceed with the waggons, on which were loaded the wounded, under the escort of a company of infantry, to a position about a quarter of a mile to the right and somewhat to the rear. The object of this movement was, if possible, to get round the piece of woods on our right occupied by the enemy, and so regain the main road and commence a retreat, which seemed the only resource to save the detachment.

Having arrived on the ground spoken of the troops were formed into close column, but from the killed, wounded and skulking our number seemed much reduced. They had marched eleven miles that morning without refreshment; they had fought three hours, the weather very warm, and consequently the troops were much exhausted. The commanding officer thought of ordering them a ration of whiskey, but some Indians getting in our rear and commencing a fire there was not time, and the commanding officer informed his troops that as the enemy were seen constantly to cross the road on which we were then formed, within long shot of them, his intention was to wait a little longer until the enemy's principal force had passed, then to rush on him with a desperate charge and if possible to gain the main road and retreat. He encouraged his troops to be resolute; these were the only means in our power, as the enemy were constantly gathering strength and we losing; added to that the ammunition low and but three cartridges of grape left for the field-pieces.

At this juncture Lieutenant FitzGibbon arrived from the enemy with a flag of truce; Captain McDowell was sent to receive him. FitzGibbon stated that we were far outnumbered; that we could not possibly escape and that they had a number of Indians from the Northwest, by no means as easily controlled as those from the vicinity, and having suffered very severely they were outrageous and would commence a general massacre; he was therefore desirous to save the effusion of blood and demanded a surrender. He was told that we knew how to die, and they should hear from us in a few minutes. He returned very shortly, repeating the summons, and added that if we did not believe we were outnumbered and could not possibly escape, an officer would be permitted to view their troops. Lieutenant Goodwin was sent and arriving at the head of the lane where a part of their force was stationed, Colonel DeHaren ordered him back, saying this was too humiliating to be permitted. On his return the commanding officer asked those under his command what was to be done. The second-in-command observed he was willing to do anything, (in other words to give no opinion.) The commanding officer said he did not ask the opinion of his officers or wish them to bear any share of the blame that might attach; he was commanding officer and therefore would take all the responsibility; he only wished to know their view of the situation. Some of them observed they did not think it possible, with such a force around us, the exhausted state of our men and seventeen miles to retreat, the road running principally through woods, that one-fourth of us could escape death, as we must retreat in regular order along the road, while the immense number of Indians would constantly hang on our flanks and rear and shoot us down at pleasure without our being enabled to injure them, more especially when our few remaining cartridges should be expended. This coinciding with the opinion of the commanding officer, Captain McDowell was directed to obtain the best terms he could, which consisted in permitting the officers to retain their side arms and horses, the militia to return home on parole and the detachment to surrender prisoners of war.

Thus terminated one of the most unfortunate and impolitic expeditions that ever was planned. Five hundred men were risked "to batter down with a twelve and six-pounder Decoo's stone house, said to be fortified and garrisoned with a company of regulars and sixty to one hundred Indians to capture or dislodge the enemy and return by the way of St. Davids and Queenston."

This intelligence was derived from a source decidedly not entitled to confidence, having long previous to this been known by many for an unblushing liar; besides he had not been within several miles of the post to be attacked, of the strength of which he undertook to give a particular detail. The situation and force of the enemy was this: Lieutenant FitzGibbon was stationed with a company of regulars at Decoo's house. Captain William J. Kerr, whose official account is within reach, states that he had four hundred and fifty warriors in the action ; Colonel Bisshopp stated their number at four hundred and eighty, that number having drawn rations at this post the evening before the engagement. Lieutenant-Colonel DeHaren with three companies of regulars, some Indians and militia was stationed at St. Catharines, that is six miles in the rear of the battleground and ten miles from Fort George, with a road leading into the mountain road at the piece of woods spoken of and the right of the scene of action, by which road his forces joined the Indians. Colonel Clark gathered all the militia he could, amongst which were a small company of dragoons. Colonel Bisshopp, commanding the whole British advance, was stationed near Twenty Mile Creek, that is seven miles from the Beaver Dams, with a road intersecting the mountain road, by which we marched, somewhat in rear of the battle ground, whither he marched during the action with four or five hundred regulars to cut off our retreat. They took their stations about the time we capitulated. They were not in the action neither did the commanding officer know of their being there until after the surrender. General Vincent with the remainder of his forces was stationed nearer the scene of action than it was thence to Fort George, and unfortunately many of his troops were advancing so as gradually to narrow our possessions around Fort George before they knew of our approach. Thus it was evident that if this detachment had possessed ammunition enough to continue the fight another hour it would have had almost the whole of the British army to contend with.

As to the policy of this measure—a detachment of five hundred men with a twelve and six pounder is ordered to proceed *via* Queenston, eleven miles nearer the enemy than their main body, to batter down a strong thick-walled two-storey house, and to capture or dislodge *a company of regulars*, (for it could never be supposed that the Indians would coop themselves up in a house when they had woods before them.) No other detachment is ordered to support the preceding one, and three thousand or three thousand five hundred men remain quietly shut up in Fort George. Yet that it was thought *dangerous* to go too near the enemy is fully proved thus : The Thirteenth Regiment, one of the best in that army, and nearly or quite of equal strength with this detachment, had been stationed at Queenston for a few days, but was ordered in two days previous to the marching of the detachment, by express, fearing it might be cut off : and as it was as near to the Beaver Dams *via* St. Catharines as *via* Queenston, why was not this detachment ordered to capture or dislodge the enemy's nearest post ? (for that it was known that the enemy had a force of at *least* two hundred men at St. Catharines will not be denied.) and this effected the detachment could proceed to

Decoo's, or, finding the enemy too strong, a retreat was secure ; or if it was thought absolutely necessary, for which, however, there appears no strong reasons, that this detachment should march by the mountain road, why was not a simultaneous movement made by another force to keep DeHaren busy where he was instead of leaving him undisturbed and at liberty to direct his force where he pleased.

An account has been published of this affair in which it is stated " why should it have been deemed proper to remain several hours in a position surrounded with woods without either risking a decisive action or effecting a retreat remains to be accounted for, as well as the *project* of waiting for a reinforcement from a distance of fifteen or sixteen miles." It can be answered that the closeness of the country and the force of the enemy prevented the action being made decisive, and in like manner the retreat, as detailed above. And as to reinforcements, the commanding officer sent for none nor is it thought that he ever did an act that would justify so mean an opinion of his understanding as this project would seem to imply—knowing the distance he had been sent from any point whence support could be expected.

And it is certainly a matter of surprise and worthy of consideration that an official statement founded on the *ipse dixit* of a runaway militiaman should be published, and that the official letter of the commanding officer of the detachment, although limited, having to pass through the hands of the enemy, sent the next day by a flag of truce, should never have been published nor even communicated to the War Department, and a copy of which has recently been obtained, although it was not *remembered* ever to have been received.

It may be added that the commanding officer of the detachment, having shortly previous to this period been twice illy treated as to commands,* was not asked how he liked this expedition, otherwise he would have decidedly opposed it, although on other occasions he always volunteered his services. But he had his written orders, enough for him. These orders were torn to pieces before the sur-

---

*Previous to the capture of Fort George Major-General Lewis called on Lieutenant-Colonel Boerstler and observed: "I am requested to recommend a Lieutenant-Colonel to lead the advance in the attack on Fort George. Will you serve?" "With great pleasure." "Very well." Three days after Lieutenant-Colonel Boerstler saw Lieutenant-Colonel Scott at the head of the advance. From motives Lieutenant-Colonel Boerstler never spoke to Major-General Lewis on the subject, feeling well convinced that the cause of this very mortifying circumstance must be sought for *elsewhere.*

About the 18th or 19th of June, Brigadier-General Boyd sent for Lieutenant-Colonel Boerstler, saying it is intended to send a regiment to Queenston to cover that part of the country, and I have made choice of yours. "Very well, Sir." At this moment Colonel Chrystie entered the room and called General Boyd into another apartment. When he returned Lieutenant-Colonel Boerstler asked: "When shall I march?" General Boyd replied: "Colonel Chrystie means to go himself." "Colonel Chrystie means to go himself!!! Does he command the army or do you, that he can go or stay when he pleases?" (No answer.) "Or, if he is to go why was I sent for? Was it to wound my feelings or

render, to prevent, possibly, the ridicule of the enemy from attaching to our plans. A copy of these orders has been written for very often but not yet obtained.

Sir George Prevost to Lord Bathurst.

Headquarters, KINGSTON, UPPER CANADA,
24 June, 1813.

(No. 71.)

MY LORD,—I have the honor to transmit to Your Lordship a copy of a letter which I have deemed it my duty to write to Major-General Dearborn, Commander-in-Chief of the American Forces, in consequence of information I had received that certain American officers who had been taken prisoners in the different attacks made by the enemy on this Province and allowed to proceed to the United States on their parole, were serving in the American army now invading this Province without having been regularly exchanged.

It may be necessary to apprize Your Lordship that during the course of last winter an application was made to me by the Government of the United States thro' Major-General Dearborn, for the exchange of these officers, together with Brigadier-General Hull and other American officers, prisoners of war, on their parole, agreeably to a tariff established at Halifax under a provisional agreement entered into for the exchange of naval prisoners by our and the agent appointed by the American Government and ratified by Sir John Warren.

Before my assent could be obtained to that agreement, as respecting prisoners taken by land and which was requested by General Dearborn at the time of the above application, and before my answer to the application was received, the Government of the United States undertook to act upon the agreement, as if I had acceded to it, by publicly declaring Brig.-General Hull and certain other prisoners of war on their parole, (among whom are those mentioned in the letter herewith transmitted,) as exchanged and free to serve in the army of United States against Great Britain and her allies.

This extraordinary proceeding called from me the general

---

insult me!" "You are warm, Sir." "Yes, Sir, it is time that the officers of the line stick out for their rights; this is twice that commands have been voluntarily offered me and twice I have been tricked." "Take care how you talk, Sir." "I know what I say, General, and am ready to take the consequences; good morning, Sir." Colonel Chrystie's regiment marched and was recalled, as already stated.

C. G. BOERSTLER,
Col. 14th U. S. Infantry.

May 25th, 1814.

(From notices of the war of 1812. By John Armstrong. New York. George Dearborn, 1836, Vol. I., appendix No. 24, pp. 250-261. Omitted in edition of 1840.)

orders* by way of protest against it, which I have now the honor of transmitting to Your Lordship. Several letters have since passed in explanation of this transaction between General Dearborn and myself, to the last of which from me, dated more than two months ago, no answer has been received.

I have, however, been much surprised to hear lately from Mr. Barclay that he had recently been informed by the American Secretary of State that the before mentioned provisional agreement had not been ratified by the President of the United States.

At this distance from my usual headquarters, where my papers are, it is not in my power to transmit to your Lordship copies of the correspondence which has taken place on this occasion, but from the view which I have endeavored to give you of the subject your Lordship will not be at a loss to discover the motives for this procedure on the part of the Government of the United States, and will, I trust, at the same time see the necessity and approve of the measure I have adopted with regard to those officers who, in violation of their parole, are now serving against us.

I have received from Mr. Barclay a copy of an agreement entered into by myself and the American Commissary, and which he says is satisfactory both to Sir John Warren and the American Government. It does not appear to me in any respect objectionable, nor have I any new article or amendment to propose.

There are at present three Brigadiers-General, about twenty-four other officers of different ranks and upwards of four hundred men American prisoners of war at Quebec, whom I shall detain as such until further and more satisfactory explanations are received by me from the American Government upon the subject of this despatch.

(Canadian Archives, Q. 122, p. 35.)

Sir George Prevost to Sir John Borlase Warren.

Headquarters, KINGSTON, UPPER CANADA,
24 June, 1813.

SIR,—As our means of equipping and manning our navy on the lakes bears no proportion to those of the enemy, who are unceasingly employed in promoting their great object of obtaining an ascendency upon them, I beg leave most urgently to request of you a supply of seamen for this purpose, without which aid, should the contest be much longer continued, we shall labor under disadvantages which no skill or valor on the part of the small band of seamen under Sir James Yeo can counterbalance. Whatever assistance you can give me on this head will, I trust, be promptly afforded, as everything will

---

*For the General Order referred to see Part V of this work, pp. 60-2.—Ed.

probably depend upon the operations of the next two months. A less reinforcement than two hundred seamen would be of little avail, and with it I should feel confident in the means of successfully opposing the American flotilla on both lakes.

The squadron under Sir James Yeo, which is now out, has been tolerably manned by the seamen arrived from England, but we are without a man either for the new brig just ready to launch here or for the ship which is in great forwardness on Lake Erie, where Captain Barclay is gone to command, and whose wants on this head, as he has very lately feelingly described them to me, are great and pressing.

(Canadian Archives, Q. 126, p. 108.)

Sir George Prevost to Lord Bathurst.

Headquarters, KINGSTON, UPPER CANADA,
24th June, 1813.

(No. 72.)

MY LORD,—I have the honor to transmit to Your Lordship a copy of a public declaration given out by the American commandant of Fort Erie, after the enemy had taken possession of that post, and the proclamation which I deemed it necessary to issue in consequence of it.

I avail myself of this opportunity of informing Your Lordship that finding upon my arrival at this place that Major-General Sir Roger Sheaffe had altogether lost the confidence of the Province by the measures he had pursued for its defence, I deemed it most conducive to the good of the public service to remove that officer to Montreal and to substitute Major-General DeRottenburg in his place. Major-General DeRottenburg has accordingly assumed the civil administration and military command in the Province. He proceeded on the 21st from hence to the head of the lake to take the command of the army there, and Major-General Sir Roger Sheaffe has returned to Montreal.

(Canadian Archives, Q. 122, p. 41.)

Brigadier-General Vincent to Sir George Prevost.

40 MILE CREEK, 25th June, 1813.

SIR,—I have the honor of transmitting to Your Excellency a report I received from Lieutenant-Colonel Bisshopp, commanding the troops in advance, of the success of a skirmish with a strong detachment of cavalry and infantry advancing with two field pieces.

To the vigilance of Lieutenant-Colonel Bisshop I feel much

indebted, and I beg leave to refer Your Excellency to his report of the conduct of the men and officers under his command, which is deserving every commendation. I cannot but particularize that of Lieutenant FitzGibbon, commanding a small reconnoitering party co-operating with the Indians, through whose address in entering into the capitulation Your Excellency will perceive by Lieutenant-Colonel Bishopp's report that the surrender of the American detachment is to be attributed.

I beg leave to recommend this officer to Your Excellency's protection.

(Canadian Archives, C. 679.)

Brigadier-General Vincent to Sir George Prevost.

40 MILE CREEK, 25th June, 1813.

SIR,—Immediately after Captain Loring left this with my letter of this morning to Your Excellency with the account of the action of yesterday, I discovered my mistake of not enclosing Lieutenant-Colonel Bisshopp's official letter but a copy of the American Colonel Boerstler's letter to Major-General Dearborn on the subject.

As I forward this in an hour after, I am in hopes it will arrive in sufficient time.

(Canadian Archives, C. 679.)

Lieutenant-Colonel Charles G. Boerstler to Major-General Dearborn.

20-MILE CREEK, 25th June, 1813.

SIR,—I am permitted to state the misfortune which has befallen myself and the detachment entrusted to my care. We proceeded yesterday morning until near the Beaver Dams when we were attacked by a large number of Indians, who were reinforced by regulars under Colonel DeHaren, while other reinforcements marched in the direction of our rear. The action lasted 3 hours, 10 minutes, during which time we drove them some distance into the wood, but finding our men not equal in that mode of fighting I changed my position twice during the engagement to get more open ground, but such was the situation that the enemy's balls reached us from every direction, while he was concealed. Our ammunition being nearly expended, surrounded on all sides, seventeen miles to retreat when my force would have constantly diminished (especially after spending our ammunition) while the enemy was gathering in from various outposts—myself, Captain Machesney, Captain Cummins, Lieut. Randall, Lieut. Marshall, wounded—I saw that in the exhausted state the men were in that the far greater part could never reach Fort George (if any), therefore was compelled to capitulate. The officers under my command will state what may be requisite as to my conduct.

The prisoners amount to :

	Majors.	Captains.	Subalterns.	Surgeons.	Sergeants.	Drummers.	Rank and File.
Artillery...................		1	1		2		31
14th Regt.		3	11	1	13	2	301
20th do	1						
6th do		1	1		3		54
23rd do		1	1		4	2	57
Dragoons...................			1		1		19
	1	6	15	1	23	4	462

You will find enclosed the articles of capitulation.

I presume my destination will be Quebec. I beg I may be exchanged as soon as possible.

(Canadian Archives, C. 679.)

Colonel Boerstler to his Father.

HEAD OF LAKE ONTARIO, UPPER CANADA,
25th June, 1813.

DEAR FATHER,—

It becomes my unfortunate lot to inform you that yesterday I was taken prisoner with a detachment under my command, amounting to about 500 men, after an engagement of about three hours. I lost not many killed, about 40 wounded, and five or six officers, myself a flesh wound of no consequence. I am on my way to Kingston. I shall write you at every opportunity. The officers under my command must say whether your son did his duty. I need only state to you that I was 17 miles from Fort George and surrounded on all sides by more than my numbers, and the enemy's force increasing while mine was constantly diminishing, ammunition nearly exhausted, men wearied with a march of ten miles without a mouthful of refreshments, then the engagement, then to fight our way back the whole distance, surrounded by woods filled by Indians. On the score of humanity I determined to capitulate, as it was extremely doubtful whether a man of us would reach Fort George. What I say above will be sufficient for you. My country must apply to those under my command.

Your son
CHARLES.

Col. Scott will please seal and forward the above.

DEAR SIR,—I pray you to believe your son is not condemned for being unfortunate.

Respectfully, Sir, your obedient servant,
W. SCOTT,

Dr. C. Boerstler,
Hagerstown, Md.
(From Niles' Register, 31st July, 1813, Vol. IV., p. 353.)

(From the Buffalo Gazette, July 29th, 1813.)

On Wednesday night last Major C. Chapin arrived in this village together with his company, escaped from the enemy on Monday preceding. The Major has given us the following narrative of the action at the Beaver Dam, &c., which we now lay before the public:

On the 23d of June last a party of the regular troops consisting of five hundred infantry and twenty light dragoons under the command of Lieut.-Colonel C. G. Boerstler, together with forty-four mounted riflemen composed of militia from the country under Major C. Chapin, were detached from the American encampment at Fort George for the purpose of cutting off the supplies of the enemy and breaking up the small encampments they were forming through the country. On the 24th, about nine miles west of Queenston they were attacked by a body of about five hundred Indians and nearly a hundred regulars, who lay concealed in the woods near the road they were passing. The attack was made upon the dragoons, who were placed in the rear. The infantry were soon brought into a position to return the enemy's fire to advantage and succeeded in driving them some distance into the woods. In a short time the Indians, having taken a circuitous route, appeared in front and opened a fire on the mounted riflemen who were stationed there. Here they met with so warm a reception that they were compelled a second time to retreat in much haste. After this every exertion was made to drive the Indians from the woods to the open ground, but without much effect. The few who were bold enough to venture out were handled so roughly that they soon returned to their lurking place. In the meantime the enemy were receiving considerable reinforcements, which at length gave them a great superiority. A retreat for a short distance was ordered and effected with very little loss.

The Indians soon made their appearance on our right and left and the regulars and militia in front. Our troops were formed into close columns for the purpose of opening for themselves a way through the enemy with their bayonets. At this juncture a British officer rode up and demanded the surrender of the American party. The demand he said was to prevent the further effusion of blood. He asserted upon his honor and declared in the most solemn manner that the British regular force was double that of the American and that the Indians were seven hundred in number. Lieut.-Colonel Boerstler, under a belief of these facts and thinking it impracticable to get off the wounded whom he was unwilling to abandon to the mercy of the savages, and deeming it extremely uncertain whether a retreat could be effected, thought proper to agree to terms of capitulation, which were at length signed by himself on the one part and Lieut.-Colonel Bisshop on the other. By these it was stipulated that the wounded should be taken good care of, the officers permitted to retain their side arms, private property to be respected and the militia paroled and permitted to return home immediately.

The articles of capitulation were no sooner signed than they were violated. The Indians immediately commenced their depredations and plundered the officers of their side arms. The soldiers, too, were stripped of every article of clothing to which the savages took a fancy, such as hats, coats, shoes, &c. It is impossible to give any correct account of the killed and wounded, as the enemy did not furnish a list. The loss of the enemy is supposed to be much greater than ours. Between thirty and forty Indians were counted that lay dead on the field. From their known practice of carrying off their killed and wounded it is believed they must have suffered severely.

The regular troops were in a few days sent to Kingston, from whence it is probable they have proceeded to Quebec. Major Chapin and his corps was detained under guard at the head of Lake Ontario and no attention paid to the article of capitulation which provided for their being paroled.

On the 12th instant they were ordered down the lake to Kingston, for which place they were embarked in two boats, accompanied by a guard of fifteen men, under command of a lieutenant. Thirteen of the men with the lieutenant were stationed in the forward boat with Major Chapin and the other officers, while the remaining two, (a sergeant and one man,) took the direction of the other boat, which contained the soldiers.

An agreement had been entered into previous to their departure of seizing the first opportunity that offered to regain their liberty, which they determined to effect or die in the attempt. When they were within about twelve miles of York the boat, which was filled with the prisoners, was moved by them alongside the other under pretence of taking something to drink. The signal being given they sprang upon the guard, who little expected such a manoeuvre, and in a short time disarmed them and gained possession of the boats.

They immediately altered their course from Kingston to Fort Niagara, and after rowing hard for most of the night and escaping with difficulty from one of the enemy's schooners, which gave them chase, arrived in safety with their prisoners at the American garrison.

When the Major and his company arrived in this village they were welcomed with suitable demonstrations of public feeling.

(File in Buffalo Public Library.)

From the Journal of Major Isaac Roach, Published in the Pennsylvania Magazine of History and Biography, July, 1893.

About the 10th of May a council of general officers was called, when it was asked by General Dearborn: "Is it expedient that we attack the enemy?" "Yes," was the unanimous reply from Generals Lewis, Chandler, Boyd and Winder and Quartermaster-General Swartwout. "Then we do attack," said General Dearborn, and the council dismissed. Nothing was done on our part for two weeks except the issuing of orders and counterorders: at one time resigning the command to General Lewis and the same hour ordering the internal arrangement of the division until confidence in our commander was very much diminished. Not wishing to go into action with the raw recruits of the 23d Infantry, I volunteered as an aid to my old friend Col. M. Porter, in command of the artillery, and was offered the appointment of aid to Brig.-General Winder. But I preferred going to the attack of Fort George with Col. Scott, who was appointed to command the advance, and although the 2d Artillery to compose the advance was to do duty as infantry, I as captain of infantry was permitted to join it with a light field piece. This was quite a compliment from the Colonel commanding and it was followed by Towson and Biddle, Hindman and others, saying: "Take what men you want for your gun from our companies." On the night of the 24th, whilst I was yet remaining with Col. Porter on the right bank of Niagara, where his command having in Fort Niagara 6 12-prs., 2 nines, some 6s and a mortar; Battery No. 2 at the graveyard, one 12-pr. and a mortar; No. 3, Lt. Murdock, 2 6-prs.; No. 4 or Salt Battery, named from furnishing it with barrels of salt covered with earth, 2 beautiful 18-prs., called rifles, 2 6-prs., 2 8-in. French howitzers and two 8-inch mortars—here we had Col. Porter, Capt Totten of the engineers, Capt. Archer and myself; No. 5, Lt. Davis, 2 12-prs.; No. 6 or Fox Point, Captain Gates, 2 12-prs.,—these batteries forming a crescent to the enemy's works, distant about 700 yards.

On the night of the 24th, when some of our boats were sent down from 5-Mile Meadows by Major Van De Venter, Directing Quartermaster General, the enemy fired on them, when Col. Porter opened his battery on Fort George for about two hours. The British were now certain we were coming, but no orders for embarkation yet, no enquiry from headquarters, 4 miles off, to know why we fired. Next morning, May 25th, Col. Porter again opened all his batteries with hot shot and in one hour we had burnt the enemy's large blockhouse in Fort George, and by 8 a. m. we had burnt four large blockhouses inside and three storehouses outside their works. But one building remained and Col. Porter directed me to proceed to headquarters and report to General Dearborn our operations. It was said the old General had not been seen to smile for a week previous but he was delighted to hear what we had done. I returned to Col. Porter with instructions for him to use his own discretion in burning the remaining buildings in Fort George.

Now the venerable Col. Porter had from the first persisted, and even swore that we could not burn a building at that distance, because when he was at Fort Mifflin in the Revolution the British fired heated shot for a week but could burn nothing. Our officers persuaded the Colonel and he said to the officers of the battery near him: "Load all the guns and I will give you one hour to burn the blockhouse." He gave the signal with his gold-headed cane. Bang went the shot and in less than ten minutes by my watch the blockhouse was on fire. The old Colonel, leaning on his cane with both hands, jumped off the ground, swearing he could set the world on fire, and said to me: "Stop the firing and let us go in to breakfast."

I would here remark that altho' the British engineers and artillery officers should have been so much our superiors, our shot and shell did double the execution. Not one of their shells burst in our battery, whilst in Fort George we could see our shells burst in the most desirable places and the weather boards of the buildings frequently flying when they burst.

On the 27th May, 1813, before daylight, we embarked to attack Fort George, and I was attached to Col. Scott's advance with a light piece of artillery. I was shot in the right arm, and before night we were in quiet possession of Fort George.

In the landing of our advance, 650 strong, after ascending the bank, which was a soft sandy soil, we formed in good order with my "grasshopper artillery" on the left. The enemy now charged and drove us off the bank where the officers of the old Second succeeded in making a stand, and with the bank for a cover opened a severe fire on the enemy. They lost in killed and wounded nearly 300, and we only one-third the number. This shows the advantage which troops of inferior numbers may find in taking a position such as the above or covered by the edge of a ravine. Brushwood, a wall or even a post and rail fence affords shelter, gives confidence to undisciplined men and disguises your actual number from a stronger enemy.

When we took possession of Fort George I had evidence enough of the effect of heated shot and shells. Every building had been burnt and even the fire engine entirely destroyed; indeed everything seemed destroyed or scattered in fragments. Every few yards was the mark of a shell and the ploughing up of our heavy shot. Nothing was saved but those articles placed in detached magazines in the ramparts. I would suggest several small magazines in a garrison, to divide the risk of explosion as well as to facilitate the serving of batteries in action.

I took up my quarters in Fort George with my veteran friend Porter, who was promoted to be a Brigadier-General, and being wounded I did not join my regiment for several weeks, but remained with my artillery friends in Fort George.

From the confusion in crossing, marching and countermarching, there was some difficulty in obtaining my company, owing to my promotion and some others. Many of the first lieutenants of infantry resigned and left the army, but an order from General Armstrong accepting all their resignations soon stopped the affair, and about the 20th [June ?] I obtained a full company in the 23d Infantry, and tho' unable to do duty proceeded to clothe and discipline my company, who, altho' now in the enemy's country, were destitute of both.

From the day of taking Fort George there had been a constant marching and countermarching of our troops, and either owing to the ill-health or age of General Dearborn it must have been evident to the enemy we wanted discipline. Almost every night we were kept under arms, and for weeks it rained very hard, until more than half our men were on the sick list. Indeed for several nights I have known the officers generally to have to turn out with muskets to patrol. General Dearborn was sick and unable to command, and yet he would not permit General Lewis to do so, who was in everything his superior.

It was the practice to send every day or two some of the battalions into the country to reconnoitre the enemy, who had taken a very strong position at Burlington Heights, and amongst the applicants for command was Col. Boerstler, commanding the 14th Infantry, who had served the year before on the Niagara with but little credit.

On the afternoon of June 23d, 1813, I was engaged in issuing clothing to my men, which I had obtained by the friendship of Col. Christie of the 13th infantry. Captain Horatio Armstrong, son of my good friend the General, had been relieved from guard and was sleeping in my tent when the adjutant, Lieutenant Burr, came in saying Captain Armstrong was detailed for command. Knowing the hard duty of our captains at that time I volunteered to go in his place, tho' I could scarcely draw my sword. In less than an hour I marched my company to the 2d Brigade. My friend, Captain McChesney of the 6th, who had been with me in 1812 at the battle of Queenston, joined at this moment and Captain McDowell of the light artillery. In a few minutes the 14th Infantry appeared and then their Colonel, Boerstler, who mounted and took command. My old friends, General Porter, Towson, Hindman, Doctor Near and Captain Totten were standing in the rear of my company to see me off, and all knew we had no confidence in the Colonel of the 14th.

I stepped to the rear and handing my pocket book to Major Hindman said: "I have no doubt we shall get broken heads before we return, and if so send my trunk and pocketbook to my family." My opinion of Colonel Boerstler was verified. He was totally unfit to command.

We moved off to Queenston where we halted that night, and next morning to the road through St. Davids and to the Beaver Dams. The road now became bad and our men were much fatigued. The column was in files—Chapin's 40 volunteers in front; next, 14th Infantry, and then Captain McDowell's light artillery company; then Captain McChesney's 6th Infantry; then Roach's 23d Infantry, and sixteen men of Burn's Light Dragoons, under Cornet Bend, forming a rear guard.

The column was halted to bring in a few men of the Canadian Embodied Militia, and the dragoons were close to my company. A soldier said, "The Indians!" and on turning to the rear I observed a large and close body of Indians moving rapidly across the road. I instantly wheeled my company into platoons and moved on the enemy, the dragoons charging them. As soon as the dragoons were close up with them the Indians fired a smart volley. The cavalry horses wheeled round and came plunging thro' the right of my platoons, knocking down and breaking about one-third of each platoon. I quickly formed in line and fired on the enemy, who broke from the road and took to the woods on each side. On the left of our line of march were four cultivated fields and a farm house, but in front and rear and right a close woods. At the moment the Indians broke Col. Boerstler rode up and ordered me to file my company into the open field, which bro't me into a close fire with that part of the Indians which had taken post in the woods. Captain McDowell now opened a 12-pounder down the road on which we had advanced. I pulled out my watch and it wanted 15 minutes of 9 a. m. Captain McChesney now took post on my right and the main body of Indians, about 300, commenced a destructive fire on our two companies, a smaller part attacking the troops which continued in the road. I noticed how useless the fire of artillery was and requested Major Taylor to have the pieces depressed, showing him how Captain McDowell was cutting off the upper limbs of the trees.

All this time I saw but one red coat, but the Indians behaved with uncommon bravery, several times dashing out of the woods to within 30 or 40 yards, as tho' confident of their numbers; they would close on us and old McChesney and myself were left to take care of ourselves. My men behaved very well. They had nearly emptied their cartridge boxes. Ammunition was bro't up and while they were firing my Lieutenant Griswold assisted me in filling up the boxes, the musicians being engaged in carrying the wounded to the rear to prevent their falling into the hands of the Indians when we should move. It is also an advantage to remove from the line the wounded, to prevent making an impression on the others. Not one of my men, I believe, had ever been in a fight; my lieutenant was direct from West Point Academy, yet he was cool and attentive.

From the division of the enemy into two parties our detachment became divided for more than an hour. Several movements were now made by Col. Boerstler to draw the Indians from the woods, but ineffectually. The enemy were now reinforcing, as we could observe, and now was the moment to have made a retreat. But the Colonel said that would never do, as we had beaten the enemy, and his orders were positive to proceed to Decou's house, which was yet 3 miles in advance.

The fire of the enemy was slackened, but he was busy in getting his Indians on our rear. Another attempt was made to draw him from cover and we moved to a by-road near the farm house. Not being able to draw him out our sapient Colonel now thought of looking towards retreat. A column of platoons was formed in a road perpendicular to the main road, placing the 14th in front, next artillery, then the waggons with wounded, then McChesney and last, in the post of honor, my company. Now, no doubt it was Col. Boerstler's object to retain his own regiment without loss, but it was decided injustice to compel my company to remain in the rear-guard so long as he did, and Captain McChesney, who ranked all of us, was remonstrating against the injustice done him, and as he was badly wounded in the wrist we both were cross enough. We encouraged our men for a charge thro' the woods and a retreating fight, and at the moment we expected the order to move on the enemy Major Taylor whispered me that he feared our Colonel was frightened, as a flag was received from the enemy and in another half hour Col. Boerstler agreed to surrender his command, reporting to the Government that he held a council of his officers, which was not true, as Major Taylor, McChesney and myself knew nothing of it.

It was now five minutes past twelve o'clock, M. and a few of Dr. Chapin's Forty Thieves, having deserted early in the action, reported to General Dearborn that Col. Boerstler had surrendered without firing a musket, and this the General reported to the Government. We were engaged three hours; twice my cartridge boxes were filled and expended. But fighting is not the hardest part of a soldier's life. Now came the tug of war. We were surrendered without discretion to a detachment of about 80 British regulars under Lieut. FitzGibbon, about 200 embodied militia under Lieutenant-Colonel DeHaren, who were equal to regulars, and a body of North-Western Indians, about 550 in number, who had that morning arrived from the upper country under the direction of Kerr, the Indian agent. Lieutenant-Colonel Bisshopp with 120 men joined them at the moment of surrender and took the command. But instead of being received by the British we were surrounded by the Indians, who commenced their business of plundering the officers. I slipped my sword under my coat in hopes to save it, but one Indian demanded it while another very significantly made a flourish of his gun over my head and took my sword.

I believe our wise Colonel now saw the snare he was in when too late, and how little dependence can at any time be placed on the promises of a British army officer. Col. Boerstler surrendered on condition that his wounded should be protected, his officers retain their side arms and be paroled to return to Fort George immediately. Not one item of this was ever complied with. Nearly all our wounded were killed by the Indians that night. The officers were marched 7 miles to Col. Bisshopp's quarters thro' various parties of Indians and protected by 2 officers and 2 men, who were more afraid and less accustomed to the Indians than ourselves. My time was occupied in attending to my friend McChesney, whose wound was very painful, as the ball passed through the wrist joint and cut off the blood vessel.

When he was shot, being near me, I had placed my field tourniquet on his arm, but he continued to bleed all that night and when quartered for the night we were surrounded by savages intoxicated by the liquor found in our waggons. I barricaded the door and armed with McChesney's sword I watched him all night. At one time I expected the Indians to break into our room, as they were in the house, and not thinking my comrade would live till morning, as his arm continued bleeding and he did not expect to live; but in the morning the bleeding stopped and his arm was saved, as the British were to have taken it off in the morning. Next day, the 25th, we were taken to headquarters at Burlington Heights and were again marched through several parties of Indians and insulted and plundered, the officers having us in charge not daring to oppose them.

Report of a Court of Enquiry on the Conduct of Lieut.-Colonel Boerstler.

BALTIMORE, 17th February, 1815.

The court met pursuant to adjournment.

The court having heard and considered the testimony adduced in this case, have the honor to report to the Honorable the Secretary of War the following statement of facts:

That on the 23d day of June, 1813, a detachment of the army of the United States, stationed at Fort George in Upper Canada, was ordered to proceed against an advanced post of the enemy at DeCoo's stone house. That a detail of 575 men in proportions of infantry, artillery, dragoons and riflemen, accompanied by a party of mounted gun-men under Captain Chapin, were ordered for the expedition, and that Lieut.-Colonel Charles G. Boerstler of the 14th Infantry was selected for the command; the riflemen were not furnished according to the detail and the expedition proceeded without them.

The infantry carried in their boxes thirty-two rounds of musket ball cartridges, and the ammunition waggon contained a reserve of 5,000 or 6,000 rounds.

The artillery, two field pieces, was well supplied with fixed ammunition of round and canister shot.

The expedition was accompanied by two four-horse waggons carrying the ammunition and provisions, without entrenching tools, and was not followed by any detachment on which it could fall back in the event of disaster. It was ordered to march upon the Queenston and St. Davids road and return upon the same route.

No copy of the commanding General's order now remains. The book in which it was entered and the original have both been destroyed by the casualties of war, but the object of the expedition is proved to have been "to batter down DeCoo's stone house, said to be fortified and garrisoned by a company of regulars and 60 or 100 Indians, and capture or dislodge the enemy stationed there."

On the same day, that is on the 23d June, 1813, the picquets of the American army covered ground to the extent of two miles in front of Fort George and no more.

And the advanced posts of the enemy, three in number, were:

1. At St. Catharines on the lake road, nine and a half miles from Fort George, and deemed the strongest. Lieut.-Colonel DeHaren commanding.

2. At Twenty Mile Creek, sixteen and a half miles from Fort George, Lieut.-Colonel Bisshopp commanding.

3. At DeCoo's stone house, seventeen and a half miles from Fort George, *via* Queenston and Sixteen *via* St. Catharines, Lieutenant FitzGibbon commanding; and in advance of this post, and one and one-half miles from it and near a road leading to it, a camp of 450 or 500 Indians, of which nothing had been known.

A plan of the ground is submitted to show the relative position of these posts; how they supported each other at a distance of six or seven miles, lying in the form of a triangle, and the point to be attacked the most distant of the three.

The intermediate country between the two armies was in general covered with thick wood.

No force was sent out to amuse or divert Lieut.-Colonels De-Haren and Bisshop while the post at DeCoo's should be attacked. A simultaneous movement had been planned against St. Catharines, (Lieut.-Colonel DeHaren,) but was not executed.

The expedition under Lieut.-Colonel Boerstler appears to have been founded upon information derived from Captain Chapin. His information is proved to have been erroneous.

The guide furnished to conduct the expedition was the same Captain Chapin, and at nine or ten miles from Fort George he was, or appeared to be, ignorant of the roads. Lieut.-Colonel Boerstler took an inhabitant of the country and compelled him to become the guide.

The detachment was ordered to lay at Queenston on the night of the 23d and march early the next morning. It did so, laying upon its arms in silence, without lights, and having taken precautions to avoid surprise and for preventing the country people from carrying intelligence to the enemy.

On the march, advance and rear guards, with flankers from each side, were kept constantly out. Captain Chapin's mounted men formed the advanced guards and frequently pushed out patrols in search of discoveries.

Between eight and nine o'clock on the morning of the 24th, at a place called the Beaver Dams, a mile and a half in advance of DeCoo's, the enemy's Indians were first discovered, issuing from the woods in rear of the detachment and moving across the road upon which it had marched. The action commenced immediately, and the column quickly forming into two lines fought at the same time to the front and rear. Lieut.-Colonel Boerstler was at the head of the first and Major Taylor at the head of the second.

The action continued upwards of three hours. The American troops contended with a superior force of Indians, British regulars and Provincials. Several changes of position, rendered necessary by circumstances, had been executed in an orderly and military manner and every officer was at the head of his command, and every company did its duty, a majority of the mounted gun-men and their commander excepted.

But the ammunition had been nearly exhausted; all the boxes had been exhausted of their cartridges, replenished from the waggon and again nearly exhausted; the waggon itself was emptied or nearly so; the artillery had but two or three rounds of canister and a small number of round shot remaining. The heat of the day was oppressive, and the men exhausted with the length of the action and the march in the morning.

Seventy or eighty of the detachment were killed or wounded. Lieut.-Colonel Boerstler, Captain Machesney, Captain Cummings and Lieutenants Marshall and Randall were among the latter.

About noon Lieut.-Colonel DeHaren arrived from St. Catharines and brought with him 120 infantry, 25 or 30 dragoons and some Provincials.

The enemy occupied in force the road upon which the detachment had marched. Lieut.-Colonel Boerstler collected the effectives of his command, formed them into column and gave in person his orders and an explanation of his object, "to clear the road by a charge, and retreat to Fort George." His force under arms was diminished by one-third, not altogether by death and wounds but partly by the various causes which conspire to thin the ranks of all troops during an engagement. All the wounded were brought to the centre of the column and there were but two waggons to receive them.

When the column was ready to be put in motion a British officer advanced and demanded its surrender. The demand was instantly and decisively rejected by Colonel Boerstler; the officer retired and presently returned with a renewal of the demand, stating the great superiority of force, and proposing that an American officer be sent to view them. Lieutenant Kearney of the 14th infantry was accordingly sent, but a senior officer having come upon the ground refused to permit the examination, but renewed the demand for a surrender. It was added that the American wounded could then be protected, but if the action recommenced they, (the British officers,) could not be responsible for the conduct of the Indians.

Lieut.-Colonel Boerstler referred to the officers about him for their opinion. They decided to surrender if honorable terms could be had, and the detachment was accordingly surrendered prisoners of war, the officers retaining their horses, arms and baggage.

The force of the enemy at the time of the surrender amounted to 700 or 800 men, comprising between 450 and 500 Indians, about 300 regulars and Provincial infantry, 25 or 30 dragoons and a small

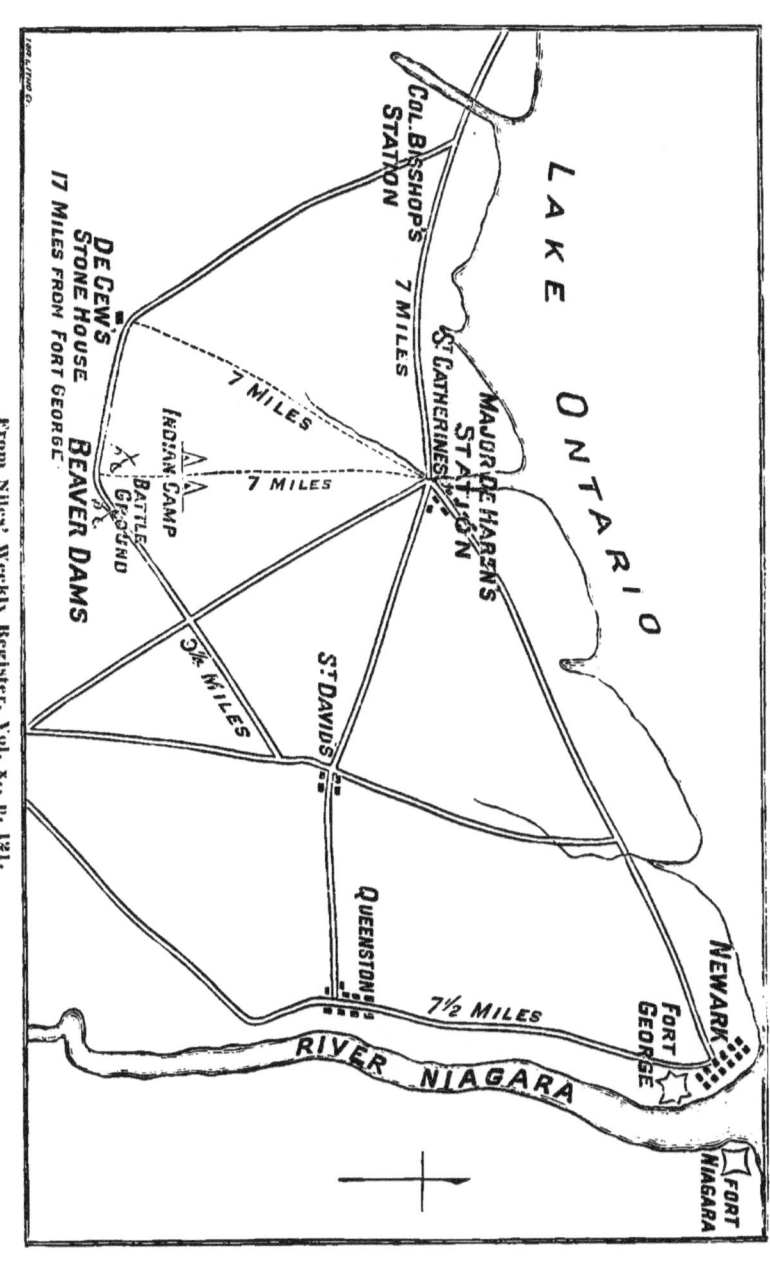

number of fencibles, exclusive of 250 infantry following Lieut.-Colonel Bisshopp from Twenty Mile Creek and arrived near the ground at the close of the action.

And it does not appear, but the contrary is proved, (so far as a negative can be proved,) that Lieut.-Colonel Boerstler sent any messenger to Fort George to demand reinforcements and to say that he would maintain his ground till they arrived.

Whereupon the court respectfully submit to the Honorable the Secretary of War the following opinion:

That the march of the detachment from Fort George to the Beaver Dams on the 23d and 24th June, 1813, under the command of Lieut-Colonel Boerstler, was made in an orderly, vigilant and military manner.

That the personal deportment of Lieut.-Colonel Boerstler in the action which followed was that of a brave, zealous and deliberate officer, and the conduct of the regular officers and men under his command was equally honorable to themselves and to their country.

That a retreat from the field after the force of the enemy had been ascertained could not be justified on any military principle, and if attempted in column must have exposed the men to certain death in their ranks, with very little means of resistance: if by dispersion the immediate massacre of the wounded and the slaughter in detail of a multitude of exhausted and tired fugitives must have been the inevitable consequences.

That the surrender was justified by existing circumstances, and that the misfortune of the day is not to be ascribed to Lieut.-Colonel Boerstler or the detachment under his command.

And the Court is unanimous in the expression of this opinion and foregoing report of facts.

    JAMES P. PRESTON,
        Colonel 23d Infantry, President.
    LEWIS B. WILLIS,
        Captain 12th Infantry, Recorder.

Extract from the Deposition of Major-General Lewis.

To the sixth and seventh interrogations this deponent answers:

That he was frequently pressed to send a detachment to the vicinity of Beaver Dams during the latter days of his command at Fort George, which he always resisted because the position and means of the enemy enabled him to reinforce with greater facility than the American army could. So strong were these impressions on the mind of this deponent that when he quitted that command he earnestly advised the gentleman on whom it devolved to resist the youthful, ardent spirits which would probably beset him on the subject, assuring him that any detachment sent on that service, unless very powerful, would probably be sacrificed, and be perhaps thereby disenabled to take possession of the Heights when the necessary transportation could be furnished, which this deponent was of opinion ought to be done.

(From Niles' Register, Vol. X., pp. 119-20.)

Brigadier-General William Bennett to Governor Tompkins.

PHELPS, June 26, 1813.

Sir,—On the evening of the 15th inst. I received information by express that the enemy had landed at the Genesee River and committed some depredations and were steering for Sodus Bay, where considerable public property was stored. I ordered out Lieut.-Colonel Swift's regiment and part of Major Granger's rifle battalion, who marched on Wednesday. Captain Dorsey's company of exempts marched at the same time and under my direction removed the public property to the safest place which time and the country afforded, and I dismissed the troops on Saturday morning. On the evening of Sunday an express arrived that the enemy's fleet had anchored off Sodus and were preparing to land. I immediately ordered those who had not proceeded with me to return and despatched an officer for the remainder. But the enemy had effected a landing before more than 40 or 50 men arrived, who, though provided only with a few cartridges, engaged with them, but owing to the darkness of the night and the superior force of the enemy were obliged to fall back to the place where the stores were secreted. We had four men wounded, one since dead. The enemy, as I am informed by the officer of the flag, on the next day had 7 men killed. In the meantime I had ordered out Lieut.-Colonel Howell's regiment, Major Rogers' battalion and Captain Rea's company of artillery, who arrived on the two following days. A number of volunteers arrived at the same time, part from Colonel Dobbin's regiment, Seneca county. On Sunday morning they set fire to and destroyed six buildings and soon after embarked and left the shore, taking with them, as I am informed by Mr. Merril, about 230 barrels of flour, a few barrels of whiskey and pork, principally private property, and then demanded the surrender of the public property and a deserter, whom they would exchange for one they had taken along shore, which was immediately refused. I ordered Lieut.-Colonel Howell's regiment and Major Rogers' battalion to Pultneyville, whither the enemy steered their course, and had previously ordered part of Lieut.-Colonel Colt's to Sodus and dismissed

Colonel Swift's, they having been on duty for some time. The property saved to the public consists of about 800 barrels of flour and pork and is now sufficiently secured from the enemy, having ordered a guard to remain and protect it. The returns of the number of men have not yet been made, but will be immediately attended to and sent to Your Excellency.

The season of the year now is so important to farmers, who compose the greater part of our country, has proved to be such a loss to those ordered out by leaving their business, that some provision in this case will be necessary to be made, and for the teams that removed the public property. The alacrity with which the *citizen soldiers* obeyed the call of their country in its defence cannot be too highly commended. The enemy, too well aware of the patriotism of our citizens, left their situation without effecting their greatest purpose, the taking or destruction of our stores, before 150 men had arrived.

(Tompkins Papers, Vol. VIII., pp. 446-8, New York State Library.)

Speech of the Indians.

FORTY MILE CREEK, IN CAMP, June (26 ?), 1813.

We, the Six Nations and the Seven Nations, thirteen in all, will now answer: We were promised in old times that whatever we took from the enemy we should be paid for by the King. We hope the King will not forget his promise, and satisfy us for what we took the other day (at the Beaver Dams.) We were accustomed to receive pay for prisoners. We have been repeatedly told not to take scalps.

BROTHER,—We have listened to your words and the Seven Nations have done the same. Perhaps the Chippewas have taken some.

BROTHER,—The King has told us that the Americans were the aggressors, that he could not keep off the war, and that he was determined to have the old French line and not to let them come so near us again. Our Western brethren have been encouraged to come forward with the promise of preserving their country for them, or not to make peace until you had those lines. The Ohio is their boundary.

BROTHER,—The Canada Indians have lands within the old lines; they hope you will not forget them. We wish to have a paper from you to say each nation will be paid. You have sent everywhere, you tell us, for shoes. You see the state we are in. We cannot go into the woods as we are, barefooted. When our people were at Detroit last summer a Shawanese chief asked the late General Brock what was to become of the things taken, and he told him that he had taken the words out of his mouth—that the Six Nations would be paid in money at Niagara and the Western Nations here. We shall see if what we were promised will be done. We understand complaints have been made of our bad treatment of the farmers. We have moved our families back and the white people are using us in the same way. We suppose what we take we are much in need of and we have no money to pay.

BROTHER,—If any of the Nations lose their men will their families be taken care of and not allowed to want? If any get wounded will they be taken care of?

BROTHER,—We suppose you wish to know whether we mean to turn our faces towards the enemy. The Seven Nations, except a few who go with the wounded, will go back. It is the same with the Six Nations, but we would be glad to know when you mean to strike at Niagara so we might collect all our forces in time.

(From the MSS. Letterbook of Colonel Claus.)

General Order.

KINGSTON, 26th June, 1813.

G. O.

On the arrival of the leading division of the DeWatteville Regiment the 2d Battalion of the 41st is to proceed by water to Prescott. The light company is to remain with the light battalion.

The detachment of the 100th Regiment is to be relieved at Prescott by two complete battalion companies of the fourth division of the Regiment DeWatteville, a Major of the corps to command this detachment.

EDWARD BAYNES,
A. G.

Garrison Order.

KINGSTON, 26th June, 1813.

(No. 2.)

One captain, two subalterns, one sergeant and 11 privates, 104th Regiment, will embark to-morrow and proceed and join their regiment with the army under Brigadier-General Vincent. The Commissary will issue six days field rations to the above party.

RICHARD LEONARD,
B. M.

Captain Leonard, 104th Regiment, having been selected for promotion is to be permitted to resign his appointment as Major of Brigade, and the Commander of the Forces having approved of the same, his appointment is to cease from to-day.

EDWARD BAYNES,
Adjutant General.

Hon. Wm. Dummer Powell to Sir George Prevost.

YORK, 28th June, 1813.

Private.

SIR,—Your Excellency's commands of the 21st instant receive the earliest attention; there can be no doubt that, if required, provision of beef and flour for the support of an army short of 2000 men can be furnished from the country depending for a market on this place. The scarcity of salt is such that little dependence can be had on a regular supply of salt pork, and the issue of fresh pork would probably be injurious to the health of the soldiers. There will be abundance of forage; large crops of rye have been raised for the purpose of distillation, which the first act of Gen. DeRottenburg's administration has prohibited. This grain affords a wholesome food both for man and horse, and will allow a larger proportion of wheat, flour and oats to be offered to the commissary.

The accommodation for troops is very little diminished, the two block houses being the only soldiers' quarters destroyed. There is timber on the ground prepared for building ways and wharf for the ship, to throw up a coarse but warm cover for a great many men at little expense. The town could not billet a thousand men without great inconvenience.

The nature of our population is sufficiently known to Your Excellency. The march of troops through the country has occasioned an obvious change in the manners and language of the people, and there can be no doubt that the permanent station of a body of troops here could have an excellent effect in confirming the loyal and overawing the disaffected, especially if a party of dragoons could occasionally make excursions through the country.

It is an invidious task to give opinions on individual character, but Your Excellency's wish is a command.

The greater or less energy of public functionaries will ever take its tone from the head. In the absence of General DeRottenburg we should not expect anything decisive in the civil administration if the measures depended on every individual, but the President has authorized the Council to deliberate any propositions supposed to be important without waiting for a special reference, so that little delay need interpose between the necessity for any vigorous proceeding and its sanction. I think I may assure Your Excellency that under this arrangement there will be no display of weakness. The sheriff is a man of personal intrepidity but extremely cautious of responsibility. Our police is weak, as must be the case where a numerous body of individuals have an equal voice.

Major Allan of the militia, although on parole, fulfils with promptitude and decision the duties of governmental agent at this place.

The Commissary is laborious and well acquainted with the resources of the country, but the habits of his department restrain in some degree the energy of personal character by its rigid regulations to ensure economy.

The Secretary of the Province is a distressed man, who has no duties to perform which call for energy. The same may be said of the Surveyor General.

The public mind, as far as I am able to judge, is depressed by the alternate apprehension of preserving or losing the superiority on the lake. There seems to be but one opinion as to keeping this port, that it depends on the fleet, and there is some regret expressed that it became necessary for the Commodore to destroy the town of Sodus from the apprehension that this place may be the subject of retaliation.

In the event of any serious disaster to His Majesty's arms little reliance is to be had on the power of the well disposed to repress and keep down the turbulence of the disaffected, who are very numerous.

I have replied to the several paragraphs of Your Excellency's letter with the frankness of a single mind which takes everything at the letter. Should I have mistaken Your Excellency's wish and wandered from its object, I assure myself that it will be excused as proceeding from an implicit obedience to your supposed desire by

Your Excellency's faithful and devoted servant,

WM. DUMMER POWELL,

(Canadian Archives, C. 679, p. 148.)

General Order.

Headquarters, KINGSTON, 28th June, 1813.

G. O.

The Commander of the Forces has great satisfaction in announcing to the army that a report has just been received from Brigadier-General Vincent of a most judicious and spirited exploit achieved on the 24th inst. by a small detachment of the 49th Regiment, amounting to 46 rank and file under Lieut. FitzGibbon, and a band of Indian warriors, which terminated in the defeat and capture of a considerable detachment of the American regular army under the command of Lieut.-Colonel Boerstler of the 14th United States Regiment, after sustaining considerable loss.

Lieut. FitzGibbon, on reconnoitering the enemy's position and finding him too numerous to oppose with his small force, with great presence of mind kept him in check while he sent and summoned him to surrender in the name of Major DeHaren, and which he was fortunately able to enforce by the prompt and timely arrival of the light division under that officer, by whose vigorous co-operation the capture of the enemy's force, consisting of one lieutenant-colonel; one major, six captains, fifteen inferior officers, twenty-five sergeants, two drummers, 462 rank and file, one 12-pounder and one 6-pounder field piece and a stand of colors was effected on the field.

Not a single British soldier is reported to have fallen on this occasion. The Indian warriors behaved with much steadiness and courage, and His Excellency has much satisfaction in learning that they conducted themselves with humanity and forbearance towards the prisoners after the action.

EDWARD BAYNES,
A. G., N. A.

General Order.

G. O. Headquarters, KINGSTON, 28th June, 1813.

The remaining detachments of the Royal Scots and 104th Regiment are to embark to-morrow in batteaux for the head of the Bay of Quinte and to proceed to join the Division of the Centre. All the men of the 8th or King's sufficiently recovered for field service are to be sent by this opportunity.

The mounted veterans and the remainder of Captain Coleman's troop of light dragoons are to march to-morrow at day break to join the Centre Division of the army.

EDWARD BAYNES,
A. G.

Garrison Orders.

ADJUTANT-GENERAL'S OFFICE,
Headquarters, KINGSTON, 28th June, 1813.

The detachment of the Tenth Royal Veteran Battalion is to be held in readiness to proceed to William Henry in the returning batteaux, for which the Deputy Quartermaster General will make the necessary distribution after the departure of the Second Battalion, 41st Regiment.

Captain F. Kishlingen of the Regiment DeWatteville is appointed Brigade Major to the forces serving in the left division of the Army of Upper Canada.

Captain Jackson, R. A., is directed to proceed to Prescott and to assume the general superintendence of the Royal Artillery on the line of communication under the command of Lieut.-Colonel Pearson. Lieut. Jones, R. A., is to proceed to Kingston.

EDWARD BAYNES,
Adjutant General.

Sir James Yeo to Hon. John Wilson Croker.

His Majesty's Ship *Wolfe*, at KINGSTON,
UPPER CANADA, the 29th June, 1813.

(No. 5.)

SIR,—I have the honour to inform you, for the information of the Lords Commissioners of the Admiralty, that on the 3d instant I sailed with His Majesty's squadron under my command from this port to co-operate with our army at the head of the lake and annoy the enemy by intercepting all supplies going to his army, and thereby oblige his squadron to come out for its protection.

At daylight, on the 8th, the enemy's camp was discovered close to us at 40 Mile Creek; it being calm, the large vessels could not get in, but the *Beresford*, Captain Spilsbury, the *Sir Sidney Smith*, Lieut. Majoribanks and the gunboats under the orders of Lieutenant Anthony, (first of this ship,) succeeded in getting close under the enemy's batteries, and by a sharp and well-directed fire soon obliged him to make a precipitate retreat, leaving all his camp equipage, provisions, stores, etc., behind, which fell into our hands. The *Beresford* also captured all his batteaux laden with stores, etc. Our troops immediately occupied the post. I then proceeded along shore to the westward of the enemy's camp, leaving our army in his front. On the 13th we captured two schooners and some boats going to the enemy with supplies. By them I received information that there was a depot of provisions at Genesee River. I accordingly proceeded off that river, landed some seamen and brought off all the provisions found in the government stores, as also a sloop laden with grain for the army. On the 19th I anchored off the Great Sodus, landed a party of the 1st Regiment or Royal Scots and took off six hundred barrels of flour and pork which had arrived there for their army. Yesterday I returned to this anchorage to victual and refit the squadron.

(Admiralty Papers, Canadian Archives, M., 389-6, p. 29.)

Brigadier-General Procter to Captain McDouall.

SANDWICH, June 29th, 1813.

MY DEAR SIR:—

I have the pleasure to inform you of the arrival of Mr. R. Dickson at Mackinac on the 11th inst., but whether he has gone to your aid or is coming here direct I do not know. Seventy-two head of cattle have been brought here by Mr. Grant, who was sent by General Vincent for that purpose. Some effort must be shortly made to procure an adequate supply of meat, which cannot be done without troops, as at present our Indian force is not a disposable one, tho' I look for a change which may, and I trust will, make it so. Our Indians very seldom get anything but bread. We are very much in want of Indian guns and ammunition, and also of goods. I do not like writing when I must dwell so much on wants. There is no money to be had here. There cannot be any payments to the troops even or in any of the departments if money is not regularly sent to the commissary. The *Detroit* will be launched in a fortnight, but her anchor was wanted at Kingston. We could lend her guns if she had seamen. I believe now that Captain Barclay is making some attempt on the enemy's vessels. We had purposed making an attempt with all our means, but I suppose he saw and learned that an immediate attempt was most eligible. We sent to Captain Derenzy* and changed his route to Long Point, where the others had better be sent also.

I may expect him to lose some men—I hope none of the staff. We are anxiously looking now in every direction. There must have been many arrivals at Quebec if we have not been very unfortunate. Mr. Grant waits. I shall write when anything interesting occurs.

(Canadian Archives, C. 679, p. 155.)

General Order.

Headquarters, KINGSTON,
Adjutant General's Office 29th June, 1813.

General Order.

At a General Court Martial held at the 40 Mile Creek on the 22d June, was arraigned Private James Gready of the 8th or King's Regiment, on the following charge :—

For deserting from Prescott to the enemy when on duty on the night of the 23d of March last, and not returning until apprehended, on or about the 7th inst., amongst the American prisoners of war taken at Stoney Creek on the 6th inst.

The Court having found the prisoner, Private James Gready, guilty of the whole crime laid to his charge, do sentence him to be shot to death at such time and place as the general officer commanding may think fit.

At a General Court Martial held at Kingston on the 26th June, 1813, was arraigned Private Terence Hunt of the 6th Regiment on the following charges :—

For deserting from the 6th Regiment of Foot from St. Johns in Lower Canada on or about the month of July, 1803.

(*Of the 41st Regiment.—Ed.)

2. For being found in arms serving with the enemy on or about the 6th of June, 1813.

Sentence.—The Court having found the prisoner, Terence Hunt, of the 6th Regiment of Foot, guilty of the crimes laid to his charge, doth therefore for the same adjudge him, the said Terence Hunt, to suffer death by being shot at such time and place as the Commander of the Forces shall be pleased to direct.

His Excellency the Commander of the Forces avails himself of this opportunity of calling the serious attention of the troops under his command to the awful consequences which, under the present circumstances of the country, must inevitably await the crime of desertion, more particularly desertion to the enemy.

His Excellency trusts that there can be found very few instances of soldiers so base and disloyal as to desert the standard of their sovereign in favour of his foes at a period when he has such powerful claims to their services in support of all that is dear and valuable to Englishmen.

The melancholy examples that are about to take place His Excellency hopes will have a due influence upon the troops under his command and at the same time convince them that no length of residence or service in a foreign country can absolve them from their allegiance to their King or secure them from the just punishment which sooner or later must attend their desertion of his cause.

His Excellency directs that the sentence of death passed upon the private of the King's Regiment and Terence Hunt, private of the 6th Regiment, be carried into execution—that on James Gready of the 8th or King's Regiment at such time and place as Major-General De Rottenburg may direct, and that upon Private Terence Hunt of the 6th Regiment be carried into execution by Brigadier-General Darroch at Kingston, and that the execution be conducted in the presence of the garrison under arms with all that awful solemnity which the occasion calls for, and at such time and place as Brigadier-General Darroch may direct.

This General Order and sentence of the Court being at the same time read to the troops and is to be inserted in the regimental books of General Orders.

By His Excellency's command,
EDWARD BAYNES,
Adjutant General.

Captain Fulton to Sir George Prevost.

Headquarters at 12 MILE CREEK, 30th June, 1813.

SIR,—Since I had the honor of last addressing Your Excellency the army, under command of General Vincent, has advanced and I now enclose you a sketch of their present position, together with a letter I received from Captain Norton, also one of the maps circulated by the American Government* and a copy of a war council held by the Indians at Forty Mile Creek.

When the Western Indians arrive, which we hope will be this evening, the whole, amounting to about five hundred, will be sent to the Four Mile Creek. This movement will totally cut off any supplies that the enemy might receive from this side the water; indeed, from everything we can learn since Colonel Boerstler's disaster they have not dared to send a patrol more than one mile from Fort George.

P. S.—General De Rottenburg arrived here late last night.

(Canadian Archives, C. 679.)

Captain R. H. Barclay to Brigadier-General Procter.

H. M. S. *Queen Charlotte*, June 29th, 1813.

SIR,—In reply to your letter requesting a statement of what is wanting to make His Majesty's squadron effective on Lake Erie, that you might transmit to His Excellency the Governor in Chief, I have to state that there is a general want of stores of every description at this post, but more especially iron for chain plates and other uses, all of which have been demanded long ago, also an abstract of former requisitions has been sent by me to hasten the supply of those things which I judged indispensably necessary.

The *Detroit* may be launched in ten days but there is no chance of her being ready for active service until a large proportion of stores and guns are sent here, and even admitting that she could be equipped there is not a seaman to put on board her. The absolute necessity of seamen being sent up is so obvious that I need hardly point it out to you. The ships are manned with a crew, part of whom cannot even speak English, none of them seamen and very few even in numbers. The enemy have two corvettes in a forward state at Presque Isle and from their resources being so contiguous I have no doubt that they will be ready to sail very soon in a much superior force than any exertion of mine can get ready to oppose them.

I have repeatedly pointed out to Commodore Sir James Yeo the manner in which the squadron under my command is manned and I have no doubt of his sending as many seamen as he can spare, but I

---

*The sketch and map enclosed by Captain Fulton have not been found.—Ed.

have little hopes of his sending a sufficient number until some method is found to get another supply of good seamen from England or Quebec. A party of twelve good shipwrights is also much wanted here. The builder represents that his present party are most ignorant of their profession and the difficulties he labors under from that circumstance must be very great. If His Excellency would cause a party to be sent here in the event of damages by action taking place they could soon be repaired and the squadron rendered effective again. At present when any repair or alteration is required, of which many are indispensably requisite from the small number of men employed, everything must stand still until that is finished. Such is the case at present, but under every disadvantageous circumstance the *Detroit* will be fully ready to receive her guns and men as soon as they are sent up.

(Canadian Archives, C. 730, pp. 27-31.)

(From the Buffalo Gazette, 29th June, 1813.)

WAR EVENTS.

On Saturday week, (19th June,) the mounted men under Major Chapin passed down to Queenston. On Sunday, (20th June,) Mr. E. Sloot of this town crossed at Black Rock with Ab. Ransom, late of this village, and proceeded for Queenston. When they had passed the foot of Lundy's Lane, (a place principally settled by the rangers who fought under Butler in the Revolution,) they were fired upon by a small party of the enemy concealed, and Ransom was made prisoner, Sloot making his escape to Queenston. For several days previous to this small parties of the enemy had been lurking about the *Lane* and were at this time supposed, from their audacity, to have been considerably reinforced. On Monday, (21st June,) a detachment of 150 infantry under Captain Myers from Fort George, with Chapin's corps marched for the Lane. When the advance came near the place where Ransom was taken they were fired upon by the enemy and Sloot was shot dead, 5 balls and a buckshot took effect. The guard retired and the enemy retreated before the infantry came up. It being apparent that the enemy had retired to draw our troops into a snare they were pursued but a short distance. N. D. Keep, belonging to Major Chapin's corps, was taken asleep by the enemy about a mile from this place. The party returned to Queenston.

On Wednesday last, (23d June,) a force marched from Fort George under command of Colonel Boerstler, consisting of 3 or 400 infantry, two pieces light artillery, 20 dragoons and about 40 men under Major Chapin and encamped at Queenston. On Thursday,

(24th June,) Colonel Boerstler marched towards the Beaver Dam. We understood from two of Chapin's men, who with four others made their escape, that an action commenced about 11 o'clock between the advance parties and continued for some time, when the enemy outflanked and surrounded our men and have very probably captured them. We know not the loss in killed but hope we may obtain some correct account this day. We learn that Joel Thorp of this town was killed at the beginning of the action.

A gentleman from Queenston states that on Wednesday last, (23d June,) a boat passed from Lewiston to Queenston with 8 persons in the boat, that when the boat landed two of the men went up the bank and were fired upon by a group of Indians, (who had concealed themselves in a barn,) and shot down. They were then dragged up the Heights of Queenston and despatched. One of the persons thus barbarously murdered is said to be Mr. George A. Tiffany of LeRoy. The other persons in the boat were made prisoners by the savages.*

P. S.—Monday evening, (28th June,) 10 o'clock p. m. Several gentlemen just from Fort George say that Colonel Boerstler had surrendered to the enemy about 500 men and 10 killed, that the picket guard at Fort George were attacked on Saturday night last, (26th June,) by the enemy, who were repulsed with loss, and that the British army were supposed to be within 3 miles of Newark—5 sail of their vessels were lying off Niagara and at Fort George, everything was in complete preparation to give the enemy a hot reception.

"LADY MURRAY" CAPTURED.

The United States armed schooner *Lady of the Lake*, under command of Lieut. Chauncey, has captured the British schooner *Lady Murray* on Lake Ontario loaded with ammunition and provisions for the British army at Burlington Bay.

The new ship *General Pike*, 32 guns, was launched at Sackett's Harbor about the 13th instant and is now undoubtedly ready for sailing.

We were misinformed last week respecting the plundering of Mr. Lay. The British officers returned a great many articles of clothing which the boats' crews had plundered.

We learn when the enemy's vessels lay near Cattaraugus, (or Canadaway,) 9 or 10 men escaped in a boat from the vessels.

The last Erie paper mentions that the British landed above that

---

*See Ducharme's narrative of this affair, p. 126—Ed.

place, killed a steer and left a half-joe* with the hide, and a written notice stating that they were not judges of cattle, but if the half-joe was not enough they would return in 2 weeks and pay the balance.

To the Editor of the Buffalo "Gazette."

FORT GEORGE, 24th June, 1813.

SIR,—You will do an act of justice by correcting a very erroneous statement of the action at Stoney Creek, which appears in your paper of last week.

I was an eye witness and engaged in the action from its commencement to its final termination. Captain Hindman is, I presume, a brave man, but the irruption of the British and Indians was so sudden that his troops were not able to form on their ground but left it before superior numbers; one of Hindman's captains immediately on the commencement of the action, his platoon having been dispersed, took the rear of the 25th Regiment and acted as file closer in that place. It is wholly incorrect that Lieut.-Colonel Milton bore a principal share in the action. Sometime after it commenced he came in contact with the enemy, but the contest was not so severe, that he lost not a single man by death. The 16th and 23d Regiments were engaged as severely as was Colonel Milton's, so were the light dragoons under that able officer Colonel Burn. But the 25th Regiment, beyond any other, was concerned in the action. That regiment was paraded even before the attack, having taken the precaution to leave its fires and take a new and commanding position, where and by this regiment the attack of the enemy was first withstood. Repeated charges of the British regulars were repulsed by its fire, and this regiment maintained its ground and was first and last in the action. The killed and wounded of the 25th Regiment was double that of all the rest of the army, 10 being killed and nearly 30 of its number wounded.

Generals Chandler and Winder were taken prisoners at the same time and towards the close of the action, merely from the accident of mistaking British troops for American. They both of them performed their duty with the utmost coolness and bravery. General Chandler's horse was shot under him in the early part of the action, after which I had the pleasure of observing him and being with him part of the time till he was taken. A braver, more industrious and excellent officer cannot be found.

(File in the Buffalo Public Library.)

---

*The Spanish coin so-called.—Ed.

From the Chiefs of the Six Nations at Alleghany to Erastus Granger.

CATTARAUGUS, 30th June, 1813.

BROTHER,—We received yours of the 22d instant two days after date, requesting us to turn out and come to Buffalo in order to aid in the present contest. We have turned out and come as far as Cattaraugus, where we are requested by the runner sent by Mr. Parrish to return home. This is twice that we have been called from our business and travelled near one hundred miles at our own expense, and leaving our business in obedience to your calls, and when we arrive here directed to return home without any explanation on the business or any reward for our trouble.

We feel ourselves injured with the treatment we receive at your hands and shall return home to our business and there remain until we receive some explanation of the cause of such trouble and disappointment. We feel ourselves ready to turn out and defend our country, but cannot be treated in this way as your brothers.

HENRY O'BEAL.
His
BLACK X SNAKE
Mark.
His
JOHNSTON X SILVERHEELS
Mark.
His
BIG X JOHN
Mark.

(From Ketchum's History of Buffalo, Vol. II., pp. 428-9.)

New York Evening Post, 13th July, 1813.

Extract of a letter from a gentleman visiting the army, dated Heights of Queenston, June 30:

The army in this neighborhood (at Fort George) consists of about 2000 effective men and are entrenched on the right of the fort, which is garrisoned pretty strongly by artillery and other troops. Fort Niagara, on the opposite side of the river, is garrisoned by about 400. Some Indians lay encamped near it, who tendered their services to the Americans. I am informed that our army expects daily the arrival of 400 or 500 Tuscaroras and Senecas. The General intends, I understand, to accept of their services, and which I think would be important against the enemy now for they are continually harassing our piquet guards and detachments sent out into the country by parties of loyal militia, Indians and a few British regulars. Every night our piquets have a skirmish with the marauders. They are very troublesome. They keep our troops under arms through the night, which exhausts and wears them fast away. Our force has decreased very much by many causes. Colonel Boerstler surrendered a few days ago, about sixteen miles from Fort George, about 600 men and officers, some cavalry and two pieces of light artillery to a motley force of militia and Indians and four companies of British regulars. I am not informed of the particulars of this disaster, but the loss on either side, I have been told, in killed and wounded was but trivial. Our men are in a wretched condition for clothing, many barefooted and half naked. The supplies of the army here from the Quartermaster's department are very irregular. The enemy's fleet plague our forces very much. It has been making demonstrations for near two weeks off Fort Niagara. There is no doubt some stratagem is going on, from its movements. It is powerful in size of vessels, number of guns and weight of metal. If the two fleets should meet the contest will be critical.

(File in Astor Library, New York.)

The Secretary of War to General Dearborn.

(Extract.)

WAR DEPARTMENT, July 1, 1813.

The leisure you now have affords a fine opportunity for the Adjutants and Inspector, General to attend to their particular duties. Some of the parties of which you speak, from the enemy, may practice a trick on those who follow them. *These last ought to be very circumspect.* Chauncey will, I hope, soon reappear on the lake. A battle will then decide which of us shall be victor for the campaign. I am afraid that we have all along acted on a belief very pleasing but ill-founded, viz.: That we were ahead of the enemy as to naval means and naval preparation on the lakes. Are we sure that our calculations as to Lake Erie have been better than those with regard to Lake Ontario? A week or two will decide this question.

(American State Papers, Military Affairs.)

Militia General Order.

Headquarters, near NIAGARA, 1st July, 1813.

The Quartermaster General of Militia will give in without delay a return of 165 days bat and forage for the general staff and regimental establishments of the militia who were on service during the last campaign. Commanding officers of regiments and corps will therefore lose no time in transmitting to him their respective returns properly certified.

By order,
ÆNEAS SHAW,
Adjt. Gen'l Militia.

Caleb Hopkins to Governor Tompkins.

CANANDAIGUA, 1st July, 1813.

SIR,—There is about $30,000 worth of public property lying at the upper landing on the Genesee river, (4 miles from its mouth,) consisting of pork, flour, corn, hay, &c., also a large quantity lying at Gerundgut (Irondequoit?) landing, also, I am informed, there is some lying at Pulteneyville, and there was some at Sodus but it was lately destroyed.

All this property is exposed to destruction by British naval enterprise from Lake Ontario.

They have visited the mouth of Genesee river already, but were repulsed by a few militia and from their fears of there being more of them. We were then informed by a deserter from them that it was their intention to have proceeded up the river at daylight next morning and burn the stores at the upper landing.

I am now informed that on their way to the river they took a sailor on the lake by the name of William Howell, (who formerly sailed under Captain Eddes of Oswego,) and they now use him as a pilot for their excursions around the south shore of the lake: that the British Commodore keeps him on board his ship, who threatens to make another visit to the port of Genesee for the purpose of destroying the property there and also of destroying the new bridge about 7 miles from the mouth of the river, having been informed that our principal baggage waggons cross it and take the Ridge Road to Niagara.

SIR,—I have been induced from my own suggestions and the advice of friends to communicate the circumstances to you, with a suggestion for you to give orders for posting a competent guard along the shore of the lake at the principal places of deposit until Commodore Chauncey shall settle the question with the British squadron respecting the superiority of the lake. Of this we have confident hopes it will be decided in a month.

Under the present circumstances no militia officer feels himself disposed to assume the responsibility without higher orders. Indeed there is a great want of ammunition and arms, and when an express is sent for them to Canandaigua under an alarm the keeper of the arsenal cannot deliver them out until a tour of 12 miles is made to obtain General Hall's order for them.

I should state the number of 300 men to be necessary to be stationed at Genesee river in order to insure its safety and the proportional number at Gerundgut, &c.

(Tompkins Papers, Vol. VIII., pp. 455-7, New York State Library.)

Earl Bathurst to Sir George Prevost.

DOWNING STREET, 1st July, 1813.

SIR,—Your despatches to No. 56 have been received and laid before His Highness the Prince Regent.

His Royal Highness approves of the early measures which you took for strengthening the line of defence in Upper Canada as soon as it was evident, from the movements of the American army, that their efforts would be principally directed against that Province, and altho' it appears that the enemy have been so far successful in that quarter as to obtain temporary possession of York, His Royal Highness sees no reason to attribute that disaster to any want of proper precautions on your part or to any deficiency in the instructions furnished by you to Sir R. H. Sheaffe.

I cannot but be most anxious to learn how far this unfortunate occurrence may influence your naval superiority on Lake Ontario. But so far as I can judge from the American newspapers, which are as yet my only source of intelligence, I derive some satisfaction from believing that the damage done by the enemy is confined to the burning of the *Sir Isaac Brock* upon the stocks and the destruction of the military and naval stores deposited at York, and that consequently the British naval superiority on that lake, tho' diminished, is not lost.

To repair the former of these losses must be the main object of your exertions, (as it is the one in which no effectual assistance from hence can be afforded.) The additional supplies of military and naval stores and of Indian presents, which I ordered for Canada on the first receipt of the intelligence, will arrive for the most part at the end of the present year and the remainder so early in the ensuing season as to repair effectually every loss of that description which may have been sustained.

It is almost unnecessary to impress upon you the extreme importance of securing Kingston against an accident similar to that which York has sustained, either by maintaining a larger force in its neighborhood during the winter months or by adding to those works which you had already provided for its defence. If it should be practicable I am sure you will not omit any opportunity for providing most effectually for its security by attacks, (similar to that made at Ogdensburg,) upon the enemy's other ports on the lake, which, if successful, would render the invasion of Upper Canada if not impracticable at least extremely difficult.

His Majesty's Government entirely approve of the force which the Legislature of Upper Canada propose to substitute for the militia of the Province, and have no hesitation in sanctioning the additional bounty which you recommend to each volunteer out of the extraordinaries of the army.

By intelligence received from Barbadoes I learn that the 13th and 64th Regiments of the members mentioned in the margin sailed from Martinique on the 2d of May. I trust therefore that they have before this reached Halifax, and as Meuron's Regiment also sailed from Gibraltar on the 2d of June, in three frigates, there can be but little doubt of their arrival in the St. Lawrence early in the present month.

13th, 750 men.
64th, 840.

As the attempt which has been made in Scotland to raise a 2d Battalion to the 49th Regt. for limited service has not been attended with the success which has been anticipated, I cannot hold out to you the prospect of any additional reinforcements during the present year beyond that which may be derived from the detachments belonging to regiments in Canada, which will be despatched from hence by the August fleet. But I have much satisfaction in learning by your despatch, No. 56, that you consider the reinforcements which have been forwarded to Canada as sufficient to enable you to act with vigor against the enemy and to convert, if necessary, your defensive into offensive operations. On this subject I have only to observe that His Majesty's Government would feel great difficulty in recommending any offensive operations which should lead you to a great distance from your frontier. If, however, any opportunity should offer of gaining any immediate or early advantage by an attack within the limits of the enemy's territory I am convinced you will be no less eager to seize it than His Majesty's Government will be ready to give to such an offensive measure their most hearty concurrence.

P. S.—Advices have been received since writing the above that the 13th and 64th Regiments arrived at Halifax on the 1st of June.

(Canadian Archives, C. 679, p. 164.)

Major-General DeRottenburg to Brigadier-General Procter.

Headquarters, 12 MILE CREEK, 1st July, 1813.

SIR,—I have the honor to inform you that I have taken into serious consideration the situation of the army under your command in the event of any disaster happening to our fleet so as to give the enemy the command of Lake Ontario, when I should be under the necessity of retreating with my division of the army upon Kingston, without perhaps being able to maintain myself long enough for your joining me at the Head of the Lake. In case of such a disastrous event taking place no other resource will be left for you than to retreat on Lake Huron and gain from thence Lake Superior, where you would find 40 canoes belonging to the North-West Company, with six Canadians in each, capable of conveying by the Grand or Ottawa river to Montreal one thousand men with their retinue and accoutrements. I have long ago made an arrangement with the North-West Company to that effect in case of the worst happening, and think it proper to communicate this plan to you as this weighty conflict between the two fleets must shortly take place.

I expect a reinforcement to-morrow or the day after and shall then immediately reinforce you with one hundred men of the 41st Regiment.

(Canadian Archives, C. 679, p. 218.)

District General Order.

Headquarters, 12 MILE CREEK, 2d July, 1813.

The Major-General having heard with much regret that several recent instances of desertion have taken place from a corps which had the honor of being placed in the advance guard of the army, feels himself called on to notice the disgraceful circumstance, and he assures the troops that he will not fail to make the most severe example of the first deserter who may be apprehended, and as a reward five pounds is promised to any person who may bring in one, dead or alive. He trusts and hopes that an effectual stop will be put to such disgraceful conduct.

Colonel William Claus to Major Givins, Captain Lorimier and Lieut.-Colonel Elliott. (Circular Letter.)

SIR,—Major Givins is to take charge of the Indians from St. Joseph, Sault La Cloche, and Lake Sinilon.

Dated at 12 Mile Creek, July 3d, 1813.

(Claus Papers.)

District Orders.

KINGSTON, 3d July, 1813.

No. 4. All the "Veterans" now here are to embark for Montreal this day in the return batteaux.

District Orders.

KINGSTON, 4th July, 1813.

No. 6. Four batteaux will proceed to-morrow morning to the Centre Division of the Army. The Deputy Qr. Mr. General will fix the hour; a detachment of an officer, two sergeants and 22 rank and file will take charge of these stores : the Eighth Regiment will furnish one sergeant and 14 rank and file, and the 104th one sergeant and 8 rank and file. Major Heathcote will name the officer to take charge of the party and will direct him to meet the Deputy Qr. Mr. General immediately. These men must be completed with everything requisite for taking the field.

Colonel Cartwright of the Embodied Militia will send one officer and eight rank and file of his corps with the batteaux to bring them back when they will have unloaded the stores.

F. KIRCHLENGEN,
B. M.

Notes by Capt. W. H. Merritt.

General Vincent moved on the army to the 12 about the latter part of June, his headquarters [being] at Mr. Adams's. On the 29th we were sadly alarmed at Decoo's by a report from Doctor —— that the whole American army were advancing by the Queenston and Chippawa roads. We were all drawn up under the command of Col. Dennis, 49th, in order of battle, expecting them on momently. I was sent on ahead to reconnoitre with a few men. The report had spread through every house; the people were all at their doors looking out for them, each saying they were at their neighbor's house. After feeling my way as far as Kilman's by by-roads a fellow told me they were at McCartey's, he had seen them. After cautiously approaching the house through the wood [I] found they had not been that far. [I] proceeded on to Knox's, heard of them being at St. Davids, crossed over to Mr. Smith's [and] found by him [that] they had not left their intrenchments that day. [I] returned in the evening, after riding 60 miles in the greatest suspense imaginable, either a slow cautious walk or full gallop.

On the 1st July our advanced posts were pushed on to St. Davids. On the same day, or rather evening, I was sent to Fort Erie to bring down Mr. Hardison who, I think, was unjustly accused of adhering to the enemy. [I] arrived at Wintermoot's at dusk [and] found a party of the enemy were at the ferry. As I had but three men I was under the necessity of avoiding them. [I] got round by the wood, made him prisoner and returned by the same road, got lost and had an infinite deal of trouble in getting back as my guide, whom I had placed as a sentry, had run away on discovering a man or two and hearing a shot at the ferry. [I] rode all night. At 9 next morning returned to Decoo's, took a nap in the afternoon, went over to the 12 where Mr. H[ardison] was liberated. [I] was presented to Major General DeRottenburg who had arrived to take the command of the army, as well as being President of the Province. He unfortunately brought with him a very great name. We expected he would have performed wonders, in fact he done nothing but eat, drink, snuff and snuffle. On the 3d, my birthday, which brought me up to a score, my kind mother had provided an excellent dinner for me and a few friends at 12 o'clock. I was sent in with a flag of truce in company with Major Fulton. Our advance picket were at the Eight Mile Creek. Near the Two Mile Creek [we] were met by Major Forsyth and his riflemen. He abused us in the most scurrilous and ungentlemanlike manner, made us prisoners and marched us into their picket at Seacord's, where we remained for 2 or 3 hours on horseback, altho' the family wished to pay us every attention in their power. Col. Fulton would have given up his sword and remained a prisoner, but they would not receive it. He called an officer [and] begged him to take notice of what had passed. We returned, dined with the Parson (Addison) and sat with him till nearly night, when we galloped back to the 12, made out a report to General DeRottenburg, who forwarded it to Gen. Dearborn, at the same time saying [that] unless Major Forsyth's conduct was taken notice of there would be an end to all communication between the two armies. The flag was sent in by one of my corporals, an answer was sent back in a few days saying he had been dismissed from the service for some time. When I heard of that fellow's death I was really pleased, a greater brute never existed. He was shot at Odelltown, Lower Canada, by a skirmishing party.

(From the Merritt MSS.)

Lieut. MacEwen, Royal Scots, to his wife at Montreal.

Woods, 12 Miles from FORT GEORGE, 3d July, 1813.

I arrived here yesterday. I can give you no idea of this place. We are in the centre of woods, which are wild in the extreme. There is nothing to be had for money and we must live on our rations, which are bad, and, I may say, too little for any man in good health. However, I endeavor to live.

The Americans are in our front, strongly fortified in Fort George, and if reports are correct they have mines in readiness to blow the place up as soon as our army gets into the garrison. I hope our

Generals will succeed in beating them out without running the risk of blowing the men up, as I have no doubt will be the case should they enter the place. Mr. Hemphill leaves this place with Captain Dudgeon's company to-morrow morning for another part of the army, distant from this place about sixty miles. This, I am sorry for, as we have always been together since we left Montreal, but in these times I cannot expect anything like comfort and this separation adds a great deal to my unpromising situation. Let me know how the garden comes on, also, if you got my sword and epaulette from Mr. Brown. I have been obliged to leave my brown trunk at York and bring my small one here with a few things, just as many as I can put in my haversack. No officer is allowed more than he can put under his arm and run with on all occasions.

(From A. Brymner's Excerpts, pp. 6-7.)

Sir George Prevost to Earl Bathurst.

Headquarters, KINGSTON, UPPER CANADA,
July 3d, 1813.

No. 73.

MY LORD,—I have the honour to transmit to Your Lordship copies of letters from Colonel Vincent and Lieutenant-Colonel Bisshopp and of the papers accompanying them, containing the highly gratifying intelligence of the capture on the 24th ulto. of a body of the enemy's forces, consisting of two field officers, 21 other officers of different ranks, 27 non-commissioned officers and 462 privates, together with a stand of colors and two field pieces. The details of this gallant affair, which reflects so much credit on our Indian allies, as well as upon Lieutenant FitzGibbon for the promptitude and decision with which he availed himself of the impression their attack had made upon the enemy, will, I have no doubt, be read by Your Lordship with great satisfaction [and afford a decisive proof of the want of perseverance in the American army.*]

Since the surprise of the enemy's camp at Stoney Creek on the 6th ulto., and their subsequent retreat from the Forty Mile Creek, in which almost the whole of their camp equipage together with a quantity of stores and provisions fell into our hands, Major-General Dearborn has withdrawn the troops from Fort Erie and has concentrated his forces at Fort George. Colonel Vincent has in consequence made a forward movement from the Head of the Lake in order to support the light infantry and Indian warriors, who are employed in circumscribing the enemy so as to make use of their own resources for the maintenance of their army. Major-General De

*Omitted in the *London Gazette.*

Rottenburg has assumed the command of the Centre Division of the Army in Upper Canada. After the squadron under Commodore Sir James Yeo had shewn itself off the Forty Mile Creek, which principally determined the enemy to retreat from that position, it was very successfully employed in interrupting and cutting off their supplies going from the Genesee river and their other settlements upon the southern shore of the lake. Five small vessels with provisions, clothing and other articles were taken and several loaded boats were destroyed.

[During the cruize Sir James had an opportunity of ascertaining that at Oswego the enemy were constructing a large floating battery according to Mons. D'Arcon's plan of admitting the circulation of water throughout, for the purpose of aiding an attack upon this place and for the destruction of our dockyard. Against any attempt of this nature all proper precautions are taking.

The force at Sackett's, from which place the attack is threatened, amounts to about 4,000 men. Commodore Chauncey with his squadron is still in port there. A bold and well conceived plan for surprising part of it was lately defeated by the desertion of two men of the Newfoundland Regiment.

Sir James Yeo with about 450 sailors and nearly 250 of the Royals and 100th Regiment had been enabled to get within ten miles of the enemy unperceived and to lay concealed in the woods for twenty-four hours intending to commence the attack the following night, the success of which seemed highly probable, but it evidently appearing by the movements of the enemy that they had taken the alarm the expedition was reluctantly abandoned and the boats returned with the party in safety to Kingston yesterday morning, the whole of Commodore Chauncey's squadron having got under weigh to attempt intercepting them.

I have just had the satisfaction of hearing that the 13th Regiment arrived at Quebec from Halifax the 28th ulto.*]

(Canadian Archives, Q. 122, p. 52.)

The Secretary of War to Major-General Lewis.

WAR DEPARTMENT, July 3, 1813.

SIR,—It is not merely possible but probable that the British fleet on Lake Ontario may, upon the fitting out of the *General Pike*, refuse a battle and take shelter under the guns of Kingston until their new brig shall restore to them the superiority. A question of much importance arises on this supposed state of things. What will be the

*Omitted in the London Gazette.

best possible employment of our force during the period we may be able to command the lake? Shall we reinforce the troops at Fort George from Sackett's Harbor and cut off Vincent, or shall we bring from Fort George the mass of the division there, and uniting them to your present command, attack the enemy at Kingston? If the latter part of the alternative be adopted two things must be done. A heavy body of militia should be assembled at Ogdensburg to draw to that point the enemy's attention, and General Hampton should move rapidly and in force against Montreal. Our assembled force at Sackett's Harbor would amount to seven thousand men independently of the naval means. The enemy's land force at Kingston is about four thousand. Could a successful attack be made here the fate of the campaign is decided—perhaps that of the war. The object is great, but in proportion as it is so the means of effecting it ought to be well considered. From the sketches I have been able to procure of Kingston and vicinity I have no doubt but that the attack should be made on the works which cover the battery on Navy Point. That gained, town, battery and harbor are all at your discretion. Beware of dividing your attack. Confine it to a single point, but let that point be a commanding one.

(American State Papers, Military Affairs, Vol. I., p. 451.)

Captain Fulton to Sir George Prevost.

Headquarters, 4th July, 1813.

SIR,—I was yesterday directed by General De Rottenburg to proceed to Fort George with a flag of truce, and never was I more grossly insulted in my life. I have the honor to enclose a copy of a letter that I addressed to General De Rottenburg upon the subject and have requested him to forward it to General Dearborn.

The army remains in the same position as when I last wrote and nothing extraordinary has occurred.

(Canadian Archives, C. 679.)

Captain Fulton to General De Rottenburg.

Headquarters, 4th July, 1813.

SIR,—Agreeable to your orders I proceeded yesterday, accompanied by Captain Merritt of the cavalry, with a flag of truce to deliver a despatch addressed to Major-General Dearborn, Commander of the American forces at Fort George. Nearly a mile on this side of Mr. Seacord's house I was stopped by a person who called himself Major Forsyth, and who seemingly had the command of about a hundred riflemen. He demanded my despatches in a most abrupt and *ungentlemanlike* manner, (I hope his expressions to me afterwards will warrant my making use of this *latter term*,) which I instantly gave him. Captain Merritt and myself were then escorted by an officer and fourteen men to Mr. Seacord's house, where I remained for nearly two hours on horseback. I was then forced to return with a similar escort, without any reply to your despatches. During the time I remained at Mr. Seacord's house I was called rascal and scoundrel by this Major Forsyth, and I appealed to an officer of the American artillery, Captain Hyndman, who was present when this expression was made use of to me, to certify to the fact.

Allow me to assure you that I in no way deviated from the usual custom of officers having flags, and that I have related a correct statement of the treatment I received, which I hope you will do me the honor to transmit to General Dearborn, that an *immediate* example may be made of the person, I cannot call him an officer.

(Canadian Archives, C. 679.)

Captain Alexander Hamilton to Mrs. Henderson, No. 1 Park Street, Edinburgh.

St. Davids, July 4, 1813.

My Dear Aunt:—

Your last kind letter of the 1st April, together with the large packet from the boys, came to hand last evening and gave us infinite pleasure. I can easily conceive how anxious you must be to hear from us at such a time, but I assure you that it is almost impossible either to write or to get letters from this when written. This must in some measure excuse our long silence. Many changes of fortune have occurred since the commencement of the war, but we are still, thank God, able to keep our heads up, and things at this moment again appear in our favor.

The first appearances were rather against us. General Hull of the Americans crossed the river at Detroit and planted their standard, but short was their triumph. Our gallant General Brock attacked them with a handful of troops, drove them from their entrenchments and in our turn crossed the river, took possession of Detroit, when the whole garrison, 2,500 men, as also the territory of Michigan, surrendered to our arms. Brock returned amidst the acclamations of an almost idolizing public.

Their next attempt was at Fort Erie. From the great extent of our lines of defence from Fort Erie to Niagara, (35 miles,) with scarcely 1,000 regular troops, you may suppose how weak our guards were. They attacked us in the middle of the night with 500 picked men, sailors, and, I'm sorry to say, most of them our countrymen, surrounded our small guards and murdered them without mercy and took possession of three of our batteries. But again their reign was short. Day arrived. The remainder of our small forces collected and drove them with precipitation into their boats and took their commanding officer and fifty men. This was nothing. Our danger only now appeared approaching. An incredible number of boats were drawn up along the opposing shore; the troops all embarked—5000 men. A few well directed shots, however, from our field pieces and the alacrity of our reinforcements coming in every moment made them first pause and at last entirely relinquish their plan. The troops were disembarked and the boats taken as far as possible out of the range of our shot.

The business of Queenston you already know; there again they were defeated with astonishing loss. One General, two or three colonels, 50 or 60 inferior officers and 1000 men. General Winchester next fell into our hands in approaching Fort Detroit, with 450 men. The command then devolved on General Harrison, who was shortly after attacked by General Procter and his fort on the Miamis invested. A reinforcement of 1300 attempted to find their way through our lines to the fort, in which they succeeded, with the loss, however, of 500 men taken prisoners.

They next appeared on Lake Ontario with seventeen sail of vessels for an attack on York, in which they succeeded, with the loss of General Pike and between three and four hundred men killed, principally killed by the blowing up of our magazine before our retreat, but, as if a species of fatality still pursued, they became afraid of an attack from our Indians and troops. After destroying all the public property they could find they decamped in a few days, bag and baggage. They then proceeded for Fort George, where, from internal enemies having gained every intelligence of our plan of defence, everything seemed now in their favor, an astonishing thick fog having spread itself over the whole river and lake, by which means they were enabled to place every vessel and boat exactly where they wished them without our being able to annoy them in the least or even knowing where they were. When the weather cleared up we found ourselves surrounded with boats and vessels on every side. They approached us in divisions, each division stronger than our whole force put together. Notwithstanding this fearful odds our advanced guard received them at the point of the bayonet and in several instances forced them again into their boats. Not content with attacking us with their men they now opened a most destructive fire of grape and canister from their vessels. Though the action lasted scarcely three-quarters of an hour, out of 500 brave fellows who entered the field scarcely 200 returned.

Finding further resistance quite in vain, our General Vincent, with tears in his eyes, gave the necessary orders for a retreat, which, in spite of six times our numbers within a few hundred yards of us, was effected without the loss of a single man.

We then proceeded to the Head of the Lake and took up a strong position at that place—our whole force consisting of about 2000 men. They, after some delay, determined upon attacking us with 5000 men, in two divisions. The first of 3000 arrived within five miles of us at a place called Stoney Creek, the other within a few miles of them. Having intelligence from a deserter of their intention to attack us early next morning with their whole force, General Vincent called together his officers, when it was determined to be beforehand with them and attack their front division that night. Eight hundred of our best troops were chosen for this attack, drove them with the bayonet from their position, got possession of three field pieces and took their two Generals, Winder and Chandler, prisoners. They immediately fell back on their rear division and the whole were making the best of their way to their boats on the lake when, to the astonishment of everybody, six vessels appeared in sight under American colors. They planted their standard on the bank and gave them three cheers, when the colors were shifted and the Royal Standard was seen flying on the vessels, which, together with a few well directed shots, put them into such confusion that they decamped with the utmost precipitation leaving everything in our hands—nineteen boats with the whole of their tents and camp equipage. They never stopped till they reached Fort George. We followed them in a day or two as far as the Beaver Dams, about eighteen miles from their fort. They determined on attacking us there, but from our intelligence we were again beforehand with them and attacked them on their way up, defeated them, and took Col. Boerstler with 420 men.

We are now within a few miles of Fort George. Our men are every hour advancing and we are fully determined, although their force is still greatly superior to ours, to make one gallant attempt to drive them from our shores; trusting to that Divine Providence which has hitherto so strongly upheld us, we have no fears. I shall not seal this till we know the event.

Robert [Hamilton] went up last winter with Mr. Robert Dickson to bring down for our support the Northwestern Indians, and is expected back every day. Some of the Indians have already arrived. George [Hamilton] and myself, with Mr. Robertson, are attached to Col. DeHaren of the 104th Regiment, who commands the advance guards, from our knowledge of the country and roads about the place to assist him in his movements, &c. James [Hamilton?] is attached as a lieutenant to the Incorporated Militia and is stationed a mile or two from this. It is with the utmost pleasure I say that although one or other of us, sometimes two or three altogether, have been in almost every action that has taken place, yet not one of our friends has been hurt. Mr. and Mrs. Clark, Mr. and Mrs. Wm. and Tom Dickson are all well. The last, you will be happy to hear, had a daughter a few days ago, as likewise Mrs. Robert Hamilton. Mrs. G[eorge] H[amilton] and son are at York with their friends, both very well. Mr. Robert Murray is still on the American shore at Presque Isle. We have not heard from him since the commencement of the war, but as he has no hand in this it is to be hoped that he will be allowed to remain quietly at home and mind his own business.

The Americans upon taking possession of Niagara allowed the inhabitants to remain in quiet possession of their homes and property, but since their last adverse fortune they have taken up almost every gentleman of respectability and sent them over the river as prisoners of war.

You will be sorry to hear Mr. Wm. Dickson is among the number. Mr. T. Dickson had to make his escape in the night. John Robertson, you will be pleased to hear, has behaved himself with great propriety and approved himself a most gallant soldier. His wife and daughter are both well. Owing to a change in councils at headquarters it is determined that no attack shall be made on Fort George until the vessels shall have decided the command of the lakes. James intends writing you after the attack is made. I shall leave it therefore to him to give you, I hope, good news.

* * * * * * * *

(From a MS. copy in Toronto Public Library, original said to be in possession of J. T. Townsend, Esq., Toronto.)

Brigadier-General Procter to Captain McDouall.

SANDWICH, July 4th, 1813.

My Dear Sir :—

Tho' I had not the pleasure of hearing from you by the last opportunity I flatter myself you are still with the army, whose movements are of so much consequence to us. In my last letter I mentioned that I conceived it requisite the whole of the 41st Regt. should be in this district with as little delay as possible. I have only to say that the detention of the force ordered here by the Commander of the Forces has prevented this district being in a state of security, which the destruction of the enemy's vessels at Presque Isle would have effected.—a service that might very easily have been completely effected a very short time since, but which, I apprehend, may now be attended with much difficulty. I should also have had it in my power to have supplied myself, at the enemy's expense, with provisions, of which we have not an adequate supply at present. I shall make the attempt unwillingly at Presque Isle except I have the *whole* of the first battalion, which I have reason to believe there is not any real intention of sending me, notwithstanding His Excellency's orders. I believe the intention is to detain a portion of the corps, whom they have found very useful as artificers, additional gunners, clerks and servants: so much consideration is there for the corps or for me. It is the inconvenience that individuals would suffer that has caused the detention of the 41st Regt. in the Niagara District so long after it was ordered here. I am sorry to tell you that the 41st has lost all its books, which were very complete, and consequently every register, every document—an irretrievable loss. The total want of military artificers in this district has been very injurious to the service here, and you know that no corps in this district can spare additional gunners to the other districts. We have not above five and twenty gunners serviceable. I feel myself fortunate that you are still with the army. If you were not, General Vincent would not be left at liberty to consider me at all. I begin to think you have Dickson with you. If he can be spared, which I suppose will soon be the case, he would be a powerful assistant to me and might soon reach Long Point. I am sorry to say from the repeated and recent treacheries of the inhabitants of the River Raisin settlement, it will not any longer be in my power to preserve it. Our safety, or rather that of the territory, is absolutely endangered by them. They sent information to the enemy by which they had nearly cut off a party of Indians. I understand that Mr. Harrison has a body of horse, and that on their vessels being ready we are to be attacked in different quarters. The enemy have certainly paid a visit last week at the said settlement, where I as certainly would have a post had I the means. I must mention the want, among others, of money and Indian powder. I hope for some agreeable information from your quarter very shortly.

July 5—Dickson left Mackina twelve days since for this place.

(Canadian Archives, C. 679, p. 177.)

Brigadier-General Procter to Sir George Prevost.

SANDWICH, July 4th, 1813.

SIR,—I have the honor to acknowledge the receipt of your letter of the 4th ulto., and am fully sensible that this district has received a due share of Your Excellency's attention. I beg to add that if I had received from the Niagara line the reinforcement which you directed should be sent, I should by this time have had it in my power, by the destruction of the enemy's vessels in the harbor of Presque Isle, to have placed the dockyard and post of Amherst in a state of security that, under existing circumstances, it cannot be said they are in at present. However, tho' certainly more difficult to be effected, it may not be too late if, agreeable to requisition, the remainder of the 41st Regt. are immediately sent to Long Point. There seems to have been with respect to the Provincial Marine a general error, which cannot rest with me, as I early reported to Major-General Sir R. Sheaffe that an entire change was as requisite on this as on the lower lake. Captain Barclay also arrived here in error. I am confident of the most cordial co-operation and aid from Captain Barclay, whose arrival lessened considerably my anxiety. I have the honor to transmit a letter from him to me for Your Excellency's consideration. I have also to mention his strong desire to have some more of the R. N'f'land Regt., as his greatest reliance is on those of that corps, at present employed as marines. The service in this district has been much impeded by the total want of military artificers. I have reason to apprehend an intention of detaining in the other district a portion of the 41st Regt., whom they have found useful as artificers, and others, which, if so, I heartily hope will not be sanctioned. We have scarcely the means of constructing even a blockhouse. I have the pleasure to acquaint Your Excellency that Mr. Dickson was at Mackina on the eleventh ulto., but whether he is on the route here or is gone by Lake Huron to York I cannot at present say. The weather has been very much against him lately. He had succeeded to the full extent of his hopes among the Indian tribes. I understand that Mr. Harrison has arrived at Fort Meigs on the Miami with a body of horse, with which he is to advance into the territory of Michigan whilst the flotilla land troops on our shore. Each of the corvettes seen by Captain Barclay he thinks equal to His Mty. ship the *Queen Charlotte.* There were eleven ships in the harbor of Presque Isle. It will not any longer, from the repeated and secret treacheries of the inhabitants on the River Raisin, be in my power to save that settlement. They endanger the safety of the territory. They conveyed intelligence to the enemy which nearly caused a party of Indians to be cut off. It is incumbent on me to acquaint Your Excellency that the service has been very much impeded by the very scanty and irregular supplies of money which have been received by the commissariat in this district.

July 5th, 1813.

P. S.—I have just had the satisfaction of seeing one of the vessels arrive from Mackina, and to learn that the other two are at no great distance. Mr. Dickson cannot be far off, having left Mackina twelve days since. If my requisition has been attended to and Sir James Yeo sends any sailors something will be done and Your Excellency's directions obeyed, which were not, however, received from M. Genl. Sir R. Sheaffe. We are much in want of Indian arms and ammunition, or rather powder. The enemy's cavalry have ventured as far as the River Raisin. Most of the Indian nations have a fear of cavalry. The inadequateness of my troops has prevented my having a post on the River Raisin.

(Canadian Archives. C. 679, p. 185.)

Sir George Prevost to Major-General Glasgow.

Headquarters, KINGSTON, 4th July, 1813.

SIR:—You will communicate to the senior officer of His Majesty's ships at Quebec my earnest desire that he should proceed promptly to St. Johns to take the command of the vessels and gunboats on the Richelieu, bringing with him as many officers and seamen as he can possibly spare from his ships and obtain from the transport and merchant service, for the purpose of cruising on Lake Champlain, with a just expectation of being enabled materially to annoy the enemy on that sheet of water and if fortunate to destroy the remainder of their shipping on it, and under all circumstances to create a powerful diversion in favor of the army in Upper Canada. I need not dwell with you on the importance of this service to His Majesty's North American Provinces if it is carried into effect with zeal and promptitude, nor do I entertain a doubt of either of these qualifications being displayed by the officers of His Majesty's Navy, providing circumstances admit of the undertaking. You will not fail in taking such precautionary steps as shall preclude the possibility of delay or embarrassment in the execution of so highly important a service as the one now entrusted to your arrangement, and I trust you will find Major-General Sir Roger Sheaffe fully prepared to perform that part in it which must devolve upon him.

(Canadian Archives, M. 389-1, p. 3.)

Lieutenant-Colonel Thomas Clark to Lieut.-Col. Harvey.

CHIPPAWA, July 5th, 1813.

SIR,—For the information of Major-General De Rottenburg please say that I last evening received a note from Lieutenant Fitz-Gibbon requesting me to assist Ensign Winder, of the 49th Regiment, with what militia I could muster, to make a descent about daybreak of this morning upon Fort Schlosser and bring off what public boats and stores we could find there. I accordingly, in the course of the night, assembled 34, including officers, who, together with Ensign Winder, Volunteer Thompson and six privates of the 49th, crossed over in three boats and arrived at Schlosser a little after daybreak, and was so fortunate as to surprise the guard, consisting of two lieutenants, one sergeant and eight privates, three civilians and three of our own subjects. In the public storehouse at and upon the wharf we found one brass six-pounder, 57 stand of arms, two and one-half kegs of musket ball cartridges, six bulwarks or musket proof curtains for boats, one gunboat, two batteaux, two anchors, twenty barrels salt, twelve casks tobacco, eight barrels pork, one barrel whiskey, with some spades, oars and axes, all of which we brought to this place. We left at Schlosser six scows, six boats— some of them very large—and about sixteen tons weight of cannon shot and shells. These scows and boats, from their being immersed in water, we could not bring off nor completely disable.

We remained at Schlosser about one hour, during which time no person appeared to oppose us. However, we had scarcely embarked in the last boat when from 12 to 15 men came to the beach, supposed to be militia or workmen from Porter's Mills. They fired about twenty shots of musketry at us, which was returned by the two last boats. No damage was done to any person in the boats and I believe little hurt was done to the people on shore.

(Canadian Archives, C. 679.)

General P. B. Porter to General Dearborn.

BLACK ROCK, July 5, 1813.

SIR,—Of the detachment of 250 militia ordered to this place from Batavia, about 210 arrived on Thursday and Friday last. On Saturday we crossed the river to select a place for a fortified camp, and returned the same day. Since that time the wind has been so high as to render it difficult to pass. This morning, however, an officer with 30 men was sent about 3½ miles down the river to bring off the family of a man who was paroled by Col. Preston, and has since been carried off to the British army and again made his escape. The officer was instructed to proceed with caution and to keep his boat near him to secure a retreat in case of being attacked by a superior force.

After marching about 3 miles he discovered a party of the enemy, consisting of about 70 infantry and 20 cavalry, and immediately retreated to the ferry, where about fifty men had been sent over to support him. He was pursued about two miles by the enemy, who, on coming near the ferry, filed off from the river into the edge of the woods. About 20 of them, however, when our troops were recrossing came down to the water's edge and fired upon them. Three or four well directed shots from our artillery actually killed one and dispersed the others.

You have had notice of the landing of the enemy this morning at Schlosser. I was not disappointed in this attack, as, I believe, I told you in strong terms that there was no possible movement of the enemy that could be predicted with more certainty than their attack upon Schlosser and this place.

(From MSS. of Hon. P. A. Porter.)

Colonel Claus to Lieut.-Colonel Harvey.

TEN MILE CREEK, 10 p. m., July 5th, 1813.

SIR,—Interpreters Fairchild and Brant have just returned from Queenston and reported the conversation with the Tuscaroras. I enclose a copy. The interpreters are of the opinion that the Indians in the American territory expect that the British troops will shortly cross and are anxious to know how they will be treated. At the Council alluded to at the Standing Stone all the Indian Nations there renewed their friendship. The Indians have not returned from the Four Mile Creek nor will they without doing something, nor have the Indians that went to Queenston this morning returned.

P. S.—A general Council is to be held at Buffalo Creek, five days from date.

(Claus Papers.)

Conversation with the Tuscaroras at Queenston, 5th July, 1813.

The Onondagas saluted the old Tuscarora chief and nine others with him.

Katwerota, an Onondaga chief, spoke :—

We understand that it was your wish to see and speak with us. We have now come to hear what you have to say.

TeKarihaga, a Mohawk chief, said :—

BROTHERS,—The Onondagas have spoken and told you we are ready to hear what you have to say. The chiefs of 16 Nations are here to listen.

Osequirison, the Tuscarora chief, spoke :—

BROTHERS,—Our desire to see you is to know whether the same sentiments of friendship exist that you expressed at the Standing Stone, (Brownstown,) two years ago. Notwithstanding we are separated by the contention between the British and the Americans our sentiments are still the same.

Katwerota spoke again :—

"BROTHERS,—You see, notwithstanding the report that the British are weak, the Great Spirit is with us and we are able to take possession again. As the King has been obliged to give ground at Niagara we wish to understand from you whether you are induced to take part with the Americans or not. We wish to know what you had to communicate with us in particular?"

Osequirison—" These times have been very hard and we labor under great difficulties, being so near the lines, and we wish to know whether your sentiments are still friendly towards us, and if you cross the river whether you will hurt us?"

Katwerota—" That will depend on yourselves. If you take no part with the Americans we shall meet you with the same friendship as we ever did, and we look for the day when you shall see our faces on your side of the water. We have no contention with you. It is the King and the Americans, and we have taken part with the King. We will contend for his rights."

Te Karihaga—Brothers, we take leave of you. The head of our army and your friend, the head of our department, salute you."

(Canadian Archives, Claus Papers.)

Left Division Orders.

KINGSTON, 5th July, 1813.

No. 1.—Colonel DeWatteville having joined the Left Division of the Army he will take the command at Kingston. All reports will be addressed to him as commandant.

No. 2.—The departure of the four batteaux under orders to proceed to the Centre Division is postponed for the present.

F. KIRCHLINGEN,
B. M.

The Secretary of War to General Dearborn.

WAR DEPARTMENT, July 6, 1813.

SIR,—I have the President's orders to express to you his decision that you retire from the command of District No. 9, and of the troops with the same until your health be re-established and until farther orders.

(American State Papers, Military Affairs, Vol. I.)

(From Buffalo Gazette, 6th July, 1813.)

To the Editor of the Buffalo Gazette:

SIR,—I could not have imagined that the concise statement of facts, which I forwarded you, relative to the capture of Fort George would have given rise to the ill-natured remarks and erroneous statements of an "Acting Aid."

It was not my intention to detract from the merits of General Lewis nor of his "Acting Aid." General Lewis is without doubt a brave officer, as he is certainly a polished gentleman. "It will not be asserted," (says the acting aid,) "that any order arrived from the ship which bore the Commander-in-Chief after the troops landed." There was an order from the Commander-in-Chief to General Lewis after the troops landed, conveyed from the ship by the Assistant Adjutant General, and the order was prompt and decisive. "When the enemy bro't his reserve into line," says the Acting Aid, "had Colonel Scott, in strict observance of his orders of the 25th, fallen back on the flanks the day had been probably lost." This is a grossly erroneous statement. It is well known to every officer of the regular army that after Colonel Scott landed, and General Boyd with part of his brigade, and they had been engaged with the enemy about fifteen minutes, the British commenced a precipitate retreat and no opportunity was afterwards presented to him, unless we had as precipitately followed him instead of hanging round the deserted village of Newark for two or three hours and being amused by the fire of Fort George, which was not defended by more than 30 men. Besides, was there a possibility of the day having been lost when 5000 men were opposed only by 1500?

* * * * * * * *
* * * * * * * *

The British fleet have again appeared off Fort George. Commodore Chauncey is shortly expected.

During the last week there has been frequent alarms at Fort George, occasioned by small parties of the enemy hovering about our picket guards. But the place is not considered in any danger, its batteries, breastworks and defences are very formidable and commanding.

A volunteer corps under Captain Bull has been enrolled in this village for defence of the place. A battery has been erected on the point of the terrace fronting the lake mounting one long 12 and a 6-pounder.

The *Queen Charlotte* and a small vessel are said to be at Long Point.

Colonel Brady from Pennsylvania with 250 regulars and 50 horse are expected every moment in the village.

About 250 militia have been drafted in Genesee County and marched to Black Rock, under the command of Major P. Adams, late of Swift's United States volunteers. The batteries at Black Rock are mounted with several fine pieces of cannon.

We were mistaken in the person killed by the Indians at Queenston. It proves to be Mr. Sylvester G. Tiffany, brother of Mr. George A. Tiffany of Le Roy.

Postscript—Tuesday morning, 6 a. m.

On Sunday night the British came across at Schlosser, surprised and captured our guard of 20 or 30 men, took some public and private property and returned. Yesterday they appeared opposite Black Rock.

(File in Buffalo Public Library.)

General Order.

Adjutant General's Office, 12 MILE CREEK,
6th July, 1813.

Militia General Orders.

His Honor the President has thought proper to direct that the great highway through the Province called Dundas Street should forthwith be put in a state for transport of troops, military stores and ordnance.

To effect this important object, in aid of the Statute Labour His Honour is pleased to direct that the militia be employed in that work; that officers commanding corps do furnish to the requisition of such persons as may be appointed to direct the labour detachments from their regiments of sedentary militia, not exceeding one-third of their strength. Each detachment of one hundred rank and file to be commanded by a captain and three subalterns; of sixty by a captain and two subalterns; of thirty by one subaltern and a non-commissioned officer to each twelve men.

The privates of the militia employed in this labour will receive two shillings and sixpence currency per day, and the non-commissioned officers three shillings in lieu of subsistence, rations, &c. The captains and subalterns the net pay of their respective ranks. The officers and men to be billeted as may be necessary.

The addition to the amount of pay and of the usual military allowance for labour is granted in consideration that each man shall bring with him an axe or other tool or implement to assist in the execution of the work.

Not to interrupt altogether the labours of husbandry, the officers commanding each party retaining one-half the number to labour may permit the other half by rotation to be absent three days in each week, if desired, to work on their farms. They will be paid only for the actual days of labour, but will be credited for the whole period in their tour of duty.

Certified pay lists will be furnished by the officer commanding the party, and the District Paymaster will make his requisitions in the usual form in each month for such sums as may be required for this service to the Deputy Paymaster General of Militia.

William Dummer Powell, Esquire, a member of the Executive Council, will, in behalf of His Honour the President, give such directions for the government of the respective officers employed in this service as from time to time may be thought necessary, and all reports and applications on the subject of this order will be made to him at York.

By order of His Honour the President and Major-General commanding.

Æneas Shaw,
Adjt. Genl., Militia,
U. C.

Memo. by Hon. Wm. D. Powell.

In the actual emergency, when the winter communication hitherto afforded by Lake Ontario is controlled by the enemy, it seems important in the highest degree that the said road over which troops, provisions and all military stores must pass should be placed in the best possible state to facilitate their passage. Circumstances have occasioned last year more than usual neglect of this object, which has never received sufficient attention on account of the geographical situation of our establishment on navigable waters. It appears to me that immediate and energetic measures should be adopted to remedy the evil, and render the road from Niagara to Kingston practicable for transport over [it] of ordnance. To conduct such a reform it will require a personal superintendence and application of all the power and energies of the Province. To enable any person to acquit himself of such an undertaking, it will be required to arm him with civil and military authority, to associate him to the commission in each district for expending the public money on roads, to be commissioned as Colonel of Militia to command as occasion may require for the special object.

A residence of 24 years, an annual progress through the colony, the gratuitous services rendered to every part of its population in the settlement of the land claims, my character as Executive Councillor and Magistrate, are calculated to give a strong impression of the importance and to add weight to such a commission.

I require no salary or perquisites, but my personal expenses for two horses, &c., I submit should, be defrayed under such limitation as might be thought decent.

I submit the project with the greatest deference.

(From MS. in possession of G. M. Jarvis.)

Sir George Prevost to Hon. Wm. D. Powell.

Headquarters, KINGSTON, 6th July, 1813.

DEAR SIR,—I have been honoured with your letter of the 28th ulto. I beg you will accept of my thanks for the able and satisfactory manner in which you have conveyed to me that information I was solicitous to obtain for the promotion of His Majesty's service.

(From MS. in possession of G. M. Jarvis, Ottawa.)

Memo. by Hon. Wm. D. Powell.

The call of the General Assembly to any other place than York necessarily removes all the public accountants as well as the officers of both Houses, and influences the administration of justice inasmuch as by law the Court of King's Bench is appointed in a place certain being the usual residence shall be determined, shall be held in the place where the last sitting of the Legislature may be held. In construction of this clause the Court of King's Bench sat at Newark from 1792 to 1798, when it necessarily removed to York, because the Lt. Governor had assembled the Legislature at that place. This removal of all the officers of that court was severely felt, and the more so because they were given to understand that York was not established as the permanent seat of Government, but that London was held out as the future metropolis of the Province. In these circumstances the call of the Legislature to Kingston must remove the establishment of the judges, clerks and inferior officers, all of whom, except the last appointed, have been under the necessity of building houses at York, from the impossibility at the first removal to here of renting them. The district in which the Court of K. B. sits must be the Home District in contemplation of law, and all the rules of practice refer to it as such, therefore the Legislature must revise its enactments to constitute the present Midland District the Home. All these difficulties may be trifling when compared with the advantages contemplated to result from assembling the Legislature at Kingston, but as they are not obvious and have not been pointed out, the reasoning on the question is hitherto all on one side.

It is certain that in relation to the war and foreign interruption, York, during the winter, is less exposed than Kingston.

There is, however, an alteration which will admit of the call of the Legislature elsewhere without drawing after it the removal of the Court of K. B. This is to declare by proclamation that York is the usual residence of the Gov'r or Lt.-Gov'r and must be so considered, notwithstanding the military commander, President and Administrator of the Gov't may not usually reside there. It is presumed that such act of Government will meet the exigence of the statute and remove all doubt as to the legal powers of the Court in its present station.

(From MS. in Hon. Wm. D. Powell's handwriting, in the possession of G. M. Jarvis, Esq., Ottawa.)

General Order.

Headquarters, KINGSTON, 6th July, 1813.

G. O.

Detachments of the Indian warriors being about to return to their homes, His Excellency the Commander of the Forces cannot suffer these brave men to depart without expressing the high sense he entertains of their good conduct, and the zeal and promptness with which they have obeyed his summons to repair to the divisions of the army in active service.

The skill and intrepidity displayed by them in battle by the defeat and surrender of a very superior body of the enemy's regular troops was principally achieved, and His Excellency has particularly to applaud the exemplary instances of discipline and forbearance evinced upon that occasion by their instantly refraining from all further hostility the moment they were informed the enemy had surrendered. The officers attached to the Indian warriors have distinguished themselves by their gallantry and good conduct. His Excellency directs that these warriors may receive on their return a liberal donation of the usual presents, and that the wounded and families of such as have fallen may receive a double proportion.

The Superintendent General of Indians will cause this part of the order to be carried into effect.

EDWARD BAYNES,
A. G., N. A.

Charles Askin to John Askin.

DUNDAS MILLS, HEAD OF THE LAKE,
June 2d, 1813.

DEAR FATHER,—

Your affectionate letter of the 2d ult. was handed me at the 40 Mile Creek without a cover, by a gentleman from Fort Erie, who picked it up somewhere there by mere accident just before he retreated from that. You must no doubt before this have heard of our misfortunes in this quarter, the loss of Fort George, after an action which lasted only fifteen or twenty minutes, and our being obliged to evacuate the whole of our fortifications from that place to Fort Erie and to destroy an immense quantity of provisions and other kinds of stores on our retreat.

On the night of the 24th ult. we commenced cannonading from the Five Mile Meadow on some boats going down the river to Niagara, which was kept up on both sides for two or three hours. We recommenced again early the next morning at some more boats going down, but the enemy had a much superior force in artillery and set fire to Fort George, which was consumed, and our troops were obliged to leave it. A great deal was burnt in it which, I am told, could have been saved, but very little exertion was made to save anything. On Wednesday everything remained quiet. On Thursday, 27th, the morning was very foggy and the enemy began to move their fleet and one hundred and fifty boats, which they had concealed behind Fort Niagara. Two or three thousand of their men landed at the same moment at 2 Mile Run, where they were met by 350 of the Glengarry Reg[imen]t who suffered very much. The enemy's vessels were anchored along our shore from 2 Mile Run on the Lake to nearly where the ferry was kept in Niagara River, and were pouring such an immense quantity of grape on our poor fellows that they were not allowed to advance to charge them, which they wished to do, until such an immense force had landed that it was thought necessary by General Vincent to order them to retire toward Queenston. From that they retreated to Beaver Dams, about 12 miles back in the country, where they were joined by about two hundred of the 41st Regiment under Colonel Bisshopp, from Fort Erie, and by two hundred of the 8th Regt., who just arrived from Lower Canada. The army remained at this place all night and the next day retired to the Forty Mile Creek, where they halted and staid two days, after which they went to the Head of the Lake, where we are now. I was stationed at Fort Erie with part of my company the day of the action, and the next day I left that with them and retreated along

Lake Erie with a small party of the 41st Regiment and some of the women of the regiment and came to   Grand River, but left the 41st behind for they came on too slow. After a great deal of fatigue I arrived at the Forty Mile Creek on the 30th ulto. alone, for all my men had stopped at their homes, and I knew that if I waited to bring them with me I should probably not be able to join the army myself, which I was very anxious to do. On my arrival at the Forty I was unfortunately taken with a fit of ague which detained me there for a day. The next day I came to this place, where part of the army lies. I am now staying at Mr. McKay's, who is extremely kind and attentive to me.

June 3d.—I yesterday had another fit of the ague, but sores are breaking out on my lips to-day and I am in hopes that I shall soon get rid of it. Since writing the above I heard further particulars of the engagement at Fort George. The enemy landed about eight thousand troops, and we had not more than two thousand five hundred to oppose them altogether, and of these there were but a very small proportion of Indians, (not one hundred), the Glengarrys, Newfoundland and 8th Regt. were the only regiments engaged with the enemy, and they suffered much. Two hundred of the 8th were killed and wounded ; nearly one-half of the Glengarry Regt. were cut off. Capt. Liddle and Mr. McLean were killed and several of the officers wounded, among which were two of Doct. Kerr's sons. The Grenadiers of the Newfoundland Regt. went into the action thirty or forty strong, but only 10 or 12 came out of it. The militia behaved as well as the regular troops and many say better. We have lost in killed, wounded and missing about four hundred and fifty men. The enemy, I believe, have not lost so many. Notwithstanding they were so superior to us in numbers they did not give our troops a chance of charging them, for the moment we advanced they would run down the bank and leave our men exposed to the grape shot from their shipping, which swept them off so fast that they were forced to fall back. A Capt. McLellan of the militia and Mr. Chew of the Indian Department were killed also. The 49th and 41st were hardly engaged at all, and our artillery did very little. We were fortunate in saving all our field pieces. All the wounded officers and men fell in[to] the hands of the enemy. Among them was Colonel Myers, a most gallant officer, and indeed the principal officer in the field and the 2d in command. The enemy did not pursue us at all, but when the army got to the Twenty Mile Creek there was a false alarm, which was the occasion of our destroying a good deal of ammunition and provision there. I must conclude this by saying that the enemy have nothing to boast of in taking Fort George, for they had an immense superiority of force.

June 4th.—I am just now going down to the camp to celebrate the day, which perhaps may be the last time, for an action I think we shall have in a very short time. Two thousand Americans are said to be at the Forty. We have a fine field to meet them on, where our army now lays, and should they advance we will probably beat them, but there will be little use in it if we should unless we get the superiority on Lake Ontario, where the chances are much against us, for we have but five vessels and the Americans fourteen. We have just had accts. from Kingston by one of Sir George Prevost's aides-decamps that an attempt had been made by Sir George with 800 men to take Sackett's Harbour, aided by Sir Lucas Yeo. Our troops landed but the vessels were becalmed and could not get into the harbour. Our troops were met by three thousand Americans, which were drove into their intrenchments. We took 150 prisoners and 3 pieces of cannon. We lost three hundred men in the affair. Col. Grey is said to have been killed and Major Evans severely wounded —two companies of the 8th suffered severely.

Our fate is decided now, for firing was heard on the lake yesterday, and it could be nothing but a fight between our fleet and that of the enemy. We hope for the best but dread to hear the result, as the chances were so much against us.

June 5th.—Our army, I think, must soon retreat from this. Whether they will go to Detroit or towards Kingston we do not know. I mean to follow it if possible. Your affectionate letter of the 24th and 31st ulto. I had the pleasure of receiving the day before yesterday. I never had an opportunity of sending up Eclipse or I should have done it. I am afraid the Americans have got him. Should Mr. Brush return to Detroit and the Americans get possession of this I hope he will try and save as much of my property as possible. A great number of our gentlemen have taken protections from the enemy since they have come in the country. I shall keep out of their hands as long as I can. I wish we had Tecumseh here to help us out of our difficulties. I received a letter from Theresa a few days ago which I am sorry I have not time now to answer. I delivered the one to Mr. Sutherland which was with it, and he has promised to send her the things she wants. You will please tell her. The Americans behaved very well to the inhabitants of York except those in any way connected with the Indian Department. Poor Mr. Selby died about the time the enemy landed at York. Poor old Mr. Warren is also dead. I was in the room when he expired, two or three days before the action at Fort George. I am sorry to hear of the death of my Uncle Grant.

The family in this quarter are well. Please give my love to my dear mother, to James, Alex. and my sisters and remember me kindly to my relatives and friends.

Believe me your dutiful and affectionate son,
CHARLES ASKIN.

John Askin, Esq.—

I beg you will excuse this scrawl, which I have had to write in haste, and not allow anyone but the family to peruse it; the contents I have no objection to have communicated.

Your affectionate son,
CHARLES ASKIN.

June 5th, P. S.—Should you wish to have any information respecting my possessions in this quarter, will please write to Mr. Wm. Lyons at the Twenty Mile Creek and address it to the care of Mr. Thomas Dickson.

Your affectionate son,
CHARLES ASKIN.

(From the Historical Collections of the Michigan Pioneer and Historical Society, Vol. XXXII., pp. 502-5.)

Charles Askin to John Askin.

DUNDASS, June 5th, 1813.

DEAR FATHER.—

I have just now met with Mr. Chisholm, who is going express to Detroit. I have requested him to stop and see you to say that I was well. I have wrote you a long letter, which I left about four miles from this. He has promised to call for it and take it up. The pistol Mr. Lewis brought down I fancy has fallen in the hands of the enemy with his things. Yesterday two American dragoons were killed a few miles from this. They have three thousand men at the Forty, about eighteen miles from our army, part of which are four miles from here.

Please give my love to my dear mother, my brothers and sisters, and remember me to my friends.

(From the Historical Collections of the Michigan Pioneer and Historical Society, Vol. XXXII., p. 505.)

Charles Askin to John Askin.

DUNDASS MILLS, June 8th, 1813.

DEAR FATHER,—

I wrote you on the 5th inst., at which time we were in a melancholy state and thought that we should be forced to surrender to a very large force which were in pursuit of us or make a precipitate retreat. An action which took place on the sixth inst., which terminated much in our favor, has quite altered the face of affairs, and the appearance of our vessels, which hove in sight last night, has put us all in high spirits again. The enemy were advancing three thousand five hundred strong, and were within six miles of us. On the evening of the 5th they took a strong position, determined to attack us next morning. General Vincent, after getting correct information of their situation, determined on attacking them that night and marched down the whole of the 8th and 49th Regt. with us and one field piece. Our force was one thousand strong. We got up to them undiscovered and bayoneted the centinels, then pushed on with the bayonet and took the enemy by surprise laying in their tents. Our troops, in order to alarm them, yelled as much like Indians as they could; this had a bad effect for it woke the enemy, who would have been [surprised?] otherwise. They kept up a warm fire on our troops for a short time with muskets and a howitzer, and killed a number of our men. Our brave fellows pushed on, took the howitzer and three field pieces, after which the Americans fled. Both their Generals fell in our hands, Generals Winder and Chandler and a number more officers and about one hundred men. Several officers who were taken, after giving their word of honour they would not run away, made their escape. They lost about two hundred in killed, wounded and prisoners. Our loss has been severe also. We had twenty-two killed on the field, about seventy wounded and thirty prisoners taken; Col. Clark of the 49th Regt. and Mr. Drury of the same regiment both mortally wounded. Mr. Taylor of the 41st severely wounded, (not the Mr. Taylor who was at Amherstburg.) Major Manners is also wounded, but slightly. Mr. Barnard was much hurt by a fall from his horse, who was shot under him. Some officers of the 8th Regt. were wounded, but their names I do not know. The night was dark and occasioned great confusion. General Vincent was missing six or eight hours after the action and was supposed to be taken, but found his way to us again. For want of horses two of the field pieces which were taken were left but a little way from the field of battle. While we were gone for horses the enemy came and took them off. The enemy retreated to the Forty. They are said to have left that and are retreating toward Niagara. I dare say the sight of our fleet does not please them much. There were no militia in the engagement and only four or five Indians. The Indians have behaved shamefully lately, and do us no service whatever. I hope they will do better. I would not give ten Hurons for two hundred of such as we have here. I fancy a stand will be made here now. Some works are going to be thrown up. Our fleet has brought us a small reinforcement and some ammunition, the last of which was wanted very much.

I am sorry to say that many of our great men below, I mean about Niagara, went and took protection from the enemy as soon as they came over.

Please give my love to my dear mother and to my brothers and sisters and

Believe me your dutiful and affectionate son,
CHARLES ASKIN.

John Askin, Esq., Sandwich.

P. S.—The action was fought half a mile this side of Stoney Creek. Messrs. Robert Grant, Wm. Kerby and five or six more gentlemen from this quarter leave this morning to buy cattle and take them to Amherstburg. I send by them a few old English papers, which are the only ones I could get.

(Historical Collections of the Michigan Pioneer and Historical Society, Vol. XXXII. pp. 505-6.)

Charles Askin to James Askin.

YIES, (YEIGH'S?) BURFORD, June 15, 1813.

DEAR JAMES,—

I am very sorry I cannot prevail on you to write me. I should be extremely glad to hear from you. Things were in a melancholy way with us here for some days but have taken a favorable change. Our army must have been destroyed but for the cowardice of the enemy. A shot from our fleet was the occasion of their making a precipitate retreat to Fort George, where they are now fortifying. Our advanced guard are at the 20 Mile Creek and the main body of our army are at the Forty. Six hundred of our troops had arrived the day before yesterday at York and fourteen hundred more are on their way. The Royals, 103d Regt., Canadian Regt., Newfoundland Regt., and a troop of the 19th Dragoons with some of the Glengarrys are the troops who are said to be on their way to reinforce us. There are 300 Indians coming also from Lower Canada, and we look for 800 from your quarter. I hope we may not be disappointed in getting them for the Indians of the Grand River are not worth a farthing. The staff of the 41st Regt. and about one hundred and twenty men are this far on their way to Amherstburg. I send you Eclipse by Mr. Lenn, who I hope will take good care of him. I shall not ask you more than thirty-five dollars for him. This sum you will please pay Mr. Smith in part of the auction acct. he has against me and send me a receipt for it from him as soon as you can. Get receipts in duplicate for fear the one you send me may be lost. The money Alex. owes me I should be happy he would pay him also as soon as possible and send me the receipt for it, for I am extremely anxious that debt should be paid.

The American fleet on Lake Ontario has not dared to meet ours yet, tho' they have sixteen vessels and we only six.

Should you be able to get me a p[ai]r of neat pistols cheap I wish you would buy them for me, and also a pair of spurs. There are no spurs to be got here, and the pistol my father was so kind as to send me I am afraid is lost, as it was in Niagara when the enemy came over. If you hear anything from Robt. Hamilton let me know as soon as possible, as ———— Hamilton is very anxious where [he is] and quite uneasy about him.

Give my love to my dear father and mother and to Alex. and my sisters.

(From Historical Collections of the Michigan Pioneer and Historical Society, Vol. XXXII., pp. 506-7.)

Major-General DeRottenburg to Sir George Prevost.

12 MILE CREEK, 7th July, 1813.

MY DEAR SIR GEORGE,—

I have had the honor of receiving successively your letters of the 22d, 29th ult. and 2d inst. I must acknowledge that the failure of Sir James's expedition is a cruel disappointment. However, *a mauvais jeu, il faut faire bonne mine*, and I am determined to procrastinate and hold my ground as long as possible, for reasons stated in my despatch to the Adjutant General. I have secured the position at Burlington Bay against a *coup de main*. That stronghold I must retire to ultimately and maintain myself until the navy will be enabled to meet the fleet on Lake Ontario. Had Sir James Yeo time to spare to co-operate with the army, Fort George would have fallen. But I do not now possess means of attacking them on both sides of the river.

Lieut. FitzGibbon is a deserving and enterprising officer and I shall forward your letter to him.

The Royals and 104th are not arrived yet, but are said to be close at hand. I am using every exertion to repair the roads. They have been much neglected by my predecessor and are the worst I ever saw any where.

Desertion is a growing evil in this army. I am trying to-day a man of the 41st. If he is sentenced to suffer death the same shall be put into execution 24 hours after.

With the exception of Lieut.-Colonel Harvey, who is a most active, zealous, and intelligent officer, the heads of the departments here are deficient in activity and cleverness, and the militia staff is most miserable. There is a vast deal to be done in this Province. Everything is unhinged and requires my utmost exertions to keep affairs in some shape or other.

P. S.—Cavalry horses may be procured here for the squadron of the 19th.

(Canadian Archives, C. 679.)

Lieut.-Colonel Harvey to Colonel Wm. Claus.

Headquarters, 10 o'clock p. m., July 7th, [1813.]

DEAR SIR,—I have Major-General DeRottenburg's directions to direct you will move forward a body of Indians to-morrow morning in the direction of Fort George. They must take post in front of [Chorus's] house* where some medicine belonging to the army was deposited, which it is the object of this movement to secure. Capt. Merritt will be sent from hence early to-morrow morning with waggons in which to bring off these medicines. A company of the King's will escort them from hence. It is therefore necessary that the officer who accompanies the Indians should point out the necessity of remaining in front of the house above mentioned until the waggons have returned.

(Canadian Archives, Claus Papers.)

Major-General Dearborn to General P. B. Porter.

Headquarters, FORT GEORGE, July 7th, 1813.

DEAR SIR,—Your letters of the 5th and 6th inst. have been received and I have had a conversation with the gentleman you refer to, who will be the bearer of this letter. I also have received the memorial of sundry citizens of Buffalo and a letter from Mr. Camp. I had hoped that you had called in an additional number of militia as authorized. The sooner you can obtain an additional number the better. I have written by the bearer of this to Col. Brady, directing him to leave at Buffalo or vicinity the company of cavalry and fifty infantry of his detachment, which, with what force you have and can muster in case of necessity, will, I presume, be sufficient for the defence of the place, &c. I have ordered Capt. Brevoort with the marines under his command to return to Buffalo as soon as practicable and to remain there until further orders. I have requested

---

*Cassel (or Castle) Chorus (or Corus), a native of Hanover, who served in one of the German regiments under Lieut.-General Burgoyne and was taken prisoner at Saratoga. He escaped and joined Lieut.-Colonel John Butler's corps of rangers on the frontier of New York in the following year, in which he enlisted and served until the end of the war, when he settled in Niagara township. On the Corus farm between Niagara and Virgil there is a tombstone bearing the inscription: "To the memory of Casper Corus, died Nov. 24th, 1835, aged 96 years."

Capt. Perry to have the detachments sent to Buffalo by water. Your proposition cannot be acceded to. The enemy's force above St. Davids would render such an enterprise as you propose more hazardous than present circumstances will permit. I hope you will not send any more parties over after inhabitants. It may cost more than you can afford.

(From MSS. of Hon. P. A. Porter.)

The Secretary of War to General Boyd.

WAR DEPARTMENT, July 7th, 1813.

SIR,—General Dearborn being about to withdraw from the command of the army until his health shall be re-established this trust will devolve upon you as the senior officer until the arrival of some person to whom it will be specially assigned. During this period you will pay the utmost attention to the instruction and disciplining of the troops and engage in no affair with the enemy that can be avoided. The orders of General Lewis and Hampton you will obey.

(American State Papers, Military Affairs.)

General Order.

KINGSTON, 7th July, 1813.

It being ordered and directed by His Majesty's Order bearing date 7th of October, 1806, that the period of service may be extended by the commanding officers of the government of colonies, islands or stations, as to non-commissioned officers and privates serving abroad for six months subsequent to the period of service for which they are serving, His Excellency the Governor-in-Chief and Commander of the Forces deems it expedient in conformity to the above stated regulations and in consideration of the actual state of hostilities in which this colony is placed, and is pleased to order, that non-commissioned officers and soldiers may not be discharged from the service until six months subsequent to the expiration of the period for which they are serving.

Commanding officers of corps are directed to see that their men are all provided with two pair of good shoes and a pair of strong serviceable pantaloons. Whatever may be required to complete the men in these articles is to be supplied from the government stores in conformity to the General Orders of the 4th instant.

Arms having arrived for the use of the Glengarry Light Infantry they will deliver up to the ordnance storekeeper the arms they now have in use. The arms exceeding the effective strength of the corps are to be kept in store for their use.

EDWARD BAYNES,
Adjutant General.

Garrison Orders.

KINGSTON, 7th July, 1813.

The headquarters detachment of the Glengarry Light Infantry with the light companies of the Royal Scots and 89th Regiment is to be held in readiness to embark in batteaux for York on Friday morning. One bombardier and four gunners of the Royal Artillery to be attached to this corps; the whole to be under the command of Lt.-Col. Battersby. The first troop of the 19th Dragoons is to join the Centre Division of the army as soon as a sufficient number of horses are received from Montreal.

EDWARD BAYNES,
Adjutant General.

Indian Council at the Ten Mile Creek, 8th July, 1813.

Sasori spoke :—

We chiefs and warriors of the Seven Nations salute you and thank the Great Spirit.

We have a great regard for the King.

We came forward and were successful. We went to the Forty and there we divided [our booty?] and you persuaded us to come forward, and that perhaps it would be but six days before we met the enemy again. We came. Our patience is at an end. The King has enemies below as well as here. This is the day our people begin to cut grass for their cattle and we must prepare not to let our people and cattle starve.

We don't mean to run away. We are too grateful. We took a good many things the other day, [i. e., at Beaver Dam.] What are we to get?

(Claus Papers.)

Charles Askin to John Askin.

10 MILE CREEK, July 8th, 1813.

DEAR FATHER,—

Your affectionate letter of the 15th ult. was handed me by Mr. Wm. Kerby on the field of battle, when six hundred of the Americans, under the command of Col. Bustler, were obliged to surrender themselves prisoners of war to us. This was on the 24th ult. The enemy had marched out of Fort George to surprise and take a party we had at the Beaver Dams, under Lt. Fitzgibbon of the 49th Regt., and probably also to attack an advance party we had at 10 Mile Creek, commanded by Col. DeHeron of the 104th Regt. The enemy were observed in the morning on their march by some Indian scouts, who gave the alarm, and about four hundred and fifty Indians, who lay at 20 Mile Creek, marched off immediately to meet them. I saw them and joined them with three more young men of the country, and in about three-quarters of an hour after, we came up to their rear-guard, which were horsemen, and attacked them, killing several. We were then pressed to retreat into a woods which was a little distance from us. Some infantry followed us across one or two fields, but we forced them to retreat. They then came along the end of the woods sheltered by a fence, but we also drove them from this. They after this came some distance in the woods, but we forced them to retire to a wheat field where the enemy remained nearly two hours firing at us from two field-pieces with canister shot, which kept the Indians from advancing on them. After a short cessation from firing the Americans began to retreat, but in very good order. The Indians followed them and the enemy soon took up a good position for their guns. While they were doing this Lt. Fitzgibbon joined us with about 48 of the 49th Regt. These were the first troops that came to our aid. The Americans gave them two or three shots from their field-pieces, but neither killed or wounded a man. Fitzgibbon's party did not fire in return for they were at too great a distance for musketry to do much execution. The Indians kept firing a few shots. Then Fitzgibbon advanced with a flag and demanded them to surrender, which, after a long parley, they agreed to do. While they were settling the terms on which they would lay down their arms, a party of our dragoons under Capt. Hall and two hundred infantry under Col. DeHeron also joined us. Fitzgibbon, who is a most active and deserving officer, gets the whole credit of the business as he was the person who demanded them to surrender, but the battle was gained by the Indians, for his party, as I said before, did not fire a shot. He is one of the most active and pleasing officers we have and has always been employed in any arduous duty. He was most always on the rear guard when we were retreating, and commanded the advance guard since we have been moving toward Fort George. While the main body of our troops were at the Forty Mile Creek he has been with a small party of the 49th in Queenston, and then would be at Chippawa, Fort Erie, and flying about in such a manner that the enemy did not know where to find him. He has had some very narrow escapes. His life was saved by Mrs. Kerby and another woman a short time since. He had by accident met two of the enemy's riflemen when he was alone. They were going to fire on him but he was in disguise and told them he belonged to their army. At the same time got near them and seized hold of their rifles, one in each hand, and was struggling to get them from them when one of his antagonists drew his sword from him and would have run him through had not a Mrs. Duffield kicked it out of the fellow's hand. The woman then threatened to kill him if he did not surrender, and they both allowed themselves to be taken prisoners. He had hardly got a quarter of a mile from the place with his prisoners when a large party of Americans came there, but he got off safe with them.

I find by one of your letters that you have understood that we have had an engagement soon after the 6th June, but there has been none since that except the one on the 24th, which I have given the best account of I could, but I omitted to mention the loss on both sides. That of the enemy was about 20 killed and nearly 46 wounded, and of the Indians six killed and ten or twelve wounded.

The enemy were panic struck by a few shots which Sir Lucas Yeo gave them at the Forty, and a few shot accompanied with a little yelling from about 20 Indians. At the same time they imagined that Genl. Procter and all the wild Indians had reinforced us, and that it was a general attack that we were about to make on them. They hurried off, left their tents, camp kettles and a number of other things behind them, and hardly halted a minute until they got into Fort George. Some troops they had at Fort Erie, Chippawa, Queenston, etc., were marched down to Fort George, so much alarmed that they hardly dared look behind them. At the same time there was not an Indian nor any of our soldiers within ten miles of them. Had we followed them we could have taken one-half of them or got some of our troops and Indians ahead of them, which could have been done easily by some bye-roads. It's the opinion of those who saw them on their retreat that the whole of this army, which was 2000 strong, would have surrendered, but we lost this fine opportunity of getting rid of them, and we have lost many others. We have been very fortunate in driving them into Fort George where they are confined and hardly dare venture out more than two or three miles. Indeed, their picket guard have been driven into the town and a number of their men at different times made prisoners. Their army are said to be very unhealthy. They have eight hundred sick and wounded, but their sick, their cannon, baggage and most everything else they have removed to the other side of the river, for they are in constant dread of an attack and are continually alarmed.

10 MILE CREEK, 19th July.

We have about one thousand men within a mile of Niagara and

our headquarters are now at St. Davids, about 7 miles from Fort George. We have good news from our fleet, which we expect in a few days. An attack will be made on the enemy as supposed the moment our shipping arrives. I am sorry to say we have lost one of our most gallant officers in the country, Colonel Bisshopp, who died of the wounds he received on Sunday, the 11th instant, at the battle of Black Rock, where we took 3 brass field pieces and some other guns. The 41st suffered much in this engagement. Capt. Saunders was supposed to have been killed but was only wounded. He is now a prisoner. Mr. Mompesson was also wounded. Col. Thomas Clark received a wound in the hand, but is doing well. We lost about forty men in killed, wounded and missing. The enemy's loss, I believe, was very trifling. Our people brought over an immense deal of stores, etc., before the engagement commenced, and could have returned without losing a man, but Colonel Bisshopp was too gallant a soldier and would not retire till he had given them battle. He was one of the last to retire from the field and was carried in the boat after receiving a wound in the thigh. His loss is universally regretted. He was one of the most gentlemanly men I was ever acquainted with and the best soldier. We have good news from Europe. Beauharnois was marching with an army of 24,000 men to burn Berlin, but was met by the Russian General Wittgenstein and defeated. He lost two thousand men and a field-piece. Bernadotte was on his march at the head of 25,000 Swedes to join the Russian army. The French were withdrawing their troops from Spain.

We have upwards of three thousand regular troops here, I think. We have the Royals, the King's, part 41st and 49th, 104th, Newfoundland, Glengarry Light Infantry and dragoons from Lower Canada. The 19th Dragoons have not yet arrived. It was not my intention to have sent this scrawl, which I am really ashamed of, but an Indian is going to Amherstburg and would not wait until I could write another. You will please not show this to anyone but my mother and brothers.

I sent Eclipse by Mr. Lewis of the 41st Regt. more than a month since. What he done with him I know not, but I am told the horse is now at the Forty. Should you write to me I beg you will send the letter by some one of my acquaintances and request the bearer to deliver the letter to myself or to one of the Hamiltons or Mr. Dickson, for some of the letters you wrote me have been lost. There is a report that Sackett's Harbour is taken but I do not believe it.

Give my love to my dear mother, my brothers and sisters, and believe me your   Dutiful and affectionate son,
CHARLES ASKIN.

John Askin, Esq., Sandwich.

P. S.—Mr. Willson of the Field Indian Dept. died on Friday or Saturday last.

The remainder of the 41st Regt. in this quarter are now on their march to Amherstburg and I believe the light company of the Newfoundland Regt. are ordered up also. I find by a letter from Theresa that you supposed me to have been in the action at Stoney Creek, but I was not. The only action I have been in was on the 24th June, which was near Beaver Dams, where we took six hundred. The battle lasted three hours and a half. I saw the whole of it.

Your affectionate son,
CHARLES ASKIN.

12 Mile Creek, July 19th, 1813.

(From Historical Collections of the Michigan Pioneer and Historical Society, Vol. XXXII., pp. 507-10.)

General Orders.

Headquarters, KINGSTON, 8th July, 1813.

Whereas General Officers commanding Divisions of the Army have frequently taken upon themselves in their published acts the style and title of Commander of the Forces, His Excellency the Commander of the Forces directs that in order to avoid confusion of persons they confine themselves to that of Major-General commanding, and that no District General Order is to be printed without having received the previous sanction of the Commander of the Forces.

All soldiers belonging to regiments serving with the Centre and Right Divisions, who are fit for field service, are to embark to-morrow morning with the detachment under Lieut.-Colonel Battersby.

EDWARD BAYNES,
Adjutant General.

Major-General Francis, Baron DeRottenburg to Sir George Prevost.

Headquarters of the Army of the Centre,
10 MILE CREEK, 9th July, 1813.

SIR,—I have the honor to forward the enclosed despatch just received from Brigadier-General Procter which, according to your orders to Brigadier-General Vincent, I have opened. It is not in my power directly to co-operate with the Brigadier-General, but I shall reinforce him as much as my means will admit. On the 6th inst. I detached 120 men [of the] 41st to Long Point, and as soon as the Royals arrive I shall send him one hundred more and the remainder of that regiment will proceed soon after. Having received intelligence that the enemy have but a very small force and considerable naval stores at Black Rock, I am now forming a plan to surprise that post and destroy the stores, upon which expedition I intend to employ the one hundred men that are to join General Procter, and if they succeed they will proceed in batteaux to Long Point. This will be a diversion in his favor, but I do not see how the superiority on Lake Erie can be obtained without seamen. Enclosed is a letter from Captain Barclay to Sir James Yeo.

I yesterday ordered a party of the King's and a body of Indians to recover a considerable quantity of medicines and surgical instruments, which were buried near Fort George when the army retreated. This brought on a skirmish between the Indians and the enemy, in which the latter lost one officer and twenty men killed and ten men taken prisoners. I am happy to state the whole of the medicines were brought off by the party of the King's, with only three Indians wounded. Captain Norton commanded the Indian warriors and behaved with great spirit. Captain Merritt of the Provincial Dragoons deserves very great credit for having reconnoitered the spot where the medicines were deposited and for conducting the party. I have not yet received the official report from Captain Norton.

(Canadian Archives, C. 679.)

Colonel Claus to Lieut.-Colonel Harvey.

TEN MILE CREEK, July 9th, 1813.

SIR,—I received your note of the 7th about 12 o'clock the same night, and I immediately went to the camp and collected a body of Indians. I gave the necessary directions to Capt. Norton. At daylight 100 and odd left camp. About 4 p. m. information was received that they were engaged with the enemy. I collected the Indians that remained in camp and was just proceeding to join them when a party appeared with five prisoners. I found that after the defeat of the foregoing party near Mr. Ball's, on the Two Mile Creek, a reinforcement of about 1,000 men advanced as far as the piquet by Mr. Butler's and returned almost immediately, as appears by the enclosed Brigade Order No. 3. The riflemen, who were out for the purpose of covering the foregoing party, retired as soon as they perceived the Indians. From what I can collect the killed and prisoners amount to upwards of 100. Of the latter there are 12. Of ours none killed; two Indians and one interpreter wounded, the other very slightly in the hand. I used every argument to get the prisoners from them. I succeeded in getting three. The remainder were to be given up to-day with assurances that no injury should be done them, but I find this morn-

near Niagara, remained safe. [I] went by way of St. Davids. Capt. Hamilton, Jervis, McKenney [and] Jno. Ball joined me. We converted it into a party of pleasure instead of danger, took turns to reconnoitre and find the coast clear. A small party of Americans had just returned from Mrs. Fry's at the X road. We took our dinners there and went on to Chorus's, found all safe. The American picket was at the end of the lane. We made a dash up it as if with an intention to charge them. They ran before we came within gun shot. They had detained two women, Mrs. Cain and her daughter, who came off in a very great fright, fearing they would be detained. H[amilton] and McK[enney] took them up behind them and galloped off. A few minutes after out came two or three hundred dragoons and infantry, when we galloped off in turn. They plundered the farms within their reach and returned. We went round by the lake road, [and] spent the afternoon with the ladies at Mrs. McNabb's, Miss Symington, Cook's, &c., &c. Most of the ladies had rendezvoused there. [We] returned to the 12 in the evening. Next day the Indians were sent to the Ten, with directions to move on under Capt. Norton by two o'clock the following morning (8th July) and place themselves in the wood fronting Ball's, in order to cover us in getting off the medicines, having received orders that night to accomplish it, as they were of the greatest importance to the army at this time. At the dawn of day I went down to the Ten. No person knew of the Indians advancing, no waggons [had been] provided, [and] everything [was] in the greatest confusion. I got a party of the King's, went on the Swamp Road, procured and sent the waggons by St. Davids. We did not reach the spot till near eight o'clock, had the medicine dug up, loaded and sent off before I learnt Norton was in the advance, sent the soldiers back with the waggons. Mr. Collis (Lt. of the King's), the subaltern, and myself went over to Peter Ball's, ate an excellent breakfast with the ladies, [and] went out to the main road to find Norton. The instant we arrived the scouting parties had commenced skirmishing. *Collis* returned to his men, Mr. Jno. Ball and myself were the only whites present except *Jno. Law*, a boy 13 years of age, whose father was a prisoner, dangerously wounded on the 27th May at Ft. George.* His elder brother was killed [in the] same action, 7 balls had passed through him. This little fellow was determined to revenge the loss his family had sustained. He would not be persuaded to leave the field till his mother, after it was nearly over, came out and took him away in her arms by force. We were very anxious to get away, as we were both mounted and had no guns. Whenever we attempted it the Indians followed. As we had come where we had no business, we were under the necessity of remaining and sharing

* Captain George Lawe, 1st Lincoln Militia.—Ed.

their fate. We were provided with a couple of red-coats, which had been left at Mrs. Lawe's, (a necessary precaution) to prevent our being shot by our own Indians. We rode on in advance and retreated to the Indians, endeavouring to bring the Americans out, as the Indians were very anxious to meet them. At length about 500 infantry with a few dragoons came out. As soon as they made their appearance the greater part of our Indians retired to the wood by Chorus's, which was far the best position. Accordingly we followed them, and lined the front of the wood and edge of the road. The enemy came on till within 300 yards of the wood, when a party of dragoons made a charge. We were ready to receive them at a few yards distance, when they boldly wheeled about and ran back. A few of our foremost men gave them a shot. The Americans returned it at 300 yards distance, which gave our men courage to advance. We had but about 60 near us, the rest were ½ a mile in the rear. B[all] and myself dismounted and urged them on. As soon as the Americans perceived they were coming in earnest they retired very precipitately. As soon as the Indians perceived this, they all ran on shouting in the most hideous manner. A party of the enemy, consisting of two officers and 50 men, were sent out from Mrs. Butler's, on Ball's road, with the intention of flanking us. I pointed them out to the Indians, who ran to the right and completely cut them off from the main body, only 7 of them made their escape. I gained my horse, left off the pursuit and turned my whole attention to the prisoners. The first one or two were brought out from the wood at the end of the lane by Blackbird, who made every gesture and threatened them with instant death. I rode up between them [and] was shortly threatened myself for interference. The poor devils were crying and imploring me to save their lives, as I was the only white they saw. After getting an interpreter they promised the lives of the prisoners should be spared; [they] *would only frighten them a great deal to prevent them coming again.* I made a solemn vow if a prisoner was killed, never to go out with an Indian again. Fortunately all that were taken except Adj. Eldridge, the officer who forfeited his life by firing at an Indian while a prisoner, [were saved.] During the whole of this affair the ladies were eyewitnesses from the windows of J. and P. Ball's. We had two Indians wounded. The American loss—50 killed and taken. The Indians followed them to Butler's meadows. Directly after, the Americans marched out nearly their whole army. We quietly retired within our pickets. For this encounter I was mentioned in General Orders, and got much more credit than I deserved, as I was most completely drawn into it against my will. Mr. Ball was taken no notice of because he happened to be a volunteer. I was rather flattered by this mark of distinction, and felt conscious the service had been well performed. Altho' I had jealous friends, jealousy and envy will ever follow a young man if he obtains notice, I most candidly and honestly confess that my first and only design in entering the situation I now hold was a desire of serving and defending my country, and not from any motives of ambition. Gen. De Rot[tenburg] lived at my father's. The house was a perfect thoroughfare for everybody for the remainder of the campaign. There never was less than 10 or 12 people constantly in it. The Indians about this time were particularly troublesome in the neighborhood where they were encamped at the Ten, [until] I removed there with the greater part of the troop, which kept them in some check.

In a few days after, headquarters of the army were removed to St. Davids, our army occupying the Four Mile Creek Road; the left at Servos's and at the lake, pickets near a mile in advance; [the] centre on the Swamp Road; those two positions were entrenched, the pickets at Ball's Fields, the American sentries within sight; our left [right ?] at St. Davids; a very strong picket on Queenston Heights. We were ordered on to St. Davids [and] remained at Mr. Smith's, an excellent quarters and very little to do, as the skirmishing was altogether at the Cross Roads.

(From the Merritt MS.)

(Independent Chronicle of Boston, August 30, 1813.)

Extract of a letter from Major B. M. Malcom, 13th United States Infantry, to Mr. Samuel Eldridge:—

CAMP, NEAR FORT GEORGE, July 18, 1813.

On the morning of the 8th inst. our advanced picket was attacked. I immediately volunteered to take command of a force sufficient to meet the enemy. Upon my having obtained this permission he (Lieut. Eldridge) nobly said: "I must go along with you." I directed him to join me at a certain point. After my departure a command of 40 men was given him with orders to join me. The battle having commenced, he was determined to meet me by a nearer route than ordered, and in endeavoring to fall on the left of my detachment he was cut off by the enemy, who by this time had gained the ground over which he was to pass, and in endeavoring to force his way he fell, having lost 20 of his little command.

(File in Philadelphia Library.)

Left Division Orders.

KINGSTON, 9th July, 1813.

All the prisoners of war are to be embarked by two o'clock this day, under the charge of Major Villatte, who will take command of the 41st detachment as a guard over the prisoners.

No 2.—The 89th Regiment is to send an officer, one sergeant and 20 rank and file at the same time to relieve the detachment of the 41st Regiment at Gananoqui, and this detachment is to proceed on with their corps to Prescott. The prisoners are to be embarked at the parade wharf and to proceed to Point Frederick, where the detachments of the 41st and 89th Regiments will take charge of them.

F. KIRCHLINGEN, B. M.

The Secretary of War to Major-General Lewis.
(Extract.)

WAR DEPARTMENT, July 9, 1813.

An order was expedited to General Dearborn yesterday, permitting him to retire from the command of the army and district. Another was sent to Boyd, forbidding him to engage in any affair with the enemy that could be avoided, and subjecting him to the orders of Major-General Hampton and of yourself. This last (for Hampton is now the oldest officer in the district) was intended to meet the contingency suggested in my last letter, viz.: that if we regained the command of the lake and Yeo retired under the guns of Kingston, this moment of superiority must not be lost, and that, bringing down Boyd's division, a blow might be struck at that place. To favor this enterprise, orders will be sent to General Hampton to push his headquarters to the position held by our army the last campaign on Lake Champlain, and a requisition for ten thousand militia from the States of New York and Vermont in reinforcement of this part of the plan will be superadded.

The moment Chauncey goes out, our stores along the south shore of the lake should be brought down to the harbor, and in that case your small posts (consisting of regular troops) drawn into your main body.

(American State Papers, Military Affairs, Vol. I., p. 451.)

Colonel Claus to Lieut.-Colonel Harvey.

TEN MILE CREEK, 10th July, 1813.

SIR,—I regret to learn that it has been insinuated that I have put complaints into Black Bird's mouth (in interpreting), and I beg that he be questioned.

(Claus Papers.)

Lieut.-Colonel Harvey to Colonel Claus.

July 10, 1813.

SIR,—The Major-General sanctions the expense of a war-feast for all the Indians engaged in the affair of the 8th.

(Claus Papers.)

Garrison Orders.

Headquarters, KINGSTON, 10th July, 1813.

Every effective non-commissioned officer and rank and file of the Royal Newfoundland Regiment is to be held in readiness to embark on board of His Majesty's ships on the lake to serve as marines, the men composing the same company are to embark on board the same vessel with their proper officers, a captain to command on board the *Wolfe* and *Royal George*. Those on board the smaller vessels to be commanded by subaltern officers. To furnish the following detail for the *Wolfe*, one captain, one subaltern, two sergeants, two drummers and fifty rank and file; *Royal George*, one captain, one subaltern, two sergeants, two drummers and fifty rank and file; *Beresford*, one subaltern, one sergeant, one drummer and twenty rank and file; *Moira*, one subaltern, one sergeant, one drummer and forty rank and file; *Melville*, one subaltern, one sergeant, one drummer and 35 rank and file; *Sir Sidney Smith*, one subaltern, one sergeant, one drummer and 25 rank and file. Total—two captains, six subalterns, eight sergeants, eight drummers and 220 rank and file. The flank companies, completed to fifty rank and file, to be stationed on board the *Wolfe* and *Royal George*, for which purpose the light company is ordered to join. All supernumerary men are to be attached to the gunboats and are to complete casualties that may occur in the detachment of marines, to which service they are to be attached. Officers, servants are to accompany their masters and attend to embark as marines.

The detachments are to be regularly mustered every 24th of the month by the respective officers, and the commanding officer is directed frequently to inspect the several detachments, to examine that the men's accounts are regularly kept and settled and that the interior economy and discipline of the corps is preserved.

EDWARD BAYNES,
Adjutant General.

Earl Bathurst to Sir Roger H. Sheaffe.

DOWNING STREET, 10th July, 1813.

(No. 7.)

Not Numbered.
20th March, 1813.
25th   "   "
No. 7, 28th March, 1813.
No. 8, 28th   "   "
No. 9, 29th   "   "
5th April, 1813.
Not Numbered.

SIR,—I have the honour to acknowledge the receipt of your despatches specified in the margin, which have been laid before the Prince Regent. His Royal Highness could not but feel highly gratified with the unanimity which has prevailed in the Legislature of the Province of Upper Canada upon all subjects connected with the defence of that country against the attacks of the enemy, and approves of the measure proposed for raising as a substitute for the militia, a corps of volunteers for service during the war. His Royal Highness willingly accedes to your recommendation of giving to each person so enrolled a proportionate grant of lands. But I must caution you against making any larger grants than those which were held out in this country to men who were willing to enter into a 2d Battalion of the 49th Regiment now raising for service in North America. The grants guaranteed to them on the conclusion of the war are 50 acres to each private, and a proportionate number to each sergeant and corporal.

I have written so fully to Sir George Prevost on military affairs that I deem it unnecessary to allude to them in this despatch, more especially as the information which I possess respecting the late disaster at York, tho' not to be doubted, is not of such a nature as to enable me to ascertain the causes which led to it or the degree of damage which the enemy's attacks have occasioned. I anxiously await for intelligence from you on the subject, and I hope at the same time to learn that it is in your power to repair the losses which the capture of the capital must have caused, and to secure it effectually against similar attacks.

(Canadian Archives, Q. 293, A. pp. 228-9.)

MEMO.
Confidential.

Headquarters, 12 MILE CREEK, 10th July, 1813.

It having been decided to detach 100 men of the 41st Regiment to reinforce Brig.-General Procter, it has occurred [to me] that after the performance of the service at Black Rock, (that is, in the event of its complete success,) the detachment might proceed in batteaux along the shores of Lake Erie (by Point Albino) to Long Point, where there is every reason to believe that our fleet as well as Brig.-General Procter himself and the greatest part of the troops under his command are at this moment or will arrive there in the course of a day or two at the furthest, for the purpose of undertaking an expedition against Presque Isle.

To Lt.-Col. Nichol.

J. HARVEY, Lt.-Col.,
D. A. G.

Major-General DeRottenburg to Mr. E. B. Brenton.

12 MILE CREEK, July 11th, 1813.

SIR,—I have the honor to acknowledge the receipt of your letters of the 5th and 7th inst. The former covering a copy of the proceedings of the several Indian nations assembled at 40 Mile Creek on 27th ulto., a board of officers will be appointed for the purpose of reporting upon the several matters therein contained. The same letter contained a copy of a letter from Captain Norton to Major Fulton. You will be pleased to inform His Excellency that prior to the receipt of that letter I have arranged all differences between Captain Norton and Colonel Claus to the satisfaction of the former. Your second letter was accompanied by a despatch for M. General Dearborn which was forwarded this morning by a flag of truce.

I transmitted a letter from General Dearborn, which I received in reply to one I wrote when enclosing Colonel Baynes's letter to Colonel Myers. It is of an old date, I having been under the necessity of returning it for his signature. I have acceded to flags of truce being sent by water, but must leave it to His Excellency to reply to what concerns prisoners of war.

(Canadian Archives, C. 679.)

Colonel Claus to Sir John Johnson, Superintendent of the Indian Department.

TEN MILE CREEK, 11th July, 1813.

SIR,—The Indians of Lower Canada are very urgent to return, complaining that their harvest would be lost. I have assured them that every assistance their families might require would be granted by you. Last night I told them that I would write to you and ask that the families of the men of the Seven Nations that remained to assist their brothers should be assisted in their hay harvest and corn by you, with which they seemed perfectly satisfied and will remain. Since I wrote from the Forty Mile Creek the Indians have been coming to us, but our people do not set them a good example. We have but half of them present. They plunder the settlers and return home to deposit what they take from the inhabitants. They destroy every hog and sheep they can meet with.

Nothing of any moment has taken place since the affair of the 24th until the 8th inst., when a party of Western Indians advanced near Fort George to cover some waggons that were sent for public property. After it was got off, they sent some men forward to induce the enemy to come out, and surrounded and cut off upwards of forty men. Twelve prisoners were taken and, I am sorry to say, a number of scalps, notwithstanding all we can say to them to prevent this barbarous custom. Our friends in the neighborhood of the last scene are, I am afraid, now suffering. They are ordered from their habitations, I am told.

I hope everything is shoved forward for us, as the demands are constant and nothing to give. It is with difficulty I can get a moment to write to you this much. I am so surrounded that I have hardly room to sit at the table.

(Claus Papers.)

General Porter to General Dearborn.

BLACK ROCK, July 11, 1813.

SIR,—At daylight this morning a party of 300 British, principally regular troops, under the command of Col. Bishop, landed a little below this place, compelled Maj. Adams, who was stationed here with 150 militia, to retreat and leave them in undisturbed possession of the place for two hours, which they employed in burning the public buildings and loading into boats and throwing into the river a quantity of provisions and other public property.

I immediately formed a force at Buffalo of about 300, and at 7 o'clock attacked the enemy and drove him with great precipitation to their boats.

The British left 7 or 8 dead on shore, a number wounded, among whom is Capt. Sanders of the 49th Regt., and several prisoners. They suffered most severely after they had embarked.

We lost 2 or 3 killed and 6 or 8 wounded, militia, and 2 Indians wounded.

I will give you particulars to-morrow.

(MSS. of Hon. P. A. Porter.)

Sir George Prevost to Major-General Dearborn.

QUEBEC, 11th July, 1813.

SIR,—I have this morning had the honor to receive Your Excellency's letter of the 2d inst., enclosing the copy of a letter you had received from the Hon. James Monroe, Yr. Secretary of State, accompanied by a copy of a list of American prisoners of war, considered as exchanged in conformity to the principles agreed on and put in practice by the British Admiral at Halifax, and requesting my approbation to that schedule, which is annexed, being an account for the exchange of Brigadier-General Hull and certain officers named, belonging to the army of the United States, for the officers, non-commissioned officers and private soldiers of H. M. 1st Regt. of Foot, captured on board the *Samuel and Sarah* transport by the U. S. frigate the *Essex*, Captain Porter.

I must confess to you that I feel some surprise at receiving this communication, and regret that circumstances will not allow me to afford my concurrence to the arrangement proposed.

So that for the ground upon which I withhold my approbation, I take care to enclose for the information of your Government the copy of an official despatch I received in the month of September last from Lt.-Gen'l. Sir J. C. Sherbrooke, commanding H. M. land forces at Halifax, and from that letter it must be inferred that the receipts from the American Agent for the crew of the U. S. sloop *Nautilus*, and a sufficient number of other seamen belonging to the U. S. have expressly been mentioned as being in exchange for the British soldiers taken in the *Samuel and Sarah* by the U. S. frigate *Essex*.

My letter of the 6th inst., to which I beg to refer you, and the instructions contained in it for Major Murray, will, I trust, convince you of my readiness to acquiesce in any arrangement within my power for the exchange of Brig.-Gen'l. Hull and such other officers as are named by your Government.

(Canadian Archives, C. 690, p. 4.)

Lieut.-Colonel Thomas Clark, 2d Lincoln Militia, to Lieut.-Colonel Harvey.

CHIPPAWA, July 12th, 1813.

SIR,—I have the honor to report to you for the information of Major-General De Rottenburg, that the detachment under the command of Lieut.-Col. Bisshopp, consisting of a detachment of Royal Artillery under Lieut. Armstrong, 40 of the King's Regt. under Lieut. Barstow, 100 of the 41st under Capt. Saunders, 40 of the 49th under Lieut. FitzGibbon, and about 40 of the 2d and 3d Lincoln Militia, embarked at 2 o'clock on the morning of the 11th inst. to attack the enemy's batteries at Black Rock.

The detachment landed half an hour before daylight without being perceived, and immediately proceeded to attack the batteries, which they carried with little opposition. The enemy heard the firing at their advanced posts, and immediately retreated with great precipitation to Buffalo.

The blockhouses, barracks and navy yard, with one large schooner, were burnt, and such of the public stores as could be got off were taken possession of and carried across the river by the troops. Before the whole of the stores were taken away, the enemy advanced, having been reinforced by a considerable body of Indians, whom they posted in the woods on their flanks and in their advance.

They were gallantly opposed by the whole of the troops, but finding the Indians could not be driven from the adjoining woods without our sustaining a very great loss, it was deemed prudent to retreat to the boats, and the troops recrossed the river under a very heavy fire.

I am extremely sorry to add Lieut.-Colonel Bisshopp fell severely wounded on our retreat to the boats. Fortunately the detachment did not suffer by it, everything having been arranged and completed previous to his receiving his wounds.

Enclosed are the returns of the killed, wounded and missing, with the exception of those of the 49th Regiment and Militia, which have not yet been received.

I have also enclosed the returns of the ordnance and other stores captured.

(Canadian Archives, Q. 122, p. 101.)

Return of killed, wounded and missing in action with the enemy at Black Rock, on the morning of the 11th inst :—

Staff—1 inspecting field officer wounded.
8th or King's Regt.—3 privates killed ; 1 corporal and 6 privates wounded.
41st Regt.—6 privates killed ; 1 captain, 1 ensign, 1 sergeant, 10 privates wounded ; 4 privates wounded and missing.
49th Regt.—4 privates killed ; 3 privates wounded ; 2 privates missing.
Militia—1 Lieut.-Colonel wounded.
Officers wounded are : — Lieut.-Colonel Bisshopp, inspecting field officer, severely, not dangerously ; Lieut.-Colonel Clark, 2nd Lincoln Militia, slightly ; Captain Saunders, 41st Regt., severely, and a prisoner ; Ensign Mompesson, slightly.

J. HARVEY, Lt.-Col.,
D. A. G.

(Canadian Archives, C. 679.)

Return of ordnance destroyed and captured from the enemy at Black Rock, July 11th, 1813 :—

Total—4 guns, 177 English and French muskets, one 3-pounder travelling carriage, 6 ammunition kegs, a small quantity of round and case shot (quantity not yet known.)

Taken and destroyed :—
Two iron 12-pounders, two iron 9-pounders.

R. S. ARMSTRONG,
Lieut. R. A.

Return of stores, &c., &c., captured at and brought from Black Rock on the 11th July, 1813 :—

One hundred and twenty-three barrels of salt, 46 barrels of whiskey, 11 barrels of flour, 1 barrel of tar, 2 large bales of blankets (about 200), 70 large blankets (loose), 5 casks of clothing, 3 cases containing 396 soldiers' caps; 16 bars of iron, 1 bar of steel, 1 side sole leather, 7 sides of upper leather (some of them marked Sergeant Fitzgerald, 41st Regiment, and taken from Fort Erie, to be returned to the 41st Regiment), 7 large batteaux, 1 large scow.

THOS. CLARK,
Lieut.-Col. 2d Lincoln Militia.

Extract from a Memorial to the Duke of York from Captain Henry Caulfield Saunders, 41st Regiment, Dated 1818.

The original intention of the expedition from the headquarters of Major-General De Rottenburg at the Twelve Mile Creek, on Lake Ontario, was for the purpose of destroying the enemy's important post at Black Rock.

Your memorialist at that time was honored with the command of 300 rank and file detached from the 41st Regiment, when he received orders to send a captain, two subalterns and 100 men, under the command of Lieutenant-Colonel Bisshopp, Inspecting Field Officer of the Militia, as part of the force for that service, the whole consisting of about 250 men with officers, including a few militia.

Your memorialist volunteered [for] the service, and left the command of his party to a junior captain.

Lieutenant-Colonel Bisshopp was successful in surprising the enemy, but while the party were destroying the blockhouses, naval yard, barracks and a large schooner, and embarking artillery and stores on board the enemy's large boats, the force driven out of the place was joined by large bodies of militia and Indians, and made a heavy attack on the right flank of the position your memorialist was ordered to take by Lieutenant-Colonel Bisshopp to cover his operations.

On the commencement of the attack Lieutenant-Colonel Bisshopp advanced to support and reinforce your memorialist, but was wounded and carried off just as he joined. On seeing him retire, your memorialist reported the circumstance to Lieut.-Colonel Clark of the militia, who had also joined him. Shortly after he received a wound, which obliged him also to retire, by which Your Royal Highness will see that your memorialist was left as commanding officer to continue the action.

Some time after, receiving information that the embarking of stores and destroying the military establishment of the place was nearly effected, and finding that the enemy from increased numbers threatened to turn his left flank, he ordered a charge, in which he succeeded and enabled him to commence his retreat, but was obliged to charge three different times, with some loss, before he was enabled completely to accomplish it.

When on the retreat to the beach, your memorialist received a rifle shot through the lungs and his right arm was much shattered; he fell, supposed dead. It was therefore impossible to recover his body, as the enemy and Indians were gathering in crowds on the beach where he lay and keeping up a destructive fire on the boats.

(Canadian Archives, Q. 150, pp. 54-7.)

221

Prize Pay List

For those entitled to share in the captures made by the Centre Division of the Army upon the Niagara Frontier* in the summer, 1813:—

	Officers.	N. C. O's.	Privates.
Staff Officers	15	—	—
Commissariat Department	4	11	—
Indian Department	13	9	—
Provincial Canadian Light Dragoons	4	7	47
Royal Artillery	4	6	71
Incorporated Militia Artillery	1	4	9
Provincial Royal Artillery Drivers	3	4	27
1st Battalion Royal Scots	27	78	660
1st Battalion 8th, or King's, Regiment	19	57	453
41st Regiment of Foot	17	51	315
49th Regiment of Foot	31	73	565
89th Light Company	3	4	53
104th Regiment of Foot	22	50	311
Glengarry Light Infantry	7	11	117
Incorporated Militia	5	6	18
2nd Regiment Lincoln Militia	15	7	33
Provincial Light Dragoons	3	6	30
Total	193	384	2709

(Abstract from Prize Lists in the Royal Hospital, Chelsea, England.)

Colonel Claus to Lieut.-Colonel Harvey.

TEN MILE CREEK, 12th July, 1813.

SIR,—I am just returning from the Indian camp at 8 p. m. I met Norton and asked him what report I should make. His reply was, that he was going to headquarters and would report that everything was settled. A party of St. Joseph's Indians [10] are just

---

* In the Prize Agent's general statement of the sources from which the Prize Money was derived, the following places are mentioned:—
  Forty Mile Creek,
  Burlington Heights,
  Fort Schlosser,
  Black Rock,
  Beaver Dam.

returned from Ball's. They have been engaged with the enemy there, in number near a hundred. One of the Indians is mortally wounded.

(Claus papers.)

Circular Letter from Colonel Claus to Major Givins and Captain Norton.

(Undated, probably 12th July, 1813.)

Captain Norton is to make requisitions for all the Indians except the following, who are to be supported by Major Givins' requisitions:

Yellow Head's band.
La Cloche band.
La Croix Rivière band.
La Trenche band.
Chippawas.
Credit Indians.

(Claus papers.)

Colonel Claus to Lt.-Colonel Harvey.

TEN MILE CREEK, 12th July, 1813.

SIR,—A party of Algonkin and Nippissing Indians, to the number of 19, with one interpreter, Langlade, who received a wound on the 8th, went forward yesterday towards Fort George and fell in with a party of dragoons near Mr. Ball's. They killed two and took the Quartermaster Sergeant prisoner with two horses. This sergeant is a Frenchman, three years from France, a shrewd, clever fellow. The Nippissing chiefs wish to carry their prisoner away with them and deliver him to Sir John Johnson. I promised to make their request known to the General and have the interpreters busy trying to get them to deliver him up.

(Claus papers.)

From the Montreal Gazette, July 12, 1813.

The Indians of Coghnawaga and the Lake of the Two Mountains, who were so instrumental in the brilliant achievement of the 24th ult., arrived here yesterday. Their short period of service with the army has been attended with eminent success, and entitles them to the warmest thanks of the country and a handsome compensation from Government, which they will undoubtedly be rewarded with.

The steamboat arrived here on Saturday morning from Quebec.

Among the numerous passengers brought up by her, we were extremely happy to see a party of volunteer seamen from the transport for the lake service.

(File in the Library of Parliament, Ottawa.)

General Peter B. Porter to Major-General Dearborn at Fort George.

BLACK ROCK, July 13, 1813.

SIR,—In giving you an account of the attack on this place of the 11th, you will pardon me if, for reasons of some moment to myself at least, I go into details which so trifling an affair may not seem to merit.

Of the troops you had ordered under my command for the defence of Black Rock and Buffalo, the following only had arrived, viz. :— 100 dismounted dragoons and regular infantry under Captain Cummings, who was stationed at Buffalo; 150 of Major Adams' Militia, stationed at Fort Gibson, half a mile above the village of Black Rock; and eight of the regular artillery under Sergeant Stevens, who was placed at the marine barracks, half a mile below the village, to take charge of the blockhouse and a piece of artillery covering the bridge over Scajaquady's Creek.

The enemy landed 300 regular troops and 40 militia, under the command of Colonels Bisshopp and Clark, some time in the night about 3 miles below the place, and by a concealed march through the woods reached the bridge at Scajaquady's a little before sunrise. A piquet of eight of Major Adams' men at the blockhouse fled on discovering the enemy without giving any alarm even to Sergeant Stevens, who was but a few rods distant. The consequence was that they immediately gained and set fire to the blockhouse and marine barracks, advanced rapidly through the town and were formed within two hundred yards of Major Adams' camp before they were discovered, and sent a flag demanding the surrender of his troops. The Major did not comply with the demand, but prudently retreated towards Buffalo *by the Beach*, leaving the enemy in possession of the barracks, one 9-pounder fieldpiece and two 12-pounder battery guns, all provided with ammunition.

This surprise, and the consequent loss of public and private property, is to be ascribed to the character of the troops (raw militia, who had not seen a week's service,) that formed the piquet. Having been most of the night on the watch, I had gone to bed half an hour before sunrise at my own house, where I did not permit myself even to keep a guard on account of the necessity of employing so great a portion of the men at other places. The enemy's advance was passing my door when first discovered, and their main body entered the house five minutes after. I escaped between them, but could not reach Major Adams by the circuitous route it became necessary to take, before he retreated. In proceeding to Buffalo, I met Captain Cummings in the Two Mile Woods, which separate it from this place. He had put his men under march with great promptitude and was advancing to the support of the militia, who had, however, by this time got into his rear by another route. Deeming it imprudent to advance with so small a force, I directed him to fall back to the first open ground in order to collect the scattered militia and employ the whole force of the neighbourhood.

In less than half an hour we added 80 or 90 of Major Adams' militia, whom the officers had kept together, 50 of the Buffalo militia under Captain Bull, and one fieldpiece under Sergeant Stevens. With this force and 30 Indians, we attacked the enemy at 7 o'clock, and drove him in great precipitation to his boats.

Our loss was 3 militia killed and 6 (4 militia and 2 Indians) wounded; 4 citizens of Black Rock and 3 sick soldiers in the hospital taken prisoners.

The enemy left 8 dead and 4 wounded on the field (among the latter Captain Saunders of 41st Regiment), and 13 prisoners. Colonels Bisshopp and Clark were both wounded, the former, supposed mortally, was carried some distance into his boat. They suffered most in their boats, particularly the last, containing about 60 men, nearly the whole of whom it is certain were either killed or wounded.

During the short time they had possession of Black Rock, they burnt the public buildings, took away 3 pieces of artillery and spiked 3 others, and were engaged in plundering the storehouses of army and navy stores and other public and private property. From appearances they must have got off about one-third of the property in store, and they expressed to the citizens their determination after taking the residue to proceed to Buffalo, where they had learnt there were large and more valuable deposits of public property.

Had I supposed that the enemy, who were the assailants with a superior force, and before effecting but a trifling part of the objects which must have suggested the expedition, would have made so faint a resistance, it is possible I might have made the whole of them prisoners by bringing the whole of our force into action at the same moment. But the advantageous position with the artillery left by Major Adams and now occupied by the enemy, covering the road or causeway to Buffalo, suggested a plan of attack in order to regain that ground which left Captain Cummings, with the regular troops and Buffalo militia, half a mile in rear. The object of the first attack, which was made with the militia, was by a sudden and bold dash through the woods to get command of the artillery and the road for the advance of the regular troops. Agreeably to the arrangement, the moment the fire commenced Major King, who had arrived a few minutes before and taken Captain Cummings' command, advanced rapidly with the regular troops and Buffalo militia, but was only able to reach the river in time to engage the enemy in his boats.

The conduct of the militia was such as would have reflected credit on veteran troops, and is not less creditable to them as soldiers and citizens than that of their companions, who basely deserted them, is disgraceful. They emerged from a thick wood, formed a line in the open field within seventy yards of the enemy, advanced under a heavy fire upon a line of double their numbers of regular troops and, with the timely assistance of the Indians, routed them and defeated two attempts made to rally. Major King, you know, has been in almost every engagement on the frontier, and on this morning he waded several miles through the swamp to take part in this. Captain Cummings gave the fullest evidence of his worth as an officer, both in the coolness and judgment with which he assisted in planning and preparing the operations of the morning, and in the zeal and exactness with which he executed his part. It is impossible to do justice to the gallantry of the Indians, who were led on by their favorite old warrior, Farmer's Brother, assisted by the hereditary chief of the Senecas, the Young King, who was badly wounded.

As this, I believe, is the first time the Indians have taken an active part with us in the war, and may become the subject of public animadversion, I feel it my duty to state that I had not solicited nor expected their assistance, nor did I know they were near until I saw them actually engaged. I had detached a party of twenty volunteers to assail the enemy on the left under cover of the woods for the purpose of throwing them into confusion and ensuring the success of the attack of the militia on the right, with which party the Indians luckily fell in and co-operated. There can, however, be no objection to the employment of them, subject as they are willing to be to the orders of our officers and the rules of civilized warfare. The cool bravery with which they fight is a sure guarantee that they will not treat a vanquished foe ungenerously. They committed no acts of cruelty, and, although some of them proposed, after the skirmish, to scalp the slain according to their ancient customs, they evinced no displeasure at meeting a peremptory refusal. How far it may be proper to employ them, or to permit them to retaliate the horrid barbarities which are daily committed by those in the employment of the enemy, it will rest with you to determine.

(From Niles' *Weekly Register*, Vol. 8, Supplement, p. 146-7.)

(From the Buffalo "Gazette," July 13th, 1813.)

On Sunday morning last Cols. Bisshop and Warren, with about two hundred and fifty of the 41st, 49th and King's Regiment, crossed the Niagara below Squaw Island and marched far above the navy yard before any alarm was given. The detached militia at Black Rock being surprised retreated up the beach and left the enemy in the undisturbed possession of the village, who immediately burned the sailors' barracks and the block house at the navy yard and barracks at the great battery. They then proceeded to the batteries, dismounted and spiked three twelve-pounders and took away three field pieces and one twelve-pounder, and also took from the beach and store-house a quantity of whisky, salt, flour, pork, &c., but to what amount is unknown. While part of them were thus engaged in disposing of the public property the remainder went through the village, entering many of the houses, but we have not heard that they committed any outrages upon private property. Messrs. Joseph Sill, A. Stannard, E. Seely and J. Caskey were taken across the river. Major Adams at the moment of retreat despatched an express to Buffalo; a part of his men came to Buffalo, the remainder left the beach and made the road leading from Buffalo to Black Rock and took post near the road. When the express arrived at Buffalo Capt. Cummins of the regular army, with one hundred infantry and dragoons, marched for Black Rock; perceiving, however, that the enemy was advantageously posted at the upper battery with a superior force, he very prudently returned to Buffalo. Capt. Bull had now collected his company, which was considerably augmented by volunteers.

From the first moment of the alarm Gen. Porter left Black Rock for Buffalo and was actively employed in arranging the subsequent operations and encouraging volunteers. The alarm came to the neighborhood of Maj. Miller's (Cold Spring) and Judge Granger's (Four Mile Creek) early, and in a short time thirty or forty volunteers came from the Plains, about twenty or thirty Indians, stationed at Judge Granger's, came down, and all the forces formed a junction within about one mile from the enemy. Gen. Porter, with about one hundred detached militia under Maj. Adams, took the left, the Regulars and Buffalo Volunteers (under Capt. Bull) the centre, and Capt. Wm. Hull, with about thirty volunteers from the Plains, and thirty Indians under Farmer's Brother, the right. It was expected the enemy had posted two field pieces at the barracks to rake the road, and it being, therefore, imprudent to advance the centre until the enemy were forced from their position, the right and left moved on the enemy's flanks; the left commenced the attack, which was quickly seconded by the right. The right being pretty well concealed they suffered but little from the enemy's fire. After a contest of fifteen or twenty minutes the enemy left his position at the barracks, and by the time the centre began to move at the sound of the bugle, he retreated precipitately with the utmost disorder and confusion to the beach at the lower store-house and embarked in several of our boats and pulled for the opposite shore. All the boats except the last, it is believed, got off without injury, but the hindermost boat was much exposed to our fire, and from the appearance of the boat the crew must have been nearly all killed or wounded.

The British lost two killed on the field and five wounded, besides those killed and wounded in the boat. We took fifteen prisoners, which are to pass on to Batavia. Capt. Saunders of the 49th was mortally wounded while stepping into the boat; he was taken to Gen. Porter's, where he now lies. He states that Col. Bisshopp was badly wounded and carried into the boat, and says that several killed and wounded were carried into the boats.

Our loss: three killed, five wounded, and probably a few militia taken prisoners. The killed were Jonathan Thompson of Caledonia, Sergeant Hartman of Riga, and Joseph Wright of Black Rock. Nearly half of the drafted militia (as Maj. Adams informs us) have gone home; those who remained did their duty like soldiers. Young King and another Indian were wounded. The Indians behaved well. They committed no act of cruelty. They fought because they were friendly to the United States, and because their own possessions, which are very valuable, were in danger of invasion. They are opposed to crossing the river to fight, but are ready to meet the enemy at the threshold in defence of the country which protects them. Major King was at Black Rock over night, and assisted in the action. It is now more than a year since the declaration of war, and this is the first attempt of the enemy to cross at Black Rock, and considering the repulse he has met with, it certainly will not redound to his credit, when his force was composed of veterans who had seen service, and ours consisting of militia and new recruits, who had very few of them been in an engagement before. The next attack of the enemy will probably be made at a different point. Some pains ought to be taken to give him a suitable reception. During the whole day the roads leading to Buffalo were filled with volunteers from the different towns.

Since the above was in type we have been informed that the enemy took a quantity of goods from Sill's store, and from buildings which were deserted some plunder was taken. Two hundred regulars have just arrived in boats from Erie, and are, as we understand, to be stationed at Black Rock.

(File in Buffalo Public Library.)

Statement by Lieut. FitzGibbon.

Knowing that the enemy had extensive barracks and stores at Black Rock, I marched my party by night to where the village of Waterloo now stands, near Fort Erie, and concealed them in barns during daylight. While next day examining the enemy's number and condition with my glass, and carefully concealed, for they did not yet expect us back to the frontier, the officer commanding our advance, with his staff adjutant and a colonel of militia, quite unexpected by me, walked up in full view of the Americans, and much to my regret, as the success of my intended project must, I thought, mainly depend upon keeping them entirely in ignorance of our having come back to the frontier. This commander then told me that he had proposed to the General Officer Commanding, General DeRottenburg, to attack Black Rock, and asked for three hundred men, but the General would give only two hundred, and he asked me if I thought the place could be taken and the barracks and stores destroyed by so small a force. I had already, the evening before, ordered four batteaux to be brought down from their place of concealment up the Chippawa Creek, and I expected to have them the following night, and in them I had determined to attack Black Rock with my party, at that time only forty-four rank and file, and I answered his question by telling him so. He laughed and said, "Oh, then! I need ask you no more questions, but go and bring the two hundred men." He ordered me not to attack during his absence, but to wait for him, and he came up the following day. He consented that my party should lead the advance and cover the retreat on coming away, should we be attacked. At two the following morning we moved off. My men being select and good boatmen soon gained the opposite shore, but owing to the strength of the current and the boats being filled with men, further down than we intended. I then saw that the other boats would be carried still further down, and must be at least half an hour later in landing than my men. Yet my orders were to advance immediately on landing. I did so, and in twenty minutes we drove the enemy out, one hundred and fifty militia men, who fled to Buffalo, and we were in full possession of all before the main body came up.

(From Col. FitzGibbon's "Hints to a Son," appendix to "A Veteran of 1812," by Miss M. A. FitzGibbon.)

Recollections of the Attack on Black Rock, 11th July, 1813, by James Sloan.

The evening previous I had shipped a part of a load of groceries, intending to drop down to Schlosser that night, but being unwell I stayed at Dr. Hawley's tavern all night. In the morning I was roused from my sleep about sunrise with musketry near and north of the house, and about the same moment the bugle just south-east of the house. I jumped out of bed and, strange to say, all the inmates had fled without my knowing it. I now saw the main body of the enemy in the road near Gen. Porter's house. The firing had killed an unfortunate Canadian baker of the name of Wright. Seeing no way of escape, I went to bed again. I had lain but a few moments [when] a man looked through the window with an exclamation of, "Sergeant Kelly! Here is a man in bed." They charged into the room, and in a rough manner ordered me out of bed. This I declined doing on the plea I was not well. This reply seemed to enrage them and they swore they would skiver me, and seemed about suiting the action to the word. I was much alarmed, and leapt over the foot of the bed and slipped into my clothes with great celerity. Sergt. Kelly now spoke to me in a kinder tone and asked for liquor. I presented him with a demi-john of excellent cherry bounce. After filling their canteens and taking a few hearty swigs, in which I joined them, we were now on the best of terms, and it was agreed I should remain and go to bed again as the most secure place. These two men belonged to the 49th Regiment, and were Irishmen. They now made their exit, and to prevent others from entering I closed the house, seemingly it being left open by the inmates in their flight. I now retired to bed again, but found it impossible to remain long. I left the bed and took a new survey of the field. The main body was near the intersection of Niagara street with Swift's Battery. The militia and volunteers had broken into Porter [and] Barton's warehouse and Nathaniel Sill's store. The military barracks at Swift's Battery, and the sailors' barracks at Conjaquety Creek, were now on fire; also, a schooner called the *Zephyr*, of about 50 tons, belonging to Jo. Carter of Cleveland. The enemy being all south of me, it was easy for me to escape from the north side of the house. I had, however, become excited, and was determined to act. Some of the officers being mounted and riding to and fro and along the road which was near the woods, I was determined to attempt the capture of one of them should I find any arms in the house. I accordingly commenced a search, and while so engaged I heard a noise on the river. This was the enemy's boats ascending the river from below Squaw Island, where the enemy had crossed over, and, strange to say, they seen me through the window. The hue and cry was raised that there were men in the house, and it was quickly surrounded on all sides and they were battering at the hall door. I unlocked it to prevent their breaking it down. Two rather pleasant officers stepped up to me and said I was their prisoner. This I demurred to on account of illness. "The Col. is at the door; speak to him," was the reply. I stepped to the door and found Col. Bisshopp mounted on Gen. Porter's horse. I now commenced putting in my old plea of poor health, when I was cut short by the Col. saying, "Young man, you must go to Canada." As my capture was unavoidable, I was pleased with the idea of seeing the country and the British army. Being an expert swimmer, I knew I could recross the Niagara river by lashing two or three rails together with strips of bark, if nothing better offered.

I was marched to Porter [and] Barton's warehouse. The Col. had preceded me there, and was quietly looking at his men rolling barrels in the river, I informed him they were destroying private property. He ordered it stopt. Col. B. was a mild humane-looking man and about 36 years of age, rather tall and well made and a man of exceeding few words. Although near him in the storehouse for some time, he did not address a single word to me, not even to ask how I knew it was private property. Indeed I have no recollection of hearing him say a single word but those I have related.

The Colonel's sands had nearly run. In the battle that took place shortly after this he was mortally wounded. My friend Sergt. Kelly was also wounded, but not supposed to be dangerous. He, however, left a few days after this with his company for Amherstburg. His wound done bad on the road, and poor Kelly was laid in the dust. I regretted the fate of these two excellent men.

(From MS. in Buffalo Public Library.)

(From the Buffalo Gazette, 13th July, 1813.)

Two hundred regulars have just arrived in boats from Erie, and are, as we understand, to be stationed at Black Rock.

On Thursday afternoon last (July 8) our picket-guard at Fort George was attacked by the British and driven in. A part of two regiments immediately passed out, and after a short contest routed the enemy. On our part there were 15 or 20 killed, wounded and taken. The loss of the British was somewhat larger.

The sickness at Fort George we learn has much abated. General Dearborn has, we believe, almost entirely recovered his health.

The British have appeared in some force at Queenston.

In the affair at Schlosser (mentioned in our last), the British took off a six-pounder, 80 or 90 barrels of salt, some property in the public storehouse, and Messrs. W. Saddler and J. Fields, tavernkeepers. The guard consisted of only 12 men, with one lieutenant and a waggon-master, Palmer, late a lieutenant in Colonel Swift's regiment. The British came over the next night, but observing a guard, they returned.

The Baltimore Blues are stationed at Lewiston and Schlosser as a guard.

On Wednesday (July 7) the enemy made their appearance opposite Black Rock. A party of the detached militia stationed at Black Rock were across the river when the British came up. The militia made good their retreat. On Thursday night (July 8) the enemy crossed the Niagara at the head of Grand Island and took off one or more citizens and some booty.

They pursued several waggons and drove the waggoners into the woods and took the waggon-harness, coverings, &c.

They entered several private houses but, we understand, they took no plunder.

(File in Buffalo Public Library.)

Major-General De Rottenburg to Mr. E. B. Brenton.

12 MILE CREEK, 14th July, 1813.

SIR,—I have the honor to transmit enclosed to be laid before His Excellency the Commander of the Forces, the official report of the affair of the 11th inst. by Lieutenant-Colonel Clark, 2d Lincoln Militia, accompanied by a return of the killed, wounded and missing and returns of the stores and ordnance destroyed and captured. I also transmit a District General Order issued on that occasion, and am happy to state that Lieutenant-Colonel Bisshopp, altho' severely wounded in his thigh and both his arms, is doing well.

(Canadian Archives C. 679.)

Militia General Order.

Headquarters, 12 MILE CREEK,
12th July, 1813.

His Honor the President and Major-General Commanding is pleased to appoint Robert Grant, Esquire, to be acting deputy paymaster general to the militia until further orders. He will receive the allowances of a captain, and the pay of ten shillings army pay per diem from the 25th June last inclusive.

Paymasters of districts will transmit to him without delay estimates in the usual form for such monies as may be required, either on the account of pay or other authorized expenditure on militia service.

By His Honor's command.

ÆNEAS SHAW,
Adjt.-Gen'l Militia.

Colonel Claus to Lieut.-Colonel Harvey.

TEN MILE CREEK, 13th July, 1813.

SIR,—Many of the Indians are without shoes. I enclose a requisition for 100 shoe-packs.

(Claus Papers.)

Colonel Claus to Lieut.-Colonel Harvey.

TEN MILE CREEK, 13th July, 1813.

SIR,—After making every exertion none of the Indians have gone to the left, but the whole, except about forty, have gone to St. Davids.

(Claus Papers.)

Major Cyrenius Chapin to Major General Dearborn.

FORT GEORGE, July 13, 1813.

SIR,—I have just arrived from my confinement in Canada with my men, without our parole. Our return happened in the following manner: I received orders at Burlington Heights on Monday morning [July 12th] to go to Kingston. We set off accordingly under the care of a guard of 16 men. I had with me 28 men. We all went very quietly until 4 o'clock in the afternoon, at which time I gave a signal to attack the guard, which were stationed in the following order: A sergeant and one man in the boat with my men, a lieutenant and 13 men in the boat with me and two officers. At a signal my men ran alongside the boat that I was in. Lieut. Showers ordered them astern; I ordered them on board, at which time the officer attempted to draw his sword. I seized him by the neck, threw him on his back —two of his men drew their bayonets upon me. I immediately seized both bayonets at the same instant and threw them on top of the officer, and kept all down together; at the same moment my men seized the guard and wrested from them their arms. We then, having possession of the arms, changed our course and arrived here this morning half after two o'clock, all safe. We have brought two boats with us.

(From Niles' *Weekly Register*, 31st July, 1813. Vol. IV., pp. 352-3.)

Major-General De Rottenburg to Colonel Baynes.

12 MILE CREEK, 14th July, 1813.

SIR,—I have the honor to acknowledge the receipt of your letter of the 9th inst., enclosing a copy of instructions for the guidance of Lieut.-Col. Battersby in the command of the corps committed to his charge to be stationed at York. These instructions are so complete that I shall have but very little to add to them. I shall forward two light field pieces to York as soon as the corps arrives there, and the two light companies of the line shall on no account be separated from the Glengarry Light Infantry. The light company of the Newfoundland Regiment left York long ago as an escort to the prisoners taken at Stoney Creek, and I trust ere this they have arrived at Kingston. At all events, the orders have been sent to York. Respecting them, I wish I had received your letters prior to the attack on Black Rock, in which case I should have employed Indians with Lieut.-Colonel Bisshopp, as you authorized me in those letters to employ Indians on the enemy's side of the water. I have hitherto refrained from so doing, His Excellency having positively forbidden my employing them beyond our lines in offensive operations. Whenever private property is to be respected, it is a very difficult thing to restrain the Indians from acts of cruelty and from indiscriminate plundering, particularly those from the westward, who are a most ferocious and savage set. As far as night attacks on the enemy's picquets are concerned, it is contrary to their custom to act in the night, and I am afraid I cannot prevail on them.

I have to lament that Lieut.-Colonel Bisshopp overstaid his time, contrary to positive instructions to that effect. Had he adhered to them, the success would have been complete without the loss of a single man, and the detachment of the 41st would have been enabled to have proceeded to Long Point without delay.

By some unaccountable occurrence the Royals and 104th have not yet arrived. I have sent an express to York to hasten them, as without them it is not in my power to take a more advanced position; it also prevents my detaching the 41st. That regiment is in rags and without shoes. I trust the promised stores of necessaries will soon arrive, and I shall forward those for General Procter without delay.

I have to request His Excellency's authority for granting the assistant-surgeons of regiments and hospital-mates the allowance for forage for one horse, as they are frequently required to attend sick militia in all parts of the country.

The enemy is much in dread of being attacked, and harass their men by continual nightly duties. They say they expect large reinforcements.

(Canadian Archives, C. 679.)

District General Order.

Headquarters, 12 MILE CREEK, 14th July, 1813.

D. G. Order.

Major Simons of the Incorporated Militia will remain at the headquarters of the army and take charge of all the militia. All requisitions for batteau-crews are to be addressed to Major Simons by the Quartermaster General's or Commissary's Department.

J. HARVEY, Lt.-Col.,
D. A. G.

(Canadian Archives, Q. 341, p. 207.)

General Dearborn to General P. B. Porter.

Headquarters, FORT GEORGE, July 14th, 1813.

SIR,—Your letter of this date has been received. I have given orders to Captain Young to march to this place with the detachment under his command. The cavalry will be left at Buffalo to assist in the defence of that place and vicinity. Am I to consider you or Major Adams as commanding the militia assembled at Black Rock? I think the enemy will not make any attempt against Black Rock after the repulse they have received.

(From MSS. of Hon. P. A. Porter.)

A. S. Clark to General Peter B. Porter.

CLARENCE, July 14, 1813.

DEAR SIR,—Since my return home I have heard many flying reports about a large British force appearing opposite the Rock. Should this be the case and you are apprehensive of an attack soon, you had better call out the militia in season, and if the militia are to be depended on to guard this part of the frontiers some measure had better be immediately taken to organize them—to be called out in the manner heretofore, without officers to command them, and have to organize after they get to the scene of action, they can afford but little assistance. Will you write me your opinion what is best, by the bearer. The gentleman I took to be Mr. Gibbons I found on enquiry is a Mr. Wilson of Onondaga, a merchant. The man that I have reference to has traded in Canada, and I was informed last winter that he was going into Onondaga Co. at or near Oswego, and from what I saw and heard of him he is a very suspicious character. He is a man as large as Mr. Wilson and much such a looking man. I am informed that a man by the name of Daily from Canada passed through this neighborhood last Friday evening going to the eastward. Did you see or hear of such a man being in Buffalo and whether he had authority to pass and repass? I think at this critical time we ought to be very cautious who we suffer to be moving through our country. This Mr. Daily, I learn, lives in Newark. Be good enough to inform me what is going on or likely to be done.

(From MSS. in Library of Buffalo Historical Society.)

General Order.

Adjutant-General's Office,
KINGSTON, 14th July, 1813.

At a general court martial held at the headquarters of the Centre Division of the Army on the 7th July, 1813, was arraigned Private Thomas Collins of the 41st Regiment of Foot for desertion from his post towards the enemy with his accoutrements on or about the 5th instant.

SENTENCE OF THE COURT.

Having found the prisoner, Private Thomas Collins of the 41st Regiment of Foot, guilty of the whole and every part of the crime laid to his charge, doth adjudge him, the said Private Thomas Collins of the 41st Regiment, to be shot to death at such time and place as the Major-General commanding His Majesty's Forces in Upper Canada may direct.

The Commander of the Forces approves of the above sentence and directs that it may be carried into execution. This order to be entered in regimental books of general orders and read to the troops on parade.

EDWARD BAYNES,
Adjutant General.

General Orders.

KINGSTON, 14th July, 1813.

Several instances of irregularity and misconduct of the light company of the 89th Regiment having come to the knowledge of the Commander of the Forces, he attributes it to a want of zeal and due attention on the part of the captain, who has, in breach of the General Orders of the Army and in violation of all regard to decency and decorum, incumbered the brigade of boats by bringing up under his protection a female of improper character. His Excellency cannot consider Captain Basden a fit officer to be entrusted with the charge of a select company in the advanced light corps, and therefore directs that Lieut.-Colonel Morrison will immediately appoint a captain to proceed to York to relieve that officer in the command of the light company of the 89th Regiment.

EDWARD BAYNES,
Adjutant General.

Lieut.-Colonel Harvey to Colonel Claus.

Headquarters, 15th July, 1813.

SIR,—With a view to prevent those acts of barbarity which others have reported have been committed by some of the Indian warriors on the persons of the prisoners who have fallen into their hands, the Major-General takes upon himself until the decision of the board which is appointed upon the subject is known, to order the payment of $5 for every American prisoner who is brought to headquarters by an Indian alive and unhurt ; only half that sum will be given for a wounded prisoner.

His Honor wishes you to communicate immediately to the assembled chiefs of all the nations the substance of this note, and that you take that opportunity of impressing on them his most anxious wish that they and their warriors should abstain from every act of cruelty and barbarity towards their prisoners, and that from the moment that an enemy surrenders he should cease to be regarded as a foe.

(Claus Papers.)

Retirement of General Dearborn.

On the morning of the 15th July, (says a correspondent of the Albany *Argus*,) there was considerable agitation in camp in consequence of a report that General Dearborn had received orders to retire from the command of the army at Fort George. This report on enquiry was found to be well grounded and Gen. Boyd and all the field officers immediately assembled and addressed to the senior general the following warm and earnest solicitation for him to remain in command, to which he made the subjoined reply :

FORT GEORGE, July 15, 1813.

To Major-General Dearborn, commanding :

SIR,—We, the undersigned general and field officers of the army, who have served under your orders in the present campaign, having heard with regret that it is your intention to retire from the present command, beg leave respectfully to address you on the subject. We are far from presuming, Sir, to interfere with arrangements made by authority when announced, but humbly conceive the present circumstances of the army are such as will, when taken into serious consideration, convince you that your longer continuance with us is of the first importance at this moment, if not absolutely indispensable to the good of the service.

We are now in a hostile country, and in the immediate neighborhood a powerful though beaten enemy—an enemy whose strength is daily recruited by the arrival of reinforcements. In our own numbers, too, we have strength and confidence; our position has been well chosen for defence, and the moment for advancing upon the enemy may be soon expected to come. But to operate with success it is necessary we should have our complement of officers. But two Generals now remain, when our numbers give full employment for three; if you too should be unfortunately taken from us, at such a period as the present, the deficiency cannot be soon supplied, and in the meantime the enemy and the period for the renewal of operations are at hand. Sir, we are far from distrusting our ability to execute the commissions with which we have been respectively honored by our government, and have no design of converting this address into one of mere personal adulation. We know your averseness to flattery, and as soldiers we are unaccustomed to flatter. But the circumstances under which we address you oblige us to say that the knowledge we possess of your numerous services and merits in the arduous struggles of our glorious revolution—not to speak of more recent events, in which we might be supposed to feel too warm a participation—has given us an infinitely higher confidence in your ability to command with energy and effect than we can possibly feel individually in ourselves or generally in those who will be placed in stations of increasing responsibility by your withdrawal from the army. As soldiers we trust we shall be found equal to our duties in any event, but as soldiers and lovers of our country we wish to perform those duties under the most favorable auspices. Therefore we do most earnestly entreat you to postpone the resolution we understand you have taken and to continue in the exercise of that command which you have already holden with honor to yourself and country, and with what is of less consequence, the approbation of those who now address you. If, however, contrary to our ardent wishes and contrary to what appears the exigencies of this army, you should still feel yourself bound from any cause whatever to withdraw from this frontier, in such event we have to beg you will please to bear with you whithersoever you may go the recollection of our great veneration for your revolutionary servicees, our respect for your political constancy and virtue and the high sense we unanimously entertain of the benefits your country has already received at your hands since the commencement of the present war.

With these sentiments and with the best wishes for a speedy and perfect restoration of your health, we have the honor to be your obedient servants.

JOHN P. BOYD, Brigadier General.
M. PORTER, Col. Light Artillery.
JAMES BURN, Col. 2d Regt. Dragoons.
H. BRADY, Col. 22d Regt. Infantry.
CROMWELL PEARCE, Col. 16th Regt. Inf.
JAMES MILLER, Col. 6th Regt. Infantry.
WINFIELD SCOTT, Col. 2d Regt. Artillery.
JOHN CHRISTIE, Col. 23d Regt. Infantry.
H. V. MILTON, Lt.-Col. 5th Regt. Infantry.
JAMES P. PRESTON, Lt.-Col. 12th Regt. Infantry.
J. L. SMITH, Lt.-Col. 24th Regt. Inf.
G. E. MITCHELL, Lt.-Col. 3d Artillery.
ABRAHAM EUSTIS, Maj. Light Artillery.
THORNTON POSEY, Maj. 5th Regt. Inf.
J. V. H. HUYCK, Maj. 13th Regt. Inf.
N. PINKNEY, Maj. 5th Regt. Inf.
R. LUCAS, Maj. 22d Regt. Inf.
F. WOODFORD, Maj. 2d Light Dragoons.
J. JOHNSON, Maj. 21st Regt. Inf.
W. CUMMING, Maj. 8th Regt. Infantry.
J. E. WOOL, Maj. 20th Regt. Inf.
W. M. MORGAN, Maj. 21st Regt. Inf.
BENJ. FORSYTH, Major rifle corps.
MAJOR CAMPBELL, 6th Inf.
MAJOR NICHOLAS, 12th Regt. Infantry.
C. M. MALCOM, Major 13th Infantry.
E. BEEBE, Maj. and Assist.-Adjt.

General Dearborn's Reply.

GENTLEMEN,—It is with sentiments of grateful feeling and liveliest satisfaction that I have observed your expressions of personal friendship and confidence. I regret that my ability to serve my country is not commensurate with the devotion and zeal I have ever felt for the cause in which it is now so honourably engaged. A cause in which the national character and the dearest rights of individuals are staked. By referring to the General Order of this day, you will perceive the necessity of my retiring from the command of the army on this frontier. Be assured, gentlemen, that a recollection of the fortitude and soldierlike deportment of yourselves and the officers and men under your command in scenes of privation and sufferings, your regularity and discipline in camp, your cool intrepidity in the hour of threatening danger, and order and bravery, will be among my most pleasing remembrances through life, and I look forward with confidence to the future glory of the soldiers who conquered at York and Fort George.

Be pleased, gentlemen, to accept my warmest wishes for your health and happiness, and your arduous services be duly appreciated by your Government and a grateful country. Accept, gentlemen, the assurance of my esteem and respectful consideration.

H. DEARBORN.

To Brig.-Gen. Boyd and the field officers of the army at Fort George.

At one o'clock the officers repaired to headquarters to take leave of their chief, who had directed their successful efforts in retrieving the honor of the American arms, and who had been present with them in scenes of privation and danger.

There was no general ever gave a firmer countenance to the army in the hour of danger than Gen. Dearborn. Disdaining to court popularity, he had acquired the confidence of every officer, as fully appears by their unsolicited expressions of it. The band had assembled on the parapet of Fort George, and as the General withdrew to the barge a salute was fired from Brock's bastion. On waving the final adieu, a recollection of the many interesting scenes which had occurred during the present campaign, and the peculiar circumstances under which the General had retired from the command, depicted a deep sensibility on every countenance. Capts. Harris and Holland with a squadron of cavalry escorted the General to Cambria.

Paragraph of General Order referred to in the address of General Dearborn.

The Major-General commanding having received orders from the Secretary of War to retire from the command of this army until his health shall be re-established and until further orders, the command devolves on Brig.-Gen. Boyd. Were the Major-General permitted to consult his own feelings, no consideration could induce him to leave the army at this important crisis, but the first duty of a soldier is to obey his superiors.

(From Niles' *Weekly Register*, Baltimore, Md., August 7, 1813. Vol. IV., pp. 372-3.)

Brigadier-General Boyd to the Secretary of War.

FORT GEORGE, U. C., July 15th, 1813.

SIR,—I have the honor to acknowledge the receipt of your commands of the 7th inst. and to inform you that General Dearborn left camp this afternoon. Conformably to your orders I have assumed the command of the army at this post.

It now becomes my duty to report to you the want of officers to this section of our army. Not long since, when our army was in high health and elated with victory, we had two Major-Generals and three Brigadier-Generals; now our force, diminished by prisoners, sickness and deaths, is left almost destitute. The enemy have been able during our *inactivity* to recruit his effective force of regulars, militia and Indians.

I shall adhere to your instructions, which prohibit an engagement with the enemy when avoidable, &c.

(From Boyd's Documents and Facts, p. 17.)

General Order.

Headquarters, KINGSTON, 15th July, 1813.

G. O.

His Excellency the Commander of the Forces has received a despatch from Major-General DeRottenburg reporting a successful attack upon the enemy's post and dockyards at Black Rock at daybreak on the morning of the 11th inst., by detachments of the King's and 41st Regiments, together with Lieut. FitzGibbon's party of the 49th Regiment and about 40 militia, the whole amounting to 240 men, under the command of Lieut.-Colonel Bisshopp.

The enemy's position was carried by a spirited attack without the loss of a single man, several large boats loaded with stores and provisions and three field pieces, a twelve and two six pounders, were brought away. A vessel and all the naval store houses have been destroyed.

Unfortunately before the evacuation of the post was completed a strong reinforcement of the enemy, aided by Indians, pressed upon this small detachment, by which Capt. Saunders and 15 men were killed, Lieut.-Colonel Bisshopp, Ensign Mompesson of the 41st and 15 rank and file wounded. The wounded were brought over.

Lieut.-Colonel Bisshopp has received three wounds, severe, but not considered dangerous.

EDWARD BAYNES,
A. G., N. A.

Additional General Order.

Headquarters, KINGSTON,
Adjutant-General's Office, 15th July, 1813.

His Excellency the Commander of the Forces has received from Major-General De Rottenburg the official report of Lieut.-Colonel Clark, of 2d Lincoln Militia, of the successful attack made on the enemy's post of Black Rock on the morning of the 11th instant, Lieut.-Colonel Bisshopp being unable to write in consequence of the severe wounds he had received.

Lieut.-Colonel Clark reports that the objects of the enterprise were achieved with the utmost gallantry, and that by the judicious arrangements of Lieut.-Colonel Bisshopp the enemy's blockhouses, barracks and dockyard, together with a large vessel, were burnt, and all the ordnance and stores that could not be removed were destroyed, and the detachment was on the point of re-embarking, without having lost a single man, when it was warmly attacked by a strong reinforcement of the enemy, aided by a numerous body of Indians, who had been enabled to approach under cover of the surrounding woods, and kept up a galling fire upon the boats.

The detachment had 13 rank and file killed; Lt.-Col. Bisshopp and Capt. Saunders, 41st Regiment, severely wounded; Lieut.-Colonel Clark, 2d Lincoln Militia, and Lieut. Mompesson, 41st Regt., slightly wounded; and 20 rank and file wounded.

The ordnance captured and destroyed consist of three 12-pounders, one 9-pounder, three 6-pounders and about 200 stand of arms; 8 large boats and scows were brought away loaded with stores.

His Excellency laments that the severe wounds of Lieut.-Colonel Bisshopp will deprive the army for a time of his able and gallant services, and is happy to learn that the wound of Lieut.-Colonel Clark is not likely long to restrain the zeal and energy with which that officer has so eminently distinguished himself.

By His Excellency's command.

EDWARD BAYNES,
Adjutant General.

(Canadian Archives, Q. 122, p. 104.)

Colonel Wm. Claus to Lieut.-Colonel Harvey.

TEN MILE CREEK, 16th July, 1813.

SIR,—I proceeded this day to St. Davids and communicated the wishes conveyed in your note of yesterday.

The Indians, with the exception of the Ottawas and the Indians from the west, state that implicit obedience has been paid to your orders. The enclosed speech by Black Bird, speaker to the Bastard, the Ottawa chief, will show His Excellency the treatment these people have received from the Americans, and he says what was done on the 8th was in the heat of the action.

(Claus Papers.)

Address from Black Bird, Speaker to the Bastard, an Ottawa Chief, to Mr. Claus, Deputy Superintendent General, 15th July, 1813.

BROTHER! At the foot of the rapids last year we fought the Big Knives and we lost some of our people. When we retired the Big Knives got some of our dead. They were not satisfied with having killed them but cut them in small pieces. This made us very angry. My words to my people were as long as the powder burnt to kill and scalp, but those behind us came up and did mischief.

Brother! Last year at Chicago and St. Josephs the Big Knives destroyed our corn. This was fair, but they did not allow the dead to rest. They dug up their graves and the bones of our ancestors were thrown away and we could never find them to return them to the ground.

Brother! I have listened with a good deal of attention to the wish of our father.

Brother! If the Big Knives when they kill people of our color leave them without hacking them to pieces we will follow their example. They have themselves to blame. The way they treat our killed and the remains of those that are in their graves to the west make our people mad when they meet the Big Knives. Whenever they can get any of our people into their hands they cut them like meat into small pieces. We thought white people were Christians. They ought to show us a better example. We do not disturb their dead. What I say is known to all the people present. I do not lie.

Brother! It is an Indian custom when engaged to be very angry, but when we take prisoners to treat them kindly.

Brother! We do not know the value of money. All I wish is that our people receive clothing for our prisoners. When at home we work and hunt to save these things. Here we cannot, therefore we ask for clothes.

Brother! The officer that we killed you have spoken to us before about. I now tell you again that he fired and wounded one of our men; another fired at him and killed him. He wished to take him prisoner, but the officer said "God Damn" and fired, when he was shot dead.

(Claus Papers.)

Captain R. H. Barclay to Sir George Prevost.

H. M. S. *Queen Charlotte*,
LONG POINT, July 16th, 1813.

SIR,—The present state of His Majesty's naval force on Lake Erie induces me to call Your Excellency's serious attention to it, more particularly as the means I possess have been so entirely misrepresented.

On my taking the command here I instantly reconnoitered the enemy's naval stations, and on finding so great a force getting ready at Presque Isle I judged that an immediate attack by land and lake would decidedly be the best mode of annihilating their naval equipments at once. Under that impression I wrote to General Vincent for a sufficient body of regulars to join what General Procter could bring with him from Amherstburg and a body of Indians, (which he could at all times command,) to enable me to attack Presque Isle at once. General Vincent having promised the remainder of the 41st Regiment, I sailed from this bay to apprize General Procter of it. He perfectly concurred in the propriety of the measure and prepared to come down with the troops and Indians, but just when all was ready General DeRottenburg gave him to understand that no assistance could be given from that quarter. He was obliged in consequence to desist from an enterprise for which he had not sufficient numbers to make success even probable.

I left Amherstburg with all the vessels that I could employ as men of war and manned with the former Canadian crews and strengthened by 50 of the 41st Regiment, but our actual force being so much inferior to that of the enemy when they get equipments for their vessels renders the situation of this squadron most hazardous.

I have further received from Lieut.-Colonel Evans 70 of the 41st Regiment and intend proceeding early to-morrow for Presque Isle and take advantage of their not being yet on the lake and endeavor to prevent it until the *Detroit* is ready for sea. But that circumstance will never take place if seamen and ordnance together with stores of every description are not immediately sent up. It is the more to be insisted on as if the enemy do gain the ascendency on this lake all supplies must necessarily be cut off.

I enclose a statement of the force of the rival squadrons, and if prompt assistance is not sent up, although my officers and men will do everything that zeal and intrepidity can do, the great superiority of the enemy may prove fatal.

I write this to Your Excellency in the hope that you will take the squadron on Lake Erie into consideration and that you will see the immense advantage that will accrue to the enemy by being enabled to transport troops either to annoy the right of the army under General DeRottenburg, or to cut off General Procter's communication with the Lower Province except by land.

Indeed, the whole line under General Procter must lay open to the enemy in the event of their being able to make His Majesty's squadron retire.

The *Detroit* will be ready to launch on the 20th instant, but there is neither a sufficient quantity of ordnance, ammunition or any other stores and not a man to put in her. If that vessel was on the lake I would feel confident as to the result of any action they might choose to risk, but at present, although for the good of His Majesty's Provinces I must attack them, I cannot help saying that it is possible they may have an advantage, though I trust not a decided one.

I have communicated with Sir James Yeo on the same subject and if he from the exigencies of the service on Lake Ontario will not admit of his sending many seamen, even fifty would be of the greatest service for the present, but it will require at least from 250 to 300 seamen to render His Majesty's squadron perfectly effective.

(Canadian Archives, C. 730, pp. 33-38.)

STATEMENT.

A statement of His Majesty's squadron on Lake Erie :—

NAMES.	Guns.	CALIBRE.	Canadians.	Nf'd Regt.	41st Regt.	Total.
Queen Charlotte..	18	24 pr. Carronades......	40	25	45	110
Lady Prevost...	12	10 12-pr. Carronades & 2 long 9's..........	30	10	36	76
Hunter........	6	4 long 6's, 2 18-pr. Carronades............	20	4	15	39
Erie...........	2	1 traversing long 12-pr. & 1 12.............	6	4	5	15
Little Belt......	2	1 traversing long 9 & 1 24-pr. Carr.........	6	4	5	15
Chippawa*.....	2	6-in. howitzers........	6	7		13
Detroit. pierced for . ... (Not yet launched).	20					
	62		108	54	106	268

*Left with General Procter.

R. H. BARCLAY,
Senior Officer on Lake Erie.

Sir James Yeo to Hon. John Wilson Croker.

His Majesty's Ship *Wolfe*,
at KINGSTON, UPPER CANADA, the 16th July, 1813.

No. 6.

SIR,—I have the honour to transmit to you for the information of the Lords Commissioners of the Admiralty a detailed account of the enemy's naval force on Lakes Ontario, Erie and Champlain, as also that of His Majesty, by which their Lordships will perceive how inadequate the force under my command is to meet them with anything like an equal force at every point, as the officers and men which came from England are scarcely sufficient to man the squadron on this lake. I have therefore appointed Captains Barclay and Finnis with their lieutenants (sent here by Admiral Sir John B. Warren) to the vessels on Lake Erie, and Captain Pring to command the naval force on Lake Champlain. I have also judged it expedient to promote two midshipmen to the rank of lieutenant to serve under these officers.

I have, ever since my arrival, been so much occupied in the equipment of the squadron, and co-operating with the army at the head of the lake, that I have not had time to communicate so fully to you for their Lordships' information as I otherwise would have done.

I have used every device in my power to induce the enemy's squadron to come out before his new ship was ready, but to no effect. I am sorry to say she is now manned, and will be ready for sea in a few days.

Our new brig *Melville* will be launched this week, when the two squadrons will be in as great force as they can be this year, and immediately we are both ready a general action must take place, as every military operation or success depends entirely on whoever can maintain the naval superiority on this lake.

I am happy to state that only one seaman has deserted to the enemy, and their conduct in general has been orderly and good; every reasonable and proper indulgence has been given them to keep them in this temper, but the encouragement that is held out by the agents of the enemy, of which there are many in this province, may, I fear, seduce them in time.

With respect to the payment of the seamen, I am sorry to say that at present it is absolutely out of my power to meet their Lordships' wishes. The provincial or old marine have always been regularly paid every two months, at the rate of 10 dollars for able seamen, and 8 dollars for ordnance and landsmen per month; most of the men of the former marine are retained in the squadron. I represented the business to His Excellency Sir George Prevost, Bart., the Governor of the Canadas, and also shewed him their Lordships' instructions on that head; at the same time expressed my anxiety to adhere as closely as possible to them. His Excellency was of opinion it would be attended with the greatest danger if not totally impracticable to make any alteration in the payment of the seamen at this momentous crisis; to make a distinction between the new and the old marine could not be done. I have therefore been obliged to yield to necessity, and what I feel I cannot take upon myself to alter.

I consequently trust that their Lordships, seeing that peculiar state of the case, will approve of the steps I have taken or furnish me with their further directions on the subject. Indeed, it has been a task of infinite labor and perseverance since my arrival to throw the former arrangement in some measure into a system agreeable to the rules of the navy.

There is one more point I wish to draw their Lordships' attention to, which is the absolute necessity of sending out more grown-up young men as midshipmen and seamen, for even a victory over the enemy would not enable us to maintain the superiority without a reinforcement being sent immediately, as the enemy from their rivers have every facility and means of obtaining whatever they stand in need of in a few days.

I beg leave further to state that the seamen will receive but one month's wages out of every two that may become due until they are six months in arrear, and enclose herewith a list of acting appointments and removals of commissioned officers between the 26th of May and 16th of July, 1813, and of warrant officers from 27th of May to this period, also an abstract of the weekly accounts of the squadron.

(Admiralty Papers, Canadian Archives, M. 389-6, p. 35.)

Left Division Orders.

KINGSTON, 16th July, 1813.

No. 2.

The dismounted men of Captain Lisle's troop and such recovered men as are now under the command of Major Heathcote and belonging to corps with the right and centre divisions of the army are to embark this day at 4 o'clock for York. The Acting Deputy Quartermaster General is to provide batteaux and the men are to take 10 days' rations.

General P. B. Porter to General Boyd.

FORT NIAGARA, July 17th, 1813.

SIR,—On leaving Fort George this morning I forgot to request you to give orders in relation to one of the principal objects of my journey, altho' I believe I mentioned the subject to you last evening.

We are entirely out of ammunition at Buffalo and Black Rock, and I have this moment received a letter from Mr. Granger informing me that not a pound of powder is to be obtained for the Indians.

I must entreat, Sir, that you will order the Q. Master to send to Buffalo without a moment's delay a supply of musket cartridges, a few barrels of cannon powder and two or three qr. casks of rifle powder for the Indians.

Permit me also to suggest to you the propriety of keeping a respectable guard at Schlosser, which would be very usefully employed as well in guarding the boats it may be necessary to send up and down the river as in preventing the enemy from occupying that place and from thence obstructing the roads in your rear, which, I confess, I have great apprehensions they will do unless prevented by a strong guard. They ought to be stopped at the threshold.

You will pardon me for expressing a studied opinion that 150 men stationed at that place will contribute infinitely more to the security of your army than double their number at Fort George.

Capt. Young will stay at Schlosser to-night with a detachment of about 220 men on their march from Presqu' Isle. Perhaps you may order part of them to remain at Schlosser. We will do the best in our power for the defence of Buffalo and B. Rock.

Some incidental charges will be incurred at B. Rock in moving and securing the public property, sending expresses, &c., &c. Having already expended a handsome estate since the war, and acting, as I have lately done, without an expectation or wish of pay for my services, it will not be convenient for me to advance more out of my private purse. Will you please to direct how these contingencies are to be defrayed, and whether a discretion is to be given to any person on this subject.

(From MSS. of Hon. P. A. Porter.)

General Peter B. Porter to Governor Tompkins.

BLACK ROCK, July 17th, 1813.

DEAR SIR,—I have the honor to enclose to you the copy of a letter to General Dearborn, giving the particulars of an attack made on this place by the enemy on the 11th inst.

The citizens of Black Rock who were made prisoners have been sent home. They state that the British in the affair lost from 100 to 120 men in killed, wounded and prisoners, that the boat which got off last contained about 60 men, only 8 of whom escaped unhurt, that Colonel Bisshopp died of his wounds on the 16th inst., and that Colonel Clark was wounded.

I have just returned from Fort George. The army are panic-struck and the affairs of this frontier are most critical. I shall write more at large by the mail.

The letter to General Dearborn was sent to Fort George the day he left that place and was not received by him. I send by the bearer a copy of it which I will thank Your Excellency to direct so that it will soon reach him. Mr. Tower will put it into the mail.

(Tompkins Papers, Vol. VIII., pp. 476-7, New York State Library.)

Captain O. H. Perry to Daniel Dobbins.

ERIE, July 17th, 1813.

SIR,—You will repair to Buffalo with the two boats and there wait until the officers and men destined for the vessels of war at this place arrive. You will upon your arrival at Buffalo endeavor to collect, in conjunction with Mr. Carter's boats, in addition to the four belonging to the navy for the transportation of the men, say three or four hundred from that place to Erie. The boats to be collected at Buffalo Creek. Great caution will be necessary on your way up to prevent being intercepted by the enemy. Should they appear off this harbor I will send an express to Cattaraugus and the 20 Mile Creek to give you information.

(From Dobbins's History of the Battle of Lake Erie, pp. 23-4.)

Major-General DeRottenburg to Mr. E. B. Brenton.

ST. DAVIDS, July 18th, 1813.

SIR,—I have the honor to acknowledge the receipt of your letter of the 13th inst., transmitting a warrant for convening General Courts Martial in Upper Canada, and authorizing me in cases where I shall think an immediate example necessary to carry the sentence into execution. Five deserters of the 104th and one of the Royal Scots have been apprehended. Two of the former and the man of the Royals will be shot to-morrow for example's sake. I shall by next express transmit to you the whole of the proceedings for the confirmation and determination of His Excellency the Commander of the Forces.

I have been informed that Lieut.-Colonel Peters is not only a drunkard but very inactive and lazy. If I was to allow him the pay of lieutenant-colonel the whole tribe would claim the same indulgence. I shall therefore settle his memorial when a favorable opportunity occurs.

(Canadian Archives, C. 679.)

General P. B. Porter to General Boyd.

MANCHESTER, July 18, 1813.

SIR,—Considerable bodies of British troops, (whose numbers cannot be ascertained for want of a glass, but some think 1,000 or 1,500,) with several pieces of flying artillery are passing up the river this morning opposite to this place. The movement and bailing of boats was heard at Chippawa the latter part of the night.

It will rest with you to discover the object of this movement and determine the means of meeting it.

Perhaps they intend an attack on Buffalo and Black Rock or a crossing to this place—possibly it may only be a feint to draw your force from Fort George. My present impression is that they intend an attack some where between the Falls and Lake Erie, probably at B. Rock.

The march of a few hundred men as far up at least as this place might defeat their object and could not essentially weaken you.

But, whatever course you adopt in respect to *this* particular movement, permit me again to recommend as a general measure of expediency the propriety of keeping a few regular troops at Schlosser and Buffalo to serve as rallying points for the militia.

Would it not be desirable to have a number of dragoons constantly patroling the river from Niagara to B. Rock, with glasses to discover the movements of the enemy. Lt. Erwin should not be without one.

I shall proceed to Buffalo to-day and if they should attack that place I hope you will send out men enough to cut off their retreat. We shall press them hard with militia and Indians.

Is there any ammunition on the way to Buffalo?

(From MSS. of Hon. P. A. Porter.)

Sir George Prevost to Earl Bathurst.

Headquarters, KINGSTON, 18th July, 1813.

No. 76.

MY LORD,—Since I had the honor of addressing Your Lordship on the 3d inst. last, the enemy has withdrawn into Fort George and its immediate vicinity such of his advanced detachments as escaped being captured, and concentrated the whole of his force in that position, where I have caused him to be circumscribed within a very small circle by the Indian warriors, supported by our light troops.

I have not considered it expedient to carry on decisive military operations against Fort Niagara and the American posts situate on the frontier of that river and on the south shore of Lake Ontario whilst the enemy are in possession of a preponderating naval force, because in my estimation the first object to be attained is to secure the naval ascendency, for, without it, to undertake a distant operation would lay open my rear and the whole of my line of communication with Lower Canada to disastrous consequences, and, moreover, expose our fleet to be met to disadvantage by being encumbered with troops and stores.

The information I have received of the state of preparation of the enemy's squadron admits of my concluding that the equipment of both fleets is nearly accomplished to the extent to which either can be prepared for some time to come. The numerical superiority being with the enemy, he may perhaps feel encouraged to attack some of our positions. Should such be his intention, it might afford an excellent opportunity of bringing on a general action, particularly if Kingston is the object he has in view.

The naval and military force here at present hold out a reasonable expectation that an attempt on this point would be repulsed with so severe a loss as would remove all restraint respecting the embarkation of troops on board the squadron, and proceeding with them against Forts George and Niagara.

My last letters from Colonel Procter are dated at Sandwich, the 5th instant. The reinforcement of the remainder of the 41st Regt., which I had directed to be sent to him, had not arrived, but was on its way, and he entertained hopes that when it reached him something might be attempted in co-operation with the squadron under Captain Barclay against the enemy's flotilla preparing at Presque Isle, and which was in a great state of forwardness.

Mr. Dickson, with a large body of western warriors, had left Michilimackinac for Sandwich about the 24th ulto., and was hourly expected. Upon his arrival Col. Procter would be enabled to advance nearer to the enemy's position at Fort Meigs, which Major-General Harrison had reached with a body of horse, part of whom had ventured as far as the River Raisin. It was said to be Major-General Harrison's intention to advance with his army into the Michigan Territory, while the flotilla from Presque Isle was to land troops on the Canada shore.

By accounts from the borders of Lake Champlain, I understand there are some movements of the enemy's troops in that quarter, and that they are collecting a considerable force at Burlington, but I rather think this proceeds more from an apprehension of an attack from us than from any plan of penetrating the frontier of Lower Canada. The naval force which we have now on the Richelieu river, being very respectable since the capture of two of the enemy's armed vessels, and such, if properly commanded, as affords a reasonable prospect of annoying the enemy on Lake Champlain, I have employed Lieut. Pring of the Royal Navy as a commander of that service. Lieut. Pring was sent, with two other officers of the same rank, during the winter by Admiral Sir John Warren to take the command of the vessels on Lakes Erie and Ontario as commanders in the navy, but the subsequent arrival of Commodore Sir James Yeo, with officers appointed by the Admiralty for this service, not having left any opening for the employment of Lieut. Pring, who is a most able and deserving officer, I have, after communicating with Sir James Yeo, with whom he has been lately serving on Lake Ontario as Captain of the *Wolfe*, entrusted him with the command of the naval force to be employed on Lake Champlain, and where he may be of material service. I have therefore respectfully to request of Your Lordship that he may be confirmed in the rank to which he was appointed by Sir John Warren.

It is extremely gratifying to me to have to report to Your Lordship, for the gracious consideration of His Royal Highness the Prince Regent, that His Majesty's troops continue to do their duty with unabated valor, and daily exhibit the advantages of a well-regulated system of discipline by their conduct in the field, notwithstanding that they experience all those privations and hardships inseparable from a campaign carried on, comparatively on a great scale, for the the defence of an extensive frontier, in a new country and against an enemy superior in numbers and contiguous to his resources of every description.

(Canadian Archives, Q. 122, p. 79.)

General Order.

Adjutant General's Office,
Headquarters, KINGSTON, 18th July, 1813.

G. O.

At a General Court Martial held at the Headquarters of the Army at the Twelve Mile Creek on the 12th July and subsequent days were arraigned severally:

William Jackson, private, 104th Regt.
Daniel Lee,   do.   do.   do.
James Bombard,   do.   do.   do.
John Wilson,   do.   do.   do.
Sayer Baby,   do.   do.   do.

On the following charge:

For deserting from the post of St. Davids towards the enemy on or about the morning of 7th July, 1813.

Also at the same Court Martial was arraigned:

Private John Courgan of the 1st or Royal Scots on the following charge:

For deserting towards the enemy with his regimental clothing and side arms on the 14th July, and not returning until brought by a party of Indians on the 15th July, 1813.

The Court found the prisoners severally guilty of the crimes laid to their charge and doth therefore sentence them the said

William Jackson, private, 104th Regt.
Daniel Lee,   do.   do.   do.
James Bombard,   do.   do.   do.
John Wilson,   do.   do.   do.
Sayer Baby,   do.   do.   do.

And John Courgan, private of the 1st or Royal Scots, to be shot to death at such time and place as the Major-General Commanding the Forces in Upper Canada may direct.

The Commander of the Forces approves and confirms the above sentences, and orders that they may be carried into execution at such time and place as Major-General DeRottenburg, commanding, may direct.

EDWARD BAYNES,
A. G., N. A.

General Peter B. Porter to Governor Tompkins.

BUFFALO, July 19, 1813.

SIR,—The highly critical and exposed situation of this frontier and the earnest solicitations of the people of Buffalo and Black Rock have induced me, with the advice of General Boyd, to send this communication by express.

The whole of our army is concentrated at Forts George and Niagara and does not afford the least protection to this part of the country. Indeed, if we should be actually invaded I have great doubts whether they would spare a man for our assistance. Considerable bodies of British troops, well supplied with artillery, were seen at different points yesterday morning upon the opposite side of the river. This may be a feint to draw our troops from Fort George, but the general belief here is (and is mine) that their object is a renewed attack upon this place. If they do come over it will be with a force greatly augmented and the conflict will be sanguinary, for I believe I may assure you we shall not add to the already accumulated disgrace which this country has suffered in its military operations.

Our force consists of 40 regulars, 100 militia under Major Adams, a few volunteer militia of Buffalo, Black Rock and vicinity, and about 200 Indians.

We are almost destitute of ammunition; the great supplies which have been forwarded to this place were all ordered to Fort George and there is none at Batavia. General Boyd has, however, promised a supply.

It will remain for Your Excellency to say whether any and what force shall be sent for our protection.

Detached militia are worth but little, and if you should devise a plan of organizing a volunteer corps to act in this quarter permit me to recommend Doctor Cyrenius Chapin for some respectable command. He is desirous of engaging, is active, bold and enterprising and would have the confidence of his men. Adjutant Stanton of Major Adams' battalion, (of whom I shall write to you more particularly hereafter,) deserves a much higher situation than he now holds.

He was in service last summer, is a good disciplinarian and is entitled to the highest praise for his conduct in the affair of the 11th inst.

(Tompkins Papers, Vol. VIII., pp. 477-8, New York State Library.)

PITTSBURG, July 21st, 1813.

Extract of a letter from a gentleman at Erie, 19th inst:—

Our town is all bustle; 5 of the enemy's vessels are now within a mile-and-a-half of the town; they appear full of men, and if they should attempt a landing I fear much our militia, from their want of discipline, would make a very poor fight. Commodore Perry has not men sufficient for a brig.

(Cited in Letters of *Veritas*. p. 64.)

Major-General De Rottenburg to Sir George Prevost.

Headquarters, Army of the Centre,
St. DAVIDS, 20th July, 1813.

SIR,—I have the honor to acknowledge Your Excellency's letter of the 13th, acquainting me with Your Excellency's decision not to undertake from Kingston any distant operations previous to obtaining an ascendency over the enemy's naval forces on Lake Ontario.

Your Excellency's desire of my circumscribing the enemy's position at Fort George in as narrow a circle as I am enabled to form round him has been anticipated by my taking up my present position on the 17th inst., which reduces the enemy to the ground he stands upon and prevents his getting any supplies from our territory. Independently of these advantages, the more forward movement became necessary on account of the Indian warriors. They must be actively employed, and are now daily engaged with the enemy's outposts, harassing and teasing them the whole day long.

The enemy has detached a few hundred men towards Buffalo Creek, and may perhaps attempt something in my rear and flank, but this causes us no uneasiness. It is surprising that with such a superiority of numbers he does not attempt to drive me from my position, but keeps perfectly quiet and passive within his lines. I strongly suspect they are waiting for reinforcements, and long for the approach of our fleet. The result of a well-combined attack on both sides of the river must lead to the capture of their army.

(Canadian Archives, C. 679.)

Lieut.-Colonel Harvey to Colonel Claus.

20th July, 1813.

DEAR SIR,—I beg that you will exert yourself to induce a party of Indians to go to the left of Colonel Young's position.

(Claus Papers.)

Brigadier-General Boyd to the Secretary of War.

FORT GEORGE, July 20, 1813.

SIR,—I have the honor to report that on the 17th inst. the enemy attacked our pickets in a body of about 200 British, besides Indians. Detachments were sent out to support them, but with instructions to act defensively. After a contest of one hour, occasionally severe, the enemy was dispersed. Our loss was trifling—only three or four being killed and a few wounded. The loss of the enemy has not been ascertained, but being exposed to some well-directed fires of our light artillery under the command of Lieutenant Smith it is probable their loss must have been comparatively great. Colonel Scott, who had the direction of the troops which were engaged, speaks highly of the ardor and steadiness of both officers and men. Being fought in detachments, many young officers had an opportunity of evincing their activity and bravery. To use the language of Colonel Scott, "this affair, though small, served to test the merits of the officers and men engaged." More ardor has seldom been displayed. Captain Vandelsen fought his detachment with good effect, and Captain Madison with his picket-guard was fully engaged. They could not lose their ardor under Major Cummins. Captain Birdsall's riflemen were nearest to the enemy in pursuit. Major Armstrong, who was officer of the day, was active in concentrating and arranging the troops and

pickets. Captain Towson of the artillery was wounded in the hand while voluntarily bearing Colonel Scott's orders, and an officer of the rifle corps was slightly wounded.
(From the Historical Register of the United States. 1814, Vol. II., pp. 246-7.)

Thomas G. Ridout to Thomas Ridout.

ST. DAVIDS, 20th July, 1813.

On Saturday, 17th, Henry Nelles and I rode down to the Cross Roads, three miles from Niagara, where the Royals, King's, and 600 or 700 Indians are posted. I understood the Americans were advancing into Ball's fields. Immediately the yell was given, and Blackbird and Norton set out with the Indians to meet them. Nelles and I rode along, and in a few minutes the skirmish began by the Western Indians getting up on the left flank and the Six Nations upon the other. The enemy consisted of 500 men. They soon retreated, firing heavy volleys upon Blackbird's party, which was the nearest. The road is so straight we could see into town, and Nelles and I rode along with the Indians to within one and a quarter miles of Niagara, when we perceived a large reinforcement join them with a piece of artillery, and they again advanced with a large front, firing grape shot. The Indians scattered in the woods, but we were obliged to keep the road. By this time three companies of the Royals and a brass six-pounder came up and posted on this side of Ball's field, the Yankees on the other side. We fired for some time, when the Americans thought fit to retreat. At one time from the farther end of Ball's field a mile and a half this way the road was covered with Indians, officers and soldiers and horses, and from the Presbyterian church they must have judged our force at 3,000 men. We had about 1,000. A good many Yankees were killed. One Indian took two scalps. A young Cayuga had his arm and side carried away with a cannon ball, and another had a ball through his arm. Some of the musket balls came pretty close to us.

The Cross Roads now are very strong. Dickson is expected here as soon as he returns from the expedition that has gone against Sandusky and Presqu' Isle, with 1,500 Indians.
(From Ten Years of Upper Canada, by Lady Edgar, pp. 203-4.)

Sir George Prevost to Earl Bathurst.

Headquarters, KINGSTON, 20th July, 1813.
(No. 78.)
MY LORD,—I have the honor to transmit for Your Lordship's information an extract from a letter addressed to me by Captain

Barclay, the senior naval officer on Lake Erie, together with the statements accompanying on the subject of what he requires to enable him to man and equip the squadron placed under his command in order that Your Lordship may be satisfied of the propriety of my demand for more seamen, both upon His Majesty's Government at home and upon the Admiral commanding on the North American station.

The great uncertainty attending my communications with Your Lordship does not encourage the hope of my receiving timely aid from England, but on the other hand I am cheered with the expectation of Sir John Warren's promptitude in affording me a sufficient supply of seamen, which is the most material of Captain Barclay's wants for the present. Lest, however, I may experience a disappointment on this head, I submit to Your Lordship the importance of guarding against the consequences of it by adopting such measures as you shall judge expedient for affording from England the supply of men required, if possible, during the present year either direct to Quebec or by the way of Halifax, from whence they may be sent on by land after the navigation of the river closes, which will not be the case until the middle of November.

The ordnance, ammunition and other stores for the service on Lake Erie had been deposited at York for the purpose of being transported to Amherstburg, but unfortunately were either destroyed or fell into the enemy's hands when York was taken by them, and the subsequent interruption to the communication by their occupation of Fort George has rendered it extremely difficult to afford the supplies Captain Barclay requires, which are, however, in readiness to forward to him whenever circumstances will admit of its being done with safety.

I have reason to think that the report Captain Barclay has received of the American force is an exaggerated one, as I do not find even from their own papers that they have any other description of vessels on Lake Erie besides the two corvettes and the schooners.

(Canadian Archives, Q. 122, p. 92.)

(From the Buffalo "Gazette," 20th July, 1813.)

General Vincent remains at Burlington Heights with not more than 150 troops. The enemy have a small garrison at that place near the lake with a few pieces of cannon. The main body of the enemy lies within 3 miles of Queenston, at a small village on the 4 Mile Creek.

At the 10 Mile Creek General Ruttenburgh, lately from Montreal, lies encamped with a body of men.

The Indians, about 800 in number, are lurking about the woods in the neighbourhood of Fort George and about the village of Queenston.

The above comes from a very respectable authority.

It appears that Col. Clark, of the Canadian Incorporated Militia, was in the affair at Black Rock on Sunday (instead of Col. Warren as reported), and was wounded in the hand. Lieut.-Col. Bisshopp of the British regular army received 4 or 5 wounds, which are considered dangerous. He was in the great battle of Talavera in Spain, under Lord Wellington, in 1809.

We stated in our last that Mr. Caskay had been taken across the river by the enemy—this was not the fact. He was taken by the enemy and put into a house with a guard of two men over him, and when the British retreated two more red coats came into the house for safety, but the Indians coming between the house and the boats, the guard surrendered.

Lieut. Eldridge was taken in the skirmish at Fort George on Thursday week, and has probably been massacred by the Indians. He was a promising, enterprising young officer. Our loss, it is said, is more severe than at first reported. Great enormities were committed on the slain by the savages.

On Friday morning (July 16) Captain Young's detachment, late from Erie, left Black Rock for Fort Niagara.

Between 3 and 400 jolly jack-tars have recently arrived at Sackett's Harbor to go on board our fleet at that place. Very important events are expected shortly to transpire on Lake Ontario.

On Lake Erie we have no doubt of the ability of Captain Perry to obtain the ascendency when his fleet is ready for cruising.

(File in Buffalo Public Library.)

From Sir George Prevost to Earl Bathurst.

Headquarters, KINGSTON,
UPPER CANADA, 20th July, 1813.

(No. 79.)

MY LORD,—I have the honour of transmitting to Your Lordship the copy of a report from Lieutenant-Colonel Clark of the militia forces of the result of an attack made by a detachment of troops from the Centre Division of the Army serving in Upper Canada, placed under the command of Lieutenant-Colonel Bisshopp, one of the inspecting field officers of militia, for the purpose of destroying the enemy's blockhouses, stores, barracks, vessels and naval establishment at Black Rock, which I have this day received from Major-General DeRottenburg.

The skill and judgment of Lieutenant-Colonel Bisshopp, aided by the valour of the officers and men placed under his command, enabled him to accomplish this enterprise in the most gallant manner, when, unfortunately for His Majesty's service, a concealed enemy at the moment of the re-embarkation of the troops in their encumbered boats threw in upon them a destructive fire, which deprived the country of some valuable men and disabled Lieutenant-Colonel Bisshopp so as to leave me no hope of again benefitting by his services during the remainder of this arduous campaign.

(Canadian Archives, Q. 122, p. 99.)

New York Evening Post, 3d August, 1813.

Extract of a letter to a gentleman in this city, dated Fort George, Upper Canada, July 20, 1813.

The skirmishing still continues. On the 17th we had a smart affair. Our picquets were briskly attacked and both sides reinforced and continued reinforcing until the business had nearly become serious. The enemy fell back about half a mile, pitched their tents and there they made a stand. This body is considered as the advanced guard and the main army probably a mile and a half in rear. Our loss was five or six killed and ten or twelve wounded, the enemy's perhaps double that.

"Thunder and Lightning" Williams is hourly expected. What a powerful reinforcement? We are placed in a strange situation, from being invaders of a territory we are now preparing to meet an attack from the invaded and our limits are so circumscribed that we scarcely hold enough of Canada to rest our wearied limbs upon. We are, however, so strongly entrenched that the result of a battle is not much dreaded. Our soldiers can beat their soldiers in fighting, but their generals can beat ours at management.

The wise ones say the battle of the fleets will decide the fate of Upper Canada. Let the long looked for battle terminate as it will, believe me, Canada will not be taken this year.

By an order from the War Secretary, General Dearborn left this on the 15th, and altho' he probably was not the most fit man to command such an army yet it was so well known that his removal was occasioned by intrigue that an universal sympathy was created in his favor, and on his departure the whole army was under arms and every honor that could be paid was paid him.

(File in Astor Library, New York.)

Thomas Barclay, Commissioner for Prisoners at New York, to Sir George Prevost.

NEW YORK, 20th July, 1813.

(IN CIPHER.)

SIR,—

* * * * * * * *
* * * * * * * *

1537 2861 650 2271 2029
It is sound policy not to
3096 2181 155 1843 808 2339 2652
parole any more prisoners.—
3060 1829 650 3060 2584 650 3060
The moment they return they
94 2744 650 24 3406 2652 3073
move against us. — This
1555 1164 1234 808 3035 3060 650
Government have told the officers
2082 808 3018 1604 3537 650
taken last year they were
3060 650 3438 650 142 808 1716
exchanged and made
3061 2744 94 2652 3060 650
them move again.—The best
299 1783 3096 1716 3060 808 127
method to make the Americans
650 3095 2077 3060 3432 3478
tired of the war will
265 386 650 1566 808 3060 1122
be by keeping their rel-
1517-21 142 650 1106 2339 2652
ations and friends prisoners.—
16 1234 650 2363 3096 3060 650
I have proposed to the Amer-
127 533 1140 2077 2339 3096
ican Commisr. Gen'l. of prisoners to
1716 140 930 2077 808 127 1058
make an exchange of prisoners for
3060 369 650 3148 650 3060
the British troops they
1234 2379 385 1234 2029 3542
have prisoners, but have not yet
650 2484 1267 151 2652
received his answer.

(Canadian Archives, C. 689, p. 195.)

Speech of Colonel Claus to the Indians.

CROSS ROADS, 21st July, 1813.

BROTHERS! I congratulate you that you have been in sight of the enemy and have not met with any severe loss, and that only some of your people have been slightly hurt.

Brothers! When so many people of different languages and nations are assembled, many bad stories are abroad. I assure you that if any news or anything worth telling occurs, I will tell you. If you are uneasy, you are to let me know. Desiré, of the La Cloche band, reported that it was their wish to turn their faces towards home. I thank you for your patience. When I came down with you I did expect that we would have struck at Niagara before, but something or other turned up to prevent it. It cannot be many days before something must take place. The ships were to sail yesterday, and when they appear we shall know the day we shall advance. I shall send a runner to our people at the Grand River, and shall add your words to mine.

Desiré complains that the change of climate made some sickness, and that makes them think of going back, and not the enemy. They have neither vermilion nor knives.

The Fisher, first chief of the Ottawas:—If you give us clothing do not put it into the hands of Black Bird. If they are sick, how can they go home? They had better stay and wait the event of the battle.

Two chiefs of the Chippewas are of the same opinion.

Yellow Head is very glad to hear what he has said, and is of the same mind.

La Cloche Chief:—We live in the interior, and do not live like the other Indians. We live by hunting, and must look out for our families. We wish you could give us a paper to get food along the road and to get our canoes across the carrying place.

Another Chief:—Since you say the vessels are out and perhaps in 4 or 5 days something will be done, I will wait and see, and my friends will do the same.

Colonel Claus:—Brothers! I thank you and will tell your father. You still hold him by the hand. The liquor you ask for you shall get, but I hope you will take it very cautiously so near the enemy.

(Claus Papers.)

General Boyd to General P. B. Porter.

Headquarters, FORT GEORGE, July 21, 1813.

SIR,—Having been informed that the threatened attack on Black Rock by the enemy has not been made, and understood by deserters that (torn) such a force as was (torn) moved up in that direction I have sent an order to Major Cummins to return with his detachment unless existing appearances should render it imprudent. This order has been dictated by the necessity we are under in the present menaced situation of our camp of preserving our force undiminished. I would again urge the immediate expediency of inducing one or two hundred Indians to join us at this post. They would enable our picquets to punish the temerity of the scouting parties of the enemy, which are constantly assailing our centries. Allow me to press this subject upon you. Ammunition has just been sent to you.

(From original MSS. in Library of Buffalo Historical Society.)

Major-General DeRottenburg to Colonel Baynes.

Headquarters of the Army of the Centre,
ST. DAVIDS, 22d July, 1813.

SIR,—The Deputy Inspector General of Indian affairs recommends Mr. Charles Spenhard, who came down with the La Cloche Chippewas, and who has been employed since 25th May last, to be placed on the pay list from the 25th June as interpreter. He also recommends Mr. George Rousseau to be appointed lieutenant, *vice* Chew killed 27th May at Niagara, the appointment to take place from 25th June. I have to request the authority of His Excellency for these appointments. You will be pleased to inform His Excellency that Captain McCoy, 41st, arrived here the day before yesterday from the Army of the Right, stating that Br. General Procter had been under the necessity of giving up his intended expedition against Presque Isle and that he was proceeding with a large body of Indians to the Miami. In consequence of this information the reinforcements for General Procter have been directed to proceed by the most direct and expeditious route to Sandwich instead of going to Long Point. Of the 120 men under Lt.-Col. Evans of the 41st, who had arrived at Long Point, Capt. Barclay had taken 70 on board the *Queen Charlotte* for the purpose of blockading the harbor of Presque Isle. He stated to Lt.-Col. Evans that without this reinforcement it would be impossible for him to manage his vessels. Lt.-Col. Evans has proceeded with the remainder to Sandwich. The new vessel at Amherstburg has been launched, but Capt. Barclay has neither guns, sails or men to put into her. The enemy's squadron on Lake Erie is supposed to consist of two corvettes, 18 guns each, and nearly ready for sea, with 10 other vessels of different sizes.

The enemy at Fort George expect reinforcements from Sackett's Harbor and General Dearborn is said to have left Fort George for that place.

P. S.—Two of our cavalry videttes were taken yesterday by the enemy.

(Canadian Archives, C. 679, p. 242.)

From Poulson's "American Daily Advertiser," of Philadelphia, 3rd August, 1813.

Extract of a letter dated Rhinebeck (N. Y.), July 26, 1813:—

I was last evening with a very intelligent gentleman from Buffalo, who gave it as his opinion that before this Fort George has been retaken by the British. He states that our effective force at that place does not exceed 2600 men; that on this side we have not one man in the service of the United States, while that of the enemy amounts, in the vicinity of the fort, to at least 5,000, exclusive of Indians. Of Indians they have 150. They frequently, to intimidate our troops, show double that number, but this increase is by the painting of white men. At Buffalo we can bring into the field about 500 warriors belonging to the Six Nations, under their chiefs,—Farmer's Brother, Red Jacket, Cornplanter, &c. The inhabitants of Buffalo were removing all their effects, under the apprehension that after the repossession of the fort, which would give the British the entire possession of Canada, they will come over and destroy the town.

In the course of the conversation I introduced the barbarities said to have been committed by the Indians. He observed that they were ten-fold exaggerated; that he had been repeatedly informed that so far as humane restraint could be laid, it was enjoined by the British soldiers to prevent any act of inhumanity by the savages to the westward, and that they never scalped any but those who were actually dead, and then it was not done when the British officers had the means of preventing it.—*N. Y. Commercial Advertiser.*

(File in Philadelphia Library.)

General P. B. Porter to General Boyd.

(BLACK ROCK, 22d July, 1813.)

SIR,—I received last evening by express your favor of yesterday, apprising me of the order you had given for the return of Major Cummins with his detachment to Fort George.

I would only so far as my personal feelings and sentiments were concerned regret that such an order was necessary. Having just before learnt that our naval force on Lake Ontario had assumed such an attitude as to remove all apprehensions of an attack on Fort George by the British fleet, I had intended to have suggested for your consideration this morning the expediency of an attack on the main force of the enemy at St. Davids, 12 Mile Creek, &c.

My idea was that a force of ten or twelve hundred men, consisting of regular troops, volunteer militia and Indians, about an equal proportion of each, with 3 or 4 pieces of artillery, might be immediately collected at this or some other place above the Falls, and being provided with boats make a landing at daylight near Chippawa, dispose of the British forces stationed there, proceed immediately to St. Davids to join and co-operate with such part of your army as you might think prudent to send out, and who might leave Fort George as nearly as possible at the same time that the party from this side does Chippawa. A sudden attack by an army thus advancing from opposite directions might confound the enemy and throw into your possession many of their scattered parties of troops, and I cannot but think that an united force of 3000 men might proceed rapidly and without difficulty through all their military stations to the Head of the Lake and capture and disperse the whole of their army. I beg, however, you will consider this in the light in which it is intended, as the mere suggestion of a citizen who pretends to no other right to advise than what arises from a long acquaintance with the country, and the tolerably correct estimates which he has hitherto been able to make of the situation, strength and views of the enemy, as confirmed by subsequent events. In estimating the force of the enemy, however, at this time, I do not pretend to any accurate information as to the reinforcements he has received within a few days past and which I presume you possess.

About 250 Indian warriors are at this place, many of them having come in this morning and more expected from distant villages. They are now in council with your proposition before them. I have great doubts whether they will be willing to go to Fort George without more distinct and better prospects than I feel authorized to hold out to them from you. But I feel confident that should they be invited to act on the offensive in company with the volunteer militia, who are their neighbors, to penetrate the enemy's country and receive a proportion of the public spoil they might acquire that nine-tenths of them would embrace the offer. They are a fine body of men and their ambition highly excited. You shall know their determination as soon as it is ascertained.

Major Chapin crossed the river yesterday with 60 volunteers, marched down to Frenchman's Creek, where he took a fine boat and one prisoner. The prisoner is a Mr. Fish, who has acted in the capacity of sailing master on one of the British armed vessels on Lake Ontario. It would be desirable to exchange him for Mr. Steers, lately acting in the same capacity on board the brig *Adams*, and who was taken prisoner at Detroit. Mr. Steers is now with Capt. Perry at Erie, is much wanted as a pilot, and may be disagreeably situated unless exchanged.

Major Chapin learnt that a party of 200 British Indians came up as high as Frenchman's Creek on Sunday last but could not learn that any regular troops were so far up.

(MSS. of Hon. P. A. Porter.)

General Boyd to General P. B. Porter.

FORT GEORGE, July 22d, 1813.

SIR,—Yours of the 21st was duly received. I am happy to learn that the cause of alarm has subsided at Buffalo. Should there be any real indications of an attack in future on the opposite side I shall be always ready to render assistance. But you must be aware that the Indians now at Buffalo receiving rations could be better employed to the benefit of the State as well as the Union by being here. Were those Indians at this post we could, by sending a body of regulars with them, clear the country for ten miles round and thereby insure safety to the opposite shore, as they are certainly the most efficient troops for such a wood country as this. I trust no local consideration will cause their detention.

(From MSS. of Hon. P. A. Porter.)

National Intelligencer, Washington, D. C., August 5th, 1813.

Died, on the 22d ult., at Fort George, Upper Canada, of fever, Colonel John Chrystic of the army of the United States, a gentleman whose bravery and talents had placed him at an early age in the rank he held.

(File in Library of Congress.)

Commodore O. H. Perry to General P. B. Porter.

U. S. Sloop of War *Lawrence*, ERIE, July 22d, 1813.

DEAR SIR,—I have this moment received your letter of the 20th inst. The enemy disappeared on the evening of Monday in the direction of Long Point. Yesterday morning they were discovered standing this way. They are still off the harbor. Having suspected them of an intention to land we are prepared to meet them. It is a most mortifying situation for me, my vessels being ready and no men yet forwarded for them, while an enemy of inferior force in vessels and guns are blockading us.

(From MSS. of Hon. P. A. Porter.)

Lieut.-Colonel Harvey to Colonel Baynes.

Headquarters, ST. DAVIDS, 23d July, 1813.

Secret.

MY DEAR COLONEL,—I am directed to enclose to you a letter containing a proposition, the object of which without explanation you may be puzzled to make out. Mr. Hogeboom is, (as his name implies), a Dutchman, who has been long resident in this country, engaged in trade with Colonel Clark of Chippawa, who has the highest opinion of his integrity and attachment to the British Government. The mercantile connection betwixt them is dissolved by the circumstances of the times, and Mr. Hogeboom is *disposeable* in any way that may best promote his *personal advantage*, of which it is not the practice of his nation to lose sight. Mr. Hogeboom's family is now and has long been resident in the *States* and he has taken it into his head that by passing there himself he might be useful to us as a secret agent. Of his zeal and fidelity I feel no doubt, but of his talents, the specimen which his epistle affords is not quite so satisfactory.

His demand appears most exorbitant *prima facie*, though if the important service he is intended to undertake was really well executed no price would be too great to pay for it.

In the event of his proposal being declined his plan is, I understand, to fix himself in trade in Lower Canada.

Clark advances him money.

(Canadian Archives, C. 679.)

Peter Hogeboom to Major-General De Rottenburg.

NIAGARA FALLS, 23d July, 1813.

SIR,—Agreeable to your request, I make a statement on the subject of re-establishment a line of intelligence between Lake Erie and Lake Ontario, and elsewhere as circumstances will admit, and also, as I have some particular friend in the neighbourhood of Sackett's Harbor, at the same time assist a man in the vicinity of that place to communicate intelligence over to Kingston or some place in that quarter. Particular persons and places to be established on the line on this side. This, of course, will be the duty of the commanders to whom the communication is to be made at either of the places. The mode to be pursued on the enemy's side to convey the intelligence must be to the person engaged, once a week, if practicable, and on particular occasions of truce, if circumstances will admit. The expense of having persons to bring over the despatches will be a separate charge ; the person employed, of course, will do his endeavor to get those persons upon the best possible terms. From the nature of the business matters may transpire that communication could not at times be made once a week. In such cases the persons engaged will be the best judge. Of course, he will do his best endeavor to send them as soon as may be. At the same time, all such newspapers as can be got from various parts of the United States will be sent over. The politics of the United States will be communicated as far as the person employed will be capable of doing it, and if the Commander-in-Chief should have occasion to send despatches overland to the seabord or New York, such matters also will be attended to, but, of course, it will be a separate charge. The sum that will be required for 12 months will be five thousand dollars, $2,000 to be advanced in order to commence the operation.

If anything further should occur to your mind, you will be pleased to communicate the same.

(Canadian Archives, C. 679.)

Plan of Campaign.

The time at which we had reason to expect an ascendency on Lake Ontario has arrived. If our hopes on that head be fulfilled though but for a short period, we must avail ourselves of the circumstance and give to the campaign a new and increased activity. For this purpose our forces on the Lake Ontario should be concentrated, because neither section of them as now located will be competent to any important object. The point of concentration is more doubtful.

1st.—If at Fort George our utmost success can but give us the command of the peninsula which if Harrison succeed against Malden will be of diminished interest, both as respects us and the enemy; to us because Malden will more completely cover our western frontier and control the savages than Forts George and Erie ; to the enemy because, Malden lost, our inroad on the peninsula will but have the effect of *shortening* not of *dividing* their line of defence ; in a word, success at this point will not give to the campaign a character of decisive advantage.

2d.—If on the other hand we make Sackett's Harbor the point of concentration Kingston may be made our object of attack, which, by the way, will but be returning to the plan of operations prescribed to General Dearborn. This post is one of great importance to the enemy and will no doubt be defended with much obstinacy and with all the resources which can be safely drawn from other points. That it may be taken by a joint application of our naval and military means is not, however, to be questioned. The enclosed diagram will show the number and character of the enemy's defences. His batteries marked No. 1 cannot be sustained but by his fleet. These carried he is open to a descent at Nos. 2 and 3. If he divides his force between the two we oppose one-half of his strength with the whole of ours. If he concentrates at No. 2 we seize No. 3 and command both the town and shipping. If he concentrates at No. 3 we occupy No. 2 and with nearly the same result.

Contemporaneously with this operation another may be made on the side of Lake Champlain, indicating an intention of attacking Montreal and its dependencies, and really attacking them if to save Kingston these posts have been materially weakened.

3d.—A different operation, to which our means may be competent, would be a movement from Sackett's Harbor to Madrid on the St. Lawrence. At this place the river may, as I am informed, be most easily crossed. The ground opposite to it is said to be a narrow bluff, skirted by the river on one side and on the other by a swamp of considerable extent and difficult passage. This gained and fortified, the fleet continuing to command the water line from the head of the river to Ogdensburg, and Lake St. Francis occupied by a few gunboats and barges, the army may march on Montreal in concert with General Hampton. The only material difficulty in the execution of this measure will be found in crossing a branch of the Grand River, which though generally deep may at this season be fordable or safely passed in rafts covered by our artillery.

Under the preceding statements it is respectfully submitted whether it will not be most advisable to make Sackett's Harbor the point of concentration and leave to the commanding General an election, (to be determined by circumstances,) between the two plans suggested under the 2d and 3d heads.

Approved, 23d July, 1813.

JOHN ARMSTRONG.

(From Notes of the War of 1812, by John Armstrong, New York, 1840, Vol. II., pp. 187-8, Appendix No. I.)

"National Intelligencer," Washington, D. C., August 7th, 1813.

ERIE, PA., July 23, 1813.

At half-past five o'clock on Monday morning last (July 19), six British armed vessels from Malden, with their decks well covered

with men, made their appearance at the mouth of our harbor. The line of sail was as follows :—
    1. The ship *Queen Charlotte.*
    2. The brig *Hunter.*
    3. The brig *Lady Prevost.*
    4. The sloop *Erie.*
    5. The sloop *Good Will.*
    6. A schooner, some distance in rear.

In this order they passed and repassed immediately at the mouth of the harbor, with a scrutinizing eye at our shipping. Commodore Perry and men enough to man one gunboat hoisted sail and played in front of them near the bar in hopes of getting a long shot, but the enemy steered a little out into the lake, where they continued until 4 o'clock, and then shaped their course towards Long Point.

On Wednesday (July 21), about 2 o'clock p. m., the enemy returned in the order above, except the schooner and in place of her they had a tender. About 6 o'clock they were near the point of the peninsula, when two of our gunboats opened fire on them, which was returned by the *Queen Charlotte, Hunter* and *Lady Prevost,* but without effect on either side. Our shots, however, were vastly superior to those of the enemy, and had not the distance been so great would have been severely felt by them. The wind at this time being very light, the Commodore was in the act of occupying a more convenient situation, at less distance from the enemy, from which his gunboats would have done some execution before they could have got under way, but a smart breeze sprung up and enabled them to put out a little further from shore.

Yesterday morning they were out some distance. In the afternoon they again came towards the harbor, but kept a greater distance than they had the day before. The enemy having a number of boats along with them, it is probable they may in some shape attempt to annoy our shipping.

(From the *Northern Centinel.*)

District General Orders.

By Major-General Francis De Rottenburg, commanding His Majesty's Forces within the Province of Upper Canada.

Whereas it has been represented to me that many farms in the District of Niagara are abandoned by their proprietors or tenants, who have joined the enemy, I have thought proper to direct, for the public benefit and for the better supplying of His Majesty's Forces in the said province, that the property in grain and stock so abandoned shall, on proof thereof before any two or more commissioners hereinafter mentioned, be taken into their hands and consigned to some proper person to husband the same; to gather in the grain and dispose thereof to the best advantage for the legal claimants; and to this end I do hereby nominate and appoint Richard Hatt, Samuel Hatt, Richard Beasely, Robert Nelles, Abraham Nelles, Wm. Crooks, Samuel Street (Senior), Thomas Clark, Thomas Dickson, John Warren, Crowell Willson and Thomas Cummings, Commissioners for that purpose in the District of Niagara.

Given under my hand at headquarters, at St. Davids, this 24th day of July, 1813.

FRANCIS DE ROTTENBURG,
Major-General.

Comparative Statement.

24th July, 1813.

Of the force of His Majesty's Squadron and that of the enemy employed on Lake Ontario :—

BRITISH FORCE.

NAMES.	GUNS.	CALIBRE.	MEN.
Ship *Wolfe*	23	1 long 24-pounder 8 long 18-pounders 4 68-lb. carronades 10 32-lb. do	175
Ship *Royal George*	20	2 long 18-pounders 2 68-lb. carronades 16 32-lb. do	155
Brig *Melville*	14	2 long 18-pounders 12 32-lb. carronades	60
Brig *Moira*	16	2 long 9-pounders 14 24-lb. carronades	92
Schooner *Sir Sidney Smith*	12	2 long 12-pounders 10 32-lb. carronades	80
Schooner *Beresford*	12	2 long 9-pounders 10 18-lb. carronades	70
			632

N. B.—The above 632 men are exclusive of 200 soldiers of the 100th and Royal Newfoundland Regts. embarked in the fleet as marines.

AMERICAN FORCE.

NAMES.	GUNS.	CALIBRE.	MEN.
Ship *Gen'l Pike*	26	Long 24-pounders	Not known.
Ship *Madison*	24	32-lb. carronades	
Brig *Oneida*	18	24-lb. carronades	
Hamilton	Unknown.	Unknown.	
Governor Tompkins			
Growler			
Fair American			
Conquest			
Pert			
Julia			
Elizabeth			
Ontario			
Lady of the Lake			
Mary and two others, names unknown			

(Canadian Archives, Q. 122, p. 122.)

24th July, 1813.

A comparative statement of the force of His Majesty's squadron and that of the enemy employed on Lake Erie :—

BRITISH FORCE.

NAMES.	GUNS.	CALIBRE.	MEN.
Ship *Queen Charlotte*	18	24-lb carronades	40 Canadians
			25 Nfd. Regt.
			45 41st do
			110
Schooner *Prevost*	12	2 long 9-prs	30 Canadians
		10 12-lb. carronades	10 Nfd. Regt.
			36 41st do
			76
Schooner *Hunter*	6	4 long 6-prs	20 Canadians
		2 12-lb. carronades	4 Nfd. Regt.
			15 41st do
			39

NAMES.	GUNS.	CALIBRE.	MEN.
Schooner *Erie*	2	1 long 12-pr.	6 Canadians
		1 12-lb. carronade	4 Nfd. Regt.
			5 41st do
			15
Schooner *Little Belt*	2	1 long 9-pr.	6 Canadians
		1 24-lb. carronade	4 Nfd. Regt.
			5 41st do
			15
Schooner *Chippewa*	2	2 8-in. howitzers	6 Canadians
			7 Nfd. Regt.
			13

Ship *Detroit*, pierced for 20 guns; supposed to be launched about this time.

AMERICAN FORCE.

NAMES.	GUNS.	CALIBRE.	MEN.
Two new brigs or corvettes, in a forward state	Not known.	Not known.	Not known.
Two brigs			
Seven schooners lying at Presque Isle			

The corvettes appeared, when reconnoitred, to be as large as the *Queen Charlotte*, but not rigged or armed, but from the vicinity of the enemy's resources were soon expected to be so.

(Canadian Archives, Q. 122, p. 123.)

General Order.

Headquarters, KINGSTON,
Adjutant General's Office, 24th July, 1813.

An express was received at Kingston on the 20th instant announcing that a brigade of batteaux loaded with provisions, under the convoy of a gunboat of the second class, had been surprised at break of day by the enemy, who had crossed the river in two armed sloops.

Three gunboats were immediately despatched from Kingston under the command of Lieut. Scott, R. N., with a view of intercepting the enemy if they should attempt to pass by the south side of the river, and a detachment of the 100th Regiment under Captain Martin proceeded by the northern channel. These parties united below Long Island, and having learned that the enemy had carried the captured batteaux into Goose Creek they immediately pushed for that place, but before they got sight of the enemy's sloop the evening was so far advanced as to preclude the possibility of attacking them before dark. It was therefore determined to defer it until the ensuing morning, and the gunboats returned to the entrance of the stream, where they met a detachment of the 41st Regiment under Major Frend, who assumed the command of the whole, and at three o'clock in the morning proceeded up the creek in the hope of gaining the enemy's position by dawn of day, when it was discovered that the enemy had removed their sloops several miles higher up the creek, where the channel became so narrow that the gunboats could not use their oars nor turn so as to bring their guns to bear upon the bank, and their further progress was here impeded by large trees felled across the stream. In attempting to remove these obstacles the party was fired upon by the sloops and from a gun in a log fort which the enemy had erected on the left bank, as well as from musketry on the same side of the creek, which was covered with thick wood and where the enemy was posted in a very strong position.

A detachment of troops had been landed on the right bank, from whence it was found to be impracticable to gain the enemy's position. These troops immediately returned and embarked in the sternmost boats to cross over to the left bank, but from the swampy nature of the soil no fit place for landing could be found. The leading boat being exposed to a heavy and galling fire and having so many of her crew wounded as to check the fire of her gun, the only one that could be brought to bear on the enemy, the troops led by Lieut. Fawcett of the 100th Regiment in the most gallant manner leaped into the water and carrying their arms and ammunition on their heads succeeded in gaining the land and instantly drove the enemy with precipitation to seek shelter within a strong log intrenchment, to which he was pursued. The undaunted gallantry displayed by the troops on this occasion was calculated to surmount every obstacle, but the enemy appearing to receive numerous reinforcements from the interior and the very great natural strength of the position in which he was posted, added to the impracticability of the gunboats co-operating, induced Major Frend to order the re-embarkation of the troops, considering the object of the service upon which he was employed as not justifying his perseverance in so unequal a contest and which would when attained have ill compensated for the unavoidable sacrifice of many valuable lives.

The detachment lost one gunner and three private soldiers of the

41st Regiment, killed; Mr. Hugo, midshipman, twelve rank and file and four seamen wounded.

Captain Milnes, aid-de-camp to the Commander of the Forces, who had been despatched to procure intelligence, met Major Frend on his route and was induced to embark in his boat, has been on this occasion severely and dangerously wounded. It is with the deepest regret His Excellency laments that the fair promise which zeal, talent and undaunted courage held forth of rising honor and eminence in the profession of arms are threatened to be untimely sacrificed in this gallant young officer.

By His Excellency's command,

EDWARD BAYNES,

Adjutant General.

Privateering on the St. Lawrence.

A few days since two private armed boats, each carrying a 6 or 8 pounder and 50 men, sailed from Sackett's Harbor to cruize in the St. Lawrence. On Monday, the 19th, they fell in with a gunboat carrying a six pound carronade convoying 15 of the enemy's batteaux, captured them without the loss of a man and brought them into Cranberry Creek, about 40 miles above Ogdensburg. The batteaux had on board 250 bbls. pork, 300 bags pilot-bread, ammunition, &c., bound from Montreal to Kingston. On Tuesday morning three of the enemy's gunboats with 250 soldiers from Prescott arrived off the Creek and landed their men. The privateersmen had hardly time to construct a breastwork of their bags of pilot-bread before they were attacked by 200 of the enemy, and, strange to tell, after an obstinate engagement in which from 40 to 60 of the enemy were killed, his force retreated precipitately to their boats, except 15 who took to the woods and were pursued. Our loss is trifling, though it is not specified; 67 British prisoners captured in the batteaux and gunboat arrived at Watertown on Tuesday evening.

(Niles' *Register*, 7th August, 1813, quoted from the Albany *Argus*.)

General Orders.

Adjutant General's Office,

Headquarters, KINGSTON, 24th July, 1813.

Every effective man of the Royal Newfoundland Regiment with a proportion of officers, sergeants and drummers are to be embarked on board the vessels on the lake to do duty permanently as marines. The proportion of the Royal Newfoundland Regiment not being sufficient to furnish the number of men required for the present emergency of service, a detachment of the 100th Regiment, consisting of two subalterns, three sergeants, two drummers and 70 rank and file is to be held in readiness as marines to embark on board the following vessels at the shortest notice after next: One subaltern, two sergeants, one drummer and 40 rank and file on board the *Wolfe*, one subaltern, one sergeant, one drummer and thirty rank and file on board the *Melville*. This detachment is to rejoin its regiment as soon as the public service will admit thereof.

Three companies of the Canadian Voltigeurs, under Major Heriot, are to be held in readiness to march to join the Centre Division of the Army; the remaining company is to be stationed at Gananoqui. All men unfit for active field service are to be transferred to that company, and all men in it fit for gunboat service are to be employed in the armed boats at that post. Soldiers serving in the gunboats are to receive free of expense their rations of provisions the same as soldiers serving as marines on board the fleet. All soldiers belonging to corps serving in the Centre Division who are fit for active duty are to be held in readiness to proceed on Monday next by water to join their respective regiments.

The troop of the 19th Dragoons at Kingston is to march on Monday next at six o'clock to join the Centre Division of the Army. Such troopers as are not provided with horses will proceed by water.

EDWARD BAYNES,
Adjutant General.

Report of Indian Council at the Cross Roads, 25th July, 1813.

Present—
Major Givins.
Captain de Lorimier.
Lieutenant de Lorimier.
Lieut. Ferguson.
Lieut. Leclair.

BROTHERS! The Seven Nations of Canada salute you. We have remained here some time and no time is mentioned when anything is likely to take place. Our young people are all going and only the old people remain. At first we were told only four or five days and we would see the fight. We have waited patiently, and a month has passed and it has not yet come. It is said it is the fleet you are waiting for, and now it is out it cannot be long before it must come and as we wish to see the end of this we will wait ten days and after that you will not think it hard if we return to do something for our families, and as the Six Nations have sent for their young men we think surely that before the ten days are out they must be down and our small numbers will not be missed.

Colonel Claus:—Brothers! I thank you. The General wishes me to speak to you on behalf of the poor people about us who have complained that they lose everything about their places, and requests that you will exert yourselves to prevent these acts of cruelty. It is very hard on these poor people. On the one hand they are injured by the enemy, on the other by us.

A Chief:—The provisions are not enough and the young men go on the hunt for something to eat. Your people take the poor people's things and our people are blamed.

Colonel Claus:—You shall not want for meat, you shall get whatever you require. If corn is to be had you shall have it.

The Echo:—I hope our brothers from the West will listen and desist. We understand that our father desires that no more liquor than the usual allowance shall be given. It is right; we see the injury it does.

We are wrong and confess our fault. It seemed as if these men (the farmers) wished to side with the strongest. We have taken many things but any that are pointed out we will give up.

(Claus Papers.)

Minutes of a Council held at Buffalo by Erastus Granger.

July 25th, 1813.

Farmer's Brother opened the council by an address to the Indians and one to me by way of compliment. He then addressed himself to the Indians, and said that as it respected the great question before them of peace or war each village must speak for themselves.

Red Jacket spoke for the Senecas as follows:—

We are once more met in council to give an answer to the speeches made by you and General Porter. It has taken time, the subject being important.

Brother! We have heard your speeches. You wanted us to assist and watch to the edge of the water. We of Buffalo have agreed to what you requested. You will now hear the decision of the old men. I speak for the Indians of Buffalo; a part will be here for a time; others will then take their places. We count the whole at Buffalo village. We count all who are to be on guard. We cannot designate numbers. Those who live in the little village will be on the ground in case of an alarm. The pay will be distributed among the whole, and be divided according to the number employed. We, the old men who have seen war, will, from time to time, instruct and regulate the young warriors. We, the chiefs of Buffalo (Senecas), turn out one hundred and sixty-two warriors to be under arms. This is all I have to say. The next who speak are the Cattaragus.

A Cattaragus chief spoke:—

Brother! You will now hear what the Senecas and Delawares from Cattaragus have to say. We have always been ready to assist in defending your boats upon the lake. We are not deceitful. We hope you will not suspect us of any want of friendship to you. We of the Cattaragus under Capt. Half-Town have for some time been in your service watching at the mouth of Cattaragus Creek. You will now hear how many we have turned out from our village, including Delawares. The number is twenty-one. If we hear you are in danger we will all rise from our seats and come forward to your defence. We expect to add to our numbers when we return home and let our young men know. We shall continue to protect your boats as they go up the lake, and we wish to know if we shall be paid for this.

Capt. Shongo from Canakedea, on Genessee River, spoke, &c. He said that eleven from their village intended to stay and fight. We have been here almost one month, and we intend to stay one month longer.

Sharp-Shins from Squakie Hill will stay alone.

John Sky from Tonawanda spoke as follows:—

We turn out none at present, but will return to-morrow and consult the rest of the chiefs. Our friendship is great for the United States.

Cornplanter spoke for the Indians at Alleghany:—

We turn out seven. We have a great deal of work to do in our village. If the danger increases we will turn out more.

He then addressed himself to those who are to stay, which was not interpreted. He then addressed himself to me and said:—

You must pay well. You must open your purse. You must pay some now; and do not let your taverns supply our warriors with spirituous liquors. We feel some anxiety that there is no provision made for the families of our men who fall in this war. There is no promise of compensation. Brother! We expect you to do your best in our behalf.

Red Jacket again spoke:—

Brother! You are now writing what has taken place this day. The part we take in this war is not voluntary on our part; you have persuaded us into it. We hope you will say so to the President. You must not be displeased with what we say. Your voice was for us to sit still when the war began, but you have beat us—you have got us into the war.

Brother! If any of our friends of the Six Nations, except the

Mohawks, fall into your hands, we hope you will treat them well; deliver them up to us; we will do the same by the white persons we take. Write to the Commander-in-Chief and let him know this.

(From Ketchum's History of Buffalo, Vol. II., pp. 430-1.)

Lieut. Edward McMahon, Acting Secretary to Major-General De Rottenburg, to Hon. Wm. D. Powell.

Headquarters, ST. DAVIDS,
26th July, 1813.

SIR,—I am directed by His Honour the President to signify to you his most anxious desire to know what progress has been made towards the amending and repairing the roads under your direction, and to request when your convenience will admit it you will be pleased to communicate the same for his satisfaction.

(From MS. in possession of G. M. Jarvis, Esq., Ottawa.)

Left Division Orders.

KINGSTON, 25th July, 1813.

No. 1. Captain Winter of the Royal Newfoundland Regiment is appointed to take the command of the Gananoqui Station. One company of the Voltigeurs and a detachment of Glengarry Light Infantry is added to the troops already there.

No. 2. The light company of the militia just arrived is to join the light battalion under the orders of Lieut.-Colonel Macdonnell.

No. 3. The light companies of the 2d Battalion, 41st, and De Watteville's Regiment are to join the 100th Regiment, and form a light battalion under Lieut.-Colonel Hamilton.

General Order.

Headquarters, KINGSTON,
26th July, 1813.

The Commander of the Forces has under consideration the report of a board of officers, of which Brig.-Gen. Vincent was president, assembled by His Excellency's order at the headquarters of the Centre Division of the army, at St. Davids, the 20th July, 1813, for the purpose of considering the claims of the Indian warriors to head money for prisoners of war brought in by them, and to the propriety of some provision being made for those who may be disabled in service, with a view to soften and restrain the Indian warriors in their conduct towards such Americans as may be made prisoners of war. His Excellency is pleased to approve of the following arrangement subscribed by that board, and directs that the same may be acted upon, viz. :—

The proceedings of a council with several Indian warriors assembled at the Forty Mile Creek on the 27th ulto. having been presented to the board, it is of the opinion that upon the subject of head-money upon prisoners of war brought in by Indians, allowance should be made for each prisoner brought in alive of five dollars. The board is of opinion that the following rates of pensions are sufficient :

To a chief for loss of limb, eye, or receiving a wound equal to loss of limb, $100 per annum.

To a warrior for loss of limb, eye, or receiving a wound equal to a loss of limb, $70 per annum.

To the widow of a chief or family of a chief killed in action or dying of his wounds, a present of $200.

To the widow of a warrior killed in action or dying of his wounds, a present of $170.

The board are of opinion that Indians ought to be entitled to prize money for the capture of Detroit in the following proportions : Chiefs as subalterns, warriors as privates. The head money for prisoners of war brought in by Indian warriors is to be immediately paid by the commissary upon the certificate of the general officer commanding the division with which they are acting at the time.

His Excellency the Commander of the Forces has been pleased to make the following appointments in the Indian Department, viz. :

Mr. Ch. Spenhard to be interpreter, to receive pay and allowances as such from the 25th June last ; George Rousseau, gent., to be lieutenant and interpreter *vice* Chew, killed in action. Commission dated 25th June, 1813.

EDWARD BAYNES,
Adjt.-Gen'l.

Captain John Hall of the Canadian Regiment, Inspector of Cavalry, to Lt.-Col. Harvey.

CAMP AT CROSS ROADS, 26th July, 1813.

SIR,—I beg leave to report for the information of the Major-General commanding, that, agreeable to the D. G. O. of the 22d instant, I have inspected the major part of Captain Merritt's troop of Provincial Light Dragoons and found the horses battered and worn up with scarcely a shoe to their feet, many being lame for want of shoeing and some of the horses unfit for light dragoon service in point of size, &c., that with the exception of a few bad half-equipped saddles and a few swords and pistols the men and horses are totally destitute of appointments. From what I have occasionally seen of the few men and horses who were on duty on the day of inspection as well as from Captain Merritt's information those men and horses are much of the same sort and in the same situation. The officers appear zealous for the service, the men tolerably good looking and if properly appointed may be made a creditable, useful corps.

If it is not exceeding the limits of my report I would, with respectful deference, observe that the present mode of feeding the horses of this troop appears to me radically bad, that if government were to take charge of feeding them a considerable advantage would be derived.

I beg leave to enclose a list of appointments necessary for the equipment of a light dragoon.

(From the Merritt MSS.)

Lieut.-Colonel Harvey to Colonel Baynes.

Hd. Qrs., St. Davids, 26th July, 1813.

My Dear Col.—Enclosed I send you by Captain Merritt of the Niagara Provincial Lt. Dragoons a report of an inspection made of this troop by Captain Hall, from which you will at once perceive the wretched state of the troop in every respect. The system of their formation is radically defective—it is the interest of the men and officers to starve their horses and even to destroy them. If Gov't fed them this would not be the case.

It is on the subject of their clothing and appointments, however, chiefly, that M[ajor] Genl. De R[ottenburg] has allowed Capt. Merritt to quit the army at this moment, as his people are literally *naked* and *defenceless*. Merritt himself is a fine young man—indeed the corps might I think be made something of if placed under the management and superintendence of Captain Hall or some smart cavalry officer.

I hope you will give him every aid in your power in attaining the objects of his journey and that the defects pointed out in Captain Hall's report may be reformed, or otherwise it would be better that the troop was disbanded altogether. To Captain Merritt I refer you for every information you can require respecting his troop.

(From the Merritt MSS.)

Lieut. MacEwen, Royal Scots, to his Wife at Montreal.

Camp, 4 Miles from Fort George, 26th July, 1813.

Many of the officers and men are very ill with fever and ague, owing to the dampness of the ground and the closeness of the woods we are obliged to occupy in this poor country.

In future you will draw what sums you want from the regimental agents in Montreal, Messrs. Gardiner, Auldjoe & Company, and they will charge same to MacGregor here. There is some mention of a peace taking place with America immediately, and if that happens we may enjoy many happy days in this country. We have been continually skirmishing with the enemy and have always beat them into Fort George where, however, we cannot attack them, as they have it mined and ready to blow up if we go in. We have certain information every day of their movements and are waiting the arrival of the fleet. The Americans sent one of their armed schooners down the other day and she fired a good many shots at us in the camp, but no lives were lost. Our artillery fired two shots into her, and finding they might be sunk if she continued much longer, she went off in a humbler manner than when she advanced. The schooner calls every day but has never cared to come near us since. Captain Gordon went out riding on the 20th and galloped into the Americans. He has written a pitiful letter but no one seems to care for him. He is now lodged as a prisoner of war, where he will remain for a little, I suppose, much to his mind.

I would advise you to keep the *carriole* until winter at all events, as there may be some change before that time. I wrote informing you that Mr. Hemphill had left this part of the army and gone with Captain Dudgeon to a place in the rear called Burlington Bay. I now live by myself in an Indian house made of branches and leaves of trees, all that defends me from cold and heat, which are very great in the night and day in these woods. If you can procure me a box of cigars, some tea, sugar, pepper, mustard and any other things you think of, send them by some careful party coming to this part of the army.

(From A. Brymner's Excerpts, pp. 7-9.)

District General Order.

Headquarters, ST. DAVIDS,
26th July, 1813.

Captains of companies are required to take and transmit an account of the number of cattle within the limits of their respective companies, distinguishing working oxen, milk cows and young cattle.

General Order.

KINGSTON, 26th July, 1813.

G. O.

The detachment of the 100th Regiment ordered to embark as marines are to parade for that purpose at 6 o'clock this afternoon, to consist of :—

Subalterns.	Sergeants.	Drummers.	Rank and File.
1	2	1	45 for the *Wolfe*.
1	2	1	45 for the *Royal George*.
Total—2	4	2	90

The Royal Newfoundland will furnish the detachment for the other vessels :—

Sub.	Sergts.	Drummers.	Rank and File.
1	1	1	35 for the *Melville*.
1	1	1	32 for the *Moira*.
1	1	1	26 for the *Sir Sidney Smith*.
1	1	1	25 for the *Beresford*.
4	4	4	118

EDWARD BAYNES,
A. G.

General John P. Boyd to General Porter.

Headquarters, FORT GEORGE,
July 27, 1813.

SIR.—I have received your letter of the 22d inst. The military suggestions you make are such as would meet my approbation were they consistent with the instructions I have received from the War Department (confidentially communicated to you when last here), which enjoin upon me for the present to act only on the defensive. The *Lady of the Lake* has just arrived, which brings news that our whole fleet is on the lake. With its co-operation something brilliant and decisive may soon be done. This ought to be communicated to the Indians, who, I understand, are assembled to the number of 3 or 400 at Buffalo, and drawing rations, as it might be an incentive to join us at this post. Their services here would be incalculably important. As there is no enemy threatening the points at which they now are, you must be aware of the importance of inducing them to tender their services where they can be so eminently useful. You will please to confer with Mr. Granger on this subject, and request him to unite his exertions with yours to persuade a part of them at least to join our army.

The British fleet is at Kingston, and believed to be partly dismantled. This may delay the final ascendency of our fleet, but will not retard our movements on land.

(MSS. of Hon. P. A. Porter.)

General John P. Boyd to Secretary of War.

Headquarters, FORT GEORGE,
July 27, 1813.

SIR,—I had the honor to address you last on the 24th inst. On the 22d instant General Lewis and Commodore Chauncey were advised by me that from intelligence received from Major Chapin and deserters, most of the enemy's captured ordnance and their principal depot of ammunition, stores, &c., are at the head of the lake. It was suggested that a small force might surprise, take, destroy and bring them off if part of the fleet might be allowed to assist in moving our troops.

Yesterday the *Lady of the Lake* brought me a letter from Commodore Chauncey stating that he approved of the enterprise and *would go himself with his fleet to the head of the lake*, and requested guides, information, &c. I have deemed it proper to detail a number of troops under the command of Colonel Scott, which will embark on board the *Lady of the Lake* with instructions to join the squadron, which is believed to be now somewhere near Little York.

(American State Papers, Military Affairs, Vol. I., p. 450.)

General Peter B. Porter to Governor Tompkins.

BLACK ROCK, July 27, 1813.

SIR,—I enclose you a copy of a letter which I have this day written to the Secretary of War, and which, as it contains some few remarks on the officers of the army, I wish may be considered as confidential. The alarm at this place has for the present subsided.

(Copy of letter enclosed.)

BLACK ROCK, July 27, 1813.

SIR,—I wrote frequently last year to the Secretary of War and to the Governor of New York, exposing, with the freedom of a Republican, what I considered to be the errors (they were then principally in that department and in the Government) which had led, and would forever lead, to disaster.

For this freedom I lost the *countenance*, if not the confidence, of the Government. But it is impossible for me to remain quiet and witness the ruin of the country while there is a possibility of rendering service by exposing facts to those who ought to know and may profit by them. History will shortly prove the justice of the speculations which I have already made relative to the conquest of Canada, and will also show, what few can now conceive, the depth of the disgrace brought upon this nation by its military operations.

If I should seem to take an improper liberty in giving my opinions, I hope you will recollect that, independently of the high responsibility which as a public man I have taken in the measures of government, I am surrounded by friends and neighbors who for more than a year have been subject to all the miseries of war, whose property has been swept away and destroyed, not only by the enemy but by our own soldiers, and whose future prospects are by the evils of which I complain rendered almost hopeless.

The truth is, (and it is known to every man of common sense in this part of the country,) that we have had an army at Fort George for two months past, which at any moment of this period might by a vigorous and well-directed exertion of three or four days have prostrated the whole of the enemy's force in this division of the country, and yet this army lies panic-struck, shut up and whipped in by a few hundred miserable savages, leaving the whole of this frontier, except the mile in extent which they occupy, exposed to the inroads and depredations of the enemy. After the evacuation of Fort George the whole of the British army might by the simplest operation in the world have been captured, and Generals Dearborn and Lewis were urged to it by all the considerations that decency would permit by those who from knowledge of the country and of the enemy's force had a claim to advise. But the opportunity was suffered to pass, and since that time there has not been a movement of the army of which a school boy ought not to be ashamed. The general officers plan nothing unless it be for their own safety, and what has been done has been done at the instigation of inferior officers. Our army is full of men fresh from lawyers' shops and counting rooms, who know little of the physical force of man or of the proper mode of its application. With them the whole of the *military* art consists in knowing how to manœuvre a regiment, how to form and display a column, and the scientific shape in which the troops are to be presented to meet a given movement or position of the enemy. With these acquirements they are sent out in quest of adventures, without object or design, without knowing where to go, what to do or when to return. The result is obvious. They break their heads against windmills.

General Dearborn has now gone home in disgrace, and notwithstanding he has done scarcely anything which in my opinion he ought to have done as a general, I do not hesitate to say that he was worth all the general officers put together that we have ever had on this frontier, and this the whole army were ready to acknowledge the moment he left them.

General Lewis is brave and capable, but he is no *veni, vidi, vici* man, and be assured he will never overrun the wilderness of Canada. He could not go 16 miles to fight the enemy, not because his force was too small but *because he had not waggons to carry tents and camp kettles for his army.* His own baggage moves in two stately waggons, one drawn by two the other by four horses, carrying the various furniture of a Secretary of State's office, a lady's dressing chamber, an alderman's dining room and the contents of a grocer's shop.

Generals Chandler and Winder are gone, *nil de mortuis.*

General Boyd is an amiable man and a good soldier, but really he has not *scope* to wield an army of 4000 men.

In short, Sir, my purpose is to tell you that unless you or General Wilkinson, or some other officer of more talent and experience than any we have yet had, come on we shall never take Canada. I ought, however, to except the possibility of Commodore Chauncey's arrival, who, by taking command of the army as he has done in every instance in which it has been successful, may save us from disgrace.

I beg, Sir, that what I have said of our general officers may be considered as confidential and not imputed to a censorious spirit in me, for I certainly feel no other sentiments towards either of the gentlemen than those of respect and esteem.

The chiefs and warriors of the Six Nations were called to Buffalo last week at the instance of General Boyd, who wishes them to join him at Fort George, not to invade the enemy's country *but to act as piquet guards to his army while stationed at that place.* After deliberating on this proposition they informed Mr. Granger and myself, through their Chief, Red Jacket, that they had unanimously agreed to reject it for reasons assigned by them at large (and intermixed with no small share of sarcasm) which could not but be satisfactory, and which it would do no credit to the *Army of the Centre* to repeat. They, however, expressed their readiness to remain here with the volunteer militia, and if thought expedient by us to penetrate the enemy's country with them. They are now in a state of complete military preparation and I hope, Sir, that you will agree that they shall remain here and receive the same pay as militia, of whom they are worth double their numbers. Mr. Granger has, I presume, written to you in relation to them.

I have made a proposition to General Boyd to give me 3 or 400 regular troops and to permit me to add to them an equal number of volunteers and as many Indians. With them I pledge myself to enter Canada and relieve his army from their *duress*. I have not yet received his answer.

You may have observed that I am acting as commanding officer at this place. But I beg you to understand that it is not done in expectation of either profit or honor, for I receive no pay or emoluments, and who could expect to gather laurels with militia and Indians in a field where our regular troops have not been able to pluck a sprig? The truth is that our wretched situation does not permit us to attend to our ordinary avocations, and *being ashamed to run away* and thereby encourage others to do the same, I offered to take charge of the few troops that General Dearborn had ordered for our defence.

(Tompkins Papers, Vol. VIII., pp. 482-7, New York State Library.)

(From the Buffalo Gazette, 27th July, 1813.)

Since our last paper there have been frequent skirmishes in the neighborhood of Fort George—foraging parties and the picket guards have been repeatedly attacked. In one of these affairs the enemy's loss was very serious—60 or 70 are said to have been killed. Sunday evening a cannonading was heard in the direction of Fort George. The pickets of the enemy are within sight of ours beyond the lighthouse, near where our troops landed on the 27th May.

Three of our armed schooners have arrived at Fort Niagara, which brought up between 2 and 300 seamen, who passed here on Friday last, (23d July,) to enter on board Com. Perry's squadron at Erie. It is said that the British fleet have gone into Kingston and that ours is now out. This probably is only a manœuvre of the enemy to get our fleet divided so as to take it piece-meal.

General De Rottenburg takes the reins of government in Upper Canada in the place of General Sheaffe.

Major-General Wilkinson is now on his way to take command of the army on the Niagara in the absence of Major-General Dearborn, gone to Albany to recover his health. Brigadier-General D. R. Williams, (lately a member of Congress from South Carolina,) will be at Fort George in a few days to take a command.

There are said to be from 4 to 6000 men at Sackett's Harbor and 3 or 4000 at Burlington.

The late threatened attack on Fort Meigs by the British was probably made to cover some other object, as no force has been seen in that quarter. General Harrison was at Cleveland at our last dates.

Lieut.-Colonel John Chrystie of the 13th Infantry died at Fort George last Wednesday, (July 21,) of a fever.

The British troops which appeared at Fort Erie in the early part of last week (and which carried much alarm in this village) have gone up the lake to join or go aboard the enemy's fleet.

Messrs. Sill, Stanard, Seelye and other citizens taken at Black Rock were released Saturday week, (July 17.) Lieut.-Col. Bisshopp has died of his wounds. The enemy acknowledge a loss in the Black Rock affair of nearly 100 in killed, wounded and prisoners.

An express arrived in this village on Sunday evening last, (July 25,) from Erie, who informs that 7 sail of the enemy's vessels had appeared before that place and menaced the shipping in the harbor, and that the militia were coming in to protect the fleet.

(File in Buffalo Public Library.)

M. T. Simpson to Horatio Jones.

BUFFALO, July 27, 1813.

Capt. Horatio Jones:

SIR,—In consideration of the gallant defence made by a party of Indians in the late attack of the British at Black Rock, I take leave to enclose you one hundred dollars, which I must request you will order to be equally distributed among them, and which I hope they will unhesitatingly receive as a proof of the respect I entertain for their brave and efficient exertions in dispersing the invading army.

In haste, but very respectfully, your most obedient servant,

M. T. SIMPSON,
of Penn.

P. S.—On reconsideration I request that the above donation may be distributed in proportion to the hazard and exposure of the individuals who led the party and showed the best example, to ascertain which I request you will authorize the nicest enquiry.

(From the Buffalo Gazette, August 10th, 1813.)

General Orders.

Headquarters, KINGSTON, 27th July, 1813.

A relaxation of regulations and discipline being frequently suffered to prevail among troops while on the march, the Commander of the Forces finds it necessary to caution officers against allowing troops a mistaken indulgence to operate to the prejudice of the service. Few situations call for more unremitting attention from the officers commanding than conducting troops en route with order and regularity, and His Excellency directs that the following instructions be strictly adhered to: The baggage and stores in charge of detachments to be prepared before the hour of march for embarkation, and no party is to be suffered to remain behind on the plea of escorting baggage.

When movements are made by water attention is to be paid to the distribution of baggage and the crews so as to ensure the boats remaining in compact order and to avoid unnecessary delay. Officers are always to accompany their respective companies or divisions and whenever they arrive at the place of halt they are not to quit it until the party is mustered and every interior arrangement is made for the accommodation of the men, the security of their arms and stores and regularity of their messing, nor are they at any time to absent themselves beyond reach of being able in a moment to superintend the conduct of their men.

Soldiers are not to be permitted to straggle on any pretence, and if for fuel, provisions or from any other cause parties are required to be sent from the post they are to be under the charge of an officer or non-commissioned officer.

Whenever soldiers are quartered on the march in the houses or barns of the inhabitants they are to be cautioned to conduct themselves in a peaceable and orderly manner, and not to presume to take any wood for fuel or anything the property of the inhabitants without their permission, and any soldier wantonly injuring or destroying the property of the settlers is, on conviction of the offence, to be punished for the same and compensation to be made to the parties injured.

The boats, baggage and stores are always to be arranged in the most compact and secure manner possible for the night.

The smallest escorts are to furnish a sentry at least, and are to be mounted at sunset, according to the strength of the corps.

Every precaution to prevent surprise or irregularity is to be taken and the utmost vigilance required of out-piquets in the face of the enemy, and is invariably to be observed by detachments on the march. Officers commanding are held responsible that these instructions are adhered to by all troops under their charge.

EDWARD BAYNES,
Adjutant General.

Lieut.-Colonel Harvey to Colonel Claus.

July 28th, 1813, 2 p. m.

SIR,—There being reason to think that the enemy is directing his views against Burlington Bay, I request you will not lose a moment in sending off to the Grand River to collect all the Indians there to assist in its defence, for which, however, we have already a considerable garrison. Collect them immediately at Bezeley's (Beasley's).

(Claus Papers.)

Colonel Claus to Captain W. J. Kerr.

CROSS ROADS,
July 28th, 1813, 9.30 p. m.

SIR,—I have to request that you will set out at once for the Grand River to collect Indians, as required by Lieut.-Colonel Harvey.

(Claus Papers.)

(From the "Buffalo Gazette," 10th August, 1813.)

Extract of a letter from a gentleman at Sackett's Harbor to his friend in this village (published in the *Utica Patriot*), dated July 28, 1813 :—

On the 21st inst. arrived the privateer *Neptune* carrying a 6-pounder, and the *Fox* an 18-pounder, commanded by Major Dimock and Captain Dixon, from a cruise to the St. Lawrence. On the 19th inst., at 4 o'clock a. m., they surprised and captured the British gunboat *Spitfire*, mounting one 12-pounder carronade, and 15 Canadian batteaux loaded with provisions, on their way up the St. Lawrence. The surprise was complete and so well arranged that not a single shot was fired or life lost on either side. The batteaux were laden with 27,000 weight of sea-bread and 270 barrels of Irish pork, intended for the British army at Kingston. Our privateersmen retired into Cranberry Creek, where, having erected a breastwork of the captured barrels of pork and hard bread, on the 21st at sunrise they were attacked by four gunboats mounting two 32-pounders, one 9-pounder and a 6-pounder, and carrying from 250 to 300 men. The attack continued about two hours, when the enemy retired with considerable loss and were pursued some distance. Our loss was but 3 killed and one wounded. However, just before this, with a view if possible to succeed by menaces and if not to cover their retreat, they sent in a flag demanding the surrender of the pork-and-bread fort, and threatening in case of a refusal to bring up a reinforcement, let loose their Indians upon them and that no quarter would be given. Major Dimock replied that they should not surrender but at the point of the bayonet, and indignantly ordered off the officer requiring the surrender. The enemy's loss must have been considerable, as our men were well intrenched behind the *substantials of life* and had a fair opportunity of dealing out the full measure of *death* to their antagonists. This is evidenced by the precipitate retreat of the enemy. The number of men engaged on our part did not exceed 60. Upon coming out of the St. Lawrence on their return to this place, they had a new and more formidable enemy to encounter. The British brig *Earl of Moira* of 18 guns was purposely stationed to intercept their return. They, nevertheless, by a vigorous and daring effort, passed her without much injury. The *Fox*, Captain Dixon, who brought up the rear, passed within half musket-shot of the brig, three 9-pound shot struck the *Fox*, one of which passed through her magazine, but without any essential injury.

The expedition reflects much honor upon the officers commanding and the men engaged in it. It was fitted out by and composed chiefly of volunteers who have been injured by the depredations of the British. It was to be hoped that the war upon this part of the frontier at least would have been conducted according to the rules of civilized warfare, and that accordingly private property would be respected. But flushed with a temporary success, the British have committed repeated acts of wanton destruction and capture of the property of individuals. This experiment will convince them that it is no longer to be continued with impunity, and that a spirit of retaliation is arising, which if it does no more will at least check their career and make full amends for the past as well as indemnity for the future.

A cannonade was heard in the direction of Presque Isle (situate about midway on the north shore of the lake) two days since, supposed to be an attempt of our fleet to destroy a large ship building there.

Extract of a letter from Major-General Lewis to the Secretary of War, dated Sackett's Harbor, July 20 :—

Our fleet has gone out of the inner harbor, and appearances are in favor of going to sea in forty-eight hours at farthest.

A little expedition of volunteers from the country, to which by the advice of Commodore Chauncey I lent 50 soldiers, sailed from hence two days since on board of two small row boats, with a 6-pounder each, to the head of the St. Lawrence, where they captured a fine gunboat mounting a 24-pounder, 14 batteaux (loaded), four officers and 61 men. Two of our schooners have gone out to convoy them in. The prisoners have been landed, and are coming on under charge of a detachment of dragoons.

On Tuesday last Chauncey's squadron arrived at Fort Niagara from a cruise. From Major Chapin (who went out in the fleet) and from other sources, we have obtained the following information :—

The fleet sailed on Thursday preceding for the head of the lake, where the troops landed and remained a day. From some unfavorable circumstances no attack was made on the enemy at Burlington Heights. Many of the Indians attached to the British army on the appearance of the fleet cleared out for the forest and went home. In the morning the fleet ran down to York ; the British troops stationed there retreated before the shipping came to anchor. Many of the inhabitants left their houses, but returned again next day. The fleet remained at York two days; 6 or 700 barrels of flour, one 24-pounder, a number of stands of arms, a variety of utensils for constructing fortifications and 53 invalids in the hospital were taken. The barracks and public storehouses were burnt. The inhabitants upon the arrival of the fleet were panic-struck, but before our forces left the place they were convinced that *women* and *children* had little to fear from our troops. For we learn that such was the discipline of the sailors, marines and soldiers that not an article of private property was plundered. A mulatto from the fleet was detected in some very uncivil conduct, and severely punished for the same in the public street. Even two or three barrels of beer which had been obtained to refresh the troops, on their departure were paid for. Many poor inhabitants and others applied for flour, which was liberally dealt out to them on condition of their withholding it from Government. Nearly 20 barrels were given out in this way. From such enterprizes as these most beneficial results may be anticipated. When the American squadron left the harbor of York the banks of the lake were lined with people of all descriptions.

Since the above was in type we learn that Colonel Scott embarked with 500 troops, and that 12 boats were taken at York.

The *General Pike* is said to be an excellent ship,—as staunch built as any in the service and outsails everything on the lake.

From Lake Ontario we momentarily expect news of the highest importance. The British fleet was discovered on Saturday morning last (August 7th) a few miles off Newark lighthouse, consisting of six sail. Commodore Chauncey was at anchor at 4 Mile Creek, below Fort Niagara, and he immediately weighed anchor and sailed up towards the enemy, when he bore down and formed his line some distance at windward; manœuvering succeeded and continued several hours, but the enemy, declining to give battle without having the advantage of position, stood up the lake, our squadron in chase. A gentleman who left Fort Niagara on Sunday afternoon states that our fleet was still in sight, but the enemy had disappeared.

On Sunday evening a young man passed thro' this town who left Cleveland on Thursday last (August 5th). He states that Commodore Perry had left Erie on Friday last (August 6th) with the brigs *Lawrence* and *Niagara*, having partly manned them with volunteers for a short cruise. He is said to have gone to Long Point. Captain Elliott with his sailors probably arrived yesterday at Erie.

Last Friday passed this place destined for Erie, Captain J. D. Elliott (who commanded at the capture of the *Detroit* and *Caledonia*

last October) with about 100 seamen, recently from Boston. Captain Elliott takes command of one of the new brigs at Erie.
(File in Buffalo Public Library.)

Lieutenant-Colonel Harvey to Major T. G. Simons, Incorporated Militia.

29th July, 1813, 11 o'clock.

DEAR MAJOR,—If you can possibly do it, the Major-General wishes you to proceed immediately with your militia to the head of the lake, collecting and taking under your command all the regular troops you may find betwixt Shipman's and Burlington, and using your utmost endeavour to forward the whole by waggons if possible. There are strong reasons to apprehend that the enemy means to attack our depot at Burlington, *which we must not lose.* It is far too valuable to this army to be lost. You must feel your way as you advance for fear the enemy may have landed *intermediately* with a view to cut off any troops advancing.

To your discretion and knowledge of the country we confidently trust for the performance of this service.
(Canadian Archives, Q. 341, pp. 207-8.)

District General Order.

Headquarters, ST. DAVIDS, July 29th, 1813.

D. G. O.

Major-General De Rottenburg having learned with great displeasure that some of the troops have committed great depredations on the property of some of the inhabitants, by forcibly taking hay and burning fences, directs any soldiers so doing to be tried by drumhead court martial.

The ready sale found for articles by the Indians having encouraged depredations by them, all officers and soldiers are forbidden to purchase anything from an Indian without permission.
(Claus Papers.)

Left Division Orders.

KINGSTON, 29th July, 1813.

No. 3.

The following men of the detachment to embark on board the fleet to-morrow morning at half past nine o'clock:

Royal Scots, 2 sergeants, 16 rank and file.
King's Regiment, 9 rank and file.

F. KIRCHLINGEN,
B. M.

Secretary of War to General Boyd.

WAR DEPARTMENT, July 30, 1813.

(Extract.)

The restriction put upon you with regard to the enemy was but commensurate with their command of the lake. So long as they had wings and you had only feet, so long as they could be transported, supplied and reinforced by water and at will, common sense as well as military principles put you on the *defensive*. These circumstances changed, the reason of the rule changes with them and it now becomes your business, in concert with the fleet, to harass and destroy the enemy whenever you can find him. Of the competency of your force there can be no doubt, provided your estimate of his be but tolerably correct.

(American State Papers, Military Affairs, Vol. I., p. 450.)

Secretary of War to General Boyd.

WAR DEPARTMENT, July 30, 1813.

SIR,—I have this moment received information that Fort Meigs is again attacked and by a *considerable regular force*. This must have been drawn from De Rottenburg's corps. His late insolence in pushing his small attacks to the very outline of your works has been intended to mask his weakness produced by this detachment. If, as you say, you can beat him, do it without delay, and remember that if you beat you must destroy him. There is no excuse for a general who permits a beaten enemy to escape and to rally. These remarks grow out of some recent events in your quarter and require no explanation. It is the President's wish you should communicate freely with Brigadier-General Williams. It is only by this kind of intercourse that the efforts of all can be united in promoting the public good.

(American State Papers, Military Affairs, Vol. I., p. 450.)

General Boyd to General P. B. Porter.

Headquarters, FORT GEORGE, July 30, 1813.

SIR,—As soon as the health of Captain Saunders will admit you will please to remove him to Buffalo or Williamsville. The latter place being more remote will be the most eligible provided it is equally commodious.

(From MSS. of Hon. P. A. Porter.)

Colonel Claus to Captain Fulton, A. D. C. to Sir George Prevost.

ST. DAVIDS, July 31st, 1813.

SIR,—I have in some measure been able to keep the Indians together, but they are getting tired and impatient. They are dropping off and in a few days I fear we will not have many. Major-General De Rottenburg has directed me to purchase everything to be had within 50 miles, but that was not sufficient for 500 men. Tobacco, in particular, is an article we cannot get. An equipment for 500 men has been forwarded to Amherstburg. I urgently request that you will send on our supply of presents.

(Claus Papers.)

General Porter to General Boyd.

BLACK ROCK, July 31, 1813.

SIR,—The men at this place and Buffalo are impatient for something to do. I have it in contemplation, if you have no objections, to gratify them by crossing the river (to-night if our boats are in readiness, and, if not, to-morrow night,) with a party of about 300 men, in two divisions, so as to secure everything on the enemy's shore for a distance of about 3 miles above and below Fort Erie. There is probably a small guard or two and a considerable quantity of live stock and other public and private property, which might in part remunerate for the property plundered at B. Rock.

I send Adjutant Stanton, who is an enterprising and meritorious officer, with this in order to know your pleasure in respect to the proposed enterprise. Should you be about to make a movement and wish to enlarge the number of men and extend the expedition to Chippawa or elsewhere for the purpose of co-operation, we can probably, by taking Indians, increase the number of the party from 3 to 500.

(MSS. of Hon. P. A. Porter.)

General Porter to General Boyd.

B. ROCK, July 31, 1813.

SIR,—Your two letters of the 22d and 27th inst. were brought to Buffalo some time last night by the mail, (due the night before,) and were not received by me until an hour after Adjutant Stanton had set out for Fort George, which will account for them not having been before answered.

Your request to have the Indians join you at Fort George shall be again submitted to them by Mr. G[ranger] and myself to-day and shall be urged by all the arguments which a sincere desire to have your wishes gratified may suggest. But I hope, Sir, if you should not succeed you will not ascribe the failure to our agency, but that you will recollect these people are peculiar for their pride and independence of opinion. That they adopt every important measure with great consideration and wariness and often persist in it with [obstinacy?]

I regret that you should suggest or even entertain the idea that "local considerations," (by which I understand an interested preference of the security of our part of the frontier over another,) could have influence in the detention of the Indians. If interest were the motive of our conduct I should long ago have abandoned the frontier and taken with me all the property exposed to hazard, except a few buildings of little value, instead of remaining here buffeting the storm and spending my time and money to no earthly profit. The truth is I have exposed myself to every hazard and remain because I was *ashamed to desert*, and by my example induce my neighbors to do the same.

The idea of interest has undoubtedly originated in the difference of opinion entertained by me and Com'g Officer at Ft. George in respect to the views of the enemy. Immediately after the affair of Stoney Creek, Gen'l D. drew all the regular force to Ft. George in expectation of an attack on that place. I at that time visited headquarters and stated to him my opinion with the freedom and confidence which I thought my acquaintance with the country and enemy's force authorized me to assume. I advised him for the honor and security of the army to attack and disperse the enemy, that if he did not they would not attack Fort George, but that they would draw a line of posts close around him, harass and amuse him there, and then commence a scene of depredations in another quarter. Indeed, my convictions of their views were so strong and I wished so much to impress them strongly on him that I well recollect having said to him that they would as soon attack *heaven* as make a sincere and general attack on Fort George, but if he remained there with his whole army they would as sure as *God lived* attack Schlosser, Black Rock and Buffalo and strike terror and consternation through the whole country. My opinion of the intention of the enemy to attack Buffalo and of consequence my wish to have some force to protect it undoubtedly led to this supposition by those who thought Fort George alone menaced that I had an interest particularly in this place. I thought this explanation due to your suggestion.

(MSS. of Hon. P. A. Porter.)

General Boyd to the Secretary of War.

FORT GEORGE, July 31, 1813.

I had the honor to address you on the 27th instant. Agreeably to the plan therein suggested, Commodore Chauncey arrived here on the 28th instant and received on board the fleet a body of men under Colonel Scott. Light and contrary winds retard their progress up the lake, but ere this the attack has probably been made on the head of the lake. No information has as yet been received. The enemy has lately kept his Indians so constantly scouring the woods of our vicinity that we gain no deserters nor intelligence of his movements.

(American State Papers, Military Affairs, Vol. I., p. 450.)

Colonel F. Battersby, Glengarry Light Infantry, to Colonel Baynes.

BURLINGTON HEIGHTS, 31st July, 1813.

MY DEAR COLONEL :—

I arrived here at half past twelve last night and left my brigade with Major Stewart, about eight miles from this, having first ascertained with certainty that the enemy had re-embarked the whole of the men he had landed in the forenoon, carrying with him what live stock and other plunder that was within his reach, and carrying off two or three of the inhabitants. What troops they have on board appear to be commanded by a Colonel Scott, and I am told that Major Chapin was the first man that landed. Their fleet got under way this morning at daylight and are now with their heads down the lake in line of battle abreast—the *Oneida* and *Pike* on the larboard quarter, the *Madison* and all the small craft on the starboard—evidently expecting to come to action, and there is report of *eight* sail of our vessels being seen yesterday from the 40 Mile Creek.

As I found it impossible to bring the guns by land, and considering that the great object was to throw myself into this place with my men, I embarked the guns at the Humber, under the charge of McKay, with directions to proceed by water as far as he could with safety, and I have now despatched a militia officer by water to conduct them in as I do not conceive there is the smallest risk, the enemy not having a *single* vessel on the lookout as has been their constant practice since first I saw them. General De Rottenburg had reinforced this post, (I think adequate to its defence,) before my arrival, and I am anxious to know where I can turn my face to next. I wish he may give me a day or two rest for I do not expect the men's packs up before to-morrow evening at sunset. I moved as light as possible but it is difficult to prevent officers and men from *encumbering* themselves with some little comforts.

12 at noon.

Lt. O'Keefe has this moment arrived from Long Point with a letter from Captain Barclay to General De Rottenburg. Captain B. has been obliged to return to Long Point owing to the weather. He represents the enemy having everything nearly ready for hauling their vessels over the bar. When that is done we must retire to Amherstburg. The *Detroit* is launched, but neither men or guns. General Procter is at Fort Meigs, and by a vessel just arrived from Amherstburg gives the following account: General Harrison had left Cleveland on his way to Fort Meigs with 800 mounted men. Colonel Elliott and Tecumseh with the flank companies of the 41st had gone to meet him and had come up his advance of 12 men, killed 10 and taken two prisoners, who said Harrison was a short distance in the rear with the above number and a large quantity of horned cattle. General Procter was at Fort Meigs with the remainder of the 41st and Indians. Report says he is about to mine one angle of the fort. Mr. O'Keefe is just returning to join the *Queen Charlotte*. He has about 150 men of his regiment on board the different vessels.

I have just learned that our guns are coming by land from the Credit and may probably arrive this night or to-morrow morning.

I believe some attempt was made upon our left at 4 Mile Creek last night or this morning. The enemy were driven back with some loss.

I am obliged to direct this under cover to His Excellency as no *extra* despatch is *permitted* to go unless so addressed and I know from a *billet* I had this morning from Col. Harvey that he conceives the communication cut off. Sir George must be anxious, and I enclose it.

(Canadian Archives, C. 679, p. 517.)

Left Division Orders.

Adjutant General's Office, KINGSTON, 31st July, 1813.

No. 3.

The Commander of the Forces is pleased to make the following appointments: Captain Jenkins, Glengarry Light Infantry, is appointed Town Major of Fredericton, New Brunswick, from the 30th instant. Assistant Sergeant Major Alexander Fraser, 49th Regiment, in consideration of his gallantry and good conduct, is appointed to act as adjutant with the rank of ensign in the New Brunswick Fencible Infantry and is to proceed to join that corps.

EDWARD BAYNES,
Adjutant General.

Major-General De Rottenburg to Captain Freer.

Headquarters of the Army of the Centre,
ST. DAVIDS, 1st August, 1813.

SIR,—I have the honor to acknowledge the receipt of your letter of the 26th ulto., and I am happy to state for the information of His Excellency, the Commander of the Forces, that the enemy has been foiled in his attempt to surprise Burlington Heights. The enclosed reports I received in the night will furnish you with the details of the occurrence. It seems the enemy's fleet is doing as much mischief as they can. We all day yesterday could perceive smoke arising from burning houses around the coast. Col. Battersby's moveable column is directed to move on again towards York and watch the enemy's operations in that quarter. Capt. Coleman's troop and the veterans will now proceed immediately for Sandwich.

I have not received any despatches from General Procter, but Capt. R. Barclay writes me from Long Point, July 30th, that he had received a letter from Amherstburg the day before, stating that General Procter had left that place on the 19th for the Miami river on his attempt to dislodge the American army at Fort Meigs, but nothing had transpired except that he had arrived within three miles of that post on the 21st. General Harrison was expected to join General Green Clay with a reinforcement of 800 men, for which purpose he was advancing by Cleveland. Brigadier-General Procter had intimation of his design and sent a party of the 41st Regt., with 800 or 900 Indians, by the lake to that river to endeavor to cut him off. He also states that the moment the seamen arrived he would proceed to General Procter, land the men of the 41st he has on board and go immediately to Amherstburg to equip the *Detroit*.

I request that you will state to His Excellency that I am perfectly recovered.

[P. S.]—The cyphered despatch of the 26th has been received. The troops the enemy sent were embarked at Fort George. By driving in the piquets yesterday the enemy's position at Fort George was closely reconnoitered. Their entrenchment [is] very strong and they had about 3,000 men under arms.

(Canadian Archives, C. 679.)

General Boyd to General Peter B. Porter.

Headquarters, FORT GEORGE, August 1, 1813.

DEAR SIR,—I have received your two letters, one by Adjutant Stanton, the last by Lieutenant Brady. The plans you propose, as I once before remarked, would gain my entire approbation were they agreeable to my instructions, which debar me from undertaking any enterprise when the hazard is not more than counterbalanced by the probability of success. The attack upon the head of the lake was approved of by Gen. Lewis because, with the co-operation of the fleet, it could hardly fail of a favorable result.

I have fully communicated with Adjutant Stanton, whom I have detained one day in the hope that the fleet would have returned. The moment it arrives and the issue of this expedition should seem to warrant any other enterprise in which you can participate you shall be informed by express.

In my extreme anxiety to have the assistance of the Indians in this quarter, expressions may have escaped me which are incompatible with the opinion I have of your patriotic sentiments and my knowledge of the sacrifices you have made since the war.

I wish it was practicable for you to occasionally visit headquarters, as your counsel and information might greatly assist in forming a plan of attack on the interior. In the event of your coming perhaps you might induce some warriors to accompany you, by whom we would endeavor to communicate a desire to the rest.

(From MSS. of Hon. P. A. Porter.)

Sir George Prevost to Earl Bathurst.

Headquarters, KINGSTON, UPPER CANADA,
1st August, 1813.

No. 81.

MY LORD,—I have the honor to inform Your Lordship that the enemy continue to occupy the position of Fort George and its immediate vicinity, within which they are still more closely circumscribed than when I had the honor of adressing you on the 18th ult., the headquarters of Major-General De Rottenburg having since been removed to St. Davids, about seven miles distant from that fort and our advanced posts being within four miles of it.

The enemy's fleet, consisting of two ships, one brig and eleven schooners, in all fourteen, sailed from Sackett's Harbor on the 23d ulto. and were seen off Niagara on the 27th and off York on the 28th and 29th, and yesterday our squadron, powerfully armed, well equipped, completely manned and ably commanded, as Your Lordship will see by the comparative statement I have the honor herewith of transmitting, left Kingston harbor in search of it. It is scarcely possible that a decisive naval action can be avoided, and I therefore humbly hope that His Royal Highness the Prince Regent will approve of its being courted by us, as a necessary measure for the preservation of the advanced positions of this army, which I have determined to maintain until the naval ascendency on Lake Ontario is decided, convinced that a retrograde movement would eventually endanger the safety of a large proportion of the troops in Upper Canada and convert the heart of the Province into the seat of war.

The operations lately carried on in the Chesapeake not having hitherto corresponded with the just expectations of His Majesty's Government by creating a diversion in my favor, and the pressure of the war continuing upon Upper Canada, I have thought it expedient to endeavor to call off the enemy's attention from this Province to the defence of their own settlements on Lake Champlain by employing Captain Everard and the officers and seamen of His Majesty's sloop of war *Wasp*, lately arrived from Halifax, to man our gunboats and the captured American vessels at Isle Aux Noix, for the purpose of joining with a body of eight hundred picked men in making a movement on that lake to arrest the progress of the reinforcements moving towards the American armies at Sackett's Harbor under Major-General Lewis and at Niagara under Major-General Dearborn. I have selected an officer of merit and enterprise for this service and he has received my instructions to destroy the vessels and boats of every description along the shore and such public buildings as are used for military purposes.

He is also to bring away or destroy provisions and warlike stores of every kind which may fall into his possession, but all private property and the persons of the unarmed and inoffensive inhabitants are to be respected and every care and precaution are to be taken to preserve both inviolate. The arrival of Mr. Dickson from the Missouri with 2000 Indian warriors has enabled me to resume offensive operations with the left division of the Upper Canada army, under the command of Brigadier-General Procter. Major-General Harrison having shewn some of his cavalry and riflemen in the Michigan Territory, a forward movement has been made by the Indian warriors, supported by a few companies of the 41st Regt., upon Sandusky, from whence they will unite with Tecumseth's band of warriors employed in investing Fort Meigs.

The occupation by the enemy of our frontier territory on the Niagara river having interrupted our usual mode of communicating with Lake Erie, I have had great difficulties to contend with in supplying the posts at Amherstburg and Mackinac. Those difficulties have, however, by great exertions, been in some measure surmounted, and I have, although at a considerable expense, been able to transport by a circuitous route by the Grand River to General Procter a small supply of Indian arms and ammunition which were indispensable and part of which I have been under the necessity of purchasing, the presents comprising the requisition of last year not having yet arrived, the inconvenience of which to the public service is severely felt.

The naval and military operations which I have above stated to Your Lordship as going on in three distinct parts of my command will evince how strong the confidence in the means, tho' comparatively small, which Your Lordship has placed at my disposal for the defence of these Provinces, and notwithstanding Mr. Madison's boastful claim to the naval ascendency on the lakes, I have the satisfaction of reporting to Your Lordship for the gracious consideration of His Royal Highness the Prince Regent, that His Majesty's flag waves on Lakes Erie, Ontario and Champlain, and with the blessing of the Almighty I hope soon to be enabled to add that it waves triumphantly, the terror of its arrogant and unprincipled enemies.

(Canadian Archives, Q. 122, p. 116.)

Sir George Prevost to Major-General Dearborn.

Headquarters, KINGSTON, 1st August, 1813.

SIR,—A period of three months has elapsed since my last communication through Your Excellency to the Government of the United States upon the subject of the exchange it had undertaken to make, without my assent thereto, of Brig.-General Hull and other officers of the American army, prisoners of war on their parole, several of whom are now serving in violation of it. As during that period a great accumulation of American prisoners has taken place in the Canadas, none of whom in the present state of the above question can be either paroled or exchanged, I have to acquaint Your Excellency that it is my intention to send the one-half of them immediately to Halifax, and in the event of my not receiving shortly a satisfactory explanation upon the subject of the communication referred to I shall be under the necessity of sending the remainder to England. Regretting, as I certainly shall, to be compelled to adopt this latter measure, I shall have the satisfaction of knowing that all the means in my power have been used to bring this subject before your Government with a view to a speedy adjustment of it, to whom alone will the American prisoners of war have to ascribe their being separated from their families and homes.

At the same time I beg leave to assure you that it will give me the greatest pleasure to find the disposition I have invariably manifested on this subject met by a corresponding one on the part of the American Government, and thereby to have the grounds of our present difference respecting it removed.

Your Excellency will, I hope, be able to afford me an early reply to this communication, but should that not be the case I have to beg you will without further delay transmit it for the consideration of the Government of the United States.

(Canadian Archives, Q. 122, p. 128.)

Extracts from Returns of the Troops at Sackett's Harbor, Fort Niagara, Fort George and Burlington.

STATION.	CORPS.	PRESENT.				ABSENT.		TOTAL PRESENT AND ABSENT.	AGGREG'TE. PRESENT AND ABSENT.
		FOR DUTY.		SICK.					
		TOTAL.	AGGRE-GATE.	TOTAL.	AGGRE-GATE.	TOTAL.	AGGRE-GATE.		
Sackett's Harbor—Light Artillery		99	103	23	23	28	28	150	154
Dragoons		235	249	138	143	46	50	419	442
Artillery		344	360	118	119	95	96	557	573
Infantry		1432	1485	545	555	46	52	2023	2092
Volunteers		303	228	111	117	57	62	371	407
Total at Sackett's Harbor		2313	2425	935	957	272	288	3520	3668
Fort George—Light Artillery		302	305	52	55	118	121	472	481
Dragoons		200	211	17	17	13	13	230	241
Artillery		162	171	70	72	33	34	265	277
Infantry		3032	3148	862	919	1486	1569	5371	5636
Total at Fort George		3696	3835	1001	1063	1650	1737	6338	6635
Burlington—Dragoons		118	122	18	18		1	136	140
Artillery		74	76	13	14	1		88	90
Infantry		2354	2441	360	367	195	209	2909	3017
Volunteers		501	530	156	159	104	117	761	806
Total at Burlington		3047	3169	547	558	300	327	3894	4053

Adjutant and Inspector General's Office, }
Washington City, August 2d, 1813. }

A. T. NICOLL, Insp. Gen.

(From Wilkinson's Memoirs, Vol. III, Appendix VI.)

Thomas G. Ridout to Thomas Ridout at York.

ST. DAVIDS, 2d August, 1813.

I received yesterday letters from you and George, giving an account of the Yankee fleet being off York threatening it with destruction. Our anxiety has not been less than yours, but since they let you remain unmolested the first day I think they'll not land until Sir James meets them. The fate of this army depends on this. Its positions are so advanced that a retreat will be impossible without losing half the men. The enemy remain cooped up in Fort George, not daring to stir beyond the common. Everything goes on steadily and regularly. Ten thousand of the enemy will not be able to start John Bull out of the Black Swamp.

Mr. Bissett went up yesterday to Long Point with £1000 in specie to buy cattle for Amherstburg.

I am very much alarmed about York for a large fire was seen in that direction all last night. The garrison at all events must be burnt, with the flour and other provisions Mr. Crookshank has been collecting. Concerning my shirts, the starch has not come to hand.

I keep my things in a pair of saddle bags that Henry Nelles lent me, ready for a march. The military chest is at present run out to $500.

More than $40,000 have been paid out within the last fortnight. Every hour is now of great consequence and I think this week will determine affairs.

Some considerable movement will take place shortly, and I hope to write you of our success.

(From Ten Years of Upper Canada, by Lady Edgar, pp. 206-7.)

Dr. Grant Powell and Revd. John Strachan to Captain Freer.

YORK, August 2d, 1813.

SIR,—We beg leave to state for the information of His Excellency the Governor General that about eleven o'clock on Saturday morning the enemy's fleet of twelve sail were seen standing for the harbor. Almost all the gentlemen of the town having retired, we proceeded to the garrison about 2 o'clock and watched until 3 o'clock, when the *Pyke*, the *Madison* and *Oneida* came to anchor in the offing and the schooners continued to pass up the harbor with their sweeps, the wind having become light, then coming to abreast of the town, the remainder near the garrison. About 4 o'clock several boats full of troops landed at the garrison, and we, bearing a white flag, desired the first officer we met to conduct us to Commodore Chauncey. We mentioned to the Commodore that the inhabitants of York, consisting chiefly of women and children, were alarmed at the approach of the fleet, and that we had come to know his intentions respecting the town, that if it were to be pillaged and destroyed we might take such measures as were still in our power for their removal and protection. We added that the town was totally defenceless, the militia being still on parole, and that the gentlemen had left it, having heard that the principal inhabitants of Niagara had been carried away captive, a severity unusual in war. Commodore Chauncey replied that it was far from his intention to molest the inhabitants of York in person or property, he was sorry that any of the gentlemen had thought it necessary to retire and that he did not know of any person taken from Niagara of the description named. Colonel Scott, the commandant of the troops, said that a few persons had certainly been taken away. The Commodore told us that his coming to York at present was a sort of retaliation for the visits our fleet made on the other side of the lake and to possess himself of the public stores and destroy the fortifications, but that he would burn no houses. He mentioned something of Sodus and the necessity of retaliation should such measures be taken in future. He likewise expressed much regret at the destruction of our public library, April 27th, informing us that he had made strict search through his fleet for books; many of them had been found which he would send back by the first flag of truce. He then asked what public stores were here, a question which we could not answer. In parting, both the Commodore and Colonel Scott pledged their honor that our persons and property should be respected and that even the town should not be entered by the troops, much less by any gentleman there. As we were quieting the minds of the inhabitants the troops took possession of the town, opened the jail, liberated the prisoners, taking three soldiers confined for felony with them. They visited the hospitals and paroled the few men that could not be removed. They then entered the stores of Mr. Allan and Mr. St. George and secured the contents, consisting chiefly of flour. Observing this we went to Col. Scott and informed him he was taking private property. He replied that a great deal of officers' luggage had been found in Mr. Allan's store and that all private property was to be respected. Provisions of all kinds were lawful prize because they were the subsistence of armies, that if it prevailed in the contest the British Government would make up the loss, and that if they were successful their Government would most willingly reimburse the sufferers. He concluded by declaring that he would seize all the provisions he could find. The three schooners which had anchored abreast of the town towed out between 11 and 12 o'clock on Saturday night and we supposed that the fleet would have sailed immediately, but having been informed by some traitor that valuable stores had been sent up the Don, the schooners came up the harbor yesterday morning. The troops were again landed and three armed boats went up the Don in search of the stores. We have since learned that through the meritorious exertions of a few young men, two of the name of Playter, everything was conveyed away before the enemy reached the place. Two or three boats containing trifling articles, which had been hidden in the marsh, were discovered and taken, but in the main the enemy were disappointed. As soon as the armed boats returned the troops went on board and by sunset both soldiers and sailors had evacuated the town. The barracks, the woodyard and the storehouses on Gibralter Point were then set on fire and this morning at daylight the enemy's fleet sailed. The troops which were landed acted as marines and appear to be all they had on board, not more, certainly, than 240 men. The fleet consists of fourteen armed vessels. One is left at Sackett's Harbor. It is but justice to Commodore Chauncey and Colonel Scott to state that their men while on shore behaved well and no private house was entered or destroyed.

(Canadian Archives, C. 679.)

Garrison Order.

KINGSTON, 2d August, 1813.

The detachment from the Glengarry Light Infantry, under orders to proceed to York, are to be held in readiness to embark in a batteau at daybreak to-morrow morning, under the command of Captain Robinson, 8th (or King's) Regiment.

Acting Quartermaster-Sergeant Prendergast, 100th Regiment, is appointed as adjutant to the Canadian Voltigeurs detachment, under Major Heriot, until further orders and is to receive the allowances of the same.

Sergeant Wm. FitzPatrick, 100th Regiment, is appointed to act as barrack master at Prescott until further orders.

Left Division Orders.

KINGSTON, 2d August, 1813.

No. 1.

Captain Washburn's company of Incorporated Militia attached to the Royal Engineers will embark this evening at six o'clock for Point Henry, and will take a week's provision. The Acting Quartermaster-General will furnish a batteau for that service.

From the Montreal Gazette, 2d August, 1813.

On Thursday last 13 American prisoners, taken by the Indians near Fort George, arrived. They were attached to a foraging party consisting of one officer and 30 men, of which the remainder were killed, and these would have probably shared the same fate had not British humanity, in the person of Colonel Young, as we are informed, rescued them by the purchase of their lives from the captors.

The steamboat arrived yesterday from Quebec. She brought up one officer and 80 prime seamen for the lake service.

(File in the Library of Parliament, Ottawa.)

Colonel Winfield Scott to Brig.-General Boyd.

FORT GEORGE, August 3, 1813.

SIR,—I have the honor to report that in obedience to your orders I proceeded on board the fleet with the detachment of troops under my command destined to act against the enemy's post at the head of Little Lake or Burlington Bay, in sight of which I arrived late in the evening of the 30th ultimo, the fleet having been greatly delayed by the almost constant calm which has prevailed since we sailed.

This delay of forty-eight hours after our destination became obvious to the enemy, enabled him to anticipate our arrival by a reinforcement of 200 men from the nearest posts on this side of the lake, of which we were early apprized. Nevertheless Commodore Chauncey, with my concurrence, thought it advisable to land the detachment from the army, together with about 250 seamen and marines from the fleet, (making a total force of about 500 men.) The better to enable us to ascertain the exact force and position of the the enemy, the landing was made on the neck of land which nearly cuts off the Little Lake from Lake Ontario. From this point we could plainly discover the enemy's position on Burlington Heights, surrounded on three sides by a creek and in front by an entrenchment and a battery of seven pieces of cannon. The Little Lake or bay is, between those points, six or seven miles across.

Perceiving the strength of the enemy's position and learning from the inhabitants that the force on the heights, independent of the reinforcement above mentioned, was nearly equal to our own, the Commodore determined not to risk an attack, especially as our boats would have been greatly annoyed in the ascent towards the head of the bay by a small schooner of the enemy's having on board one 18-pound carronade. The channel connecting the two lakes did not afford water for the passage of either of our schooners. In the above opinion I fully concurred with the Commodore. It may be added that the enemy received a further reinforcement the same evening by land from Kingston.

On our return to this harbor the fleet put into York, at which place we burnt the barracks and public stores and brought off one piece of ordnance, (24-pounder,) eleven batteaux and about 400 barrels of flour and hard bread. The barracks and stores had been repaired since the 27th April. Thirty or forty sick and wounded in the hospital were paroled and four prisoners (regulars) brought off. There had been no garrison at the place for the few days previous.

(American State Papers, Military Affairs. Vol. I., p. 450.)

From the Buffalo Gazette, 3rd August, 1813.

Our Ontario fleet, consisting of 15 sail, with Commodore Chauncey on board, arrived at Niagara on Wednesday last, (July 28.) The fleet on Thursday evening sailed up the lake. It is understood there were 1,000 troops on board. Colonel Scott, Major Chapin and Captain Phelps went on board the fleet.

Runners on Sunday evening last stated that the troops had landed at the head of the lake or at Little York,

The British fleet left Erie on Thursday last, (July 29,) for Long Point.

In our paper of the 13th ult. we stated that the British Captain Saunders, wounded in the affair at Black Rock, was not likely to recover. One of his physicians attending him has requested us to mention that his wounds were doing well and that he is in a fair way of recovery.

BEAVER, PA., July 17.

The British have had the impudence to threaten that Congress shall hear the thunder of their cannon. From this has arisen the strong anxiety expressed by General Baird in his toast of the 5th inst., for the safe return of General Tannehill to Grove Hill. It is presumed that the General stands in as much danger from the British in Congress Hall as he intended to place himself in when he went to Black Rock. —*Crisis.*

Since the arrival of the British prisoners in this place seventeen of the regulars have escaped from their guard.

—*Geneva Gazette.*

(File in Buffalo Public Library.)

General Order.

Adjutant General's Office,
Headquarters, KINGSTON,
3d August, 1813.

G. O.

The Commander of the Forces is pleased to direct that the following movements take place in the distribution of the troops:—

The flank companies of the line to join their respective corps in Lower Canada. The flank companies of the 4th Battalion of embodied militia, under Major Perrault, to be attached to and do duty with the Canadian Voltigeurs, under Lieut.-Colonel De Salaberry.

The 103d Regiment is to proceed to Quebec to relieve the Regiment de Meuron, which is to be stationed at Chambly. The 13th Regiment is to be stationed at St. Johns and Isle Aux Noix, to relieve the detachment of the 100th Regiment under Major Taylor, who is to proceed to join his regiment at Niagara.

The detachment of the Royal Scots and the detachment of lads of the 41st, 2d Battalion, and 89th Regiment are to proceed, under the command of Major Deane, to join their respective corps.

On the arrival of the Regiment de Meuron at Chambly, the Canadian Fencibles will march to Laprairie and the 3d Battalion of embodied militia will proceed to Montreal.

These movements will commence at Quebec by the detachment under Major Deane, Royal Scots, followed by a division of De Meuron's Regiment, the last division of which will leave Quebec on the arrival of the first division of the 103d Regiment.

The movements in the Montreal District are to commence by the 103d Regiment proceeding to Quebec in two divisions, and the flank companies joining their respective corps.

The 13th Regiment will march to St. Johns as soon as the commanding officer of that corps is returned, and the detachment of the 100th Regiment is to proceed to Kingston, without delay, as soon as relieved.

Lieut.-Colonel Murray will deliver over the command of the post of St. Johns to Lieutenant-Colonel Williams, 13th Regiment, and repair to the headquarters of the army to receive His Excellency's further instructions.

EDWARD BAYNES,
Adjutant General.

Brigadier-General Boyd to the Secretary of War.

(Extract.)

FORT GEORGE, August 4th, 1813.

SIR,—Since I had the honor to address you last two deserters have come in from the enemy, by whom we learn that he is entrenching in the woods in expectation of an attack, rather than having an intention to make one himself. His position in the woods, where his red auxiliaries are so formidable, may render him strong. But *we trust* when you shall deem it proper to *allow* the army to act offensively that we shall be able to dislodge, *perhaps*, with the *co-operation* of the fleet, to capture or drive him to his stronghold at the head of the lake.

(From Boyd's Documents and Facts, p. 18.)

Commodore Chauncey to the Secretary of the Navy.

U. S. Ship *General Pike*,
at anchor off Niagara,
August 4, 1813.

SIR,—After leaving Sackett's Harbor I stretched over for the enemy's shore and from thence stood up the lake. The winds being light I did not arrive off this post until the evening of the 27th ult. On the 24th I fell in with the *Lady of the Lake*, on her return to Sackett's Harbor with prisoners from Fort George. I transferred the prisoners to the *Raven* and ordered her for Sackett's Harbor. The *Lady of the Lake* I despatched to Fort George for guides for the head of the lake. General Boyd having informed me that the enemy had a considerable deposit of provisions and stores at Burlington Bay, I was determined to attempt their destruction. On the 25th I was joined by the *Pert* and on the 27th by the *Lady of the Lake*, with guides and Captain Crane's company of artillery and Colonel Scott, who had handsomely volunteered for the service. After conversing with Colonel Scott upon the subject, it was thought advisable to take on board 150 infantry, which by the extraordinary exertions of that gallant officer were embarked before 6 o'clock the next morning, and the fleet immediately proceeded for the head of the lake, but owing to light winds and calms we did not arrive at an anchorage before the evening of the 29th. We sent two parties on shore and surprised and took some of the inhabitants, from whom we learned that the enemy had received considerable reinforcements within a day or two, and that his force in regulars was from 600 to 800 men. We, however, landed our troops and marines and some sailors the next morning, and reconnoitred the enemy's position; found him posted upon a peninsula of very high ground and strongly intrenched, and his camp defended by about 8 pieces of cannon. In this situation it was thought not advisable to attack him with a force scarcely half his numbers and without artillery. We were also deficient in boats, not having a sufficient number to cross the bay with all the troops at the same time. The men were all re-embarked in the course of the afternoon, and in the evening we weighed and stood for York; arrived and anchored in that harbor at about 3 p. m. On the 31st, ran the schooners into the upper harbor; landed the marines and soldiers, under the command of Colonel Scott, without opposition; found several hundred barrels of flour and provisions in the public store-house, five pieces of cannon, eleven boats and a quantity of shot, shells and other stores, all of which were either destroyed or brought away. On the 1st inst., just after having received on board all that the vessels could take, I directed the barracks and the public store-houses to be burnt. We then re-embarked the men and proceeded for this place, where I arrived yesterday. Between 400 and 500 men left York for the head of the lake two days before we arrived there. Some few prisoners were taken, some of whom were paroled; the others have been landed at Fort George.

(From the Historical Register of the United States, 1814, Vol. II., pp. 280-2.)

Lieut. Patrick McDonogh, 2d U. S. Artillery, to his Parents.

FORT GEORGE, August 4th, 1813.

. . . .

. . . .

I have nothing worth writing to you about except to tell you that I am well and that we still remain here doing nothing, nor do I know when we shall move. Our fleet is now lying off this place, expecting the British fleet every hour. We hear they are building another forty-four gun ship; if so I do not think they will venture out until she is finished. Col. Scott went on an expedition to the Head of the Lake and from there to York in search of British stores, but it seems they were apprised of our intentions before the fleet reached there, as they had almost everything removed. We took 4 or 500 barrels of flour and some officers' baggage at York, burnt their barracks and returned. It is reported that Gen. Wilkinson and the Secretary at War are coming on. If this be true we may yet do something. Genl. Williams arrived here some days back; he commands our brigade. I think if things go on no better than they have done I shall be ashamed to return to Philadelphia next winter, even should I get permission to do so. War characters must rank mighty low there.

P. S.

Col. Scott has resigned his appointment as Adjutant-General.

Major-General DeRottenburg to Sir George Prevost.

Headquarters of the Army of the Centre,
ST. DAVIDS, 5th August, 1813.

SIR,—Mr. Hagerman arrived here in the afternoon of the 3d with Your Excellency's letter of the 31st ulto., announcing the joyful tidings of our fleet being under weigh and transmitting a few signals to be established at my different posts to enable Sir J. Yeo to distinguish our positions from those that might be occupied by the enemy. These signals have been communicated to the various officers in command of posts.

Commodore Chauncey continues at anchor off the Niagara river and it is my opinion that if Sir James comes upon him with a fresh easterly breeze he will seek refuge in the river. Nothing has as yet been seen or heard of Sir James. I suppose he keeps away waiting for a breeze, the wind ever since his sailing having been very light. It is probable that both Commodores want to play their own game, the one must endeavor to avoid an engagement in a calm and the other will decline it in a gale. Should the enemy's fleet be driven into the Niagara river I shall most cordially co-operate with Sir James in such manner as may appear practicable for its destruction. The appearance of the enemy's fleet has caused great uneasiness to the Indian warriors. Your Excellency may rest assured that no personal exertions of mine are spared to retain them. I gave them a great war feast the other day and I have again a great talk with them this evening. The orders relative to rewards, &c., have been immediately forwarded to Brigadier-General Procter. I have no detailed report as yet of our losses sustained at York. For the purpose of re-establishing order there and protecting our remaining stores I have directed Lieut.-Colonel Battersby to detach 100 men to re-occupy York. I am glad Your Excellency has decided to erect blockhouses there in order to render the place tenable.

I have given orders to the acting-barrack-master to contract for the erection of log barracks for 1000 men at Burlington Heights.

(Canadian Archives, C. 679.)

General Porter to General Boyd.

BLACK ROCK, August 5th, 1813.

SIR,—I should have written to you sooner but that until the arrival of Major Chapin I had intended to go to Fort George myself this morning.

On Saturday last Mr. Granger and I renewed to the Indians your request to have them join you at Fort George. They agreed to take it into consideration and give an answer in the course of the day, which they did in the afternoon to Mr. Granger, being absent myself at the time.

Red Jacket told him that the Indians still adhered to their determination not to go to Fort George and leave their own village exposed to the incursions of the enemy, and made some free observations on the conduct of the Government or of Mr. Granger toward them, which led to harsh reflections on both sides, and ended in Mr. Granger telling them that he found their only object in staying here was to eat the public provisions and the sooner they went home the better it would be for the United States.

On Sunday morning a great part of them were prepared to start for home. Believing, as I always have, that there was no difficulty in leading them into the war and that their services might be very useful, I requested them to remain a day or two, when I should have something to propose to them. On Monday I told them that I was about to cross the river and should probably go as far as Chippawa for the purpose of learning the situation of the enemy and taking some guards I supposed were stationed along shore, and that I should be glad to have part or the whole of them go with me to look for the enemy, and invited as many of them as chose to go along, promising them that if they conducted themselves well and observed the instructions given them that they should have some public cattle and horses, which I intended to take from the opposite shore.

On Tuesday morning at 3 o'clock we crossed 200 regular troops and militia and 200 Indians, being all that were then here, and with the exception of 10 or 15 of the Indians their conduct was remarkably good. We marched four miles down the river from Fort Erie. They were extremely active and expert in taking prisoners and did not offer the least violence to the persons or property of the citizens. While they were engaged in taking the cattle and horses across the river a few unprincipled rascals from our shore crossed the river and with a few Indians strayed off, unknown to the officers, and plundered several private houses.

This disgraceful conduct is highly disapproved by the respectable Indians and they are now collecting it to be returned, and I am doing the same in respect to that taken by the white people, altho' the whole amount taken could have been but of trifling value.

As to the horses and cattle, all of which were found on the common, I find that a considerable part of them are claimed as private property, but under the assurance I had given the Indians I cannot with propriety take them away. The whole value of property taken cannot exceed 1000 dollars, and it would perhaps be best for the Government to pay for it than to take it away. The soldiers, of course, will not be permitted to retain any.

The expedition was undertaken with a view to subserve a public purpose and not for private plunder. But if the Indians have taken more than of strict right an army should take we have the consolation to reflect that they offered no abuse to the persons of the citizens and that the plunder taken from our citizens at their private houses in Black Rock by the regular troops was of three times the value of all we have brought from the other shore.

We took 20 prisoners, principally citizens, some of them under parole, but some of the most troublesome.

(MSS. of Hon. P. A. Porter.)

General Boyd to General P. B. Porter.

Headquarters, FORT GEORGE,
August 5, 1813.

Confidential.

SIR,—An expedition is on foot against the enemy which will require the co-operation of the fleet. Gen. Williams and Col. Scott are now on board with the Commodore to confer with him. If he can be persuaded to stay long enough to go as far as the 40-Mile Creek 1000 men will be landed at that point; if not, at the 12-Mile Creek; two columns will move at the same time from this place, one by the way of Queenston, another by the Lake Road. Your participation is earnestly desired. The principal force of the enemy being at St. Davids, it is thought not advisable for you to descend on this, but you will please to join us by the other with as great a force of *Indians* as you *can* assemble. I need not repeat the importance of such a force. As the Commodore will probably be unwilling to protract his stay longer than two or three days, you will be pleased to make known your decision as soon as possible.

(From MSS. of Hon. P. A. Porter.)

Handbill.

KINGSTON GAZETTE OFFICE,
5th Aug., 1813.

The following account of the enemy's late visit to York is published by authority:—

At 11 o'clock on Saturday morning, the 31st ult., the enemy's fleet, consisting of 12 sail, were seen standing for the harbor. About half-past 4 the *Pike*, the *Madison* and the *Oneida* came to anchor in the offing—the schooners continuing to pass up the harbor with their sweeps. About 4 o'clock three of them came to, near the town, and the remainder near the garrison, and immediately afterwards several boat-loads full of troops landed at the garrison and proceeded from thence to the town, of which they took possession.

They then opened the jail, liberating the prisoners and taking three soldiers confined for felony. They then went to the hospital and paroled the few men that could not be removed. They next entered the stores of Major Allan and Mr. St. George and seized the contents, consisting chiefly of flour, the same being private property. Between 11 and 12 o'clock on Saturday night the three schooners which had anchored abreast of the town towed out, and it is supposed that the fleet would have sailed immediately; but information having been given by some traitors, whose names it is hoped will be discovered, that valuable stores had been sent up the River Don, the schooners went up the harbor on Sunday morning, the troops were again landed and three armed boats proceeded up the Don in search of the stores. In consequence of the meritorious exertions of a few young men, amongst whom were two by the name of Playter, everything was conveyed away and the boats sunk before the enemy reached the place. Two or three boats containing trifling articles, which had been hid in the marsh, were discovered and taken, but in their main object the enemy was completely disappointed. As soon as the armed boats had returned the troops went on board, and by sunset both sailors and soldiers had evacuated the town, the barracks, the woodyard and storehouses on Gibraltar Point having been first set on fire by them, and at daylight on the following morning the enemy's fleet sailed.

The troops which were landed were acting as marines and appeared to be all they had on board the fleet, and did not exceed 240 men. They were under command of Com. Chauncey and Lieut.-Col. Scott, an unexchanged prisoner of war on his parole, both of whom landed with the troops. The town, upon the arrival of the enemy, was totally defenceless; the militia were still on parole, and the principal gentlemen had retired, from an apprehension of being treated with the same severity used towards several of the inhabitants near Fort George, who had been made prisoners and sent to the United States. Lt.-Col. Battersby, with the troops under his command, had, upon the first appearance of the enemy's fleet off York, on the 29th, proceeded from thence, with his guns, to Burlington Heights, where he had joined Major Maule and concentrated his force on the following evening. The enemy had, during the course of the day, landed from the fleet 300 men near Brandt's house, with an intention of storming the heights, which they hoped to carry, but finding Major Maule well prepared to receive them and being apprized of Lieut.-. Col. Battersby's march, they re-embarked and stood away for York

The plunder obtained by the enemy on this predatory expedition has been indeed trifling, and the loss has altogether fallen upon individuals, the public stores of every description having been removed; the only prisoners made by them being confined felons and invalids in the hospital. We are sorry to be obliged to observe that there is too much reason to believe that the enemy was furnished with exact information respecting the movements of our troops and the state of York and the position at Burlington Heights from traitors amongst ourselves; from men, too, who are holding public situations in the country, and whose names we trust, when correctly known, will lead to their conviction and punishment, and hold them up to the just detestation of every loyal subject of His Majesty.

(From Niles' *Weekly Register*, Baltimore, Md., September 4, 1813. Vol. 5, pp. 11-12.)

Colonel Claus to ———

CROSS ROADS, 6th August, (1813).

SIR,—I have waited in vain for the Indian presents which usually come in June. It is absolutely necessary to have the following to keep them together:

  1200 yards cotton.
  1000 yards linen.
  200 yards broadcloth.
  1000 yards sateen.
  200 lbs. vermillion.
  1000 lbs. tobacco.
  800 yards strouds.
  1,344 lbs. ball.
  400 butcher knives.
  400 clasp knives.

A list was given to Major Fulton to complete 500 men, but I have not heard anything of it.

(Claus Papers.)

E. Granger to Gen. Boyd, Commanding American Army.

BUFFALO, August 6th, 1813.

SIR,—I wrote you the result of a council held at this place the 1st inst. with the Indians. Some were of the opinion that the firm ground I took with them would induce them all to go home. I knew better. I knew that they were in a state of starvation at their villages and would not leave us. On the Sunday following they went forward to Gen. Porter and offered to cross the river with him and the troops of this place.

An expedition, as I afterwards understood, was agreed on to take place on the Tuesday morning following. The result of that expedition I shall not have to explain to you in detail, for you had the planning and execution of it. I shall only observe that being in principle opposed to it, and believing that no advantage would be derived from crossing the river and plundering the inhabitants, I did not think it proper to say anything to them or give directions on the subject. By the directions of Gen. Porter I assisted in furnishing the Indians with arms and ammunition for crossing. I believe the object of General Porter was to get information, apprehend some obnoxious characters and bring off some cattle running on the commons. He had not the most distant idea that the Indians would go to plundering the houses of individuals, nor did I if the example had not been set to them by individuals who crossed for the sake of plundering.

General Porter is trying to collect the household furniture and clothing taken from individuals for the purpose of returning them to the rightful owners, but as a number of the militia have deserted and gone home with a part of the booty and some gone into the Indian village, I fear but little will be collected.

Major Chapin, (Dr. Cyrenius Chapin,) has stated to me that you contemplate a movement into Canada, the fleet co-operating, and still wish some Indians to be with the army. Since the expedition from this place into Canada the Indians feel alarmed; they fear the British will retaliate upon them. They, of course, are unwilling to have their houses and women and children exposed. I still think that as they have now committed themselves, have in fact crossed the river, they may be persuaded to join you. But it will be necessary to encourage certain chiefs with presents of clothing, etc., in order to induce them to go. Some Indians have said that I was illiberal in issuing provisions, but these complaints come from Indians with families to live upon us, without any intention of rendering service.

I have never been authorized to draw upon the contractor for rations to Indians; I have, however, done so and take the responsibility on myself. I think that a liberal distribution of provisions among the Indians at this time, and an encouragement that their wives and children will receive some rations during their absence would have prevailed upon them to comply with your wishes. What instructions you think proper to give me on the subject of joining you at Fort George, or as it respects the issuing provisions, or the gratuity to certain chiefs, I shall consider the governing rule of my conduct and shall use my exertions to carry into effect your wishes.

If the Indians should join you they must not have much time to reflect; the business must be arranged with a few confidential chiefs. Pray, Sir, give me three days notice of the time you want them at Fort George. Mr. Parrish, the interpreter, is here and I hope will be faithful, and indeed have no reason to think otherwise.

Major Chapin is, I understand, in the service of the U. S. I think he will make an excellent Indian fighter and leader; the Indians have an excellent opinion of his prowess.

Shall I be permitted to suggest to you the idea of a communication of the British Commander-in-Chief, that if he will send his Indians home and not employ them any longer we will do the same; that our Indians are coming in from all quarters and are determined to take an active part in the war; that there is but one way to restrain them and that is for them to send them home; that when our Indians know they have disbanded theirs they will return home, and not before; that we wish not to let loose our Indians on the defenceless inhabitants on that side, but if they are determined to follow their present measures we shall not any longer refuse the services of the Indians. I would not be thought to be dictating what shall be done with the communication on this subject, or whether it is proper to make one at all—I shall merely take the liberty of suggesting the idea.

This is written while attending to the business of the Indians and I have no time to take a copy or make corrections. Be assured, Sir, that whatever you think proper to give me, or in whatever way I can be useful to my country, my best service will be rendered.

Believe me, &c., &c.,

ERASTUS GRANGER.

General John P. Boyd.

P. S.—The British must know by this time that the Indians are determined to fight. What a noble act it would be on our side to arrest the ferocity of the savage.

E. G.

(MSS. of Col. J. N. Granger, Buffalo.)

Robert Gilmore, D. A. C. G. to Edward Couche, Deputy Commissary General.

Deputy Assistant Commissary General's Office,
AMHERSTBURG, 6th August, 1813.

Edward Couche, Esq.:

SIR,—Your letters of the 26th ultimo, with two thousand pounds currency in army bills, were delivered to me by Mr. Charles Askin on the 29th.

I am extremely happy to find that I may expect liberal supplies of flour from Long Point, the more so as the two principal mills (McGregor's and Arnold's*) are not now going—the dams are broke, and I am informed it is more than probable will not be prepared and filled with water till late in the fall; thus the wheat on hand and that now cutting in this district will be of little immediate service to me for want of mills to grind it. The windmills at this season of the year do very little service.

I have been abundantly supplied with cattle for some time past, though my issues have averaged about 17 per diem,—but should the Indians remain with us, and in addition to the quantities of meat, &c., issued by me continue their wanton and extensive depredations on cattle of all descriptions, a short period will put an end to our supplies of this article. I have now in my possession, to be submitted to Brig. Gen. Procter, accounts to near two thousand pounds for working oxen, milch cows, sheep, hogs, &c., killed by Indians, and I presume accounts to at least as much more will be given in addition thereto. Some of these cattle have been killed without any meat having been taken from them; in other instances the horns and tail seem to have been the cause of shooting down the animal—these being cut off, the carcass is left to the dogs. In addition to about 14,000 rations per day can a new conntry like this supply sufficient provisions for our consumption? The Commissary General cannot expect from me any particular accounts of the resources of the country under such circumstances. I can only say that for 2000 men I could easily supply provisions for six months, in conformity to general orders mentioned in your letter of the 18th ult. Since then I have been feeding about 15,000 troops, Indians, &c., from which, I presume, the Commander-in-Chief has as little idea of the provisions required for this post as others have of the difficulties to be surmounted by me and the immense labor to be performed, otherwise I can scarcely suppose that I should have been so long without more assistance. I have now given up the idea of making up my accounts till the assistants as required by me are sent.

---

* The former was burnt by the Indians in the skirmish of the 4th October at the Forks, the latter on the 5th October.

I find such difficulties in procuring flour, corn, etc., sufficient to feed such hordes of savages, in paying therefor and money to do so, finding materials for all departments of the army here, that the business of the day is more than sufficient to employ the whole of the time of myself and my small establishment. Hence my reason for applying for an officer of the department to be put over me. I find more expected of me than all my abilities and zeal can perform—my accounts getting in arrears and the miserable prospect before me of getting embarrassed beyond the possibility of extraction—of perhaps involving myself and my family in ruin from getting so involved. I was in hopes that as a number of officers of the commissariat, superior to me in rank and likely in abilities and practice, had arrived from England—others promoted in this country—that one of them might have been sent here to take charge of a district which I consider inferior to none in Canada in point of responsibility and commissariat duties. At the same time I should be far from wishing more than can be asked with propriety or granted without ruining my prospects in the department after 15 years' faithful services.

I am very happy that you are sending me a supply of oats. In addition to the 30 barrels mentioned by you I will require about 60, provided you can spare so much. I beg to be informed what quantity of that article is issued to the troops in your district. Brigadier-General Procter requires some for their horses though I cannot get him to give out a general order on that subject. I have to acknowledge your letter of the 24th ult. and beg leave to state that on the renewal thereof I could not pay the accounts of the 41st Regiment on account of the paymaster as well as the commanding officer being at the fort of the Rapids. Since their return I have been prevented from making payment for want of money, a supply of which I hope to receive on a larger scale than hitherto. The escort of dragoons with the 4,000 dollars in specie has not yet arrived.

P. S.—I sincerely hope that the transport *Mary* will soon arrive with more flour—I am really out. I have sent Mr. Reynolds and one of my clerks to Detroit to purchase the whole of the flour and corn that they can get in the Michigan territory and in the neighborhood of Sandwich. I pay $10 per bbl. of 196 lbs. for flour and 7s 6d per bushel for corn. I understand that the schooner *Ellen* is to be sent for provisions to Long Point in a few days.

(From Niles' *Weekly Register*, Baltimore, Md., 15th January, 1814, Vol. V., pp. 328-9. Said to have been taken in General Procter's baggage on 5th October, 1813.)

Left Division Orders.

No. 1.   KINGSTON, 6th August, 1813.

Proceedings of a Division Court Martial held at Kingston, August 4th, 1813:—

The court being duly sworn, proceeded to the trial of Sergeant William Patterson of the Grenadier Company of the 100th Regiment, confined for neglect of duty while on command, in joining with the men under his charge to plunder Miss Simons, and not using his best endeavors to prevent it; also, allowing the men to act in a riotous manner, and although repeatedly ordered to put a stop to it, that he did not make any attempt to put a stop to it.

2d Charge. Disobedience to orders given him by Lieut. Nowlan on the morning of 1st instant.

Sentence. The court, having duly considered the evidence brought forward in support of the prosecution, as well as what the prisoner has alleged in his defence, is of opinion that the prisoner, Sergeant William Patterson, 100th Regiment, is guilty of the whole of the charges exhibited against him, and do therefore sentence him to be reduced to the rank and pay of a private soldier; and further, to receive four hundred lashes on his bare back, at such time and place as the Brigadier-General commanding shall direct.

No. 2.

The Brigadier-General commanding observes with regret by the sentence of the above court martial that great irregularity existed among the boats' crew, many of them being in a state of intoxication and fighting with one another.

Had the officers and non-commissioned officers not permitted more liquor to be brought than the regulated quantity (which is very ample), this would not have happened, and what Captain McIntosh said respecting Miss Simons being a suspicious character and that her goods ought to be confiscated, could not have been construed into a permission to plunder the raft.

It does not seem to be clearly understood that plundering is positively forbidden. By His Majesty's regulations and the articles of war, any man found plundering is liable to be hanged, and that without being brought to court martial.

When a seizure or a capture is ordered to be made it is ordered in the name of His Majesty, and as soon as the legality of the seizure has been ascertained it is distributed according to the established regulations, and by order from the proper authority.

The 100th Regiment have so high a character and have conducted themselves in such a soldierlike manner since they have been in this command that the Brigadier-General regrets much that his duty obliges him to bring one of that gallant corps before a division court martial. The sentence is approved and confirmed, and the prisoner deserves every lash, but in consideration of his former good conduct, and in the hope that he is the only non-commissioned officer in that regiment that could be guilty of such a crime, that part of the sentence that awards corporal punishment is remitted, and the prisoner, William Patterson, is directed to join his regiment as a private soldier.

The articles brought from the raft are to be returned to their proper owners, and the division court martial is dissolved.

F. KIRCHLINGEN,
B. M.

Speech of Major General De Rottenburg to the Indians.

CROSS ROADS, 7th August, 1813.

BROTHERS! I come among you to express my regret at the accident that happened to one of your people last night, and to condole with you.

I cannot pass unnoticed your patience. You have waited day after day in expectation of seeing our ships. Nothing but want of wind now keeps them away.

(Claus Papers.)

(From the Diary of Thomas Ridout.)

YORK, 7th August, (Saturday).

This morning our fleet consisting of six vessels were seen. In the afternoon they passed with a light breeze to the westward and in the evening were between the Humber and Etobicoke. The enemy's fleet of fifteen sail were seen on the lake opposite the town about eight or ten miles out. As it was calm they approached our fleet with sweeps.

(From Ten Years of Upper Canada by Lady Edgar, p. 207.)

General Order.

Adjutant General's Office, Headquarters,
KINGSTON, 7th August, 1813.

It being desirable that every means should be resorted to to promote and uphold the power and influence of the principal leaders of the Indian warriors, His Excellency directs that the officers of the Indian Department who do not accompany the warriors to the field of battle but whose duties have been confined to the care and distribution of presents shall no longer exercise their discretion in allotting articles as presents to the Indian warriors, but be guided in their distribution by such tokens or certificates of fidelity and bravery produced by them from the officers or chiefs of renown who witnessed their gallant conduct before the enemy; and should a general officer in command of a division to which Indian warriors are attached deem it advantageous to His Majesty's service to place a proportion of the presents in the Indian store at the disposal of an officer or chief of renown, enjoying his confidence and possessed of influence over the warriors, to enable him to reward his warriors according to their merit, he is hereby authorized to do so and the officers of the Indian Department are to comply with his requisitions. Presents made to sedentary Indians or to the wives and children of warriors absent in the field are not affected by this order but are to remain under the existing regulations.

EDWARD BAYNES,
Adjutant General.

Left Division Orders.

KINGSTON, August 7th, 1813.

No. 3.

Major Heathcote will hold all the disposable officers and men of the Royal Newfoundland Regiment in readiness to embark for Gananoqui at an hour's notice.

Brigadier-General Boyd to the Secretary of War.

Headquarters, FORT GEORGE,
August 8, 1813.

SIR,—By Thursday's mail I had the honor to receive your commands of the 30th.

Conceiving myself at liberty to act offensively on the arrival of the fleet, an expedition was immediately concerted against the enemy, and acceded to by Commodore Chauncey. One thousand men were to embark on board the fleet, under the command of Brigadier-General Williams, to land at the head of the lake. The army at this place was to move in two columns against the enemy's front, while General Williams assailed his rear and cut off his retreat. Yesterday morning when the troops were to have embarked, the enemy's fleet was discovered off this place. Commodore Chauncey weighed anchor, approached him and by every indication that a leeward position would afford offered to engage. Sir James, after manœuvring for some time at a distance, bore away for the head of the lake, whither he was pursued by the Commodore. This morning our fleet was seen off in the lake, while the enemy is near the shore, on which his army is encamped, still having the wind in his favor.

I am sorry to be obliged to report that the unusually warm weather has increased our sick list. The officers in particular have suffered.

(From Boyd's Documents and Facts. pp. 18-19.)

General Boyd to General Peter B. Porter.

Headquarters, FORT GEORGE,
August 8, 1813.

SIR,—Important military operations will be speedily undertaken on this side the Niagara, and it is desirable to augment our force as much as the shortness of the time will permit.

In pursuance of conversations we have had on this subject, I have to request that you will engage as many volunteers and of the Indians who have been acting with you and others as may be willing to cross and join this army in Canada, and can be ready to march from Buffalo by Wednesday next. You will organize them on their arrival in the best manner that time and circumstances will admit.

They will be allowed rations by the U. S. while in service.

If it shall be thought that your departure from Buffalo and Black Rock will leave those places too much exposed, there will be no objection to your ordering the contractor to issue provisions to such of the neighboring militia as may come in for their protection.

As your late expedition across the river with the Indians was intended to effect a desirable public object in respect to these people, I approve of the proposition to sell the cattle and horses taken at that time from the enemy's side at vendue, and divide the proceeds among the Indians who were engaged in the expedition.

(From MSS. of Hon. P. A. Porter.)

From the Secretary of War to Major-General Wilkinson.

WAR DEPARTMENT, August 8, 1813.

SIR,—I have given to your observations of the 6th instant all the consideration they so justly merit.

The main objection to any plan which shall carry our operations wide of Kingston and westward of it, is that in the event of its success it leaves the strength of the enemy unbroken; it but wounds the tail of the lion, and of course is not calculated to hasten the termination of the war, either by increasing our own vigor or by diminishing that of the enemy. Kingston is the great depot of his resources, and so long as he retains this and keeps open his communication with the sea, he will not want the means of multiplying his naval and other defences and of reinforcing or renewing the war in the west.

Kingston, therefore, as well on grounds of policy as of military principle, presents the first and great object of the campaign.

There are two ways of approaching this: By direct or indirect attack; by breaking down the enemy's battalions and forcing his works, or by seizing and obstructing the line of communication, and thus drying up the sources by which he is nourished and maintained.

Circumstances must govern in choosing between these different modes. Were our assembled land and naval forces competent to the object, a direct attack would no doubt be the shorter and better way; but if on the contrary our strength be inferior or hardly equal to that of the enemy, the indirect attack must be preferred. These considerations have suggested the third plan, to be found in my note of the 23d ultimo. To give execution to this, I would collect my force at the head of the St. Lawrence, make every demonstration of attacking Kingston, proceed rapidly down the river, seize the northern bank at the village of Hamilton, leave a corps to fortify and hold it, march upon Montreal with the main body, effect there a junction with Hampton and take a position which shall enable you to secure what you gain. In this plan the navy would perform its part by occupying the mouth of the river and preventing a pursuit by water, by clearing the river of the armed boats of the enemy, by holding with its own the passage at Hamilton and by giving support to that position. If the enemy pursues it must be by land, without subsistence (except what he carries on his back), and without artillery. If he remains stationary his situation must soon become even more serious, as the country in which he is cannot long subsist him. It will then but remain to him to fight his way to Quebec, to perish in the attempt or to lay down his arms. After this exposition it is unnecessary to add that in conducting the present campaign you will make Kingston your primary object, and you will choose (as circumstances may warrant) between a direct and indirect attack upon that post.

(From Memoirs of my own times, by General James Wilkinson, Philadelphia, 1816. Vol. III., pp. 187-9.)

Sir George Prevost to Earl Bathurst.

KINGSTON, August 8th, 1813.

No. 83.

MY LORD,—I have the honor to acquaint Your Lordship that the enemy's fleet of twelve sail made its appearance off York on the 31st ulto. The three square rigged vessels, the *Pike, Madison* and *Oneida*, came to anchor in the offing, but the schooners passed up the harbor and landed several boats full of troops at the garrison and proceeded from thence to the town, of which they took possession. They opened the gaol, liberated the prisoners and took away three soldiers confined for felony. They then went to the hospital and paroled the few men that could not be removed. They next entered the store houses of some inhabitants and seized their contents, chiefly flour, the same being private property. Between eleven and twelve o'clock that night they returned on board their vessels. The next morning, Sunday, the 1st instant, the enemy again landed and sent three armed boats up the river Don in search of public stores, of which being disappointed, by sunset both sailors and soldiers had evacuated the town, the small barrack, wood yard and storehouses on Gibraltar Point having been first set on fire by them, and at daylight the following morning the enemy's fleet sailed. The plunder obtained by the enemy upon this predatory expedition has been indeed trifling and the loss has altogether fallen upon individuals, the public stores having been removed and the only prisoners taken by them being confined felons and invalids in hospital.

The troops which were landed were acting as marines and appeared to be about 250 men. They were under the command of Commodore Chauncey and Lt.-Col. Scott, an unexchanged prisoner of war on his parole, both of whom landed with the troops. The town upon the arrival of the enemy was totally defenceless, the militia were still on their parole and the principal gentlemen had retired from an apprehension of being treated with the same severity used toward several of the inhabitants near Fort George, who had been made prisoners and sent to the United States. Lieut.-Col. Battersby of the Glengarry Fencibles with the detachment of light troops under his command, who had been stationed at York, was, upon the appearance of the enemy's fleet off that place on the 29th ulto., ordered with his detachment and light artillery to proceed for the protection of the depots formed on Burlington Heights, where he had joined Major Maule's detachment of the 104th Regiment and concentrated his force on the following evening.

The enemy had during the course of that day landed from the fleet five hundred men near Brandt's house, with an intention of storming the heights, but finding Major Maule well prepared to receive them and being informed of Lieut.-Col. Battersby's march, they re-embarked and stood away for York.

My last accounts from Major-General DeRottenburg are to the 3d instant, when the enemy's fleet had marched off Niagara.

I have received no tidings of our own squadron under Sir James Yeo since its sailing from hence on the 31st ultimo.

(Canadian Archives, Q. 122, p. 131.)

Lieut. Patrick McDonogh, 2nd U. S. Artillery, to his Sister.

FORT GEORGE, August 9th, 1813.

. . . .

We (the 2d brigade) were to have embarked on board the fleet on Saturday last, where for we knew not, but judged for Kingston; but the sudden appearance of the British fleet changed the scene. At daylight they were discovered 8 or 10 miles from here, rather above us. They came up during the night along their own shore and cut across it is supposed with the intention to surprise and board our ships, which were at anchor 4 miles below here. They succeeded in getting to windward, but daylight appeared too soon for them to do more. Our gallant Commodore immediately weighed and made for them notwithstanding their favorable position. Sir James's object just now appeared to be to get ours in a position where he could attack the *Pike* with two vessels at once, but Chauncey manœuvred too well for him, and had the wind been in his favor would have brought him to action long before this, but the wind has been constantly wavering or shifting as if it were to be allied against him. He is yet in pursuit of him. I think before I close this I will be enabled to give you an account of the battle, in spite of Sir James's endeavor to avoid it.

I am sorry to say that two of our schooners upset in a gale the night before last, (the *Paul Hamilton* and the *Scourge*, commanded by Lieutenants Winter and Osgood,) while hanging on the left of the British fleet, and the officers and sixty of the crew are lost.

. . . .

Tuesday, August 10th.

This is the fourth day the fleets have been in sight of each other and no engagement yet. We are all anxiety here and will be so until we know the issue. . . . . . .

P. S. . . . . .

We have to divide our time—begin writing in the morning, and before you are well seated you have to attend a call of the pickets or other party. I was out all the afternoon and had a few shots at the Indians, but I believe they are very weak in this neighborhood now, as they will not stand a fight. Ours are coming over to-morrow or next day to the number of four or five hundred.

Erastus Granger to the Secretary of War.

BUFFALO, August 9th, 1813.

SIR,—A letter from General Dearborn, dated at Fort George June 21st, 1813, was received by me and in it a request was contained that I would immediately bring forward to Fort George one hundred and fifty Indians on condition they were willing to join the army and enter into the service of the United States. The Indians did not choose to give a positive answer as to what part they would take in the war until they had seen the General. A few of the principal chiefs with some warriors repaired with me to Fort George. The General wished them to stay, but as they had, at the request of our government, taken a neutral part, and the unfortunate affairs at Stoney Creek and the Beaver Dams had recently taken place, the Indians thought their safest course was to continue their neutrality. They urged in their private councils that the invitation for them to go to war did not come through the right channel; that it was necessary that it should come from the great war chief of the United States, meaning the Secretary of War. They, however, agreed to return home and call a council of the confederacy and take up the question and let General Dearborn know the result.

In the communications which I had heretofore received from the War Department I had been instructed to use my influence in keeping the Indians quiet by telling them that they had nothing to do with the war; that the quarrel was ours, etc.

In the situation I was placed, anything I would say in favor of their taking an active part in the war would come with an ill grace from me unless I had something to show from you on the subject. Believing, however, that General Dearborn was authorized to accept their services, I was determined to promote his wishes.

The Indians returned and sent runners to the distant villages, inviting them here with their arms to attend a council for the purpose of deciding the question of peace or war.

Soon after my return from Fort George I was informed from deserters and others who came from Canada that an attack was meditated on Black Rock and Buffalo, and my person and property were threatened by the British—a reward offered for my head, etc.

The evening before the attack was made at Black Rock I invited a few Indians to come to my house, being convinced the British would be over the next morning. As our force was small and a large quantity of public property at Buffalo and its vicinity, I thought the step a prudent one. Thirty-seven Indians, with Farmer's Brother at their head, came to my house on Saturday evening at eleven o'clock. So confident was I of a visit from the enemy that I got the Indians armed that night.

About sunrise the next morning Major Wm. King came to my house through the woods from Black Rock and informed me that the enemy had landed a considerable force. My residence is three miles from Buffalo and two from Black Rock.

Farmer's Brother on being informed that the enemy were on our shores told the warriors they must go and fight the redcoats. He told them that our country was invaded : that they had one common interest with the people of the United States : that they had everything dear at stake ; that the time had arrived for them to show their friendship for their brethren of the United States, not only in words but in deeds. He led off his little band, and when they came in sight of the enemy they prepared for action and he directed the warriors to follow his example. He was instantly obeyed, and the action was commenced and continued on the part of the Indians with the greatest coolness and intrepidity. Their personal bravery greatly contributed in routing and defeating the enemy. They showed no disposition to commit any improper acts on the field of battle—not offering any abuse to the wounded prisoners.

(From Ketchum's History of Buffalo, Vol. II., pp. 431-2.)

Sir James Lucas Yeo to Sir George Prevost.

H. M. S. *Wolfe* off YORK, the 9th of August, 1813,
¼ past 11 a. m.

MY DEAR SIR,—I am sorry I have no good news to give Your Excellency as yet, and must fear Mr. Chauncey will not engage if he can help it except in his own port or in a calm, where his schooners would give him the victory without his having a shot fired at him.

We arrived off Niagara Saturday morning, having had nothing but calms and light airs all the way from Kingston. The enemy's squadron was at anchor, but got under weigh immediately on seeing us and stood out. I shewed every disposition to engage, but on coming within four miles of him he fired his broadsides, (which did not reach half-way,) wore round and stood close in with Niagara. On Sunday it was calm, when he sent all his schooners to sweep after us, but about two o'clock, a breeze springing up, we stood for them, and it was with some difficulty he gained the anchorage off the river, where he remained all night.

The *Pike* is a very fine large ship, but appears to be very unwieldy and unmanageable, and from the manner she is worked [I] should judge she is not complete with seamen. The *Madison* is about the size of the *Wolfe*, sails well and is managed better than the *Pike*. The *Oneida* is small and sails bad, and the schooners, though formidable in a calm, are very contemptible otherwise, as they have not the least shelter for their men.

My hope is that they may remain out at night, when we may be able to close with them before they see us, and from their numbers they may be much dispersed.

The *Royal George* sprung a leak last Friday, by which a great part of her powder was lost; however, we have been able to supply her, and tho' we cannot find out the leak it does not as yet get worse. Last night it blew fresh and the *Melville* sprung a leak, but reports it of no consequence.

Procrastination is to us a great evil, as I never witnessed such enthusiasm as there is in every ship in the squadron.

I communicated with General DeRottenburg yesterday, but nothing new.

Your Excellency may rest assured that no opportunity shall be lost of bringing them to action and giving you the first information of anything interesting.

(Canadian Archives, C. 730, pp. 78-80.)

Major-General Morgan Lewis to Mrs. Lewis.

SACKETT'S HARBOUR, 9th August, 1813.

We are lying here on our oars waiting the arrival of the Secretary of War, when, it is presumed, we shall know the future course of the campaign.

The fleet has been out now nineteen days—it went up to the head of the lake, where it remains cruising. At York it landed a party and destroyed some public stores. The *Lady of the Lake* arrived here yesterday morning from the fleet, and departed again in the evening with a reinforcement of marines and seamen. The captain informed us that yesterday our army intended a general attack on the enemy, and that many of our savages had joined and would be in the action.

The British fleet put to sea a few days after ours, cruised about at this end of the lake for some days and went into port again without going in quest of Chauncey, notwithstanding they mount nineteen guns more than he does and of heavier metal. Our advantage is in having long guns and braver men; and I think if they dare fight they will be beaten.

Our health here is improving, owing to the introduction of a strict police, which has removed the filth,—certainly the cause of the sickness—and prevents its future accumulation.

You can form no conception of the abominable nuisances that everywhere assailed us on our arrival. It was difficult to breathe, and you could literally taste the putridity in the atmosphere. Had the weather been warm pestilence would have been inevitable. We have now a purer atmosphere and few, if any, cases of disease.

(From the Biographies of Francis Lewis and Morgan Lewis, by Julia Delafield, Vol. II., pp. 85-6, New York, 1877.)

From the Secretary of War to General Wilkinson.

WAR DEPARTMENT, August 9th, 1813.

DEAR SIR,—In answer to that part of your letter of the 6th instant which calls for information, &c., on certain enumerated points, I have the honour to state:—

1st,—That General Hampton's instructions go only to assemble and organize his division at Burlington. It is intended that he shall operate contemporarily with you and under your orders in prosecution of the plan of the campaign which has been given to you.

2d,—The senior Major-General, commanding the principal army, is entitled to the services of a private secretary.

3d,—The ordnance and other departments of supply within the district (No. 9) are subject, of course, to your orders.

4th,—The Quartermaster-General of the army will supply the funds for secret service.

5th,—All orders to subordinate officers pass from the War Department to the Adjutant-General, to be communicated by him to the general commanding the district in which the subordinate officer may serve.

6th,—No specific permission is necessary for removing factious or disorderly men. All such will properly become subjects of the confidential reports to be made by inspectors. To detach such men from one district to another is only shifting the evil; the better way is to report them for dismission.

7th,—If the corps at Fort George be recalled, the works should be razed or occupied by a force competent to hold it against an assault. There is a corps of militia (to whom the Six Nations of Indians have associated themselves) at Black Rock which may be kept in service. They are commanded by General Porter and Mr. Parish.

8th,—The Secretary of War will decline and forbid all improper communication, and particularly any such as may bear any color of insubordination.

9th,—Besides the ordinary mode of communication, expresses may be employed in extraordinary cases.

10th,—The dragoons and light artillery corps shall be made efficient. Horses may be bought for both. An officer from each corps should be directed to superintend the purchases. Price (average) not to exceed one hundred and twenty dollars.

(From Wilkinson's Memoirs, Vol. III., Appendix XXXIV.)

Earl Bathurst to Sir George Prevost.

DOWNING STREET, 10th August, 1813.

SIR,—I have had the honor of receiving your several despatches of the dates and numbers specified in the margin and have laid them before His Royal Highness the Prince Regent.

It gives me great satisfaction to be able to assure Your Excellency that your conduct meets with His Royal Highness's approbation. I am also commanded by His Royal Highness to direct Your Excellency to inform M. General Procter that His Royal Highness is fully sensible of the judgment, spirit and perseverance manifested by M. General Procter in the course of his arduous exertions to keep in check M. General Harrison's army.

You will convey to Brig. General Vincent His Royal Highness's approbation of the enterprising spirit and professional ability displayed by Lt.-Col. Harvey in suggesting and by Br. Gen'l Vincent in making the attack on the advance of the American army on the 6th of June near Burlington.

The attack on Sackett's Harbor, under the command of Col. Baynes, (altho' from circumstances which could not be prevented it was not ultimately successful to the utmost,) appears to His Royal Highness to reflect great honor on that officer and I am most particularly commanded by His Royal Highness to direct you to convey to the officers and also to the non-commissioned officers and men serving in the several divisions of your army above mentioned His Royal Highness's sense of the essential services which the skill of the former and the discipline of the latter and valor of all have contributed to the defence of His Majesty's possessions in the Canadas.

(Canadian Archives, C. 679, p. 395.)

APPENDIX.

Since the foregoing pages were in print, Mr. H. H. Robertson has kindly furnished me with the following return found among the papers of the late Lieut. Thomas Taylor of the 41st Regiment, Fort Major of Fort George in 1813, and afterwards Judge of the District Court for the District of Gore, who died at Hamilton in December, 1837.—EDITOR.

State of Troops in Cantonments, head of Burlington Bay, 3d June, 1813.

	M.	C.	L.	E.	Sergt.	Dr.	Fit for duty.	Sick.	Total.
R. A............		2	2		1		56	——	56
Drivers.........		1	2		2		30	——	30
8th............	2	2	7		14	5	357	3——	360
41st...........		5	8	1	29	2	369	9——	378
49th...........	2	8	9	6	38	14	554		554
R. N. I........		2	3		3	2	60	——	60
G. L. I.........		1	1	2	3		58	8——	66
Color Corp.....		1			3		29	1——	30
Dragoons......		1		1	2		29	——	29
Militia.........	1	2	3	2	7	1	55	——	65
	5	25	35	12	102	24	1607	21	1628

ERRATA.

P. 119, for Memorial to Captain Wm. J. Kerr, *read* Memorial of Captain Wm. J. Kerr.

P. 147, for Cornet Bend, *read* Cornet Burd.

P. 154, for Brigadier-General William Bennet, *read* Brigadier-General William Burnet.

INDEX.

A.
Page.

Abino, Point..29, 108, 109, 122, 124
Adams, brig of war..264
Adams' house..173
Adams, Major Parmenio.................................189, 216, 223, 224, 226, 227, 234
Addison, Rev. R...174
Agnier Indians..124, 126
Aickman's house..45
Albany, N. Y...285
Albany Argus..71, 236, 273
Algonkin Indians..222
Allan, Major Wm...56, 157, 303, 313
Alleghany, N. Y..3, 102, 167, 276
American State Papers..........6, 25, 28, 56, 69, 76, 77, 78, 95, 96, 168, 177, 187,
    201, 212, 282, 292, 295, 306.
Amherstburg............10, 74, 89, 97, 101, 121, 183, 197, 198, 205, 206, 230, 243,
    256, 261, 293, 296, 297, 299, 302, 317.
Anderson, Lieut. Charles..97
Anderson, Lieut. Thos. G..65
Anglo-American Magazine..128
Anthony, Lieut..160
Archer, Capt..26, 75, 144
Armistead, Major...56
Armstrong, Capt. Horatio...146
Armstrong, Lieut. R. S..217, 219
Armstrong, Major..24, 254
Armstrong, Major-General John...3, 137, 146, 267
Armstrong's, Major-General John, Notices of the War of 1812...........4, 137, 267
Arnold's Mill...317
Artillery drivers, corps of..73, 331
Ashtabula River..96
Askin, Charles...193, 196, 198, 202, 205, 206, 317
Askin, John..193, 196, 198, 202, 205
Astor Library...103, 104, 168, 258
Aughquaga Indians..122
Aurora, Philadelphia newspaper..38
Aylwin, Mr..128, 129
Aymard, Charles...122

B.

Baby, Sayers..251, 252
Baird, General..306
Ball's fields...211, 255
Ball's house..207, 209, 210, 222
Ball, John..209, 210
Baltimore Blues..231
Baltimore Whig newspaper..30, 46, 103
Barbadoes..171
Barclay, Capt. R. H..........79, 84, 89, 91, 139, 161, 163, 183, 207, 243, 244, 245,
    250, 256, 261, 296, 297.
Barclay, Thomas,...138, 259
Barnard's house...45
Barnard, Lieut. J...112, 122, 197
Barstow, Lieut..217
Barton's warehouse..229, 230

B—Continued.

Basden, Capt. J. L. 235
Bastard, an Ottawa Chief 242
Batavia, N. Y. 101, 185, 227, 253
Bathurst, Earl .... 22. 52, 58, 79, 137, 139, 170, 175, 214, 249, 255, 257, 298, 323, 330.
Battersby, Lieut. Col. F. 70, 202, 206, 232, 295, 297, 310, 314, 324
Baynes, Col. Edward .... 5, 7, 54, 65, 66, 67, 69, 70, 74, 84, 87, 90, 91, 92, 97, 100, 104, 110, 115, 116, 156, 159, 162, 192, 202, 206, 213, 215, 232, 235, 236, 240, 241, 252, 261, 265, 273, 274, 278, 279, 281, 287, 295, 296, 307, 321, 330.
Beasely, Richard 269
Beaver, Pa. 306
Beaver Dam .... 16, 112, 117, 121, 122, 123, 124, 125, 126, 128, 129, 130, 135, 140, 142, 147, 151, 153, 155, 165, 180, 193, 202, 203, 206, 221, 326.
Beebe, Major E. 238
Bentley, Elijah 81
Beresford, schooner 150, 213, 269, 280
Bezeley's (Beasely's) house 287
Bibaud, Michel 123
Bibliothèque, Canadienne 123
Biddle, Capt. 23, 48, 49, 75, 144
Big John, Indian Chief 167
Bird (Burd), Cornet 115, 121, 147
Birdsall, Capt. 254
Bissett, Mr. 302
Bisshopp, Lieut.-Col. Cecil ...... 10, 66, 98, 110, 112, 119, 122, 135, 139, 140, 143, 149, 151, 153, 175, 193, 205, 216, 217, 218, 219, 220, 223, 224, 226, 227, 230, 231, 233, 240, 241, 247, 257, 258, 286.
Blackbird, Ottawa Chief 208, 210, 212, 242, 245
Black Rock, N. Y. .... 30, 55, 92, 96, 108, 120, 184, 185, 189, 205, 207, 214, 216, 217, 218, 219, 221, 223, 224, 226, 227, 228, 230, 231, 233, 234, 240, 241, 247, 249, 252, 253, 257, 260, 261, 262, 282, 286, 293, 294, 301, 311, 312, 322, 326, 327.
Black Snake, gunboat 53
Black Snake, Indian Chief 167
Black Swamp 302
Boerstler, Dr. C. 142
Boerstler, Lieut.-Col. C. .... 110, 111, 112, 113, 115, 118, 120, 121, 123, 124, 125, 126, 127, 130, 131, 136, 137, 140, 141, 143, 146, 147, 148, 149, 150, 151, 152, 153, 158, 163, 164, 165, 168, 180, 202.
Bombard, James 251, 252
Boston Patriot newspaper 37, 50
Boyd, Brig.-Gen. John P. .... 6, 28, 29, 31, 47, 51, 56, 77, 95, 107, 108, 130, 136, 144, 188, 201, 212, 236, 238, 239, 240, 246, 249, 252, 253, 254, 261, 262, 264, 281, 282, 284, 292, 293, 295, 297, 305, 308, 311, 312, 315, 316, 321, 322.
Boyd's, Brig.-Gen. J. P., Documents and Facts 240, 308, 322
Boyd, Lieut. 11
Brady, Col. H. 189, 200, 238
Brady's house 8
Brady, Lieut. 297
Brandt's house 56, 314, 324

B—Continued.

	Page
Brant, John	122, 124, 126, 127, 186
Brant, Mrs. Joseph	120
Brenton, E. B.	83, 215, 231, 248
Brevoort, Capt.	200
Brock's bastion	239
Brock, Major-Gen. Sir Isaac	18, 19, 59, 86, 119, 155, 178
Brock, Paymaster	10
Brown, Mr.	175
Brownstown, Mich.	186
Brush, Mr. E.	195
Bruyeres, Lieut.-Col. R. H.	69
Brymner's (Alex.) Excerpts	92, 93, 175, 280
Buffalo, N. Y.	88, 92, 96, 100, 117, 120, 167, 200, 201, 218, 223, 224, 226, 227, 228, 234, 235, 247, 248, 249, 252, 253, 262, 264, 275, 286, 292, 293, 294, 315, 322, 326, 327.
Buffalo Creek	109, 186, 248, 254
Buffalo Gazette, newspaper	28, 85, 105, 106, 142, 164, 166, 188, 226, 230, 256, 285, 286, 288, 306.
Buffalo Historical Society's Library	102, 235, 261
Buffalo Plains	226
Buffalo Public Library	30, 86, 109, 144, 166, 189, 227, 230, 231, 257, 286, 291, 306.
Bull, Capt.	188, 224, 226
Burford	198
Burgoyne, Lieut.-Gen. John	200
Burlington, Ont.	66, 291, 330
Burlington, Vt.	250, 285, 301, 329
Burlington Bay	12, 22, 32, 53, 54, 59, 79, 165, 199, 280, 287, 305, 308, 331.
Burlington Heights	7, 8, 11, 12, 16, 32, 41, 146, 149, 228, 232, 256, 289, 295, 297, 305, 310, 314, 324.
Burn, Col. James	6, 23, 32, 33, 34, 37, 40, 47, 48, 75, 78, 147, 166, 238.
Burnet, Brig.-Gen. Wm.	154
Burr, Lieut.	147
Butler, Col. John	164, 200
Butler's house	207, 210

C.

Cain, Miss	209
Caledonia, N. Y.	227
Caledonia, brig.	290
Cambria, N. Y.	239
Cameron, Capt.	56
Camp, Mr.	200
Campbell, Justice Wm.	61
Campbell, Major	238
Canadakea	276
Canadaway	165
Canadian Archives	8, 10, 11, 22, 23, 53, 54, 59, 60, 63, 64, 65, 68, 71, 72, 74, 80, 83, 85, 89, 90, 91, 92, 101, 102, 112, 113, 115, 120, 121, 122, 138, 139, 140, 141, 158, 160, 161, 163, 164, 171, 172, 176, 177, 178, 182, 184, 185, 187, 200, 207, 208, 214, 215, 217, 218, 220, 231, 233, 234, 241, 244, 246, 248, 251, 254, 256, 258, 259, 262, 265, 266, 270, 271, 290, 296, 297, 300, 304, 310, 324, 328, 330.
Canadian Courant, newspaper	60
Canadian Dragoons	98

iv.

C—Continued.	Page.
Canadian Fencible Regiment	5, 198, 278, 307
Canadian Voltigeurs	70, 274, 277, 304, 307
Canandaigua, N. Y.	3, 93, 103, 109
Carrying Place	93
Carter, J.	228, 248
Cartwright, Colonel R.	53, 173
Caskey, Mr.	226, 257
Cattaraugus, N. Y.	97, 248, 276
Cattaraugus Creek	109, 165, 276
Cattaraugus Indians	103, 276
Cayuga Indians	122, 255
Chambers, Capt. F.	88
Chambers, Captain P. L.	10, 66, 101, 110
Chambly	5, 307
Champlain Lake	21, 184, 212, 245, 251, 267, 299, 300
Chandler, Brig.-Gen. John	6, 8, 9, 12, 14, 16, 23, 24, 25, 28, 29, 30, 31, 32, 33, 37, 38, 40, 41, 42, 43, 44, 47, 48, 49, 50, 51, 74, 75, 78, 85, 86, 105, 106, 107, 108, 144, 166, 180, 197, 284.
Chapin, Major Cyrenius	98, 109, 117, 118, 122, 123, 130, 131, 132, 133, 142, 147, 149, 150, 151, 164, 165, 232, 253, 263, 264, 282, 289, 295, 306, 311, 315, 316.
Charlotte, N. Y.	93
Chauncey, Com. Isaac	3, 20, 28, 29, 31, 55, 64, 67, 79, 95, 96, 104, 108, 109, 168, 169, 176, 187, 188, 212, 282, 284, 289, 290, 295, 303, 304, 305, 306, 308, 310, 312, 321, 324, 325, 327, 328.
Chauncey, Lieut. Wolcott	95, 165
Chautauqua	96
Chew, Mr.	194, 261, 278
Chicago, Ill.	242
Chippawa, Ont.	62, 98, 100, 117, 118, 120, 121, 122, 130, 173, 184, 203, 204, 217, 249, 263, 265, 293, 311.
Chippawa Creek	228
Chippewa Indians	155, 222, 260, 261
Chippewa schooner	244, 271
Chisholm, Mr.	196
Chorus, Casper, (Cassel)	200, 208
Chorus's house	200, 209, 210
Christie, Lieut.-Col. John	41, 71, 76, 100, 136, 137, 146, 238, 264, 280
Church, The, newspaper of Cobourg	128
Churchill, Col.	101
Clarence, N. Y.	234
Clark, S. S.	234
Clark, Capt.	69
Clark, Lieut.-Col. Thos	118, 119, 205, 217, 218, 219, 220, 223, 224, 231, 241, 247, 257, 265, 269.
Clark, Mr.	181
Clarke, Lieut.	115
Claus, Col. Wm	97, 110, 111, 120, 121, 124, 126, 172, 186, 200, 207, 212, 213, 215, 221, 222, 232, 236, 241, 242, 254, 260, 275, 287, 288, 299, 314.
Claus, MSS	110, 111, 156, 172, 186, 200, 202, 208, 212, 213, 216, 222, 232, 236, 242, 254, 260, 275, 287, 288, 290, 293, 314, 320.
Claus, Mrs.	56, 57, 156
Clay, Brig.-Gen. Green	297

C—Continued.

	Page.
Clerk, Major Alex	6, 11, 15, 47, 86, 106, 197
Cleveland, Ohio	229, 285, 290, 296, 297
Clyne, Lieut.	92
Coffin, Lieut.-Col.	56
Cognawaga Indians	98, 123, 222
Cold Spring, N. Y.	226
Coleman, Capt. Thos.	159, 297
Collins, Thos.	235
Collis, Lieut.	209
Colored Corps	73, 331
Colt, Lieut.-Col.	154
Conjaquity Creek	229
Conner, Maj. S. S.	69
Conquest, schooner	270
Cook's house	209
Coot's Paradise	54
Cornplanter, Indian Chief	262, 276
Cornwall, Ont.	5
Couche, Dy. Commissary Gen. Edward	85, 317
Courgan, John	252
Cranberry Creek	273, 288
Crane, Capt.	308
Credit Indians	222
Credit River	296
Crisis newspaper	306
Croker, Hon. John Wilson	160, 245
Crooks, Wm.	269
Cross Roads	209, 211, 255, 260, 274, 278, 288, 314, 320
Cummins, Capt.	115, 140, 152, 223, 224, 225, 226
Cummins, Major	238, 254, 261, 262
Cummings, James	122
Cummings, Thomas	269

D.

Daily, Mr.	234, 235
D'Arcon, Mons.	176
Darroch, Brig.-Gen.	162
Davis's Mills	7, 12, 45
Davis, Lieut.	144
Davy, Capt.	53
Deane, Major	307
Dearborn, Major-Gen. Henry	3, 6, 19, 23, 25, 28, 29, 31, 32, 40, 51, 55, 69, 72, 74, 77, 81, 92, 95, 99, 102, 103, 106, 109, 137, 138, 140, 144, 145, 146, 163, 174, 177, 178, 184, 185, 187, 200, 201, 212, 215, 216, 217, 223, 230, 232, 234, 236, 238, 239, 240, 247, 248, 258, 262, 266, 283, 285, 294, 299, 300, 326.
De Boucherville, Lieut.-Col.	70, 78
Decamp, Mr.	128
DeCoo's (or DeCou's) house	98, 111, 122, 123, 130, 131, 134, 148, 150, 151, 173, 174.
Defield, (or Duffield), Mrs.	98, 117, 203
DeHaren, Major, P. V.	5, 53, 54, 98, 111, 112, 113, 115, 118, 119, 124, 125, 126, 127, 134, 135, 136, 140, 149, 150, 151, 152, 158, 180, 203.

D—Continued.

	Page.
Delafield's, (Mrs. Julia) Biographies of Francis Lewis and Morgan Lewis	329
Delaware Indians	122, 276
Dennis, Col., U. S. A	48
Dennis, Major and Lieut.-Col. J. B	11, 15, 56, 59, 62, 63, 173
Derenzy, Capt	161
DeRottenburg, Major-Gen. F	5, 97, 101, 139, 157, 162, 163, 171, 174, 176, 177, 198, 200, 206, 208, 211, 215, 219, 228, 231, 232, 240, 241, 243, 244, 248, 252, 253, 256, 257, 261, 265, 268, 269, 277, 279, 285, 291, 292, 293, 295, 296, 298, 310, 320, 324, 328.
De Salaberry, Lieut.-Col. L	307
Detroit, Mich	18, 55, 80, 155, 178, 179, 195, 264, 278, 318
Detroit, ship of war	89, 161, 163, 164, 244, 271, 290, 296, 297
De Watteville, Col. L	187
Dickson, Robert	18, 64, 85, 160, 180, 182, 183, 250, 255, 299
Dickson, Thomas	181, 196, 205, 269
Dickson, William	181
Dimock, Major	288
Dixon, Capt	288, 289
Dixon, Captain Manly	82
Dobbin, Lieut.-Col. H	154
Dobbins, Daniel	248
Dobbins, (Daniel) History of the Battle of Lake Erie	248
Dominique, Sobrigen	91
Don River	304, 313, 324
Dorsey, Capt	154
Dox, Capt. A	94
Drummond, Lieut.-Col. Wm	53
Drummond, Sir Gordon	119
Drury, Ensign	11, 15, 197
Ducharme, Captain Dominique	123, 125, 127, 165
Dudgeon, Capt	175, 280
Dundas	45, 196
Dundas Mills	193, 196
Dundas street	189

E.

Eastman's house	99
Echo, Indian Chief	275
Eddis, Mr	169
Edgar, Lady J. D.—Ten Years of Upper Canada	255, 302, 320
Eight Mile Creek	174
Eighteen Mile Creek (Lake Erie)	109
Eighteen Mile Creek (Lake Ontario)	76, 93
Eldridge, Lieut	76, 210, 211, 257
Eldridge, Samuel	211
Ellen, schooner	3, 8
Elizabeth, schooner	270
Ellicott, Joseph	101, 102
Elliott, Capt. J. D	290, 291
Elliott, Capt. Matthew	97, 208
Elliott, Lieut.-Colonel Matthew	97, 172, 296
Erie, Pa	96, 108, 165, 227, 230, 248, 253, 264, 267, 285, 286, 290, 291, 306
Erie, gunboat	244, 268, 271

E—Continued.

Erie, Lake..........30, 55, 79, 97, 101, 139, 163, 168, 194, 207, 214, 243, 244, 245, 249, 251, 256, 257, 265, 270, 299, 300.
Erwin, Lieut..249
Essex, frigate..217
Etobicoke Creek...320
Eustis, Major..108, 238
Evans, Major and Lieut.-Col. Thomas...56, 57, 59, 62, 63, 67, 100, 120, 121, 195
Evans, Lieut.-Col. Wm...69, 243, 261
Everard, Capt..299

F.

Fair American, schooner..270
Fairchild, Interpreter, Benj...186
Farmer's Brother, Indian chief......................................225, 226, 262, 275, 326, 327
Fawcett, Lieut...272
Ferguson, Lieut...274
Fields, J..230
Finnis, Capt...89, 90, 245
Fish, Mr..264
Fisher, Indian chief..260
Fitzgerald, Sergeant...219
FitzGibbon, Lieut. James..........12, 16, 98, 99, 111, 112, 115, 116, 118, 119, 120, 121, 122, 123, 124, 125, 127, 128, 129, 130, 133, 134, 149, 151, 158, 175, 183, 199, 203, 217, 228, 240.
FitzPatrick, Sergeant Wm..304
Five Mile Meadows..107, 145, 193
Fleming, Capt..115
Fleming, Dr...99, 117
Forsyth, Major Benjamin..28, 107, 174, 177, 178, 238
Forsyth's Wood..98
Fort Erie............16, 29, 55, 62, 74, 82, 86, 100, 110, 117, 122, 139, 173, 175, 178, 193, 203, 204, 228, 266, 285, 293, 311.
Fort George..........4, 6, 7, 16, 20, 22, 29, 30, 32, 33, 40, 44, 46, 48, 50, 54, 55, 59, 62, 69, 70, 71, 74, 80, 81, 86, 88, 89, 90, 93, 94, 95, 98, 100, 103, 106, 107, 114, 121, 124, 126, 130, 135, 141, 142, 144, 145, 146, 149, 150, 151, 152, 153, 163, 164, 165, 166, 167, 168, 174, 175, 177, 179, 180, 181, 188, 193, 194, 195, 198, 199, 200, 202, 203, 204, 205, 207, 208, 209, 211, 216, 222, 223, 230, 232, 234, 236, 239, 240, 246, 247, 248, 249, 250, 252, 253, 254, 256, 257, 258, 261, 262, 263, 264, 266, 279, 280, 281, 282, 283, 284, 285, 292, 293, 294, 295, 297, 298, 301, 302, 305, 308, 309, 311, 312, 314, 316, 322, 324, 325, 326, 331.
Fort Gibson..223
Fort Mifflin..145
Forty Mile Creek..........6, 7, 8, 14, 24, 25, 29, 30, 32, 41, 46, 47, 49, 53, 54, 56, 59, 62, 63, 64, 66, 67, 71, 74, 75, 79, 81, 86, 87, 91, 100, 102, 105, 111, 122, 124, 139, 140, 155, 160, 161, 163, 175, 176, 193, 194, 195, 196, 198, 202, 203, 204, 215, 221, 278, 295, 312.
Four Mile Creek..163, 186, 211, 220, 256, 290, 296
Fowler, Capt..10
Fox, Lieut..92
Fox Point..144

F—Continued.

	Page.
Fox, Privateer	288, 289
Frazer, Lieut	40, 42, 43
Fraser, Private	14, 17
Fraser, Sergt. Alex	14, 16, 17, 22, 23, 296
Fredericton, N. B.	296
Freer, Capt. Noah	297, 302
Frenchman's Creek	263
Frend, Major	69, 272, 273
Frey's House	209
Fulton, Capt. James P.	91, 163, 174, 177, 215, 293, 314
Furry, John	91

G.

Gage's fields	45
Gage's house	46, 61, 66
Gamelin, Lieut	148
Gananoqui, Ont	90, 212, 274, 321
Garden, Lieut	89
Gardiner, Auldjo, & Co	280
Gates, Capt	109, 144
Gaucher, Lieut. Gedeon G.	124, 125, 126, 127
General Pike, ship of war	165, 176, 270, 290, 295, 302, 308, 313, 323, 325, 327
Genesee County, N. Y.	189
Genesee river	51, 88, 93, 109, 154, 160, 169, 170, 176, 276
Geneva, N. Y.	94
Geneva Gazette newspaper	306
George, Ensign James	45
German Meeting house	98
Gerundgut (Irondequoit ?)	169, 170
Gesso, Mrs.	99
Gibbons, Mr.	234
Gibraltar	171
Gibraltar Point	304, 313, 324
Gilmore, Robert	317
Givins, Major James	172, 222, 274
Glasgow, Major-General George	5, 184
Glegg, Major James B.	9, 12, 73, 86, 87, 111
Glengarry Light Infantry	5, 10, 52, 66, 70, 73, 84, 88, 193, 194, 198, 201, 202, 205, 221, 233, 277, 295, 296, 324, 331.
Goldrick, Capt	111
Good Will, sloop	268
Goodwin, Lieut	115, 134
Goose Creek	272
Gordon, Assistant Commissary	45
Gordon, Capt	280
Gordon, Major	90, 92
Governor Tompkins, schooner	270
Grand Island	231
Grand River	41, 47, 55, 90, 111, 194, 198, 260, 267, 287, 288, 299
Granger, Erastus	103, 167, 226, 247, 275, 281, 284, 293, 313, 315, 316, 326
Granger, Major	154
Granger, MSS. of Colonel J. N.	103, 316
Grant, Commodore Alexander	195
Grant, Robert	160, 161, 198, 231

G—Continued.

	Page.
Gready, James	161, 162
Green, Jeremiah	91
Grey, Col. (Capt. Alex. Gray)	195
Griswold, Lieut	148
Grove Hill, Pa	306
Growler, schooner	270
Gruserat, Jacob	97

H.

Hackett, Assistant Surgeon	10, 22
Hagerman, Mr	310
Halftown, Captain, Indian Chief	276
Halifax, N. S.	21, 171, 176, 217, 299, 300
Hall, Captain John	5, 6, 98, 112, 118, 122, 125, 127, 203, 278, 279
Hall, Major-General Amos	170
Hamilton, N. Y.	323
Hamilton, Captain Alexander	178, 209
Hamilton, George	180
Hamilton, James	180
Hamilton, Robert	180, 199
Hamilton, Lieut.-Colonel	5, 277
Hamilton, schooner	270, 325
Hampton, Major-General Wade	6, 177, 201, 212, 267, 323, 329
Hardison, Mr. Benjamin	173, 174
Harris, Capt.	239
Harrison, Major-General Wm. H	47, 55, 72, 80, 85, 179, 182, 183, 250, 266, 285, 296, 297, 299, 330.
Hartman, Sergt.	227
Harvey, Lieut.-Colonel John	7, 8, 9, 11, 23, 24, 36, 44, 45, 54, 62, 66, 67, 71, 79, 88, 120, 184, 185, 199, 200, 207, 208, 212, 213, 215, 217, 218, 221, 222, 232, 234, 241, 254, 265, 278, 279, 287, 288, 291, 296, 330.
Hatt, Samuel	269
Hatt, Richard	269
Hawley's tavern	228
Heathcote, Major	90, 105, 173, 246, 321
Hemphill, Lieut	175, 280
Henderson, Capt.	48
Henderson, Mrs.	178
Hendrick, Lieut.	92
Heriot, Major G. F.	274, 304
Hildreth, Mr	94
Hindman, Capt.	23, 48, 75, 105, 106, 144, 147, 166, 178
Historical Register of the United States	25, 95, 255, 309
Hogeboom, Peter	265
Holcroft, Major Wm	10, 11, 57, 66
Holland, Capt.	239
Home District	191
Hooker, Lieut.	11, 15
Hopkins, General Caleb	169
Horn (Haun) Tice	122
Howell, Lieut. Colonel	154
Howell, Wm	169
Hugo, Mr.	273
Hull, Brig.-General Wm	18, 137, 178, 217, 306
Hull, Capt. Wm	226

H—Continued.

	Page
Humber river	320
Hunt Thomas (or Terence)	12, 161, 162
Huron Indians	197
Huron Lake	172, 186
Huyck, Major J. V. H	238

I.

Incorporated Militia	53, 58, 180, 221, 234, 257, 304
Independent Chronicle Newspaper	71, 211
Ingersoll, Ensign	88
Ingersoll, Lieut	71
Ingersol's tavern	109
Irondequoit, N. Y	169
Iroquois Indians	124, 126
Isle Aux Noix	5, 6, 21, 299, 307

J.

Jackson, Capt	159
Jackson, Wm	251, 252
James, C. C	130
Jarvis, G. M., MSS. of	102, 191, 192, 277
Jarvis Papers	87
Jarvis, Wm	87
Jason, ship of war	52
Jenkins, Capt	296
Jervis, Lieut	209
Johnson, Major John	25, 35, 38, 40, 41, 49, 78, 238
Johnson, Mr	117
Johnson, Sir John	124, 126, 215, 222
Johnston, Lieut	92
Jones, Capt. Horatio	286
Jones, Major	25, 40
Jones, Lieut	159
Julia, schooner	270

K.

Katverota, Onondaga Chief	186, 187
Kearney, Lieut	115, 152
Keep, N. D	164
Kelly, Sergt	229
Kerby, Mrs. James	98, 99, 117, 203
Kerby, Wm	198, 202
Kerr, Capt. Wm. J	110, 112, 119, 120, 121, 122, 124, 126, 127, 134, 149, 288
Kerr, Dr. Robert	194, 208
Ketcheson, Lieut	69
Ketchum's History of Buffalo and the Senecas	3, 167, 277, 327
Kirchlingen, Capt. and Brigade Major F	159, 173, 187, 212, 291, 320
King, Captain and Major Wm	72, 100, 225, 227, 327
King's Regiment	5, 7, 8, 9, 10, 11, 12, 13, 14, 15, 22, 41, 44, 45, 66, 68, 70, 73, 112, 161, 162, 173, 193, 194, 195, 197, 200, 207, 209, 217, 218, 220, 226, 248, 255, 291.
Kingston, Ont	4, 15, 18, 19, 20, 21, 22, 52, 53, 54, 61, 65, 68, 69, 70, 71, 72, 74, 79, 81, 83, 84, 87, 91, 92, 93, 94, 95, 96, 97, 99, 100, 101, 102, 104, 110, 115, 137, 138, 139, 141, 143, 144, 156, 158, 159, 161, 170, 172, 173, 175, 176, 177, 184, 187, 190, 191, 192, 194, 197, 201, 202, 206, 212, 213, 232, 233,

K—Continued.

	Page.
Kingston, con.	235, 240, 241, 245, 246, 249, 250, 251, 253, 255, 257, 265, 266, 267, 271, 273, 274, 277, 281, 282, 286, 288, 291, 296, 298, 300, 304, 306, 307, 319, 320, 321, 322, 323, 327.
Kingston Gazette Newspaper	313
Knight, Charles	91
Knox's house	173

L.

Lachine	124, 126
Lacloche Indians	222, 260, 261
La Croix Riviere Indians	222
Lady Gore, transport	56
Lady Murray, transport	95, 165
Lady of the Lake, schooner	95, 111, 165, 270, 281, 282, 308, 328
Lady Prevost, schooner	108, 244, 268, 270
Lake of Two Mountains	24, 126, 222
Lake Road	98, 312
Lake St. Francis	267
Langlade, Lieut. and interpreter Louis	124, 125, 126, 127, 208, 222
Laprairie	307
La Tranche River	18
La Tranche Indians	222
Lawe, Capt. George	209
Lawe, John	209
Lawe, Mrs. George	209
Lawe's house	210
Lawrence, sloop of war	264, 290
Lay, Mr.	109, 165
Leclair, Lieut. Isaac	124, 126, 274
Lecroy, Mr.	88
Lee, Daniel	251, 252
Legg, Abram	81
Lenn, Mr.	98
Lenox Library	71
Leonard, Capt. L.	23, 24, 75
Leonard, Major Richard	105, 156
LeRoy, N. Y.	165, 189
Lewis's house	122
Lewis, Major-General Morgan	3, 6, 28, 31, 32, 38, 39, 40, 44, 51, 56, 69, 70, 74, 77, 88, 100, 106, 108, 109, 136, 144, 156, 176, 188, 201, 212, 282, 283, 284, 289, 298, 299, 328
Lewis, Mr.	196, 205
Lewis, Mrs. Morgan	328
Lewiston, N. Y.	120, 165, 231
Library of Parliament, Ottawa	223, 261, 305
Liddle, Capt.	194
Lincoln Militia, 2d Regt. of	217, 218, 219, 220, 231, 241
Lincoln Militia, 3d Regt. of	217, 218, 219, 221
Lisle, Capt. R.	246
Little Belt, gunboat	244, 271
Little Lake	305
Logan, Alex	91
London, Ont.	191
London Gazette	175
Long Island	272

L—Continued.

	Page
Long Point	....85, 89, 108, 161, 182, 183, 188, 206, 207, 214, 233, 243, 261, 264, 290, 296, 297, 302, 306, 317, 318.
Lorimier, Capt.	274
Lorimier, Lieut. J. B. de	124, 126, 129, 172, 274
Loring, Capt. R. R.	140
Louth, township of	100, 111
Lower Canada	122
Lucas, Major R	238
Lundy's Lane	98, 117, 122, 164
Lyons, Lieut. and Interpreter, Barnet	97, 208
Lyons, Wm	96
Lytle, Capt	23, 105

M.

Macomb, Col. Alex	28, 31, 55, 108
Madison, Capt	254
Madison, President	300
Madison, Ship of War	29, 107, 207, 295, 302, 313, 323, 327
Madrid, N. Y	267
Majoribanks, Lieut	160
Malcom, Major B. M	211, 238
Malden, Ont	29, 55, 95, 266, 267
Manchester, N. Y	88, 249
Manners, Capt	11, 15, 106, 197
Markham, township of	81
Marshall, Lieut	140, 152
Martin, Capt	272
Martin, George	122
Martinique	171
Mary, schooner	270, 318
Maule, Major	314, 324
Meigs, Fort	183, 250, 285, 292, 296, 297, 299
Melville, brig	213, 245, 269, 274, 281, 328
Merrill, Mr	94, 154
Merritt, Capt. Wm. H	98, 111, 122, 173, 177, 178, 200, 207, 208, 278, 279
Merritt, MSS. of Capt. Wm. H	98, 123, 174, 211, 279
Meuron's Regiment	171
Miami Rapids	318
Miami River	179, 183, 261, 297
Michigan	17, 178, 183, 299, 318
Michigan Pioneer and Historical Society, collections of	196, 198, 199, 206
Michilimackinac	55, 85, 160, 182, 183, 250, 299
Midland District	87, 191
Miller, Col. James	51, 72, 238
Mills, Capt	71, 106
Milnes, Capt. H. B. O	8, 9, 36, 66, 273
Milton, Lieut.-Col	24, 27, 43, 48, 51, 78, 106, 131, 166, 238
Milton's house	56, 59
Mississauga Indians	41
Missouri River	299
Mitchell, Lieut.-Col. G. E	238
Mockler, Capt	82
Mohawk Indians	122, 123, 124, 126, 127, 277
Moira, Earl of, schooner	213, 269, 281, 288
Mompesson, Ensign	205, 218, 240, 241
Monroe, Hon. James	217

xiii.

M—Continued.

	Page.
Montonier, Elijah	91
Montreal	4, 5, 12, 16, 17, 21, 25, 60, 65, 69, 92, 93, 97, 100, 104, 139, 172, 174, 175, 177, 256, 273, 279, 307, 323.
Montreal Gazette, newspaper	116, 122, 305
Moodie, Major	69
Morgan, Major Wm	238
Morris, Lieut	115
Morrison, Lieut.-Col. J. W	236
Mudd, Lieut	115
Munday, Capt	11, 37
Murdock, Lieut	115, 144
Murray, Lieut.-Col. John	307
Murray, Major	72, 117
Murray, Robert	181
Myers, Capt	164
Myers, Lieut.-Col. C	28, 194, 215

Mc.

Macaulay, Dr	104
McCartey's house	173
McChesney, Lieut. and Capt	39, 50, 75, 115, 140, 147, 148, 149, 152
McClure, Lieut.-Col. F	108
McCoy, Capt	261
McDonald, Sergt	12
Macdonell, Major George	84, 88, 277
McDonogh, Lieut. Patrick	309, 325
McDouall, Capt. Robt	9, 54, 64, 66, 80, 81, 91, 160, 181
McDowell, Capt. A	112, 113, 115, 118, 131, 132, 134, 147, 148
McEwan, Capt	12, 39, 51, 279
MacEwen, Adjt	92, 93, 174
McGillivray, John	17, 22
MacGregor	280
MacGregor's Mill	317
McIntire, Angus	91
McIntosh, Capt	53, 69, 319
McKay's house	194
McKay, Mr	295
McKee, Lieut. Alex	97
McKenney, Cornet Amos	45, 98, 111, 122, 209
McKenzie, Lieut	115
McLean, Mr	194
McLellan, Capt. Martin	194
McMahon, Lieut. Edward	277
McNabb's house	209
McTavish, Simon	17

N.

Nanticoke Indians	122
National Intelligencer	264, 267
Nautilus, sloop of war	217
Navy Point	177
Near, Dr	147
Nelles, Abraham	269
Nelles, Henry	255, 302
Nelles, Robert	269
Nelles's house	122

N—Continued.

	Page.
Neptune, privateer	288
Newark, Ont	28, 86, 103, 107, 109, 130, 165, 188, 191, 235, 290
New Brunswick Fencible Infantry	286
New York Commercial Advertiser	262
New York Evening Post	103, 167, 258
New York Society Library	49
New York State Library	155, 170, 248, 253, 285
New York Statesman, newspaper	48
Niagara	9, 17, 19, 20, 22, 29, 52, 57, 71, 74, 77, 87, 93, 94, 97, 100, 102, 103, 109, 144, 155, 156, 165, 178, 181, 182, 190, 193, 197, 199, 200, 204, 209, 249, 261, 298, 299, 303, 306, 308, 324, 327.
Niagara District	64, 80, 182, 268
Niagara Falls	249, 265
Niagara Fort	29, 74, 120, 144, 167, 193, 246, 249, 250, 252, 257, 285, 289, 290, 301.
Niagara Frontier	119, 120, 121, 221
Niagara River	16, 124, 126, 226, 231, 285, 299, 310
Niagara, sloop of war	290
Nichol, Lieut.-Col. Robert	63, 64, 67, 85, 208, 215
Nicholas, Capt	23, 48, 75
Nicholas, Major	238
Nicoll, Inspector General A. T.	301
Niles' Weekly Register	38, 45, 48, 50, 78, 82, 142, 154, 225, 232, 299, 314, 318.
Nippissing Indians	222
Norfolk Militia, 2d Regiment of	91
Northern Centinel	268
Northwest Company	172
Norton, Capt. John	52, 53, 123, 163, 207, 208, 209, 215, 221, 222

O.

O'Beal, Henry, Indian Chief	167
Odelltown	174
Ogdensburg	19, 80, 171, 177, 267, 273
Ogilvie, Major James	9, 11, 15, 44, 66, 71, 92
O'Keefe, Lieut	291
Oneida, brig of war	295, 302, 313, 323, 327
Oneida Indians	122
Onondaga County, N. Y	234
Onondaga Indians	122, 186
Ontario Lake	8, 10, 11, 16, 29, 32, 50, 51, 52, 101, 124, 126, 143, 165, 169, 170, 172, 176, 179, 190, 195, 199, 219, 244, 245, 249, 251, 253, 257, 263, 264, 265, 266, 269, 270, 290, 298, 300, 306.
Ontario, schooner	270
Osgood, Lieut	325
Osgoode Hall	81
Osiquirison, Tuscarora Chief	186, 187
Oswego, N. Y	55, 88, 93, 169, 176, 234.
Ottawa Indians	208, 241, 260
Ottawa River	172

P.

Palmer, waggonmaster	230
Parrish, Jasper	3, 167, 316
Patterson, Andrew	80, 81

P—Continued.

	Page.
Patterson, Sergt. Wm.	319, 320
Pearce, Col. Cromwell	48, 238
Pearson, Lieut.-Col. Thos.	159
Penfield, N. Y.	94
Perrault, Major J.	307
Perry, Capt. O. H.	55, 96, 97, 108, 110, 201, 248, 253, 257, 264, 268, 285, 296.
Pert, schooner	270, 308
Peters, Lieut.-Col.	248
Phelps, N. Y.	154
Phelps, Capt.	306
Philadelphia Library	30, 52, 93, 94, 95, 97, 211, 262
Pike, Brig.-Gen. Z. M.	3, 179
Pike, ship of war	165, 176, 270, 290, 295, 302, 313. 325, 327
Pinkney, Major	238
Pinkney, Col.	40
Pittsburg, Pa.	253
Plattsburg, N. Y.	51
Playter, Messrs.	304, 313
Plenderleath, Major and Lieut. Col. C.	9, 11, 14, 15, 16, 17, 22, 44, 66, 71, 92
Plenderleath, Rev'd W. C.	16, 17
Point Frederick	212
Point Henry	304
Porter, Augustus	88
Porter, Capt. David	217
Porter, General Peter B.	88, 92, 101, 109, 185, 200, 216, 223, 226, 227, 234, 245, 246, 247, 249, 252, 261, 262, 264, 265, 275, 281, 282, 292, 293, 297, 298, 311, 312, 322.
Porter, MSS. of Hon. P. A.	88, 92, 110, 186, 201, 216, 234, 247, 249, 282, 292, 293, 294, 312, 315, 322.
Porter, Lieut.-Col. Moses	28, 56, 144, 145, 238
Porter's house	229
Porter's mills	185
Posey, Major T.	238
Poulson's American Daily Advertiser	93, 94, 96, 262
Powell, Anne	56, 57
Powell, Grant	302
Powell, John	57
Powell, Justice Wm. D.	56, 57, 102, 157, 158, 190, 191, 192, 277
Powell Papers	57, 58
Prendergast, Sergt.	304
Prescott, Ont.	5, 87, 104. 156, 159, 212, 273, 304
Presqu' Isle (Erie, Pa.)	55, 64, 74, 84, 89, 90, 91, 163, 181, 182, 183, 215, 243, 247, 250, 255, 261, 271, 289.
Preston, Lieut.-Col. J. P.	29, 82, 83, 86, 185, 238
Prevost, Lieut.-Gen. Sir George	8, 19, 22, 36, 53, 54, 59, 70, 72, 78, 79, 82, 83, 91, 101, 102, 112, 137, 138, 139, 146, 151, 163, 170, 177, 182, 184, 195, 199, 206, 214, 216, 243, 245, 249, 253, 255, 257, 293, 296, 298, 306, 310, 323.
Pring, Capt. D.	245, 251
Procter, Major-Gen. Henry	17, 18, 29, 45, 47, 60, 64, 74, 78, 80, 81, 82, 84, 87, 89, 90, 91, 95, 101, 160, 163, 171, 179, 181, 182, 204, 206, 207, 214, 215, 233, 243, 244, 250, 261, 296, 297, 298, 299, 310, 317, 318, 330.

P—Continued.

	Page
Provincial Cavalry (dragoons)	112, 207, 208, 278, 279
Pultney, schooner	92
Pultneyville, N. Y	154, 169

Q.

Quebec	305, 307, 323
Quebec Mercury, newspaper	64
Queen Charlotte, ship of war	89, 90, 96, 108, 163, 183, 243, 244, 261, 268, 271, 296
Queenston	32, 48, 52, 62, 88, 100, 127, 128, 131, 134, 135, 136, 142, 147, 150, 151, 164, 165, 173, 179, 186, 188, 196, 203, 204, 230, 256, 257, 312
Queenston Heights	29, 32, 154, 165, 167, 211
Quinte, Bay of	68, 69, 70, 100, 159

R.

Raisin River	183, 184, 250
Randall, Lieut	115, 140, 152
Rangeworth, Lieut	105
Ransom, Ab	164
Raven, transport	308
Rea, Capt	154
Rea, Brig.-Gen	101
Red Jacket, Indian Chief	262, 275, 276, 284
Rees, Capt	94
Regiment, 1st Foot or Royal Scots	70, 90, 92, 95, 99, 100, 159, 160, 176, 198, 199, 202, 206, 217, 220, 248, 252, 255, 291, 307
Regiment, 6th Foot	161, 162
Regiment, 8th Foot or King's	5, 7, 8, 9, 10, 11, 12, 13, 14, 15, 22, 41, 44, 45, 59, 66, 68, 70, 93, 112, 159, 161, 162, 173, 193, 194, 195, 197, 200, 205, 207, 209, 217, 218, 221, 226, 240, 255, 291, 331
Regiment, 13th Foot	171, 176, 307
Regiment, 19th Light Dragoons	198, 202, 205, 274
Regiment, 41st Foot	10, 12, 56, 59, 60, 62, 64, 65, 66, 68, 69, 73, 74, 84, 90, 101, 104, 156, 159, 161, 172, 181, 193, 194, 197, 198, 199, 205, 206, 212, 214, 217, 218, 219, 221, 226, 233, 235, 240, 241, 250, 272, 277, 307, 331
Regiment, 49th Foot	5, 6, 7, 8, 9, 10, 11, 12, 13, 14, 15, 22, 23, 24, 28, 44, 45, 48, 56, 59, 62, 66, 73, 79, 91, 106, 112, 115, 116, 118, 125, 127, 129, 130, 158, 171, 184, 185, 194, 197, 203, 205, 214, 216, 217, 218, 221, 226, 227, 229, 240, 277, 331
Regiment, 64th Foot	171
Regiment, 89th Foot	87, 202, 212, 220, 235, 236, 307
Regiment, 100th Foot	5, 6, 87, 104, 156, 176, 272, 274, 281, 307, 319
Regiment, 103d Foot	5, 307
Regiment, 104th Foot	5, 52, 69, 84, 90, 92, 96, 98, 100, 104, 110, 112, 119, 156, 159, 173, 199, 203, 205, 221, 233, 248, 251, 252
Regiment, Canadian Fencible	5, 307
Regiment, Canadian Voltigeur	70, 274, 277, 304, 307
Regiment, Glengarry Light Infantry	5, 10, 52, 66, 70, 73, 84, 88, 193, 194, 198, 201, 205, 221, 233, 277, 295, 296, 304, 331
Regiment, New Brunswick Fencible	296

xvii.

R—Continued.   *Page.*

Regiment, Royal Newfoundland..........10, 66, 73, 89, 90, 176, 194, 198, 206, 213, 233, 269, 271, 273, 277, 281, 321, 331.
Regiment, de Meuron..171, 307
Regiment, de Watteville...104, 156
Regiment, 2d United States Dragoons..................23, 25, 32, 34, 37, 40, 47
Regiment, 5th United States Infantry..........23, 24, 25, 26, 27, 32, 34, 35, 39, 42, 43, 47, 75, 106.
Regiment, 6th U. S. I..................50, 76, 114, 115, 131, 132, 141, 147
Regiment, 9th U. S. I..32, 33, 37
Regiment, 13th U. S. I.......................................24, 26, 32, 33, 36, 135, 211
Regiment, 14th U. S. I..........25, 26, 32, 33, 114, 115, 131, 132, 141, 147, 152, 158
Regiment, 15th U. S. I..28, 107
Regiment, 16th U. S. I..........23, 24, 32, 34, 37, 39, 42, 43, 44, 48, 51, 166
Regiment, 20th U. S. I..114, 115, 141
Regiment, 23d U. S. I..........23, 24, 26, 27, 32, 34, 35, 36, 37, 39, 42, 43, 44, 51, 75, 114, 131, 132, 141, 144, 166.
Regiment, 25th U. S. I.......—..23, 24, 25, 26, 32, 33, 34, 35, 39, 40, 41, 42, 43, 44, 47, 75, 166.
Renvoisey, Capt..119
Retaliation, gunboat..105
Reynolds, Mr...318
Riall, Major-General P...119, 120
Rice Lake..122
Richelieu River...184, 250
Ridge Road..169
Ridout, Thos..255, 302, 320
Ridout, Thos. G..255, 302
Riga, N. Y...227
Ripley, Lieut.-Col. E. W..55
Roach, Capt. Isaac...115, 144, 147
Robertson, H. H...331
Robertson, Mr...180
Robinson, Capt. Wm...304
Robinson, Lieut..115
Rogers, Major..154
Rousseau, George..261, 278
Royal Artillery..10, 11, 73, 159, 202, 217, 221, 331
Royal George, ship of war...213, 269, 281, 328
Royal Veteran Battalion 10th...23, 159, 172
Rutledge, Lieut..92

S.

Sackett's Harbor............19, 20, 29, 51, 55, 57, 64, 80, 84, 95, 96, 109, 111, 165, 176, 177, 257, 265, 266, 267, 273, 285, 288, 289, 298, 299, 301.
Saddler, W...230
Samuel and Sarah, transport...88, 217
Sanders, Edward..81
Sandusky, Ohio..255, 299
Sandwich, Ont...64, 84, 160, 181, 182, 205, 250, 261
Sappers and Miners..87
Sasori, Indian chief...202
Sault LaCloche..172
Sault St. Louis..124, 126
Saunders, Capt. H. C.....................216, 217, 219, 224, 227, 240, 241, 292
Saunders, Lieut..115
Sayers, Lieut. Edward..97

S—Continued.

	Page
Scajaquady's Creek	223
Schlosser, Fort	120, 184, 185, 186, 189, 221, 228, 230, 231, 247, 294
Scott, Chief Justice Thos.	81
Scott, Lieut.	271
Scott, Lieut.-Col. Winfield	28, 31, 32, 56, 70, 71, 77, 78, 88, 100, 106, 107, 108, 136, 142, 144, 145, 188, 238, 254, 255, 282, 290, 295, 303, 305, 306, 308, 309, 312, 313.
Scourge, schooner	325
Seacord's house	174, 177, 178
Secord, Charles B.	129
Secord, James	130
Secord, Laura	127, 130
Seeley, Mr. E.	226, 228
Selby, Prideaux	195
Selden, Capt.	23
Seneca County, N. Y.	154
Seneca Indians	122, 167, 225, 275, 276
Servos's house	211
Seven Nations	110, 155, 156, 202, 215, 281
Sharp Shins, Indian chief	276
Shaw, Major-Gen. Æneas	169, 190, 223
Sheaffe, Major-Gen. Sir R. H.	3, 4, 5, 19, 21, 58, 61, 78, 97, 119, 139, 170, 183, 184, 214, 215.
Shell, Lieut.	115
Sherbrooke, Lieut.-Gen. Sir J. C.	217
Shipman's Tavern	291
Shongo, Capt., Indian chief	276
Shortt, Lieut.-Colonel	65
Showers, Lieut.	232
Sill, Joseph	226, 286
Sill's (Nathaniel) Store	227, 229
Silverheels, Johnston, Indian chief	167
Simons, Miss.	319
Simons, Major T. G.	234, 291
Simpson, M. T.	286
Sinilon Lake	172
Sir Isaac Brock, ship of war	170
Sir Sidney Smith, brig of war	160, 213, 269, 281
Six Nations	103, 110, 120, 122, 123, 155, 156, 167, 255, 262, 284
Sky, John, Indian chief	276
Sloan, James	228
Sloot, E.	164
Sodus, N. Y.	93, 94, 154, 158, 160, 169, 303
Soldier's Companion	123, 125
Somerville, Rev'd. James	12, 16
Smelt, Major	5
Smith, Capt. E.	109
Smith, Lieut.	254
Smith, Lieut.-Col. J. L.	238
Smith, Major	24, 27, 36, 40, 42
Smith, Mr.	110, 198
Smith's house	173, 211
Smyth, Brig.-Gen. Alex	19
Spalding, Mr.	94
Spectateur, Canadien	123, 125
Spenhard, Charles	261, 278

S—Continued.

	Page
Spilsbury, Lieut.	160
Spitfire, gunboat	288
Squaw Island	226, 229
Squakie Hill	276
Standing Stone	186
Stannard, A.	226, 286
Stanton, Adjutant	253, 293, 297, 298
Stearn, Adjt.	11, 15
Steers, Mr.	264
Steele	12, 39, 47, 48, 51
Stevens, Sergeant	223
Stiver, John	99
Stoney Creek	7, 8, 11, 12, 16, 23, 25, 30, 32, 33, 38, 39, 41, 46, 50, 51, 78, 79, 86, 87, 105, 161, 166, 175, 180, 206, 233, 294, 326.
Strachan, Rev. John	302
Street, Samuel, Sr.	269
Stuart, Col.	92, 100
Sturgeon Point	108
Sugar Loaf Hill	91, 122
Sutherland, Mr.	195
Swamp Road	123, 209
Swartwout, Brig. Gen. S.	77, 78, 144
Swearingen, Lieut.	12
Swift, Col. Philetus	93, 94, 154
Swift's Battery	229
Swift's Volunteers	189
Symington, Miss	209

St.

St. Catharines	130, 132, 134, 135, 150, 151
St. Davids	22, 32, 111, 117, 130, 131, 147, 150, 173, 178, 205, 209, 232, 241, 248, 251, 253, 255, 263, 265, 269, 277, 279, 280, 291, 297, 298, 302, 310, 312, 313.
St. George, Quetton	303
St. George's house	57
St. Germain, Lieut. E.	65, 134
St. Johns, Que.	161, 184, 307
St. Joseph	55, 172, 242
St. Joseph Indians	221
St. Regis	124, 126
St. Lawrence River	82, 171, 267, 273, 288, 289, 323

T.

Talbot papers	91
Tannehill, Brig. Gen. A.	306
Tappan, Ensign	43
Taylor, Lieut., and Fort Major Thomas	10, 197, 331
Taylor, Major	5, 6, 307
Taylor, Major	113, 132, 148, 149, 151
Tecumseh, Indian Chief	195, 296, 299
Te Karihaga, Mohawk chief	186, 187
Ten Mile Creek	98, 186, 202, 203, 204, 206, 209, 211, 212, 215, 221, 222, 232, 241.
Thames river	65, 85, 122
Thompson, Jonathan	227
Thompson, Volunteer A	185
Thorold township	130

T—Continued.

	Page
Thorp, Joel	165
Thunder, gunboat	53
Tiffany, George A	165, 189
Tiffany, Sylvester G	189
Tobey, Capt.	31
Tompkins, Governor D. D.	154, 169, 247 252, 282
Tompkins Papers	155, 248, 253, 285
Tonawanda, N. Y.	276
Toronto Public Library	57, 58, 87, 127, 181
Totman	123
Totten, Capt.	56, 75, 144, 147
Tower, Mr.	248
Townsend, J. T.	181
Towson, Capt.	23, 43, 75, 147
Troup, Samuel	91
Turner, Lieut.-Col. G. V.	12, 73
Turney's Cross Roads	98
Tuscarora Indians	122, 167, 186
Tutulie Indians	122
Twelve Mile Creek	165, 171, 172, 189, 199, 206, 208, 214, 215, 219, 231, 232, 234, 251, 263, 312.
Twenty Mile Creek (Lake Erie)	248
Twenty Mile Creek (Lake Ontario)	62, 81, 98, 124, 126, 140, 152, 153, 194, 196, 203.
Two Mile Creek	174, 207
Two Mile Woods	224

U.

United States Gazette	50
Utica Patriot	288

V.

Vandelsen, Capt.	254
Vandeventer, Major	12, 27, 51, 86, 145
Van Vechten, Capt.	12, 51
Veritas, Letters of	253
Vilatte, Major	212
Vincent, Brig.-Gen. John	5, 6, 7, 8, 11, 15, 18, 20, 22, 36, 45, 46, 47, 50, 52, 53, 54, 56, 57, 59, 60, 61, 62, 63, 64, 65, 66, 67, 68, 69, 70, 71, 74, 78, 79, 83, 84, 88, 89, 91, 94, 95, 100, 102, 112, 115, 116, 119, 120, 138, 139, 140, 156, 158, 160, 163, 175, 177, 180, 193, 197, 206, 243, 277.
Virgil, Ont.	200
Voltigeurs, Canadian	70, 274, 304, 307

W.

Wallace, Capt.	53
Warburton, Lieut.-Col.	82
Warren, Ab.	94
Warren, Lieut.-Col. John	226, 257, 269
Warren, Mr.	195
Warren, Sir John B.	137, 138, 245, 251, 256
Washburn, Capt.	304
Waterloo	228
Watertown, N. Y.	273
Western Indians	111

W—Continued.

	Page
Weyland, Lieut.	11
Whartenby, Major.	251
Whitchurch, Township of.	80
Wideman, Jacob	81
Wideman, John.	81
Widner, John.	91
Wilkinson, Major-General James	284, 285, 309, 322, 323, 329
Wilkinson's Memoirs.	301, 330
William Henry, Fort.	159
Williams, Brig.-Gen. D. R.	258, 285, 292, 309, 312, 321
Williams, Lieut. Titus.	91
Williams, Lt.-Col.	307
Williams, Major	26, 33
Williamsville, N. Y.	292
Willis, Capt. Lewis B.	153
Willson, Crowell.	269
Willson, Mr.	206
Wilson, Capt.	92
Wilson, James.	251, 252
Wilson, Mr.	234
Winchester, Brig.-Gen. James.	179
Winder, Brig.-Gen. W. H	6, 8, 9, 12, 14, 16, 17, 23, 24, 25, 26, 27, 28, 29, 31, 32, 33, 35, 36, 42, 43, 47, 48, 49, 50, 51, 68, 74, 85, 105, 106, 166, 180, 197, 284.
Winder, Ensign.	184, 185
Winter, Capt.	277
Winter, Lieut.	325
Wintermoot's house.	173
Wolfe, ship of war.	59, 68, 160, 213, 245, 251, 269, 327
Wood, Alexander.	81
Woodford, Major F.	238
Wool, Major J. E.	238
Wright, Joseph.	227, 229
Wycan, Mr.	94

Y.

	Page
Yellow Head, Indian Chief.	260
Yellow Head's band of Indians.	222
Yeo, Sir James L	20, 22, 29, 53, 57, 59, 62, 63, 64, 67, 68, 74, 76, 83, 89, 94, 95, 100, 138, 139, 163, 176, 195, 199, 202, 204, 207, 212, 244, 245, 321.
Yie's (Yeigh's) house	198
York	20, 21, 32, 53, 54, 56, 60, 61, 64, 81, 91, 95, 100, 102, 120, 143, 151, 170, 183, 184, 191, 192, 214, 233, 236, 246, 256, 282, 289, 290, 298, 302, 303, 306, 309, 310, 313, 320, 327.
Young, Capt.	234, 247, 257
Young, Colonel.	254, 305
Young, Surgeon.	115
Young King, Indian Chief.	225, 227

Z.

	Page
Zephyr, schooner.	229

www.ingramcontent.com/pod-product-compliance
Lightning Source LLC
Chambersburg PA
CBHW020242240426
43672CB00006B/611